ALGERIA

THE MAKING OF THE MODERN WORLD

This group of narrative histories focuses on key moments and events in the twentieth century to explore their wider significance for the development of the modern world.

PUBLISHED

SERIES ADVISERS

PROFESSOR CHRIS BAYLY, University of Cambridge
PROFESSOR RICHARD J. EVANS, University of Cambridge
PROFESSOR DAVID REYNOLDS, University of Cambridge

ALGERIA: FRANCE'S UNDECLARED WAR

MARTIN EVANS

OXFORD
UNIVERSITY PRESS

OXFORD
UNIVERSITY PRESS

Great Clarendon Street, Oxford OX2 6DP

Oxford University Press is a department of the University of Oxford.
It furthers the University's objective of excellence in research, scholarship,
and education by publishing worldwide in

Oxford New York

Auckland Cape Town Dar es Salaam Hong Kong Karachi
Kuala Lumpur Madrid Melbourne Mexico City Nairobi
New Delhi Shanghai Taipei Toronto

With offices in

Argentina Austria Brazil Chile Czech Republic France Greece
Guatemala Hungary Italy Japan Poland Portugal Singapore
South Korea Switzerland Thailand Turkey Ukraine Vietnam

Oxford is a registered trade mark of Oxford University Press
in the UK and in certain other countries

Published in the United States
by Oxford University Press Inc., New York

British Library Cataloguing in Publication Data

Data available

Library of Congress Cataloging in Publication Data

Data available

Typeset by SPI Publisher Services, Pondicherry, India
Printed in Great Britain
on acid-free paper by
Clays Ltd, St Ives Plc

ISBN 978–0–19–280350–4

1 3 5 7 9 10 8 6 4 2

To Abdul with love

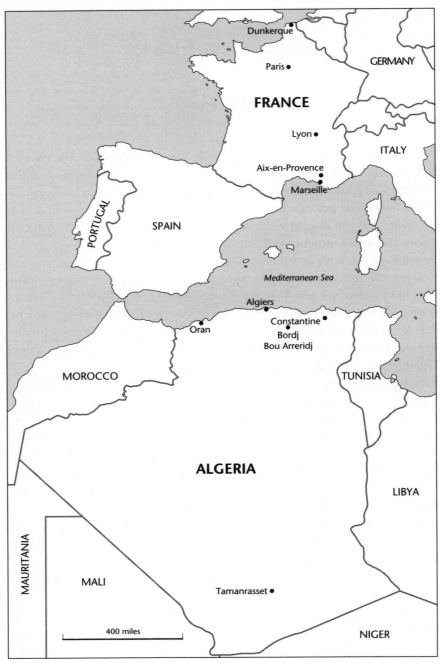

Contemporary Algeria and France

Acknowledgements

B ordj Bou Arreridj is a small city of 169,009 inhabitants in eastern Algeria. Well known for its food and hospitality, Bordj is situated in the midst of a countryside that produces the bulk of the country's wheat and barley: hence the area's nickname as Algeria's bread basket. To walk down the streets of Bordj Bou Arreridj, as I did in April 2010, is to feel the hand of history. There is a museum dedicated to the veterans who fought against the French between 1954 and 1962; a cemetery for the fallen martyrs; a monument to the national liberation struggle; a statute commemorating Mohammed El-Mokrani who led a huge revolt in the region against the French in 1871. In this manner Bordj Bou Arreridj is typical. Every village, town, and city in Algeria has the same type of monuments: an ever-present public memory that is encapsulated in the massive memorial—the 97-metre-high Riad-El-Feth—that dominates the Algiers skyline. Inaugurated on 5 July 1982, exactly twenty years after independence from the French, at the base of the abstract monument are three huge male bronze figures, proud and defiant, which represent 'popular resistance to the French occupation'; the 'National Liberation Army'; and the present 'Popular National Army'. Underneath the monument, the Museum to the National Liberation Struggle climaxes with a domed room, decorated in gilded verses from the Qu'ran, that contains a single illuminated stone: the symbol of the 'unity of the Algerian people and its heroic resistance'.

In contrast, across the Mediterranean in France, there is no equivalent public memory. Unlike World War One, or the World War Two Resistance, public monuments have been local, piecemeal affairs. Those that exist are the result of pressure from below by specific communities who want recognition of how they suffered during the Algerian War. Significantly, too, the diversity of these monuments is testament to the ongoing memory war over Algeria within contemporary France. Thus, in Paris we can find a Place Maurice Audin dedicated to the memory of an Algerian Communist Party member who disappeared at the hands of French paratroopers in

Algiers in 1957 and a plaque on the Pont Saint Michel bridge to Algerians who were murdered by French police there on 17 October 1961. While in Aix-en-Provence there is Place Bachaga Boualam, marking the life of the most prominent pro-French Algerian from the late 1950s, and in Nice a memorial to the French settlers which also includes a plaque to fallen members of the extremist pro-French Algeria organization the Organisation Armée Secrète (OAS) who are called 'the martyrs of French Algeria'.

Two different patterns of remembering; measures of the enduring significance of the subject of this book, namely the origins, experience and legacy of the Algerian War of Independence 1954 to 1962—a seminal event in twentieth-century world history. As such the book will be dealing with broad issues—colonialism, nationalism, war, the impact of transnational ideals—but it will also be attuned to the particularities of Algerian history: a combination of the generic and specific that is absolutely vital in understanding the Arab world as this region experiences the tumultuous events of the 'Arab Spring'.

In completing this book I must first thank the British Academy which awarded me a Leverhulme Senior Fellowship in 2007–8. In addition the British Academy also financed fieldwork in France, participation in the Rudé Seminar on French History in Adelaide in 2006, and a three-year project on an oral history of Algerian and Senegalese veterans from the Algerian War of Independence (Oral history across generations: a research programme with the universities of Dakar and Algiers, <http://www.port.ac.uk/research/africanoralhistory>). In the last case this facilitated workshops at the Universities of Algiers and Dakar in 2010 and 2011 that produced fascinating insights into the complexities of memory and history in contemporary Africa. Equally I must thank the Arts and Humanities Research Council which financed the research leave that allowed me to write up the bulk of this book. And finally I must thank the Centre for European and International Studies Research at the University of Portsmouth which generously financed research trips to Algeria, Belgium and France.

In terms of colleagues I must thank Megan Vaughn who first approached me with the idea for this book on the advice of Mark Mazower. Thereafter I could not have begun to trace the long and complex history of Algeria without the ideas of stimulating colleagues at the University of Portsmouth, above all Walid Benkhaled, Tony Chafer, Emmanuel Godin, and Natalya Vince, each of whom commented on the manuscript. Equally, writing this book gives me a chance to thank a generation of graduate students at Portsmouth—Enrico Cernigoi, Marianne Durrand, Fiona Haig, Manus

McGrogan, Tobias Reckling, Monica Riera, and Jo Warson—each of whom has brought new understandings to the vital realism of contemporary history, as well as those final-year students in the School of Languages and Areas Studies who took my final-year option in Algerian history and participated in the annual Algeria workshops. Again this teaching experience has done so much to deepen my knowledge and understanding of the subject.

Beyond Portsmouth, in the rest of the UK, Algeria, Australia, Canada, Senegal, and the USA, I must also thank Richard Evans, Alistair Horne, Jim House, Roderick Kedward, Sylvie Thénault, Martin Thomas, and Ryme Seferdjeli who read the manuscript. For their insights and suggestions I am sincerely grateful. A special mention must also be made of those who were so helpful at the Socialist Party Archive in Paris—Frédéric Cépède, Denis Lefebvre, and Gilles Morin. Thanks also to Naomi Graham, who so kindly gave me much of her late husband's (Bruce Graham) personal archive on the French Socialist Party, which proved invaluable. Importantly, too, I have benefited from conversations with Attika-Yasmine Abbes-Kara, Robert Aldrich, Martin Alexander, Robert Baldock, Catherine Barry, Christopher Bayly, Badia Benbelkacem, Raphaëlle Branche, Michael Brett, Phoebe Clapham, Claire Eldridge, Mohammed Harbi, Julian Jackson, Malika Kebbas, Cheikh Ahmadou Bamba Khoulé, John King, Zineb Lalaouine, James McDougall, Margaret Majumdar, Clare Marynower, Cheikh Anta Mbaye, Gilbert Meynier, Samia Mitchell, Clive Myrie, Sabrea Oughton, Malika Rahal, Eugene Rogan, Lydia Aït Saadi, Cherif Khaled Sabeur, Méziane Saïdi, Sokhna Sané, Gavin Schaffer, Ibrahima Seck, Martin Shipway, Daniel Stone, Ibrahima Thioub, Stephen Tyre, and Michael Willis. Significantly, too, I would like to thank the team at the magazine of *History Today*—Sheila Corr, Charlotte Crow, Peter Furtado, Kathryn Hadley, and Paul Lay—who in bringing informed, well-researched history to a wider audience have always been open to all things Algerian. Then at Oxford University Press Matthew Cotton has been a superb editor throughout, incredibly patient and always encouraging, while Jeremy Langworthy did a fine job of copy-editing, and Emma Barber and Clifford Willis played a crucial role during the final production process. Emmanuelle Péri succeeded admirably in tracking down the illustrations. Finally, as regards, my family—Lucy, Hannah, Calum and Skye—I cannot begin to thank them enough for their love, patience, and support.

Martin Evans

Algiers
April 2011

Preface

The end of empires is a defining feature of twentieth-century history. From the Austro-Hungarian, German, Ottoman, and Russian in World War One, through to the Japanese, Fascist, and Nazi in World War Two, the Europeans in the post-1945 period and the Soviet in 1989– 91: the collapse of these different empires has shaped the modern world in a profound manner. In this complex and diverse process, the demise of the French Empire—the world's second largest in 1920—occupies centre stage, and within this particular history the Algerian War of 1954 to 1962 is *the* key event. This was one of the longest and bloodiest wars of decolonization, partly because Algeria was considered to be an integral part of France, but also because of the heavy settler presence (by the mid-1950s 1 million settlers coexisted with 9 million Algerians). These factors explain why Algeria became such a major international crisis: an event that led to the fall of four French governments and the collapse of the Fourth Republic in 1958, and produced huge tensions, both amongst the Western powers, and between the West and the Muslim World.

This book is a chronological narrative of the Algerian War's origins, intensification, and consequences. It is structured around three analytical threads, the first of which is *the long hatreds* produced by the original French invasion in 1830. Defeat, when added to the subsequent material and cultural dispossession of land, produced a bedrock of Muslim anger which never went away. Large numbers felt that their land and their religion, Islam, had been defiled and they were never reconciled to French rule under any circumstances. Although in the intervening century and a quarter a complex world of contact and interaction did emerge between France and the indigenous population, one that cannot be reduced to two undifferentiated blocks of colonizer and colonized, in the eastern part of the country and the mountainous interior this relationship was no more than superficial. Two societies existed uneasily in conditions of mistrust, segregation, and mutual incomprehension; a divide that was exacerbated by a further

fundamental factor: the demographic time bomb which meant that, by
1954, the Muslim population outnumbered the Europeans by 9 million to
1 million. The result was a society at breaking point which, in denying
Muslims an economic and political space in French Algeria, slid into an
undeclared conflict in the decade after the end of World War Two.

The second analytical thread is the emergence of *modern Algerian nationalism* from the 1920s onwards. Algerian nationalism was made of four
strands: assimilationists, a religious clerical movement, communists, and
radical nationalists, each of which looked beyond Algeria for inspiration.
The supporters of assimilation drew upon French republican models and
language to condemn the inequalities of French Algeria. Religious clerics
looked towards the ideas of a pan-Muslim renaissance emanating from the
Middle East. Communists invoked the example of the 1917 Russian Revolution. Radical nationalists were inspired by a mixture of ideas derived from
the French Communist Party as well as the ideology of pan-Arab nationalism. Significantly, these movements fed into, and fed off, a much broader
current in Algerian society which witnessed a flowering of sporting and
cultural groups and associations throughout the 1920s and 1930s: the assertion of a separate identity which was a reaction against the 1930 centenary
celebrations of French Algeria. Algerian nationalism, therefore, did not
begin with the Front de Libération Nationale (FLN) insurrection in November 1954. It was a pluralistic movement whose development is vital to
understand the emergence and shape of the FLN. Because of this the
relationship between Algerian nationalism and the French left during the
years 1918 and 1954 was a crucial determining factor for the subsequent
eight-year conflict. The failure of the Popular Front in 1936 and the early
Fourth Republic in 1947 to engage with Algerian demands produced a
further layer of anger and disappointments that made the relationship of
Algerian nationalism with the French Socialist Party (French Section of the
Workers' International—Section Française de l'Internationale Ouvrière—
SFIO) into a major source of conflict. This legacy shaped the FLN's political
culture, ensuring that it instinctively opposed any proposal of reform or free
elections. Instead, the armed struggle was sacrosanct right up until independence in 1962.

This brings us on to the third analytical thread: *third-way reformism*. French
rule in Algeria was never a continuous block. For its first seventy years, it
went through three different phases, commencing with army rule between
1830 and 1870, followed by a limited integration into the Third Republic's

structures, and then financial autonomy for a settler-dominated Algerian Assembly in 1900. Nor was French rule in French Algeria ideologically unified. Ideas of the inherent inequality of races coexisted with others based upon paternalist notions of the protection of the indigenous people. Within this unfolding argument over how to rule in Algeria, one crucial stage was the emergence of a third-way reformist perspective inside the Radical and Socialist Parties in the years immediately after World War One. This perspective was embodied above all by Maurice Viollette, the left-wing Radical Party politician, who, as Governor-General in Algeria from May 1925 to November 1927, sought to chart a third way between hard-line settlers, opposed to any reform, and a nascent nationalist movement which he saw as communist controlled. In rejecting these extremes, Viollette wished to assimilate a Muslim elite as equal citizens, who would form the basis of a more equal and, therefore, more durable French Algeria. These ideas were also reflected in the arguments of fellow Radical Party members, notably Albert Sarraut, Governor-General in Indochina between 1912 and 1919, and Albert Bayet, historian and human rights activist. Bayet, speaking with Viollette in May 1931 at Vichy in a conference on 'Colonization and the Rights of Man' organized by the League of the Rights of Man, was unequivocal:

> Colonization is legitimate when the people who colonise bring with them a treasure of ideas and feelings which will enrich other peoples; from that moment colonization is not a right, it is a duty . . . It seems to me that modern France, daughter of the Renaissance, inheritor of the seventeenth century and the Revolution, represents in the world a valuable ideal which can and must be spread across the universe.[1]

Clear in its belief in French sovereignty and the 'civilizing mission', as well as its opposition to nationalism and communism, much of the third-way reformist tradition was imprecise. Beyond the grand rhetoric, it was unclear how big ideas such as the values of the French Revolution, 'humanism', and the promotion of women's rights would translate into practical policy. Yet, vague as they were, these ideas framed the failed Popular Front reforms in Algeria in 1936 initiated by Viollette himself. They were fundamental to the Fourth Republic in its transformation of the French Empire into the associative French Union (proclaimed in the 1946 Constitution as a new entity based on equality of rights and obligations without distinction of race or religion), and in the new political structures introduced to Algeria in 1947.

These ideas, it will be argued, reached their apogee with the left-of-centre Republican Front government which emerged from the 2 January 1956 elections. Under the leadership of the Socialist Party Prime Minister Guy Mollet, this was the point when the contours of third-way reformism took on their clearest shape. Imprecision gave way to clarity as Guy Mollet's government combined repression and reform into a single policy designed to defeat the FLN and win the 'hearts and minds' of the Algerian majority.

This policy was encapsulated in the Special Powers Act, voted through by the French National Assembly on 12 March 1956 by an overwhelming majority, 455 votes against 76. Through it, the deputies (including the communists) gave the Republican Front government virtual carte blanche to stop the terrorist violence which had spread across Algeria since 1 November 1954. As article five of the special powers explicitly stated, the government now had the legal right to take any measure deemed necessary for the 're-establishment of order'.[2] Side by side with repression, the first four articles of the special powers promised far-reaching reforms that would ensure Muslim advancement through equal political rights and greater economic prosperity. These included the creation of a special fund to expand the number of small Muslim farm owners and train them in modern agricultural techniques, more access to posts in the civil service, and an industrialization programme designed specifically to create jobs in the Muslim community.[3] This made the special powers into a double-edged sword. The intention was to defeat the insurrection and anti-Muslim racism at the same time. The Republican Front government wanted to create a 'Franco-Muslim community' that rejected the extremism of 'Arab nationalism' on the one hand, and the most reactionary settlers on the other. It was defending a third-way perspective which did not see itself as colonial.

The special-powers vote was backed by the call-up of 70,000 additional reservists which further underlined the wider geo-strategic significance of the Republican Front's policy. For the Mollet government, Algeria was to be the key to France's standing as a world power. Victory would secure the newly discovered oil resources in the Sahara. It would allow France to fashion a Franco-African Union, stretching from Paris to Brazzaville in the Congo, that could confront the challenges of the cold war, Western European integration, and rival Anglo-Saxon imperialisms. Moreover, by bringing about harmony between the 1 million Europeans and 9 million Algerians, this solution aimed to maintain France's moral standing across the globe. By following a three-point agenda that would begin with a cease-fire, proceed to elections, and then end in negotiations, such a policy, Mollet emphasized, was one of peace not war:

> The reservists must know . . . that they are not going to Algeria to prosecute a war, but to carry out a work of peace. Few men would be needed to do the work of destruction. Many are necessary to restore peace. If we were looking for war, the power of modern arms is such that small numbers of troops, using all of the means at their disposal, could quickly achieve a bloody and destructive military victory. That France does not want and will never want. On the contrary, to guarantee security everywhere, to affirm our presence and our strength in order to use it as little as possible, numerous troops are indispensable . . . I solemnly affirm that at no point will we impose on the Algerian people a solution by force.[4]

These events of spring 1956 are at the centre of this history of France's war in Algeria between 1954 and 1962. This was the moment when the conflict really took hold on both sides of the Mediterranean. By means of these emergency measures the Republican Front government hoped to bring about a rapid solution, but in reality they dramatically deepened the war. By giving the army a free hand, the special powers intensified the hatred of the Algerian population because, in their search for FLN militants, French soldiers subjected the population to large-scale arrests, internment, and combing operations. This produced a dramatic response from the FLN. In military terms, the FLN sought to match French actions with a mass mobilization of its own, urging students and young men to take to the maquis. Politically the FLN renewed its drive to predominate, either through argument or violence, over all other rival organizations and to become the sole voice of Algerian nationalism.

The Republican Front government lasted until May 1957, making it the longest-serving administration of the Fourth Republic. During these sixteen months in power the Republican Front embodied the clash between third-way reformism and the FLN. This clash was the *casus belli* behind the Republican Front's decision to ally itself with Britain and Israel and attack Egypt in November 1956, whose leader, General Gamal Abd Nasser, was seen to be the hidden hand behind the FLN. It was also at the heart of the 'Battle of Algiers' in 1957, when the Tenth Paratrooper Division ruthlessly dismantled the local FLN networks operating out of the tiny trap-like streets of the Casbah, using methods of torture that included 'the bathtub' (repeatedly plunging a prisoner's head into water soiled with urine), 'electricity' (electric shocks to feet, ears, and genitals), 'the bottle' (forcing a prisoner to sit on a bottle while soldiers pushed down on their shoulders), and 'the rope' (suspending a prisoner with a slipknot above the jaws).[5]

In recovering the absolute centrality of 1956, this book peels back the layers of a fast-evolving epoch. It does not see the period from January 1956 as the beginning of the death throes of the Fourth Republic. It does not fast-forward to de Gaulle's return to power in May–June 1958 as the decisive event in the eight-year conflict. During 1956, 1957, and early 1958 the Fourth Republic bubbled with projects about Algeria. Algeria was seen to be France's future: the lynchpin of a geo-strategic strategy which would uphold France's role as a global actor.

These three analytical threads running through the narrative explain the political context for the Algerian War. They situate the ideas which justified the violence on all sides. However, they go beyond the notion of Algerians and French as two indiscriminate entities. On the Algerian side, they show how the conflict drew in a myriad of actors whose motivations ranged from pro-French sentiments through to communism, liberalism, and nationalism. On the French side, they differentiate between the settlers, conscripts, professional soldiers, as well as socialists, Gaullists, and anti-colonialists. No less importantly, these analytical threads go beyond a narrow Franco-Algerian perspective. The Algerian War was a pivotal episode in the break-up of empires, and to be fully understood it needs to be clearly placed within this international framework. Algerian politics was profoundly altered by the impact of wider transnational ideologies such as pan-Arabism, pan-Islamism, communism, and Third World non-alignment. At the same time, French policies in Algeria were shaped by events within other parts of the French Union: the threat of fascism and communism; the cold war; the drive for Western European unity in the 1950s; and rivalry with Britain and the USA.

Lastly, a note on terminology. In this book I have studiously avoided anachronism. So, during the first two chapters looking at the period up to 1918, I refrain from the term 'Algerian' to describe the indigenous population, preferring 'Muslim', because this was how they would have understood themselves. Notions of popular Algerian nationalism did not emerge until the 1920s: a modern concept which it would be wrong to confer on an earlier generation. Equally, to describe the settlers I use the term 'settler' or 'European', carefully avoiding *pied-noir*, a phrase of uncertain origin which did not emerge until the 1950s and only became dominant when they 'returned' to France in 1962.

Contents

List of Illustrations

List of Maps and Table

Maps

Table

List of Abbreviations

ALN	Armée de Libération Nationale (1954–62)
AML	Association des Amis du Manifeste et de la Liberté (1944–5)
CCE	Comité de Coordination et d'Éxécution (1956–8)
CNRA	Conseil National de la Révolution Algérienne (1956–62)
CRUA	Comité Révolutionnaire pour l'Unité et l'Action (1954)
ENA	Étoile Nord Africaine (1926–37)
FAF	Front de l'Algérie Française (1960–1)
FIS	Front Islamique du Salut (1989–92)
FLN	Front de Libération National (1954–)
GRPA	Gouvernement Provisoire de la République Algérienne (1958–62)
MNA	Mouvement National Algérien (1954–62)
MTLD	Mouvement pour le Triomphe des Libertés Démocratiques (1946–54)
OAS	Organisation de l'Armée Secrète (1961–2)
OS	Organisation Spéciale (1947–51)
PCA	Parti Communiste Algérien (1936-66)
PCF	Parti Communiste Français (1920–)
PPA	Parti du Peuple Algérien (1937–54)
PSU	Parti Socialiste Unifié (1960–89)
RPF	Rassemblement du Peuple Français (1947–55)
SAS	Section Administrative Spécialisé
SFIO	Section Française de l'Internationale Ouvrière (1905–69)
UDMA	Union Démocratique du Manifeste Algérien (1946–56)
UDSR	Union Démocratique et Socialiste de la Résistance (1947–64)

Some Key Characters

Abbane, Ramdane (1920–57) Born in Kabylia. Joined PPA at age of sixteen. Member of the OS after 1947. Arrested in 1950. On his release in January 1955 joined the FLN. Architect of the Congress of the Soummam. Murdered in Morocco in December 1957 as a result of internal struggles within the FLN.

Abbas, Ferhat (1899–1985) One of the leaders of the assimilationist movement during the 1930s. By 1943 he was calling for political autonomy for Algeria. During 1956 he joined the FLN and in September 1958 was president of the Provisional Algerian Government in Tunis. In September 1962 he became president of the Algerian National Assembly, but resigned in August 1963 in protest at the authoritarian nature of the new regime. Thereafter he retired from public political life.

Aït Ahmed, Hocine (1919–) Member of the OS and one of the nine leaders who coordinated 1 November 1954. Arrested and imprisoned in October 1956, he opposed the dictatorial rule of Ben Bella and then Boumediène with the foundation of the Front des Forces Socialistes (FFS). Still a key figure in Algerian politics.

Amirouche, Aït-Hamouda (1926–59) Originally an activist in the MTLD, Amirouche rose to become the commanding colonel of Wilaya 3 (Kabylia) where he imposed an iron discipline on his own troops and the local population. Killed in an ambush in March 1959.

Ben Bella, Ahmed (1916–) One of the historic FLN leaders who planned 1 November 1954. An OS member, he was arrested by the French in 1950, but escaped in 1952. Arrested and imprisoned in October 1956, he was the first president after independence. Overthrown by Boumediène in June 1965, he was imprisoned until 1980 whereupon he went into exile. Ben Bella returned to Algeria in 1990.

Ben Boulaïd, Mostefa (1917–56) OS member who was in charge of the November 1954 FLN insurrection in the Aurès Mountains. Killed in March 1956 by a booby-trapped parcel parachuted into the maquis by the French army.

Ben Khedda, Ben Youcef (1920–2003) Politicized by the Algerian Scouts, he was a leading member of the MTLD who opposed Messali Hadj's leadership in 1954. Arrested after November 1954, he immediately joined the FLN upon his release in April 1955. Became president of the Provisional Algerian Government in August 1961, but lost out to Ben Bella in the struggle for power after independence in July 1962.

Ben M'Hidi, Larbi (1923–57) OS member, he was one of the FLN founders in 1954. Arrested by the French paratroopers during the 'Battle of Algiers' on 25 February 1957, he died in custody shortly afterwards.

Ben Tobbal, Lakhdar (1923–2010) Activist in the PPA and then the OS, he was one of the FLN's founders in 1954. A military man above all, he was Minister of Interior in the first Provisional Algerian Government in September 1958. A key negotiator in the Evian negotiations, Ben Tobbal was on the losing side during the FLN in-fighting in the summer of 1962.

Bitat, Rabah (1926–2000) Member of the PPA and then the OS, he was one of the FLN's historic leaders. Arrested in March 1955, he was not freed until 1962.

Boudiaf, Mohammed (1919–92) Member of the PPA and then the OS, Boudiaf was one of the FLN's founding leaders and the architect behind 1 November 1954. Arrested in October 1956 he remained in prison until 1962. Opposed to Ben Bella's taking of power in 1962, he went into exile in Morocco. Recalled to become head of state in January 1992, he was assassinated in June 1992.

Bouhired, Djamila (1935–) Joined the FLN in 1956. Acted as a liaison agent during the 'Battle of Algiers' 1956–7. Planted bombs in specified parts of the European Quarter.

Boumediène, Houari (1932–78) Born near Guelma in eastern Algeria into a poor peasant family. Studied at the prestigious Al-Azhar University in Cairo and was very influenced by the Egyptian Revolution and the rise to power of Nasser. Joined the National Liberation Army in Morocco in 1955 and rose to become the military leader of the army of the frontiers. Joined with Ben Bella in the summer of 1962 to defeat the Provisional Government. Overthrew Ben Bella in 1965 and became head of state.

Bouteflika, Abdelaziz (1937–) Born in Oujda in Morocco into an Algerian family, Bouteflika joined the National Liberation Army in 1956 and became a key member of Boumediène's entourage. Became Minister for Foreign Affairs in 1963, remaining in this position until Boumediène's death in 1978. Marginalized during the 1980s, he returned to Algeria in 1989. Elected president in dubious circumstances in 1999 and again in 2004, he changed the constitution in 2008 so that he could run for a third term. Re-elected president in 2009.

Boussouf, Abdelhafid (1926–80) Member of the PPA and then the OS, born in eastern Algeria. Minister in the Provisional Algerian Government, he was instrumental in establishing the secret police which became the spine of the military and continues to dominate Algerian politics. After independence he retreated from political life and pursued business interests.

Chadli, Bendjedid (1929–) Born in eastern Algeria, he joined the maquis in 1955. As an obscure military man, he was the compromise candidate to succeed Boumediène in 1979. Forced out of office in January 1992 by a *coup d'état*.

Challe, Maurice (1905–79) The French government's military representative to Britain during the Suez campaign in 1956. Commander-in-chief of French forces in Algeria 1958–60. Led the failed military coup against de Gaulle in April 1961.

Dahlab, Saad (1918–2000) PPA veteran, he was part of the anti-Messali Hadj opposition that emerged within the MTLD in 1954. Joining the FLN he became Minister for Foreign Affairs in the Provisional Algerian Government in 1961 and was involved in the final negotiations with the French. After independence followed a business career and established a publishing company.

Debré, Michel (1912–96) A fierce defender of French sovereignty in Algeria, he was prime minister under the new Fifth Republic from 1959 to 1962. After the referendum on 8 April 1962 ratifying the peace accords with the Provisional Algerian Government, he was replaced by Georges Pompidou.

Didouche, Mourad (1922–55) One of the historic FLN leaders, he was killed in January 1955.

Gaulle, Charles de (1890–1970) Historic leader of the World War Two French Resistance, head of the French government during the May 1945 repression in Algeria. In 1954 de Gaulle had 'retired' from politics, but the Fourth Republic's inability to solve the Algerian problem catapulted him back to power in 1958. Initially continued with the Fourth Republic's policy of reform and repression, before accepting the need to negotiate with the Provisional Algerian Government, which led to final peace accords in March 1962.

Fanon, Frantz (1925–61) Born in the French Caribbean, Fanon worked as a psychiatrist in Algeria between 1953 and 1956. Siding with the FLN, he worked for the Provisional Algerian Government in Tunis and became one of the leading intellectual writers of the Algerian struggle.

Harbi, Mohammed (1933–) Activist in the MTLD and FLN, Harbi was imprisoned under Boumediène, but escaped in 1973. As a university academic in Paris, he has become the leading historian of Algerian nationalism and the FLN.

Khider, Mohammed (1912–67) Born in eastern Algeria, Khider was a veteran nationalist who participated in the PPA, the OS, and was one of the founding members of the FLN. Arrested in October 1956, he sided with Ben Bella and Boumediène in 1962 against the Provisional Algerian Government. Falling out with Ben Bella he went into exile in 1963. Assassinated in Madrid in 1967.

Krim, Belkacem (1922–70) Took to the maquis in Kabylia in 1947. One of the historic FLN leaders, he dominated the FLN in 1958 and 1959 as vice-president of the Provisional Algerian Government. Took a leading role in the final negotiations with France. Marginalized at independence, he was found dead in hotel room in Frankfurt in West Germany in 1970 after being sentenced to death by the Boumediène regime.

Lacoste, Robert (1898–1989) Socialist Party member, highly decorated for his service in the two world wars. Minister Resident in Algeria between 1956 and 1958, he pursued a ruthless policy of reform and repression.

Lejeune, Max (1909–95) Socialist Party member and prominent member of the Republican Front government 1956–7. Fervent defender of the decision to intensify the conflict in Algeria in spring 1956.

Mendès France, Pierre (1907–82) Radical Party member who was prime minister in November 1954, responding to the FLN with a mixture of reform and repression.

Messali Hadj, Ahmed (1898–1974) One of the historic figures of Algerian nationalism. A key founder of the first party committed to outright independence in 1926, he founded the PPA in 1937 and the MTLD in 1946. In response to November 1954, he founded the MNA in December 1954, which became involved in a bloody struggle with the FLN. Excluded from negotiations in 1961 and 1962, Messali went into exile post-independence.

Mitterrand, François (1916–96) Minister of the Interior in November 1954, Mitterrand was an advocate of reform and repression. As Justice Minister supported the special powers and the guillotining of Algerian prisoners. Opposed the return of de Gaulle in 1958. Became president of France in 1981.

Mollet, Guy (1905–75) Prime minister during the Republican Front government 1956–7, Mollet oversaw the intensification of the war against the FLN with the voting of the special powers, the recall of the reservists and the attack on Egypt. Supported the return of de Gaulle in 1958.

Soustelle, Jacques (1912–90) Anti-fascist during the 1930s, Soustelle joined de Gaulle's Free French in 1940. As Governor-General of Algeria between 1955 and 1956, he sought to introduce reform while simultaneously repressing the FLN. Supported de Gaulle's return to power in 1958, but accused him of betraying French Algeria and broke with de Gaulle in 1960. Went into exile in 1961, but was amnestied in 1968.

Yacef, Saadi (1928–) Joined the FLN in 1955. One of the FLN leaders during the Battle of Algiers 1956–7. Condemned to death but pardoned, he sided with Ben Bella in 1962.

Chronology

1830: Capitulation of Algiers to French invasion.

1847: Abd el-Kader surrenders.

1848: Algeria divided into departments.

1871: The El Mokrani revolt, which ends in defeat for the insurgents.

1881: Algeria integrated into the administrative structures of the Third Republic under the Minister of the Interior.

1889: Law giving foreign settlers French nationality.

1926: Establishment of the Étoile Nord-Africaine—the first party committed to Algerian independence.

1930: Celebrations of centenary of French rule.

1936: Failure of the Popular Front reforms that would have extended the Muslim franchise, albeit very modestly.

1940: Fall of France.

1942: Allied landings in Algeria and Morocco.

1945: Sétif revolt followed by severe repression.

1947: New administrative structures in Algeria.

1948: Fraud robs Algerian nationalists of electoral victory.

1954: 7 May. Fall of Dien Bien Phu in Indochina.

1 November. Attacks by Front de Libération National (FLN) across the country.

1955: 25 January. Soustelle appointed Governor-General.

6 February. Mendès France government falls.

18–24 April. FLN delegation present at Bandung Conference.

20 August. FLN violence in eastern Algeria involving massacres of Europeans at Philippeville.

12 September. Algerian Communist Party dissolved.

30 September. Algeria discussed at the United Nations for the first time.

1956: 2 January. Victory of the Republican Front in national elections.

26 January. Mollet becomes prime minister.

6 February. Mollet bombarded with tomatoes by Europeans in Algiers.

10 February. Robert Lacoste appointed Minister–Resident in Algeria.

16 March. Special Powers voted through by the French National Assembly.

19 June. First execution of FLN prisoners.

20 August. FLN conference at Soummam.

30 September. FLN bombing of European cafés in Algiers.

22 October. Ben Bella hijacked and imprisoned by the French.

5 November. Anglo-French landings at Suez.

1957:   7 January. French paratroopers take over police powers in Algiers.

28 January. General strike begins in Algiers—broken by the French paratroopers.

14 March. Announcement of the 'suicide' of Larbi Ben M'Hidi.

26 March. Announcement of the 'suicide' of Ali Boumendjel.

21 May. Mollet government falls.

8 October. Ali la Pointe killed by French paratroopers.

27 December. Abbane Ramdane liquidated in FLN in-fighting.

1958:   8 February. French bomb Sakiet in Tunisia.

13 May. European demonstrations in Algiers.

1 June. De Gaulle becomes prime minister.

4 June. De Gaulle makes triumphant visit to Algiers.

19 September. Algerian Provisional Government formed in Cairo.

3 October. De Gaulle announces the Constantine Plan to modernize Algeria.

1959:   22 July. Climax of the French offensive against the FLN.

16 September. De Gaulle offers Algeria 'self-determination'.

1960:   20 January. Massu transferred from Algeria for attacking de Gaulle's policy.

24 January. European revolt in Algiers.

29 January. European revolt collapses.

25–9 June. Franco-FLN talks end in failure.

9–13 December. De Gaulle visits Algeria—huge Algerian nationalist demonstrations.

1961:   January. OAS founded in Madrid.

20–6 April. Army putsch against de Gaulle ends in failure.

20 May–28 July. First peace talks at Évian end in failure.

17 October. Repression of Algerians in Paris.

1962:   7–18 March. Second Évian peace talks lead to agreement.

19 March. Ceasefire.

1 July. Referendum on Algerian independence.

3 July. De Gaulle recognizes Algerian independence.

25 September. Algerian Republic proclaimed.

1965:   19 June. Boumediène overthrows Ben Bella.

1978:   Death of Boumediène.

1988:   October. Riots in Algiers.

1992:   Cancellation of elections in Algeria.

1993:   Violence between army regime and Islamist guerrilla groups.

1999:   Bouteflika becomes president.

2009:   Bouteflika re-elected president after changing the constitution so that he could run for a third term.

2011:   Arab Spring.

2012:   Fiftieth anniversary of Algerian independence.

'We want the men of Algeria to be more free, more fraternal, more equal, that is to say more French.'

Max Lejeune (Socialist Party Deputy for the Somme and Armed Forces Minister), 15 March 1956.

PART I

Origins 1830–1945

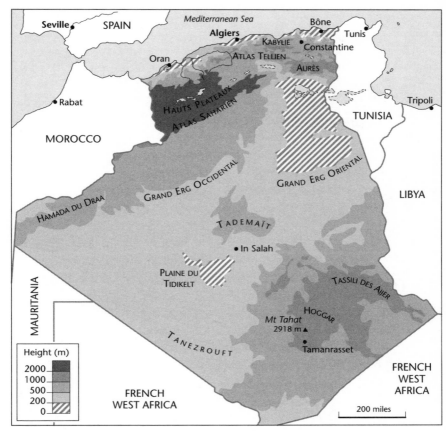

Map A 1954: French Algeria.

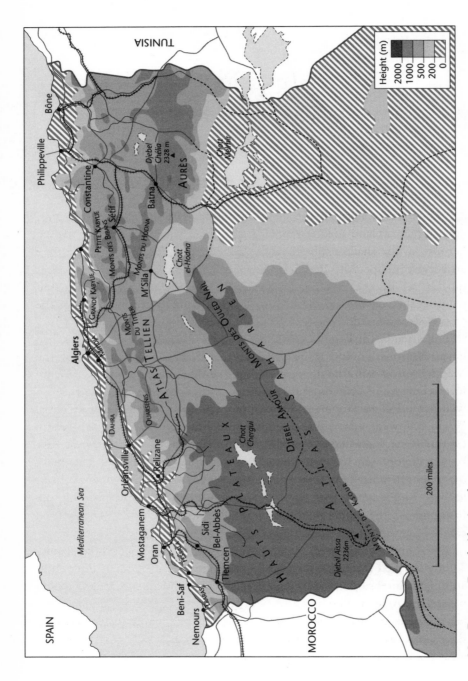

Map B 1954: French Algeria—the coast.

I

Invasion

Monday, 14 June 1830

The invasion began in the early hours of the morning at Sidi-Ferruch, a tongue of land 30 km to the west of Algiers. The spot had been chosen because of the shallow, sheltered beach. This was ideal for landing light artillery from specially designed flat barges and once ashore these units quickly set up the gun emplacements to repel any enemy attack, thus securing the way for the eighty-four ships and small vessels to disgorge the 37,000-strong force.

This armada, the largest expedition since the Napoleonic campaigns, had departed from Toulon three weeks earlier and under the glare of the Mediterranean sun the troops executed a well-prepared plan. Within forty-eight hours the immediate hinterland had been transformed into a well-defended encampment with hospitals, bivouacs, stables, and wells. What followed were five days of skirmishes before a 35,000-strong Ottoman force attacked on 19 June. Superior firepower led to an easy French victory which transformed the Ottoman retreat into a rout. Staouéli, the main Ottoman camp on the plateau overlooking the bay, was overrun, leaving the French to pick through the military debris while planning the final push on the capital. Not knowing what to do with the sixty captured camels, they ate them.

With nothing to stop the French, Algiers was gripped by panic. Thousands fled the city either to the east or to the mountains just south, an exodus intensified by news that the Ottoman sultan in Istanbul would not defend Algeria. The final advance began on 29 June and at midday on 5 July French troops entered Algiers. The French commander, General Bourmont, gave guarantees that the religious beliefs and customs of the local population would be respected and on these grounds the Ottoman

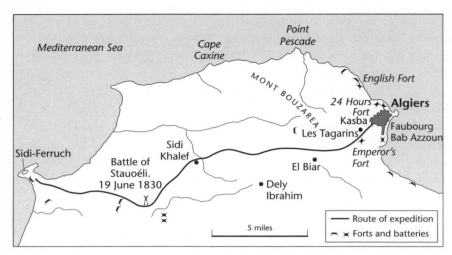

Map 1.1 1830: The Conquest of Algiers.

Dey, Khodja Hussein, agreed to depart. The campaign had lasted just twenty-one days at a cost of 400 casualties (see Map 1.1).

The pretext for invasion was the 'flywhisk incident' three years earlier. Since 1820 the Regency, nominally part of the Ottoman Empire but to all intents and purposes independent, had been plagued with financial troubles whose root cause was the decline in the flow of wealth from piracy operating out of Algiers.[1] To compensate for these losses the Regency tried to extract more taxation from the local population, but when this produced widespread resistance the crisis reached breaking point. Confronted with a desperate situation the Dey wanted loans, made to the French during the Napoleonic Wars, repaid. However, when the French consul refused, Khodja Hussein attacked him with a flywhisk calling him a 'wicked, faithless, idol-worshipping rascal'.

The incident soon blew up into a major diplomatic crisis. In France the press was clamouring for revenge. National honour had to be upheld; the 'nest of pirates' had to be given a bloody nose. Support for invasion came, too, from the Marseille business community. Having already established trading posts on the coast at La Calle and Bône, they had long seen Algeria as an inviting economic prize. And finally there were King Charles X's cold political calculations. He reasoned that foreign adventure would be a useful diversion from his domestic unpopularity.

Initially a blockade was instigated in the hope of bringing the Dey to his knees. However, once it became clear that this was having little impact France was left with a stark choice: either lose face or launch a full-scale attack. Invasion plans were drawn up based on originals made by Napoleon in 1808.[2] Yet, the French admiralty hung back, partly because of cost, partly because the fleet was deployed in Greece, but mostly because Charles X did not want to antagonize the British by raising the spectre of French expansion. When the decision to invade was made three years later the international situation seemed more favourable. Britain was in no position to intervene because the country was beset with social and political problems. Austria, Prussia, and Russia were supportive because foreign conquest would strengthen the hand of the conservatives against the liberals across Europe. Like Charles X they hoped that victory would sideline the liberal opposition and open the way for a return to absolute rule.

On 2 March 1830, Charles X announced to the National Assembly that France would invade. His public justifications: the need to punish the 'grave insult' of the flywhisk, end piracy, and reclaim Algeria for Christianity. This was a message which the officer corps, frustrated by barrack life in the provinces, relished. In Algeria they saw the opportunity to relive the Napoleonic era and win enduring military glory. But although the initial invasion was a success, it was not enough to save the Bourbon monarchy, which fell weeks afterwards in the July Revolution. This left the new liberal king, Louis-Philippe, shackled with Algeria where the army, forced to survive off the land and ravaged by dysentery, had lost a clear sense of purpose. In a bid to restore morale, the new commander, General Clauzel, launched a fresh offensive into the mountains just south of Algiers. There the 10,000-strong force was met by ferocious resistance forcing the army to take the town of Médéa street by street and house by house. Clearly the military had underestimated the size of the task in front of them and in November 1830 the National Assembly conducted a wide-ranging debate on the next step to take. Withdrawal, limited occupation, or full-scale conquest; all three were discussed without one scenario winning out over the others. Similarly, to the question 'why was France in Algeria?' nobody came up with a clear and unambiguous answer. The lack of consensus was striking, underlining the salient fact about these early years, namely that France stumbled into Algeria with no grand design.

Conquest

Political indecision left the commanders on the ground with a free hand. So, the promises that Islam would be respected were continually broken. Mosques were made into churches and cathedrals, often at gunpoint in the face of local protests, as the army leaders pressed into the rest of the country, presenting each victory as a fait accompli that Paris had to retrospectively sanction. But a quick victory proved elusive principally because the army had to cope with a treacherous landscape. This was a place of dramatic extremes where the intermittent coastal plains—an often unbearably hot zone of marshland, flooding, and malaria—gave way to the Tell Atlas ranges, followed by a high plain, the Saharan Atlas mountain ranges, and then inhospitable desert, comprising nine-tenths of the country's surface. In the case of the northern Tell Atlas, where much of the fighting between 1830 and 1847 was concentrated, the terrain was made up of deep gorges, narrow passes, and mountain peaks, some of which rose to over 2,000 feet. It was ideal country for ambushes and 'hit and run' attacks and soon the army was bogged down in an elusive war where the enemy deployed their local knowledge of the place to deadly effect.

As the French pressed on into the rest of the country they were confronted not only with a treacherous landscape, but a complex society made up of 3 million people.[3] Aside from a minority of 25,000 largely impoverished Jews living in towns and cities, the overwhelming majority was Berber in origin which, following the Arab expansion from the Middle East into North Africa between the seventh and ninth centuries, had largely absorbed Arabic culture and Islam and made them their own.[4] They saw themselves as belonging to the western tip of the Arab word (*Maghreb* in Arabic) which looked instinctively to their Arab roots in the east (*Mashriq* in Arabic). Although this process was self-evident right across North Africa, it really took root on the coast and along the plains, so that by 1830, it is vital to stress that the distinctions between Arab and Berber could not be reduced to two easily identifiable groups. The local population was a complex intermingling of the two, stretching back over 1,000 years, even if the Arab speakers were associated with the plains and the Berber speakers with the mountains. Of this population about 30 per cent spoke a variant of Berber made up principally of the Kabyles in Kabylia in the north, the

Shawiya in the Aurès region to the south-east, the Mozabites around Ghardaïa in the south, and the Tuaregs in the Saharan Hoggar region, while the rest spoke a local form of Arabic.[5] A tiny minority, principally the religious elite, spoke and wrote classical Arabic. For the most part the population was rural with the biggest city being Algiers with 30,000 inhabitants, followed by Constantine, 25,000; Tlemcen, 8,000; and Oran with just less than 6,000.[6] It was also a place characterized by religious homogeneity. All were Sunni Muslims; nor was there a Christian population. Christianity had died out by the twelfth century.[7]

The end of Ottoman rule did not mean that the local population wanted to be ruled by the French. However, in explaining their resistance it would be wrong to talk about a national consciousness. The populations did not describe themselves as Algerian even if Ottoman rule, in place since 1529, had delineated the outline of modern Algeria. What motivated their resistance was religion. In the century following the arrival of the Arabs in 647, part of the extraordinary expansion of Islam out from the Arabian peninsula after the Prophet Mohammed's death in 632, the Muslim religion became deeply rooted, assuming a central position in everyday life. Within the countryside the predominant form of Islam was Sufism: a mystical theology based around the cult of local saints, known as marabouts, that emerged in the twelfth century. The various orders were centred on refuges (*zawiyas*) and by the seventeenth century the most important were the Rahmaniya in Kabylia, the Tijana in the Sahara, the Darqawa in the area around Oran, and the Qadiriya, the local offshoot of the more widespread Shadhiliya. This identity produced a strong sense of religious place, blending the larger transnational Muslim community, the *umma*, with a notion of belonging based on the tribe, the *zawiya*, and their immediate surroundings. They inhabited the 'world of Islam' and it was their sacred duty to defend where they lived from what, in popular Arabic, was known as *al-Roumi*: the Christian invader.

Resistance based on Islam also fused with resistance to central authority. Throughout North African history a basic division had existed between the mountains and the plains. The mountains have functioned as natural fortresses where the power of the plains stopped abruptly. This was the world of the outlaw and the rebel. This was the world, too, of tribes, lineages, and families where great stress was placed upon male honour and respect for arms. Opposition to the French, therefore, was the expression of a deeply ingrained mindset, namely the hatred of any outside authority.

Figure 1.1 Abd el-Kader, lithograph by Auguste Bry.

It was the Sufi orders that led the large-scale revolts against Ottoman rule at the beginning of the nineteenth century when increased taxation of the countryside produced widespread resentment. It was the same Sufi orders that now led resistance against what was seen as a Christian invasion. In the western part of the country resistance was organized by a charismatic holy man, just 25 years old, Abd el-Kader.[8] Paintings and engraving depicted him as a handsome figure. Tall, imposing, always endowed with flowing robes, his religious legitimacy derived from the fact that he was part of the Qadiriya religious order and from a family that claimed descent from the prophet Mohammed. On this basis, he proclaimed himself commander of the faithful and called for a mass jihad to chase out the unbelievers, inflicting on the French a series of embarrassing reverses.

By 1836 the French were facing catastrophe, at which point they dispatched Marshal Thomas-Robert Bugeaud. Born in 1784, the now white-haired Bugeaud mixed military ruthlessness with cunning and guile, the product perhaps of his peasant upbringing and being a keen duellist. As deputy for the Dordogne in the new National Assembly he had voiced scepticism over Algerian colonization. These doubts, however, were cast aside as Bugeaud dedicated himself to total victory. Like most of his fellow officers, he had learnt about the harsh realities of guerrilla warfare during the Peninsula campaign in Spain between 1808 and 1814, lessons that he now applied to Algeria.[9] Called 'father Bugemar' by his troops, who penned songs about his peaked cap that was supposedly made out of camel hair, Bugeaud told them to give no quarter, an uncompromising attitude that produced victory against Abd el-Kader at the battle of Sikkak in July 1836. The Treaty of Tafna that followed, signed on 20 May 1837, then freed the French to defeat opposition in the east.

In theory, Tafna conceded sovereignty to Abd el-Kader of over two-thirds of Algeria, but this was an uneasy peace. The frontiers were ill-defined and, in response to French incursions into his territory, Abd el-Kader declared war in November 1839. Faced with renewed war Bugeaud returned as Governor-General in February 1841 and, drawing again on his Spanish experience, he introduced ever more ruthless tactics. This was the point when the Arab word *razzia* (scorched earth) entered the military lexicon as pro-Abd el-Kader villages were razed to the ground, captured Muslims beheaded, and prisoners forced to write on their clothes 'Subjugated Arab' ('*Arabe Soumis*').

Hemmed in on all sides, the situation was desperate for Abd el-Kader. In an attempt to stave off defeat Abd el-Kader looked for support from

Morocco, but when Moroccan troops were routed at the Battle of Isly on 14 August 1844, a crowning moment for Bugeaud, surrender became a matter of time. This came on 23 December 1847 in the hills just above Oujda on the Moroccan border. Imprisoned in France, Abd el-Kader went into exile in Damascus in December 1855.[10] It was without doubt a decisive moment in the conquest process, but not one that brought an end to resistance. In the east, Greater Kabylia would not be conquered until 1857 and in the west there were uprisings in 1864 and again in 1881.

Early settlement

The invasion did not lead to mass colonization. Fear of Muslim violence, combined with the threat of typhoid and cholera, were great deterrents and by 1839 the European population stood at 25,000, still less than a French provincial city like Limoges. Of these only 11,000 were French with the rest from Spain, Malta, Italy, Germany, and even Switzerland. The majority clung to the coastal towns and cities. This was where they felt most secure. With men outnumbering women by five to one this was a macho, frontier world which, in the eyes of mainland France, was looked down upon as a magnet for brothels, bars, and low-life swindlers.

Out of this initial European population only 10 per cent ventured into the countryside to establish pocket settlements. There were aristocratic settlers who, wishing to remain faithful to the Bourbon line after the July Revolution, acquired large tracts of land with a view to recreating a pre-1789 regime in Algeria.[11] There were soldier settlers who were given land concessions at the end of their military service.[12] And there were religious settlers such as the Cistercian monks who were granted over 1,020 hectares to build a monastery and farm on the Staouéli plateau, midway between Algiers and Koléa.

There was, too, a strong left-wing strain to colonialism. Disciples of the socialist Saint Simon saw Algeria as a blank space for their utopian schemes. Workers and artisans, deported to Algeria after the failed June 1848 Paris uprising, established model villages. The revolutionary Louis Blanc welcomed the invasion in the name of France's world mission to free oppressed peoples. In a similar vein Friedrich Engels justified French rule on the grounds that this was opening the country up to the forward march of history. By sweeping away old structures and introducing capitalism France was laying the basis for Algeria's ultimate eventual social and economic liberation. Writing in the English Chartist newspaper, the *Northern Star*, in 1848, he applauded Abd el-Kader's surrender:

> Upon the whole it is, in our opinion, very fortunate that the Arabian chief has been taken. The struggle of the Bedouins was a hopeless one, and though the manner in which brutal soldiers, like Bugeaud, have carried on the war is highly blameable, the conquest of Algeria is an important and fortunate fact for the progress of civilisation . . . after all, the modern bourgeois, with civilisation, industry, order, and at least relative enlightenment following him, is preferable to the feudal lord or to the marauding robber, with the barbarian state of society to which they belong.[13]

Military rule

In France the Orleanist monarchy gave way to the Second Republic in 1848. This in turn was swept away by Louis-Napoleon's *coup d'état* on 2 December 1851 and the establishment of the Second Empire. This instability allowed the army to transform Algeria into a military fiefdom where violence became the standard instrument of French rule. However, coercion went hand in hand with a reaching out to the people through the creation of the 'Arab Affairs Bureaus' (Bureaux des Affaires Arabes) in 1844. Headed by officers who spoke Arabic, the Bureaux adapted Ottoman structures in order to institutionalize patterns of control and communication with the various tribes: a world of contact between rulers and ruled which, although highly paternalistic, displayed a concern for the local population.

The establishment of military rule was bitterly resented by the settlers. They saw the army policies as pro-Arab and wanted civil rule in Algeria. Initially they hoped Napoleon III would be an ally, but when in 1863, he proclaimed the vision of an Arab kingdom and underlined the need to bring the two communities together, he too became a hate figure. Thus, Napoleon's capture at Sedan in the early weeks of the Franco-Prussian War on 2 September 1870 was greeted with widespread enthusiasm. Even if they wanted to continue to fight the Prussian invaders, the streets of Algiers were swamped by crowds of settlers singing the Marseillaise. Inspired by the proclamation of a republic in Paris on 4 September, a republican committee was established on the following day. This Algiers Commune, establishing a tradition of settler revolt that was to continue right up until 1962, then set about the purging of Bonapartist civil servants and demanding liberation from military rule.

The incendiary atmosphere had a different impact upon the Muslim population. Suffering from economic misery, worried by the end of military rule which had afforded some protection, and convinced that defeat at the hands of Prussians was a sign from God, a huge revolt erupted in Kabylia led by the local leader Bachagha El-Mokhrani. The final straw had been the Crémieux decrees giving citizenship to Jews on 24 October 1870, placing Muslims below Jews, and on 16 March 1871 150,000 answered Mokhrani's call for a jihad against French rule. At first the French army was over-whelmed by the sheer magnitude of the uprising. By the end of May all the major towns in eastern Algeria were under siege. In the end, however, there was no coordination and by the end of 1871 the revolt had ended in complete failure. The repression that followed was very harsh. A total of 450,000 hectares of tribal land was confiscated; the leaders were either executed or deported to New Caledonia in the Pacific; and Qur'anic schools put under surveillance. Then, to humiliate still further, Arabic was categorized as a foreign language.

The Mokhrani revolt was the climax of thirty-one years of bloodshed that devastated Muslim society. This violence, if the military losses are combined with that of the 1867 famine, left nearly 1 million dead, in other words a third of the population. It also destroyed many of the outward pillars—mosques, religious schools, communal stores of food put aside for hardship—as well as a generation of Muslim elites. In terms of scale the destruction was much more total than in either Tunisia or Morocco, annexed as protectorates in 1881 and 1912. Here the Bey in Tunisia and the Sultan in Morocco remained in place and specific treaty obligations gave them both, in theory at least, some measure of authority.[14] In Algeria no such structures ever existed. The country's leaders were just too weakened to be a serious political force and this meant that, in contrast to Tunisia and Morocco, Algerian nationalism would come from beyond the traditional elites.

Ultimately, however, the most profound legacy was a psychological one. Stunned by the magnitude and visibility of the disaster Muslims carried with them the trauma of the 1830 invasion. They had been overrun by a Christian country and in a society that was profoundly Muslim this left a lasting hatred. It became an oral memory handed down the generations.

Muslims were told to remember the brutality of Bugeaud.[15] They were told to remember the humiliation of Islam, such as the conversion of the Ketchawa mosque, one of the largest and most beautiful in Algiers, into a cathedral on 18 December 1832.[16] They were told, too, to remember the dispossession of their land. The original sin of invasion could never be forgiven. All their subsequent ills—racism, religious humiliation, material dispossession—were seen to flow from this event and on this basis a large part of the population could never accept French rule under any circumstances.

Without doubt the failure of the Mokhrani revolt was a nadir. From this psychological low point it took Muslim society some fifty years to recover.

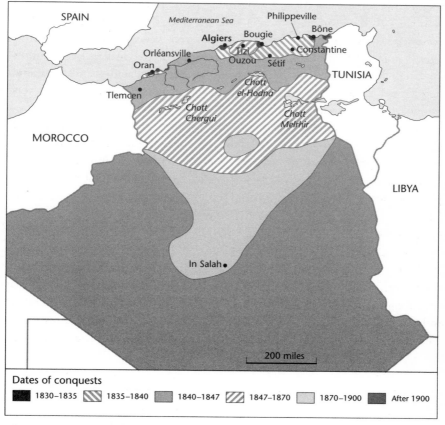

Map 1.2 1830–1900: The Conquest of Algeria and the Sahara.

During these decades there were still periodic revolts and the conquest of the Sahara was not complete until the 1920s, but for the most part the Muslim population turned in on themselves. Islam remained at the centre of their personal lives, expressing a basic and formidable barrier. This was a private world that was unconquerable, ensuring that Muslim and European society remained separate.

2

The Long Hatreds

Friday, 26 August 1881

O n this day the French government, led by arch colonialist Jules Ferry,
announced a momentous step to the National Assembly.[1] Henceforth
Algeria would be administered as an integral part of France under the Third
Republic's 1875 constitution.[2] Any confusion about Algeria's status was
ended. In the eyes of the law the country was sovereign territory under the
control of the Ministry of the Interior, whose civil servants and officials
were accountable to the various government departments in the metropole.

In debating the legislation no doubts were expressed about the legal or
moral legitimacy of this action. The consensus from right to left was that
France had a right to be there. Algeria was declared to be French in the same
way as Normandy, Brittany or the Savoy. To leave would be to dismember
the essence of the nation state, an unthinkable scenario for any future
government.

On hearing the news the settlers were jubilant. This is what they had
been fighting for all along. At last they felt protected. This was an unbreakable bond because the Third Republic introduced the building blocks of
rule with departments (Oranie in the west, Algérois in the centre, and
Constantinois in the east), prefectures and communes. Yet, despite the
principle of a unified republic, practices in Algeria were very different
from those in the metropole. In Algeria republican structures were applied
with one aim in mind: to exclude the Muslim majority from political
power. Within the mixed communes (communes mixtes), which held sway
in Muslim-dominated areas, there was no voting. All the Muslim administrators were appointed by the administration. Equally, each department's
size, ten times greater than the average metropolitan equivalent, meant that
French rule was always overstretched. To cope, civil servants, confronted

with the day-to-day problems of governance, adapted the Ottoman system, just as the army had done with the Arab bureaux (*bureaux arabes*), searching out compliant local leaders amongst the tax collectors (*qaïds*), judges (*qadis*), and tribal leaders (*bachagas*) who would administer the law and raise taxes in return for concessions. Key legislation too was never applied in Algeria. So, the separation of Church and State in 1905, a major victory in the establish-ment of a secular state, was not extended to Algeria. Why? Because the authorities wanted to control the appointment of Muslim preachers in Algeria, as well priests within the Spanish and Italian communities of the European population. And finally there was the anomaly of the Sahara. This remained a territory apart under military rule.

Furthermore, Algerian territory might have been assimilated into France but the populations were not equal.[3] Throughout the Third Republic until its fall in 1940, the law enshrined exclusion. It defined who had citizenship and voting rights and who did not. Within this discriminatory system neither women, as in France itself, nor Muslims could vote. They were not considered to be part of the body of citizens who made up the active nation. This meant that electoral politics was race- and gender-specific. It was dominated by a narrow band of male European settlers.

These numbers swelled in 1889 when, to mark the hundredth anniversary of the French Revolution, the Third Republic conferred citizenship on the non-French settlers, mostly from Italy and Spain, who made up just over half the 430,000 *colon* population.[4] This made 1889 into *the* moment when a collective settler identity came into being. In political terms this identity was to be expressed through the election of six deputies. They were the settlers' eyes and ears, the backbone of a colonial lobby whose reach was formidable. Within this lobby two parliamentarians came to stand out as the undisputed masters of the Algerian scene: Eugène Étienne and Gaston Thomson. As near contemporaries (Étienne was born in 1844 and Thomson in 1848), the two men had much in common. Both were born in Oran in western Algeria. Both radiated late nineteenth-century bourgeois political respect-ability with their suits and whiskers. Both styled themselves as left-wing republicans who enjoyed long and prolific parliamentary careers. Étienne was deputy for Oran between 1881 and 1919, and, at various times, vice-president of the Assembly, Minister of the Interior and Minister of War. Thomson, eleven times elected deputy for Constantine, occupied the post of Navy Minister on three separate occasions between 1905 and 1908. In each case they used government to champion the 'age of empire'. To those who argued that colonialism was a diversion from the real issue, the recovery of Alsace-Lorraine from the Germans, they invoked the national greatness, 'civilizing mission' and the need for resources.

By sidelining the role of the Governor-General as it did, the 1881 settlement handed over the reins of power to the Algerian deputies. Their six seats became personal fiefdoms, the hubs of patronage at all levels of the political process. Constantly vigilant, inherently conservative, they were the gatekeepers of colonial Algeria. All legislation was carefully vetted to ensure that settler interests were ruthlessly defended, while pushing for French imperial expansion into the four corners of the globe.[5] The lobby's effectiveness in pursuing these aims was reflected in Étienne's standing amongst fellow deputies. Nicknamed 'le Grand Marabout' and 'Kingmaker', these soubriquets were testaments to his skills as an operator. They also recognized a basic political fact, namely that the settlers monopolized power in Algeria.

Below the Europeans were the Jews. At the time of the invasion there were 25,000, mostly living in dire poverty. With names like Daniel, Derrida, Nouischi, and Stora, Jews had existed in North Africa for over 2,000 years. Some arrived with the Phoenicians between 1100 and 146 BC. Others came after the expulsion of Jews from Spain in 1492.[6] Under Islamic law they were accorded a protected status as the 'people of the book'.[7] This meant that in return for a tax they were allowed to practise Judaism. From the outset French governments saw Jews as potential allies. This view was championed by French Jews who sought to convince their co-believers of the need to embrace French culture. The most passionate advocate of this position was Isaac Moïse Crémieux. Born in Nîmes in 1796, going under the name Adolphe, Crémieux was a lawyer, freemason, and several times deputy. For him, republicanism embodied personal and collective liberation for Jews and as Justice Minister in the government of National Defence he passed the Crémieux Decrees on 24 October 1870, which conferred citizenship onto the Jewish community, then totalling around 37,000. It was his crowning achievement and in the following two decades Jews embraced assimilation. In terms of dress, manner, and language most, but in particular the new generations, adopted modern French styles and distanced themselves from Hebrew and Arab culture. The French Republic was their home, a sentiment that was reflected in the way in which Jews became prominent in the League of the Rights of Man, the freemasons, trade unions, and left-wing political parties. But, despite the law, Jewish status remained problematic. On the one hand, Europeans saw Jewish advancement as a threat to their own privileges, thereby making anti-Semitism into a permanent feature of settler political culture. On the other, the Muslim majority resented Jewish enfranchisement because it reinforced their own lack of rights. As a result the Jewish minority came to occupy a vulnerable position between Europeans and Muslims. Their citizenship was always fragile.

At the bottom of the system were Muslims. In reviewing the legal status of the populations, the 1865 *sénatus-consulte* defined Muslims simply as voteless French subjects. Citizenship was separated from nationality, but also linked to race and religion. Islamic culture was seen to be incompatible with citizenship and this ensured that Muslims, although defined as French nationals, were permanently shut out of French Algeria.[8] The schema was justified on the grounds that it upheld local customs. Non-criminal justice related to marriage or inheritance was administered by Muslim judges rather than French officials. In practice this was an insurmountable barrier, for to become citizens Muslims had to sign away this right, an act of apostasy few were willing to make. Between 1865 and 1899, a mere 1,309 requests for citizenship were made out of a population of approximately 4 million by 1901 and within wider Muslim society this tiny minority were viewed with suspicion.[9] In popular Arabic they were referred to as *muturni*, a pejorative word meaning someone who had turned their back on their own culture: in short a Muslim seduced by colonialism.

Without citizenship Muslims could not vote in national elections, but even this was not considered enough to keep them in check.[10] Further legislation ensured that Muslims were excluded from positions of power. By law a Muslim could not be a court judge. Even more emphatically disenfranchisement was reinforced by the 1881 'Native Code' (*Code de l'indigénat*), a uniquely repressive set of laws, that applied only to Muslims and was designed to ensure complete submission.[11] The *indigénat* reached into every cranny of the Muslim majority's life. Under its twenty-seven provisions Muslims were controlled by legislation right down to requiring permission to go on pilgrimage to Mecca. They could be imprisoned for making rude remarks about French authority; holding public meetings without authorization; opening schools without a permit; refusing to supply colonial administrators with transport, food, water, or fuel; not registering a weapon; tax avoidance; even giving refuge to vagabonds.

The *indigénat* served as a reference point for the rest of the French Empire—similar systems of crime and punishment were introduced in New Caledonia and Senegal in 1887, Tahiti in 1897, Cambodia in 1898, and Madagascar in 1901—and in these countries, as in Algeria, the laws inspired universal loathing. This was because they cut across class barriers. They not only chained the peasant, but also paralysed and gagged the landowner, intellectual, doctor, and lawyer. They unified Muslims more strongly than softer laws could ever have done, creating disaffection right across the political spectrum.

When added together these laws, creating as they did hierarchies of power, ensured that French Algeria was rigidly segregated.[12] Exclusion was a defining principle. Political separation produced physical separation. Europeans, Jews, and Muslims inhabited different spaces, coexisting but never truly intermingling. Marriages between these different groups were very rare indeed, and the result was a society that was deeply divided and deeply unequal, defined by hatred, conflict, and tension. This fault line, running right through the history of French Algeria, was to be the major cause of the 1954 to 1962 war.

Settler society

The imposition of French law was central to the settler seizure of the best land. For example, the 1873 Law, introduced by August Warnier, simplified the buying and selling of land by enshrining private, rather than tribal, ownership. Warnier believed that the introduction of these principles would benefit Muslims, opening the path to 'progress' and 'civilization'. It would allow them to adapt to free-market principles, discard outmoded techniques and raise living standards through efficient and productive use of the land.

In reality, the law became the instrument for an all-out land grab. Even if some Muslims did have a notion of private ownership, none understood the French concept of a legally binding property contract, in particular the way in which contracts had to be signed by a surnamed individual. The possibility for fraud was legion with the result that between 1880 and 1908 vast estates, totalling 451,000 hectares, were purchased by Europeans at little cost. This dispossession accelerated a process that had been in place since the 1830s. Already by 1870 settlers had acquired 481,000 hectares and this was supplemented by 687,000 hectares of land, most of it annexed as punishment for the 1871 uprising, which was granted directly to *colons* by the state. In the case of the settlers from Alsace, 100,000 hectares of the best land was given to them in 1871 in recognition of their patriotic decision to flee German rule after the annexation of Alsace-Lorraine.

Moreover, this acquisition of land was facilitated by a banking system which was always tilted in favour of the settlers. Founded in 1851 and given the right to print money, the Bank of Algeria introduced French principles. This handed an inbuilt head start to those settler speculators who understood the system of borrowing and credit, an advantage reinforced by the fact that usury was forbidden by Islamic law. This access to finance capital was the final pillar in a system that dispossessed Muslims on a grand scale. By 1936, settler ownership stood at 7.7 million hectares, that is 40 per cent of the land possessed by the indigenous population before the French invasion.

Specializing in wine, cork, and alfalfa, this settler land was primarily concentrated on the coastal plains and in the west. It was also the preserve of a tiny group of individuals and companies. They were the winners in the colonial system whose aim was to produce a modern agricultural economy, a French California, driven by profit and not subsistence. Out of the 26,153 properties, one-fifth accounted for three-quarters of the total land owned by Europeans. It was a huge statistic and the public faces of this entrenched minority were Jacques Duroux, Henri Borgeaud, and Laurent Schiaffino. Duroux, the richest man in Algeria in the 1930s, was a senator and the owner of a flour industry, a shipping company and huge vineyards, as well as head of a press empire that included the most widely read daily newspaper *L'Écho d'Alger*. Henri Borgeaud, owner of the famous La Trappe wine company, was also a senator, while Laurent Schiaffino was a shipping magnate and the president of the Algiers Chamber of Commerce. All three oligarchs symbolized the connection between politics and economics. Driven by self-interest, they built a maritime export economy—all the roads and railways led to the major ports—whose base was an endless reservoir of cheap labour amongst the Muslims.

The conversion of the land into a profitable entity was part of a global economic phenomenon and the same processes could be seen in French Tunisia and Morocco or the British territories of Kenya, Rhodesia, and South Africa.[13] This transformation became the foundation stones of French Algeria. The settlers had a right to remain in Algeria because the land had been 'rightly' acquired in law. Equally they had, so the argument ran, made a wilderness bloom through tender care and attention. The new

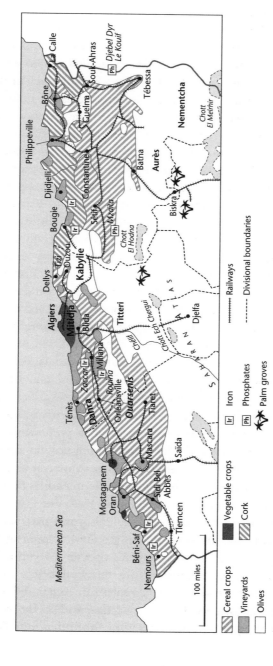

Map 2.1 The Colonial Transformation of Algeria: Patterns of European Farming and Industry at the beginning of the Twentieth Century.

Algeria of irrigated plains, ripened vineyards, and intensive farming was testament to their pioneering spirit; the decisive reason why they, and not the original inhabitants, should own this land.

This image of the settlers as tough frontier people rooted in the soil was central to their self-identity. Yet, paradoxically this image was a myth. The majority were urban. They lived in the coastal cities and were located in the west of the country, in particular Oran, the only city with a settler majority right up until 1961.[14] Few had any direct experience of farming. Rather they were employed as manual workers, white collar employees, small-trades people and in local government.

It was the last three decades of the nineteenth century that witnessed the arrival of the settlers en masse. Motivated by the desire to escape poverty and make a better life, this migration was part of a general pattern throughout Europe.[15] What led these migrants to choose Algeria over the USA was the close proximity of North Africa. This made travel cheaper and less hazardous. They were also reassured by the fact that after forty years of colonization the French presence seemed permanent and secure. Sociologically most settlers were from Southern Europe. They were Italian, Maltese, or Spanish.[16] In the case of those French people who crossed the Mediterranean they mostly came from the Midi. For them Algeria was a new start after a phylloxera epidemic had destroyed a large part of the wine industry in Languedoc and Provence between 1875 and 1889.[17]

This meant that the settlers were never homogeneous. There was a top and a bottom. At the apex were the rich *colons*, a tiny clutch of people who wielded economic and political control over French Algeria. The overwhelming majority, however, were poor. Even by the 1950s, living standards were 20 per cent lower than the metropole and within this majority social status was carefully indexed. Given that French was the language of authority and education, those who were French in origin enjoyed the most prestige. This was especially true of the natives of Alsace-Lorraine. In choosing to come to Algeria in 1871 rather than live under German rule they were the living embodiment of republican patriotism, constantly lionized within official ceremonies.[18] In turn the French looked down on foreign settlers. Marked out by names like Martini, Martinez, Lopez, Gomez, or Ortiz, they were seen as vulgar and uneducated. Enormous pressure was put on them to forget their countries of origin and assimilate into French culture. For example, Andrea Chazot was born in 1921 and lived in Hussein Dey, a predominantly Italian and Spanish *quartier* of Algiers.

At home she spoke Spanish, a phenomenon frowned upon by her primary school: 'Our teacher was French, she did not want our parents to speak Spanish, she made my parents come and see her to tell them: "Your children are going to live in France, they must speak French, if not it will be a handicap for them, do not speak to them in Spanish."'[19]

Judgements of this nature explain why the settlers were always finely attuned to difference. They knew that to be French, Italian, Maltese, and Spanish was not the same, even if all European men enjoyed citizenship after 1889, and this was reflected in the way in which each group became identified with specific *quartiers* in the major towns and cities.

This also explains their ambiguous relationship with France and Frenchness. On the one hand, the settlers were intent on recreating day-to-day French life. They built cafés, churches, and town halls. They baked baguettes and played boules. They gave French names to villages, towns, and cities. But, on the other, they knew that amongst metropolitan French they were seen as coarse and uncouth, emotional hotheads who would act on impulse and think later. Marie-Louise Pons was born in 1932 in Affreville in the west of the country into a modest Spanish family. She remembers:

> We always had a complex relationship in Algeria with the people from the metropole. We found that they spoke better . . . we had the impression that we were less well mannered, less educated. In Algeria, all the senior posts, the prefects, sub-prefects, lawyers . . . were taken up by metropolitans with their know-how, their qualifications. We the Spanish, the foreigners, we came over as labourers.[20]

These fears and insecurities produced a separate settler identity. This was articulated through an explosion of the regional and national press. By 1914 all the major cities had a daily newspaper.[21] It was also reflected in the opening of Algiers University in 1880, followed by the Opera House three years later, signalling Algiers's intention to be a major centre of culture to rival Paris.[22] But it was captured in *Cagayous*, a series of popular humorous novels by Auguste Robinet with illustrations by Salomon Assus.[23] First serialized in the satirical review *Le Turco* in the 1900s, Cagayous, a street urchin from the Bab-El-Oued *quartier* of Algiers, was a warm-hearted pig head, sporting a Breton top, plaited trousers and slip-on espadrilles. Louche, loud, and macho, his language was angry, mixing French with Spanish, Italian, and Arabic. It was also very proud. If asked, 'Are you French?', Cagayous would retort, 'We are Algerian.' He was the embodiment of the

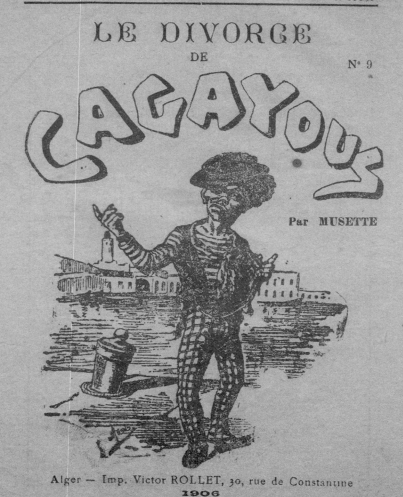

PRIX : 10 Centimes   Mercredi, 25 Avril 1906.

LE DIVORCE
DE
CAGAYOUS
N° 9

Par MUSETTE

Alger — Imp. Victor ROLLET, 30, rue de Constantine
1906

Figure 2.1 *Cagayous*: these novels celebrated the specificity of the European settlers as Algerians.

settlers as Algerians, sentiments that were at the heart of Robert Randau's 1911 novel *Les Algérianistes* and the writings of Louis Bertrand, both of whom proclaimed Algeria to be a new civilization, more vibrant and alive than the metropole.[24] Bertrand in particular portrayed the Europeans as a Latin melting pot that was taking up the heritage of the Roman Empire in North Africa. In this perspective the settler presence was not an invasion or occupation. It was the recovery of a land that was rightfully theirs.

Bertrand, Robinet, and Randau give us an insight into the European world. This was a world that championed the ordinary settler (*les petits*) against big power interests (*les grands*). It was a very male world that rejoiced in male prowess on the sports field and relegated women to the domestic sphere. And finally it was a world that disliked meddling from French politicians. 'Algiers is not Paris' was a familiar refrain amongst settlers, indicating a hostility to centralized control which, although evident elsewhere in Brittany and the south of France, was particularly entrenched in Algeria because the settlers saw Parisian interference as a threat to their privileged position.

Figure 2.2 French Algeria: settlers in front of a post office with the tricolore, Alma, near Algiers, 1910.

The Jewish and Arab 'other'

If disavowal of Paris was one way in which Europeans found unity, the other was in opposition to Jews and Arabs. Generalizations peppered daily conversation. These became the basis of a collective 'we' and 'they', reinforcing attachment to the Roman Catholic Church. Looking down on the indigenous populations made them feel superior, especially when so many had so little themselves. The lower down the scale the more virulent was the racism. Their sense of being poor Europeans demanded relief and this was to be found in denigrating Jews and Arabs—an embittered comfort, a defence against their own deracination.

Anti-Semitism tapped into the settler perceptions of themselves as ordinary, hardworking people. Jews were held up as a rich and exploitative breed intent on dominating French Algeria. The Crémieux Decrees were seen as evidence of this grand plot and throughout the 1870s and 1880s prejudice became more and more open, before exploding in 1897 when settlers sacked the Jewish *quartiers* in Mostaganem and Oran. In part the movement was fuelled by anger over the Dreyfus Affair and on 18 and 19 January 1898 settler students burnt effigies of Alfred Dreyfus and Emile Zola while shouting 'Long live the army! Down with Jews!'[25] Then on the following day they looted Jewish shops in central Algiers under the watchful gaze of the police who did not intervene. This violence left two Jews dead and dozens injured. It created a momentum that saw settlers elect four anti-Semitic deputies, including the notorious Edouard Drumont, in the May 1898 national elections.[26] Like anti-communism in 1950s USA, anti-Semitism was now a permanent feature of settler politics, reflected in a surge of publications such as *Le Combat Antijuif, Le Colon Antijuif Algérien*, and *Le Petit Anti-Juif.*

This anti-Semitism was indissolubly linked to the calls for separatism. Already Félix Dessoliers, professor of law and former deputy for Oran, had brandished this spectre in his 1895 book *L'Algérie libre.*[27] Reminding Paris that taxation and representation was at the origin of the 1776 American Revolution, the settlers, he argued, did not want to be economically and politically subordinate to the metropole. They wished to administer their own budget. Bolstered by the anti-Semitic movement, such threats forced the French government to devolve financial power to an Algerian Assembly on 19 December 1900. Through intimidation they had got all they wanted: the right to run Algeria with limited interference from Paris.

This was a constitutional arrangement that suited the rich settler lobby perfectly because it understood the limitations of the USA analogy. With the American War of Independence between 1776 and 1783 the thirteen colonies reimagined their identity in a fundamental way. They were not colonists dependent on the prerogative of the British monarchy but owners of the continent by inherent right, even if this was based on the exclusion of slaves, Native Americans, and women. European settlers reconceived their identity at the end of the nineteenth century in a similar fashion. They were Algerian and they were different from the metropole. Yet, ultimately the settlers never went as far as the thirteen British colonies. Why? Because they felt increasingly outnumbered as the Muslim demographic curve recovered from the shock of 1830–71 to move steadily upwards. Between 1871 and 1936 the Muslim population trebled from 2 million to 6 million, increasing to 9 million in 1954 (Table 2.1). During the same period the settler population rose to 1 million, creating a fundamental imbalance. In the last resort the *colons* knew that they needed the protection of the metropole. With France they were the majority. Without France they were the minority.

Like anti-Semitism, anti-Muslim racism was endemic to settler society. To hold an attitude of antagonism towards Muslims was inbred from childhood. Constantly demeaned through phrases like *melon, bougnoule,*

Table 2.1 1836–1960: The Demography of French Algeria.

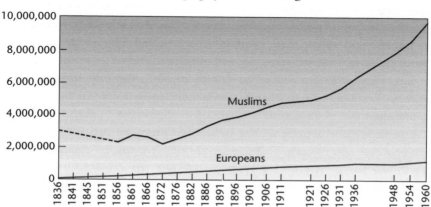

bicot, and *raton*, Muslims were seen to be uncivilized, stupid, and untrust-worthy, or some mixture of all three. One book by a French doctor, published anonymously in 1891, was typical of settler generalizations: 'The Arab is thieving and cruel. We see how groups form in order to pillage, and how their blood runs in attack or defence. Everyone must be on their guard, especially in respect to the stealing of cattle.'[28]

Such prejudices made the settlers constantly vigilant. The smallest favour to Muslims on the part of the authorities released huge resentment. For them Muslims had to be kept in rigorous submission which was one of the reasons behind settler anti-Semitism. They saw Jewish citizenship as the thin end of the wedge. It was the first step on the road to Muslim enfranchise-ment and the end of the status quo.

Anti-Muslim prejudice also created a siege mentality. The settlers, espe-cially those living in isolated pockets in the interior, wanted to feel pro-tected by the strong arm of the French state. In Guelma in the east of the country the local authorities were inundated with settler complaints at the end of the nineteenth century.[29] All testify to an all-pervasive atmosphere of insecurity. Settler farmers in the surrounding region, notably Nechmeya, Millésimo, and Héliopolis, reported a constant stream of criminal attacks, including death threats and murder. One letter dated 27 March 1890 from A. Bailleul, a beleaguered settler in Guelaât-bou-Sba, was typical of settler exasperation. Replying to a questionnaire sent out by the local agricultural organization asking for details of crime, he listed what he had been subjected to during the decade 1880–90. These included two attacks on the house; the theft of wheat and cattle; the vandalizing of vineyards and trees; and burning down of a haymaking machine. Despite each incident being carefully reported only one person had been brought to justice. Frustrated, Bailleul concluded that to go to the police was a waste of time: 'We must ask ourselves where we are going to. Indubitably to the liquidation of coloni-zation, if a prompt and energetic remedy is not brought to bear on such a serious situation; this is a truth which is obvious to all, apart from the government.'[30]

For the settlers, such attacks on people and property were symptoms of a criminal mentality which, if allowed to continue, would ignite their greatest fear: generalized Muslim insurrection. Despite the crushing of the 1871 revolt, this image remained a constant anxiety. Settlers were worried that Muslim violence was always just below the surface; an impression re-inforced by the events of 26 April 1901 when a hundred people from the

Righa tribe 16 km from the town of Miliana to the south-west of Algiers attacked the village of Margueritte Bourgade. Taking the *qaïd* hostage and murdering a Muslim policeman, the assailants forced the captured Europeans to convert to Islam, killing five who refused. Troops alerted by telegraph wire quickly quashed the rebellion, but within settler society the 'Margueritte incident' had a lasting psychological impact. It showed why the settlers had to be permanently on their guard. As a boy growing up in French Algeria, Jules Roy remembers how in the years before World War One his uncle, the owner of a small farm on the Mitidja plain, always carried a gun: 'The natives feared us because of the gendarmes, and we feared the natives—the Arabs. My uncle Jules always carried a hunting rifle, another was hanging up in the dining room, a third in my grandmother's bedroom. We never travelled in a car without a gun.'[31]

Within French Algeria, Muslims, therefore, were seen as a law-and-order problem. They were not part of the historical and political landscape. Growing up in the 1930s in Blida, just to the south of Algiers, into a Jewish family that had assimilated into French culture, Jean Daniel remembers this invisibility as one of the unspoken assumptions of daily life.[32] The notion that the Arab and Berber populations might have legitimate political opinions, which should be taken account of, was inconceivable. Instead student discussions centred on politics in the European community. Nor did settlers like anything that upset this invisibility. Daniel cites the example of a Muslim doctor who established his surgery in the European *quartier* in 1935. The barriers for this were enormous. To register a practice a Muslim had to dress in a European manner, be the son of an ex-serviceman and speak French without an accent. However, his presence was even then perceived as a threat. Settlers hated Muslim middle-class advancement as a threat to the status quo and on this basis they shunned his surgery. One day, though, parents of one of Daniel's friends, left-wingers who according to him treated their Muslim farm labourers humanely, had to use this doctor for an emergency prescription because their child had suddenly fallen ill:

> The father of my friend kept turning over the prescription in his hands, embarrassed at having had to resort to an Arab doctor and vaguely sharing the suspicion that a Muslim would not be able to cure her child. They waited forty-eight hours for the return of a European doctor, despite a growing worry for the health of my friend.[33]

Such prejudice reflected the way in which those on the left also looked down on Muslim culture as backward and unsophisticated. Roger Rey, for example, was born on the Franco-Swiss border in 1925. His father (a customs officer posted to Oran in 1931) and mother were proud members of the left. Fiercely anti-clerical, a trade-unionist and freemason, Rey's father joined the French Socialist Party (Section Française de l'Internationale Ouvrière—SFIO) in 1936. Echoing Engels's sentiments a century earlier, Rey remembers how they saw themselves as the standard bearers of 1789 and the Paris Commune whose role was to elevate Muslims into the realm of modern 'civilization': 'They looked down on Algerians because they considered themselves to represent a political culture and tradition which was superior to that of the Algerian peasantry. It did not enter their heads to question the French presence in Algeria. For them Algeria was three French departments.'[34]

Although there was a common pattern of power, relationships did vary from region to region. Jules Roy remembers how his father, the owner of a small 8-hectare farm on the Mitidja plain, could converse in basic Arabic with his labourers. In the same vein Bernard Coll, interviewed about his childhood in 1930s French Algeria, underlined the difference between urban settlers, and those in the countryside like himself, who mixed with Muslims and spoke some Arabic, pointing to the way in which away from the coastal cities a world of contact, connections, and exchange did exist.[35] Yet, even if barriers were crossed in some places, the evidence, both contemporary and retrospective, points to a strong sense of geopolitical place on all sides. French Algeria might not have been as rigid as the apartheid system in South Africa, but ethnic segregation structured society. Under this unwritten schema Muslim space was comprised of the Casbah, the mountains, the interior, and the east, while that of the settler was made up of the coast, the city, and the west.

Muslim dispossession

Ottoman rule between 1529 and 1830 did not lead to the expropriation of land or the imposition of a new economic and legal system. Nor did it involve mass settlement or an attack on indigenous religious beliefs.[36] The consequences of French colonialism were on a different scale entirely.

The private purchase of the best land by Europeans created two unequal agricultural systems that led to the collapse of Muslim rural society. On the one side there were the settler farms, in the main huge mechanized enterprises concentrated in the west and fixated by profit and export, while on the other there was a Muslim system made up of small family-run holdings. In 1901, the latter had to feed 1,768,000 mouths or a staggering 55 per cent of the agrarian population.[37] Not surprisingly this subsistence economy, forced to make do with the worst land and reliant upon traditional methods that were highly inefficient—often fields would be left fallow for two years—began to buckle in the face of a demographic curve that, as previously noted, saw the population triple to 6 million between 1871 and 1936. Just for a family of six to exist they needed an area of 10 to 30 hectares and in the Constantine department in 1914, 54.7 per cent of the peasants worked on areas under 10 hectares in extent. The result was a precariously balanced system that tipped over into famine conditions at regular intervals, notably in 1905, 1908, and 1912.

This produced a downward spiral whose outward sign was the collapse of the small farm as families, in one last bid to ward off destitution, decided to sell up. Forced off their land, this pauperization process created a permanently antagonized rural proletariat numbering hundreds of thousands who, clothed in little more than rags, stalked the countryside in search of work. Large numbers flocked to the cities and towns or, ironically, the Mitidja plains where the settler farms, in particular the vineyards, needed a reservoir of cheap labour. By 1930, 428,000 Muslims were employed by these large farming enterprises but, as the country divided into European 'haves' and Muslim 'have-nots', this new state of affairs produced elemental anger. To Muslim minds they had been robbed of their land and thrust into poverty through the imposition of an alien system.

In 1891 this basic point was made by a local Muslim official, Cheikh Ben Sliman, when replying to an inquiry from the French Senate on the impact of law on rural society.[38] In his letter he explained how three tribes adjacent to him in Righan near Sétif had been dispossessed of their land since the 1860s because they did not accept French law based upon individual ownership and a surname. Equally Islam meant that they were opposed to any form of borrowing with interest. Allied to this, Ben Sliman reported, there was a widespread belief that the banks were swindlers since they supposedly charged Muslims 30 per cent interest as against just 2 per cent for French people. Disorientated by a system they both distrusted and did

Figure 2.3 A group of Muslim musicians begging in Bougie, 1915.

not fully comprehend, the three tribes had watched their land being expropriated until in 1891 a mere 33,203 hectares sustained 36,000 people.

This land question was an open wound in French Algeria. It created a fundamental conflict between the European landowners and the dispossessed. For Muslims this land was their land, which explains why settler farms were vandalized on regular occasions. It also explains why land became a rallying cry for Algerian nationalism from the 1920s onwards; a point underlined by Rabah Bitat, born in 1926 in the rural east and one of the original founders of the FLN: 'I was born into a peasant milieu which, during the years of colonization, saw the land left to us by our ancestors shrink away. Very young, I knew that the land, the country was ours and had been usurped from us by the French. Everything in our daily lives reflected this truth.'[39]

The subsistence economy made the problem of food into a daily agony. Hunger was always with people. It made them weak. It made them short tempered. It made them resentful. In the winter of 1877, Camille Sabatier was a justice of the peace in the region of Mila in Kabylia where there had been a number of thefts. In response Sabatier went with a detachment of troops to a nearby 'native' village:

> In the sixty dwellings that were successively searched, I found no food provisions apart from a small sack of barley in one of them, and in the others, piles of wild-lily roots known as *kérioua*. These wretches after having cooked the bulbs, crush them, wash them several times then boil and eat them. I know by experience that a European would not be able to taste such a dish without being overcome with vomiting and a pain in the entrails. For the last two months *kérioua* has been the only food for the poor population in this region.[40]

After World War One there was no let-up in this hunger. With famine striking again in 1920 and 1937, malnutrition continued to be an endemic condition. In Kabylia in 1937, known popularly throughout North Africa as the 'year of the great hunger', stick-like figures, close to starvation and vulnerable to disease, literally dropped dead on the road as families tried to survive on wild roots and rotting animal remains.[41] Ali Zamoum was born in 1933 in Boghni at the foot of the Djurdjura mountains in Kabylia. He remembers that at school during the 1930s appeasing hunger was the continual topic of conversation. At playtime he would hear friends asking insistently 'give me a fig' or scouring the ground for discarded food. In the case of Horeb Ali, he would surreptitiously knock the arm of the French school teacher's son, Pierre Lurati, to make him drop his slice of bread: 'Pierre would run immediately to replace his slice of bread which, having fallen on the ground, could not be eaten . . . On Pierre's return, Horeb had already eaten his free bread. "With jam as well", he used to say, in a deadpan way.'[42]

Anger over land and hunger went hand in hand with a sense of religious and social dispossession. Muslims believed that they and their religion were treated with contempt. The most obvious expression of this contempt was the *indigénat* but, describing the 1930s, Ali Zamoum recounts how his fellow villagers were convinced that their values were being defiled on a daily basis. The rumour that to become a French citizen Muslims had to spit on the Qu'ran in an official ceremony had the status of an invulnerable truth. Equally they were outraged at the presence of Catholic missionaries at nearby Ouadhai who had converted Muslims to Christianity and given their children Latin surnames. This feeling of humiliation—*hogra* in spoken Arabic—was talked about on a daily basis. Restricted to positions such as shoe-shine boys, agricultural workers, and servants, their lot in French Algeria was summed up in one word: servitude.

Rather than acquiesce in extreme poverty, many Muslims, particularly those in the poorest parts of Kabylia, chose to go into the French army or emigrate to France. As early as January 1856, three infantry regiments were established in Algeria and during the nineteenth century Muslim troops would distinguish themselves on far-away battlefields including the Crimea, Mexico, and Madagascar. Emigration really took off during and after World War One to become part of the fabric of rural society. Yet, once again, in both the army and emigration inequality was built into the system. Within the army, recruits knew that their chances of promotion above a certain rank were absolutely nil. Their role was to follow orders.[43] In France, Muslims tended to be allotted menial, poorly paid jobs in construction and the car-building industry.

Muslim resistance

Colonialism was not uniform. Relationships varied from region to region. Born in 1933, Mohammed Harbi grew up in the village of El-Arrouch in rural Constantinois in the east of the country in a relatively well-off family who owned a sizeable amount of land.[44] Where he lived there were few settlers. He was surrounded by Muslims. This meant that in contrast to Algiers or Oran he had no direct contact with crude day-to-day racism. He was not being made to feel inferior on a regular basis. Consequently he and those around him retained a strong sense of pride and dignity. In their minds they remained unconquered. They took the long view. They never believed that the French presence was permanent. Life was a question of holding on to their separate identity until the French left.

In resisting French rule, Harbi remembers, Islam remained at the centre of their personal lives, the most formidable barrier separating them from European society. This was a sanctuary sustained by women where, within the privacy of the family, Islamic practices reminded them on a daily basis that they were not French. They organized religious festivals, circumcisions, marriages, and funerals. They oversaw rituals of cleanliness. They passed down stories and songs that instilled notions of a separate religious identity. All of this was expressed in popular Arabic, providing a powerful counterpoint to the language of official authority, namely French.

Across rural society, but particularly in the eastern part of the country, opposition was fuelled by a millenarian Islam.[45] This rural Algeria was an otherworldly place where, in people's imaginations, beliefs in spirits and legends coexisted with a rudimentary knowledge of the Qu'ran. Within this world the dispossessed peasantry waited for an event or person that would arrive from elsewhere and destroy French rule. Stories described a divine figure or *mahdi* that would save Muslim society, an image deeply ingrained within popular Islamic culture. This 'man of the hour' or *mûl al sa'a* was to appear on the last day and establish the reign of justice across rural Algeria. And the more these rural masses suffered, the more they complained about the misrule of the Christian infidel, and the more these rumours circulated. There were stories about imminent earthquakes that would cause the settlers to disappear into the sea. There were stories about an Ottoman invasion in 1914. There were stories, too, about the mythical powers of Kaiser Wilhelm of Germany or Hadj Wilhelm as he was known.[46] Later there would be stories about the US and British forces in 1945 and Egyptian forces in 1955 landing to disarm the French. The attraction of these rumours was simple: it allowed Muslims to reinvent the colonial world as different and better—one where their land and religion had been recovered.

If hope was sustained by the 'man of the hour', it was also fortified by the image of the honourable outlaw, a long-standing tradition within North African society. Invariably male figures, the bandits of the mountains were lionized in folklore. Through wit and cunning they had turned the tables and made the authorities of the plains, whether Roman, Arab, or Ottoman, look ridiculous. Under French rule these 'primitive rebels' instilled feelings of pride and revenge because they were not prepared to act out a subservient role.[47] In the case of Bou-Zian, leading a band of men that attacked convoys and farms in the Sahara in the 1870s, it took years to finally track him down.[48] With the authorities powerless to apprehend him, stories and songs championed Bou-Zian as a saintly presence protected by God. The enemy of colonialism and the poor Muslims' friend, he was the emblem of freedom in a chained society.

Bou-Zian was so difficult to capture because everywhere in rural Algeria the French met with the law of silence. For Camille Sabatier, justice of the peace in Kabylia in the 1870s, this silence was a perennial problem.[49] Nobody would answer questions. In part this was because of fear. People feared retribution from the bandits themselves. But it was also the product of an instinctual hostility to outsiders. People felt that it was wrong to talk because there was a strong sense of identification with these 'bandits of honour'. They were seen to embody community resistance to colonialism and this unspoken bond made silence into a 'weapon of the weak'.[50] Not to speak was a mechanism for thwarting authority. It was also a way of signalling the illegitimacy of French rule; a deeply embedded reflex that was passed down from one generation to the next.

Alongside silence, a further 'weapon of the weak' was humour. Ali Zazoum remembers that in Boghni in the 1930s the Europeans, referred to collectively as 'el-colon', were an endless source of jokes.[51] The Europeans were mocked for their lack of hygiene. They were said to wear perfume to hide their bad smell. They were said to only clean their hands and face. They were said not to wash after using the toilet. At school Zazoum and his friends developed subversive rituals that expressed their hostility to the French primary school system. When performing traditional French songs they deliberately sang out of tune. Similarly when asked to recite Victor Hugo's patriotic poem 'Aux Morts' they spoke the final line 'Long live eternal France' in a resigned and downbeat way.[52]

Like laughter, music sustained Muslim self-belief. Andalucian-style classical orchestras made up of a fiddle, oud, kamenjah (violin-type instrument played vertically on the knee), zither, darabouka, and tambourine were testament to a rich musical heritage derived from the fusion of Arab, Jewish, and North African styles in Muslim Spain.[53] Within North Africa, this tradition included *malhûn*, a semi-classical form of sung poetry made up of an overture followed by solo verses, interspersed with refrains from the chorus. At the core of this poetry was word play, where metaphors and allusions, drawing upon oral story-telling and poetry traditions as well as mystical religious influences, were twisted to fit the flow of the music. French culture would try to absorb this music as 'exotic', but for Muslims this tradition was the embodiment of a different history and identity. It showed how North Africa was linked definitively to the Middle East and the heritage of Andalucian Spain.

Significantly, too, these musical traditions were not revered as monuments. They were open to adaptation and improvisation and in the early twentieth century new forms of popular songs talked explicitly about French misrule, poverty, and unemployment, mixing together aspects of the classical tradition and the *malhûn* canon with spoken slang. This was the case with the street poets who went from village to village and performed in the open air. It was the case too with the *cheikhas*, women drawn from the vast Muslim underclass in Oran, who sang in cafés, bars, and bordellos from the 1920s onwards. Sections of Muslim society were shocked by what was seen as their licentious behaviour and at times sexually explicit lyrics. Yet, despite this hostility women like Cheikha Djenia, Cheikha Grélo and, most famous of all, Cheikha Remitti El Reliziana were unrepentant. Their music was not for respectable society. Expressing themselves in an Algerian Arabic that few French people would have understood and usually accompanied with a flute, violin, and some percussion, they provided a snapshot of what is was like to be the lowest of the low in colonial society. They sang of pain. They sang of suffering. They sang of exclusion. Shared emotions that pointed to the way in which popular music and theatre, increasingly monitored by the authorities, became a measure of Muslim anger.

Religion, crime, silence, ridicule, music: all reflected deep hatred of French rule. However, the lasting and most significant act of resistance was the rising population. For Muslims a large family was a sign of prestige and this factor, when added, ironically, to the impact of French medicine particularly in the 1940s and 1950s, produced a huge demographic increase. By the mid-1930s Muslims outnumbered the settlers by six to one and this ultimately was their strength. The sheer weight of numbers meant that the aspirations of the Muslim majority could not be ignored.

Rulers and ruled: the hope of assimilation

Although the Muslim evidence is overwhelming, it would be wrong to reduce French Algeria to a single story of resistance. Despite huge prejudices on both sides the settler minority and the Arabo-Berber majority were not two immovable blocks. In between, as Harbi's memoirs underline, there was a grey area where a minority interacted, either as government officials or through the army or school, and the result was a complex set of entanglements where emotions ranged from hatred and anger through to loyalty, affection, and even love.[54]

On the French side the basic problem was how to rule. They had to break down the wall of silence, but to achieve this they needed intelligence. On this basis the authorities carried out a systematic inventory of Muslim society during the early 1880s because, as the original circular on 11 August 1880 explained: 'One of the principal difficulties that civil servants or military personnel newly appointed to administer a district encounter . . . consists of the absence of precise information on the natives with whom they have to deal.'[55]

The authorities wanted a 'who's who' of the rural elite. They wanted to identify which people had power. So, detailed forms identified political figures, religious figures, and other people of influence, such as ex-servicemen, categorizing their attitude to French authority. Armed with this knowledge the authorities sought to establish lasting bridges. They cultivated allies, recruiting a minority of loyal Muslims into the lower tiers of government and administration, so that alongside resistance there was also accommodation, cooperation and allegiance; bonds that were equally prevalent in the army where many ex-servicemen came to equate loyalty to a particular regiment with loyalty to the French nation.

A further point of interaction was education. Muslim exclusion from schools and universities is undeniable. In 1890, only 10,000 out of a population of 3.5 million attended primary school Moreover, education for Muslims was designed differently from that for the settlers. It was about preparing Muslims for manual labour and instilling respect for French authority.[56] Yet, even these limited numbers made an impact. Mouloud Mammeri, one of Algeria's most significant novelists who, post-independence, became Professor of Anthropology at Algiers University, was born in 1917 in Kabylia. He remembers how the village was cut off by the mountains.[57] There were no roads, electricity, or telephones. However, the village did have a school, built in 1883, that he remembered as a window on the world. Even if he later came to realize the shortcomings of this education, notably the concept that the 'Gauls' were his ancestors, it gave him a start that led him to study at the prestigious Louis-le-Grand Lycée in Paris. In the same way Harbi remembers a change of attitude in El-Arrouch in the 1930s.[58] Previously Muslims had boycotted French schools. Now, as French became the language of social advancement, they sent their children. However, far from instilling respect for French rule, the experience, notes Harbi, instilled a spirit of reading, criticism, and questioning that made El-Arrouch into a bastion of nationalism.

Engaging with French rule, therefore, did have a complex impact. For instance, it transformed the Arabic language. In day-to-day parlance Muslims developed versions of French words, like *mîr* (mayor), *boulisiya* (police), *lici* (lycée), *miri* (town hall) and *el-caserna* (barracks), that reflected their relationship with colonial authority.[59] It also led a minority of Muslims, either through school or the army, to learn to read and write in French. Expressing themselves thus led them to engage with French ideas. In particular they began to perceive a tension between the image of 'France the colonizer' and 'France of the Rights of Man'. They began to reflect on how the message of 'liberty, equality, fraternity' could be applied to them. This thinking, reflecting the aspirations of an emerging Muslim middle class of teachers, doctors, lawyers, and landowners, led to an assimilationist movement in the 1900s. Painfully aware of racism and exclusion, they wished to be treated with dignity and respect. Appealing to the 'France of the Rights of Man' they wanted to become equal citizens in the French nation.

Transforming horizons: World War One

The leader of the assimilationist movement was Emir Khaled. A grandson of Abd el-Kader, a blood connection to the original opponent of French rule that conferred on him enormous prestige, Khaled was a graduate of the military academy in Saint Cyr.[60] Attacking the old elite, dismissed as the 'old turbans' bought off by colonialism, Khaled was inspired by the 'Young Turks' movement in the Ottoman Empire. Styling himself and his followers as the 'Young Algerians', Khaled drew upon French models of political action. Consequently, when the French introduced conscription for Muslims in 1911, the 'Young Algerians' replied with a Manifesto calling for an end to the *indigénat*, equal taxation, enlarged suffrage for Muslims, and representation in the National Assembly.[61]

In June 1912 a delegation, some attired in traditional robes, others in suits, went to Paris and presented their demands in person to the Prime Minister Raymond Poincaré. There they reiterated the point that duties could not be separated from rights. Assimilation should not be partial, they argued. If Muslims were being asked to spill blood for France, then they must be treated as French citizens.

Given these arguments it was not surprising the colonial lobby was opposed to native conscription. They were petrified that 'native conscription' would not only lead to full political rights but also train Muslims to fire on settlers, and the first proposals, elucidated in 1908, produced a storm of protest. Numerous town halls refused to carry out the necessary census of the Muslim population; Gaston Thomson, deputy for Constantine, resigned from government as Navy Minister; and the press attacked the 'Young Algerians' as troublemakers in the pay of the Ottoman Empire. Equally there was opposition amongst Muslims. Petitions against conscription were organized and in 1908 4,000 Muslims from Tlemcen, anxious that they might be called to fight fellow-believers in Morocco, chose to go into exile in the Middle East.[62] Then, during World War One itself, in late 1916, the Shawiya people in the Aurès mountains to the south-east rejected conscription and proclaimed an independent republic. The repression that followed lasted five months and left between 200 and 300 insurgents shot.

Despite this opposition huge numbers of Muslims did submit to the call-up. Some 173,000 conscripts fought between 1914 and 1918. Of these 25,000 died and 57,000 were wounded. In addition 120,000 workers contributed to the war effort in armament factories. This physical mobility, representing a third of the male population and a stark counterpoint to their political immobility, transformed horizons. They left Algeria for the first time and this confronted them with new experiences. They encountered French people in the metropole who were perceived to be different from the Europeans in Algeria, more welcoming and much less racist. They met others, Moroccans, Tunisians, and West Africans, from the French Empire. They witnessed French military failures that undermined the aura of imperial invincibility. All of this provided points of comparison with their own lives in French Algeria. They were also exposed to new political ideas. There was the impact of German and Ottoman anti-French propaganda. There were the reverberations of the October 1917 Russian Revolution, with its call for the imperialist war to be transformed into a global class war, and in the USA President Woodrow Wilson's Fourteen Point Declaration for a new world order based on national self-determination. There was, too, interaction with French trade unions and the 1920 split within the Socialist Party (SFIO) and formation of the French Communist Party—events widely debated and discussed, underlining the way in which the world war was a crystallizing moment in Algerian history.

French reformism

In the wake of their blood sacrifice these Muslim soldiers wanted to be recognized; a pattern that was also reflected in West Africa, Indochina, Morocco, and Tunisia as there too veterans made political demands.[63] In

Paris in 1918 the Prime Minister Georges Clemenceau, the 77-year-old veteran republican patriot and architect of final victory, was receptive. Although he had been hostile to colonialism in the 1880s, arguing that imperial expansion was a diversion from the recovery of Alsace-Lorraine, as war leader from 1917 onwards nobody had done more to harness the empire to the French effort. He wanted to recognize this contribution and shortly after the November 1918 Armistice he introduced a system of fiscal equality, one of the 'Young Algerians' demands', for Muslims and settlers. Then in February 1919 the Clemenceau government introduced laws that made it easier for certain categories of Muslim men—ex-servicemen, farmers, those who could read and write French—to become citizens. These laws also widened Muslim access to posts in the administration and raised the percentage of Muslim representation on departmental and local councils to up to one third.

Although these changes fell far short of the 'Young Algerians' demands', they were loathed by settlers. It was seen as another example of Parisian meddling. They wanted protection not interference. Fearing for the status quo, the settler press focused upon Emir Khaled as a target of hatred because it was he, in the wake of Clemenceau's laws, who took up the mantle of reform. Elected to the Algiers municipal council in 1919, Khaled continued to argue for assimilation, calling for the right of Muslims to acquire citizenship without renouncing Qu'ranic law. However, the more Khaled pressed these demands, the more the hate intensified and in 1923 settler opposition forced him to resign and go into exile in Syria.

Timid as Clemenceau's reforms were in Algeria, they were part of a wider phenomenon in post-1918 politics, namely a new evaluation of the overseas territories, and what they meant for France by the mainstream left. Hitherto the colonies had not been a dominant preoccupation for either Clemenceau's Radical Party or the SFIO, formed in 1905 out of the various strands of the socialist movement. With 33,000 members, the SFIO's dominant reference point was the class struggle. Blending Marxism with the French revolutionary tradition, the SFIO understood society as a fight between the proletariat and the bourgeoisie. This meant that colonialism remained marginal. When it was discussed, members stopped well short of a blanket condemnation. Abuses, usually criticized as the consequences of capitalism, were set against the need to spread the values of 1789. French socialism, it was believed, was the cradle of civilization, the pinnacle which the peoples of the empire should aspire to.

These attitudes were also prevalent amongst the far-left. Writing in 1905, for example, Ernest Girault, a revolutionary anarchist, could not have been more condemnatory about French Algeria.[64] After a fact-finding visit he made to Algeria with Louise Michel (a veteran of the 1871 Paris Commune who was also on the far-left of the political spectrum), the book, entitled *A Colony of Hell* (*Une colonie d'enfer*), was intended as an attempt to alert metropolitan left opinion to the huge injustices suffered by the Muslim majority.[65] However, in portraying their plight Girault tended to depict them as victims: impoverished, child-like, and resigned. He also had little sympathy for Islam, denigrated as backward and superstitious, two assumptions that were typical of French Left thinking at the time.

Post-1918 there was a reappraisal of Algeria and the empire within the SFIO and centre-left that accepted the need for change and pushed the issue further up the party agenda. Reaffirming the civilizing mission and blaming the right for any abuses, this reformist perspective believed that the empire could be transformed for the better. By bringing the peoples of the empire into the orbit of French civilization, the goal was to spread human liberation to all corners of the globe. Articulated thus, it was a view that saw no need to consult with the local populations. French sovereignty and the right to impose these reforms were unquestioned. It was a view, too, that justified the 'civilizing mission' as a struggle against the despotism of the local elites and the ill-treatment of 'native' women by 'native' men. The Third Republic's role was to end this feudal domination and introduce greater liberty and equality.

Within this emerging reformist position there was an inherent suspicion of anti-colonial nationalism. This suspicion was derived from the acrimonious split at the Congress of Tours in December 1920, when just over two-thirds of the delegates broke away from the SFIO to form the Parti Communiste Français (PCF) and adhered to the Third International, launched by Lenin in March 1919. One of the key points by which the Communist Third International had differentiated itself from socialists was in unconditional support for national liberation struggles in the colonies. This, it was proclaimed, was the duty of all communists which meant that, in the eyes of the minority who vowed to preserve the SFIO's existence, Bolshevism and anti-colonial nationalism became synonymous. The SFIO saw the hidden hand of Moscow everywhere as the SFIO leader, Léon Blum, condemned the Communist Party's anti-imperialism as a 'race war' which would endanger the lives of both settlers and natives throughout the French

Empire.[66] In rejecting the Communist Party stance, Blum talked of a third way between colonialism and anti-colonialism which would rule in the interests of both settlers and natives. He talked, too, of the need for a more nuanced approach which, in mapping out forms of government, distinguished between the different parts of the French Empire: the League of Nations mandates, the older colonies, the protectorates, Algeria, Indochina, and Black Africa. In this respect the consensus amongst the SFIO membership was of the need for more equal rights between European and Muslim in Algeria.[67]

Within the mainstream centre-left the person who embodied this post-World-War-One reformist perspective more than anybody was the Radical Party member Maurice Viollette. Bearded, stout, well dressed, he was born in 1870 into a solidly middle-class background. A rising star in Parisian law circles by 1898 Viollette had become the socialist mayor of Dreux to the west of the capital. During this time he had also marked himself out as a rare breed on the left: a person with a detailed knowledge of the colonies. A talented debater, he quickly became an eloquent adversary of the colonial lobby within the National Assembly, condemning violence in Congo in 1902 and exposing corruption in Indochina in 1910. But in opposing the colonial lobby Viollette was not an anti-colonialist. He believed in assimilation. This he conceived of as a gradual process rooted in practical reality. The people in the colonies were children who had to be patiently guided, step by step, through a long process of education, towards emancipation.

In 1925 Viollette was appointed Governor-General in Algeria by the *cartel des gauches* government, a non-communist coalition of radicals, socialists, and smaller left-wing groups that had come to power in the previous year. On his arrival in Algiers on 27 May Viollette proclaimed that he would astonish the world by demonstrating the generous benefits of republican rule. First, this meant defending French sovereignty against the communist menace. In April Emir Abd el-Krim, leader of the Rif insurgency against Spanish rule in Northern Morocco, had attacked the French Protectorate, claiming national status for the Rif and entry into the League of Nations. Settlers in Algeria feared that the Rif revolution could spill over the border—a scare bolstered by Communist Party calls for French soldiers to fraternize with Krim's fighters—and this led to strong measures on Viollette's part. Conjuring up the image of a patriotic sacred union (*union sacrée*) against internal and external enemies, Viollette cracked down hard on the

Communist Party, repression that earned him the soubriquet 'Viollette the tyrant' within far-left circles.

If repression was one side of Viollette's policy, the other was the attempt to win over Muslim 'hearts and minds'. Viollette wished to chart a third way which opposed communism and nationalism, while studiously striving to reform the status quo. He wanted to reach out to a Muslim elite, calculated as around 100,000, and include them as equal citizens. It was an ambitious agenda that would define left-of-centre thinking for the next thirty years. But it was also one that quickly provoked settler opposition. They disliked his increased spending on Muslim health and education. They disliked his talk of increasing Muslim citizenship, stirring up a campaign against 'Viollette the Arab' that forced him to resign in November 1927. Unrepentant, Viollette's parting shot was a warning: 'The natives of Algeria, because of your errors, do not have a country. They are looking for one. They are asking to become part of the French *patrie*. Give it to them quickly or without that they will make another.'[68] Muslims, he underlined, could not be shut out forever. They had to be given a shared future or otherwise the end of French Algeria was inevitable.

3

The Making of Algerian Nationalism 1930–45

Monday, 5 May 1930

At 10.30 a.m. President Gaston Doumergue, proudly attired in his republican regalia, stepped forward to unveil a grandiose monument, 9 metres high, celebrating the one hundred years of French Algeria. Situated on the beach of the 1830 landing, the monument's centrepiece was comprised of two female allegorical figures: on the one side France, maternal and generous, and on the other Algeria, looking upwards for protection and guidance. It was an emphatic statement about the civilizing mission encapsulating the wider message of the centenary, namely that France had bestowed justice, health, and prosperity on a willing population.

Retracing the steps of the invasion, Doumergue had left by boat from Toulon on 3 May, exactly one hundred years to the day after the original French force. Given that he had started his career as a civil servant in the Oran department, the whole event had a strong personal dimension and over the following nine days Doumergue visited Algiers, Constantine, Bône, and Oran. Following a carefully prepared choreography, Doumergue was greeted everywhere by waving crowds as he reviewed military parades, handing out medals to loyal Muslim soldiers and opening buildings and exhibitions, including the new art museum in Algiers which celebrated the orientalist tradition in French painting. Throughout these official celebrations Doumergue reiterated one point above all others: the loyalty of the Muslim population who had been won over by the civilizing mission. Speaking to an assembled crowd in Constantine on 7 May he proclaimed: 'The celebration of the centenary will show in a decisive fashion the human,

Figure 3.1 Poster celebrating one hundred years of French Algeria.

peaceful, just, and beneficial character of the French colonization methods and of the work of civilization that she is pursuing.'[1]

Doumergue's official visit was the high point of a cycle of centenary celebrations that had begun on 1 January 1930 when French and 'native' soldiers laid a wreath and lit a flame at the tomb of the unknown soldier in Paris. Seven years in the making, the centenary glorified one hundred years of achievement. To this end it was marketed to the wider public in a meticulous manner through posters, stamps, postcards, school textbooks, and the cinema.[2] The intention was to make Algeria into an integral part of the national consciousness and here 800,000 tourists responded by visiting the country to see the monuments, the ceremonies, and the Exhibition in Oran. Covering 5 hectares and devoting a pavilion to each part of the empire, this exhibition allowed people to tour 'Greater France' in a day. It underlined how the Third Republic was engaged in a heroic endeavour that had instilled loyalty and gratitude amongst the 'native' populations: themes that were replicated on an even grander scale at the Colonial Exhibition in Paris in May 1931.

Sheikh Abd al-Hamid Ben Badis: Muslims into Algerians

In contrast to the settlers, most Muslims found the centenary nauseating. Forced to relive the shame of defeat, they felt that they were being forced to accept what they could never accept. Even the moderate middle classes were shocked by the sustained note of triumph. Why did the French tell such a one-sided story? Why was there no mourning for those who had been killed or displaced? Why was there no talk of the successive famines since the 1860s? Such questions underlined the undercurrent of anger summed up in the popular assertion: 'The French celebrate the centenary of French Algeria. They will not celebrate a second.'[3]

Nobody felt the centenary's triumphalism more acutely than Sheikh Abd al-Hamid Ben Badis. Born in Constantine in 1889, Ben Badis came from a well-connected family, which although it had taken a pro-French stance during the nineteenth century—his grandfather was a *qadi* decorated by Napoleon III, while his father was awarded the Légion d'Honneur—sent him to the prestigious Zitouna University in Tunis. Zitouna was well known as one of the centres of the Islamic renaissance which had begun during the second half of the nineteenth century and drew upon the theological ideas of Jamal al-Din al-Afghani (1838–97), Mohammed Abduh (1849–1905), and Rashid Rida (1865–1953). Belonging to a current of thought that became known as the *salafiyya* movement, all three were determined to challenge the dominance of Western ideas and called upon Muslims to return to the purity of early Islam.[4] Without doubt Ben Badis's educational experience at Tunis was a turning point. Convinced of the need for reform, he returned to become the movement's leading voice in Algeria.

Basing his manner and dress on the Prophet Mohammed, Ben Badis cultivated a dignified image. Bearded, invariably dressed in flowing robes, he chose his words carefully. Feigning not to speak French, he expressed himself in classical Arabic. Determined to reawaken the country's Muslim and Arab roots, a conclusion that was deepened by pilgrimage to Mecca in 1914, Ben Badis was instrumental in the explosion of the Muslim press during the 1920s and 1930s in Algiers and Constantine.[5] His most significant act, though, was the formation of the Association of Algerian Ulema in May 1931, familiarly known by its shortened Arabic name, the *Jam'iyat al-'Ulama*. Bringing together a small group of like-minded elite arabophone clerics, such as Bachir Ibrahimi, Ahmad Tawfiq al-Madani, Moubarak al-Mili, and Tyeb al-Okbi, the Ulema wished to bring about a religious and cultural rebirth that rejected the centenary. Drawing upon concepts such as people (*cha'b*), nation (*watan*), and nationality (*qawmiyya*), the Ulema underlined the existence of a separate Algerian nation based on Muslim and Arab values and intimately connected to the world Islamic community (*umma*). Light years away from the settlers' sense of what it was to be Algerian, this national identity, Ben Badis stressed, could never be assimilated into France.

For the Ulema the justification for this rejection was to be found in the past and between 1929 and 1932 both al-Mili and al-Madani produced detailed *national* histories that were a direct challenge to the colonial narrative. Tracing the past, present and future, they wanted to show that a Muslim Algeria did exist. Al-Madani's study, *The Book Algeria* (*Kitāb al-Jazā'ir*), in particular was to become a cornerstone of the upsurge in nationalist and religious sentiment during the 1930s.[6] Describing a national consciousness forged through successive struggles against Christian Spain and France, the book's cover carried the epigram: 'Islam is our religion, Algeria is our homeland, Arabic is our language.'[7]

Figure 3.2 Sheikh Abd al-Hamid Ben Badis, leader of the Association of the Algerian Ulema.

No less important was the cultural battle. The tongue of the foreigner must not be allowed to triumph. It was held to be an outrage that the Arabic language, the language of God, was categorized as foreign by the colonial authorities. To counter the advance of French the Ulema established a network of schools to teach Arabic that was complemented by a hub of cultural and social associations. Including sports clubs, theatres, a scouting movement, and a thriving press, this was a vibrant, alternative society which, the Ulema hoped, would instil national pride in a new generation. In the case of Muslim scouts, formed when French leaders refused to accept Arabs into their ranks in 1935, they held regular camping weekends and open-air activities that popularized Ulema ideas.[8] One scouting song, 'From our Mountains', proclaimed: 'From our mountains rise up the cries of free men. They demand the independence, the independence of our country.'[9]

By 1935 the Ulema had 10,000 adherents in the Constantine department.[10] Styling themselves as scrupulous orthodox, the Ulema were determined to root out what they saw as anti-Islamic practices, whether it be the marabouts, accused of being both pagan and the servile creatures of colonialism; inappropriate female behaviour; or the drinking of alcohol. Fired up with this missionary zeal, groups, often armed with clubs, went out into the countryside to spread the Ulema message.[11] Through argument or force they wanted to convince people that the worshipping of saints was not true Islam; a campaign which left the French authorities worrying that whole swathes of the countryside in eastern Algeria had been won over to the Ulema cause.

The stridency of the Ulema in the 1930s cannot be separated from the broader context. The rise of Arab nationalism stoked up by World War One, the disintegration of the Ottoman Empire, the emergence of independent states like Iraq: all of these events produced intense debate across the Arab and Muslim world.[12] The issue was leadership. What was the right course in the face of continued British and French dominance? How were Muslims to extract themselves from foreign rule? One response was the Muslim Brotherhood in Egypt founded by the schoolteacher Hassan al-Banna in 1928.[13] Situating itself within the lineage of the modern reform movement initiated by al-Afghani, the Brotherhood was dedicated to a return to original practices of the Prophet that would allow Egyptians to overcome division, shake off British control and establish an Islamic state based on sharia law. Another response was the one disseminated by Emir Shakib Arslan, the unofficial representative of Syria and Palestine at the

League of Nations in Switzerland from 1921 onwards. Similarly moulded by al-Afghani, Arslan preached pan-Arab and pan-Islamic solidarity from Morocco to Iraq through an intellectual review published in French, *La Nation Arabe*, a message that made him into a hate figure for successive French governments who accused him of stirring up anti-French feelings. Wired into these arguments, both al-Banna and Arslan exerted a huge influence on Ben Badis. He was impressed by their credo of doctrinal and organizational unity which he sought to replicate in Algeria.

The rise of Ulema led the authorities to monitor Ben Badis's activities. This surveillance was stepped up on 16 February 1933 when Ferdinand-Jules Michel, in charge of the 'native affairs' desk at the Algiers Prefecture, called for an even closer watch on meetings, Qu'ranic schools, and all international links. The 'Michel circular' set the tone and in the following weeks Ulema mosques and schools were closed on the grounds that they were a threat to French sovereignty. By propagating Arslan's pan-Islamism, the authorities claimed, they were converting loyal Muslims into anti-French agitators.[14] In response the Ulema accused the French of yet another attack on Islamic culture, views that led more than 1,000 demonstrators to protest outside the Algiers prefecture on 3 March 1933.

Ferhat Abbas

In asserting a separate identity Ben Badis's primary target was assimilation. With the demise of Emir Khaled this political current organized itself into a 'Fédération des Elus' in 1927. Proudly proclaiming their independence from the French administration, particularly strong in the Constantine department, the Fédération was a coalition of elected officials rather than a formal party. By the early 1930s the leading exponent of their cause was Ferhat Abbas who would rise to become one of the most significant figures in twentieth-century Algerian politics.

Born in 1899 in the village of Affirs in the Djidjelli region in the east of the country, a particularly beautiful area in Algeria, Abbas was the son of a local official (*qaïd*).[15] This privileged background led him to do a degree at Algiers University where he became elected president of the Association of Muslim Students. Jovial, approachable, fluent in French and married to a French woman, his trade-mark double-breasted suits exuded the air of a well-heeled provincial bourgeois. As the proprietor of a chemists shop in

Sétif, made up of a population of 30,000, two-thirds of whom were Muslim, 'Monsieur Abbas' quickly became the rising star of local politics. This was his fiefdom and in 1933 he was elected as a municipal councillor and as a representative on the 'Financial Delegation' (Délégations Financières) in Algiers.

Although determined to engage with the political process, Abbas, too, had been shocked by the centenary. He was particularly dismayed by the manner in which Viollette's proposals to extend the Muslim franchise—a grand gesture that would have reinforced the generosity of French rule— had been sidelined by the colonial lobby. These frustrations, though, reaffirmed his belief in the 'France of 1789' and in 1931 he made the case again for total assimilation with his book *The Young Algerian* (*Le Jeune Algérien*).[16] Algeria had to be transformed from a colony into a French province. Through an end to discrimination Muslims had to be allowed entry to the French nation.

Abbas's model of action was political lobbying rather than mass action. By persistent pressure Abbas and the Élus wanted to bring home to the government the extent of their grievances and the most acceptable way of removing them. With this aim in mind a delegation from the Fédération went to Paris in June 1933 calling for an end to the repression against the Ulema, greater press freedom, and more primary schools so that Muslim children could learn French. In by-passing the colonial administration and talking directly to the government, the delegation hoped that their demands would be met. They were quickly disappointed. The Minister of the Interior refused to meet them and, returning empty handed, some chose to resign in protest. However, the political momentum was maintained through success at local elections in October 1934, and in early 1935 the Fédération published a further political programme. The key demands were 'native' representation in parliament, the attachment of the three departments to the metropole, and a greater voice in local government. But, once again, the Minister of the Interior, the Radical Marcel Régnier, chose to ignore the Fédération. Instead he listened to the colonial lobby. Placating the latter's fears about law and order, the 'Régnier decree' on 30 March 1935 was particularly draconian, making any opposition to French authority punishable by two years' imprisonment. Not surprisingly it created uproar amongst the Fédération.

Messali Hadj

If Ben Badis represented religious renaissance and Ferhat Abbas symbolized assimilation, the other strand was political nationalism, which was encapsulated in the third figure of the 1930s: Messali Hadj. Born in Tlemcen on 16 May 1898 in the west of the country, the bearded Messali was the son of a shoemaker and a member of the Derkawa brotherhood, a sufi suborder. Resilient, famously disciplined about keeping fit, Messali was an autodidact—attendance at both French and Qu'ranic schools produced no formal qualifications—whose perspectives were transformed by his time in Bordeaux as a conscript at the end of World War One. Utterly opposed to French rule, Messali reflected with his compatriots on the implications of the final demise of the Ottoman Empire. Seeing this as a temporary setback, Messali argued that Islam's torch would now be taken up by the 'rise of the Arabs'.[17]

In France Messali was also struck by the differences between French people in the metropole and settlers in Algeria. He found that the French people he met on the mainland were much less prejudiced and much more welcoming.[18] He was also greatly impressed by the ideas and strategy of the French left, in particular the trade union movement. He admired their emphasis on mass action which reinforced his disappointment with the 'Young Algerians'. For Messali the latter were too moderate, too bourgeois, promoting a reformist agenda that, in his opinion, reinforced the colonial status quo. Determined to learn more about revolutionary politics Messali returned to France in 1923. Living in Paris as a worker, he met and fell in love with his life-long companion, Émilie Busquant, the eldest daughter of an anarchist miner, who deepened his knowledge of French working-class struggles. He also forged links with Algerians in the French Communist Party that led to the formation, in July 1926, of the first political party committed to independence: the Étoile Nord-Africaine (ENA)

The social context for the ENA was Algerian emigration to France. Desperate to escape poverty, 68,000 war workers had remained in 1919, followed by 21,000 in 1920, 44,000 in 1922, and 71,000 in 1924—a wave of emigration which, because it was so much larger than that from Morocco and Tunisia, was a measure of the greater depth of the colonial pauperization process in Algeria.[19] Principally made up of young men from Berber

Kabylia, these immigrants remained for a few months or a year as unskilled workers in the metal and chemical industry or seasonal labourers in agriculture.[20] Usually concentrated in the Paris region, particular neighbourhoods became linked to Algeria as immigrants replicated home life through cafés, barber shops, grocery stalls, and makeshift mosques. Cafés in particular became hubs of support where people were pointed in the direction of work, lent money and given advice on how to adapt to French life; especially important as Algerian emigration became the focus of organized police surveillance in the mid-1920s.[21] In these ways immigration created bonds of solidarity. Pushed to the margins, Algerians had an obligation to support each other. It also created a new awareness of what it meant to be Algerian in terms of dress, food, and music.[22] French society became the measure of their difference, instilling a sense of a separate national identity.

The political context for the ENA was communist anti-imperialism. Staying faithful to the Third International's unconditional support for anti-colonialism, the French Communist Party reached out to workers from the colonies within the metropole, the largest number of which were Algerian.[23] Here the driving force was Hadj Ali Abd el-Kader, born in 1883 in western Algeria and from 1923 onwards the head of the party's Colonial Section (*Union Intercoloniale*), who in 1924 and 1925 took a leading role in organizing immigrant opposition to the Rif War and the repression in Tunisia, denouncing Herriot's centre-left government as an agent of 'imperialism' and 'colonial fascism'.[24] Capitalizing on this upsurge in militant activism, Abd el-Kader and Messali now looked to create a political party, establishing the Étoile Nord-Africaine, theoretically independent of the Communist Party but with a strong communist faction, whose inaugural meeting took place on 14 July 1926 in a trade union meeting hall in rue de la Grange-aux-Belles in Paris. Attended by more than 300, for the most part Algerian, the ENA's programme called for the political emancipation of North Africa, and the redistribution of land to peasants.

Nationalism and communism

On 10 February 1927 Messali Hadj arrived in Brussels to attend the 'Congress of Oppressed Peoples'. Organized by the Anti-Imperialist Movement, based in Berlin and supported by the Comintern and the French Communist Party, the four-day Congress, attended by 175 delegates, was a meeting of ideas where it was possible to rub shoulders with Albert Einstein, the world famous physicist, Henri Barbusse, writer and communist intellectual, and Jawaharlal Nehru, India's future first post-independence prime minis-ter. In this atmosphere Messali thrived. Listening to others he was able to refine his arguments, reflected on how Algeria was similar to, or different from, other colonial situations. It also gave him the perfect platform to launch a clear and unambiguous call for Algerian independence.

Lasting just fifteen minutes Messali's speech was a tour de force whose centrepiece was an eight-point political programme that included indepen-dence, the withdrawal of French troops, the establishment of a Constituent Assembly based on universal manhood suffrage, the restitution of confis-cated land to the peasantry, and the recognition of Arabic as an official language.[25] Significantly in exalting the aspirations of the dispossessed masses, Messali accorded no place to the settlers, a silence which further reinforced his image of a Muslim Algeria. By any standard it was a revolu-tionary call to arms which, in looking to the people, went much further than either Ben Badis or Abbas. Vigorously applauded, the speech propelled Messali onto the international stage.

On his return to Paris, however, the speech produced the first strains with the PCF. For the Communist Party leadership, Messali was too indepen-dent. They wanted someone who would remain subservient to the party line, not a political rival. On the other side many ENA members were increasingly ill at ease with the idea that their party was a front for atheist communism. By 1928 the ENA's membership stood at 4,000 and many wanted to assert their organizational and ideological independence by breaking the PCF link.[26] Increasingly cut off from the PCF, the ENA also had to contend with police repression.[27] Everywhere Messali was tracked by the authorities.[28] Regular reports recorded what he said, where he went, and who he met and on 20 November 1929 the ENA was proscribed as a threat to French sovereignty.

In the face of this crackdown Messali was resilient. Modelling itself on the French Communist Party, all the ENA's decisions went through Messali as general-secretary, a power base that allowed him and others, notably figures such as Khider Amar, Banoune Akli, Si Djilani, and Yehiaoui, to hold the party together. In October 1930 Messali launched a monthly paper in French: El-Ouma. In choosing this title Messali explicitly situated the Algerian struggle within that of the wider transnational Muslim community (umma), underlining the way in which Islam and nationalism now came to the fore. Like all Muslims, Messali argued, Algerians had to recover their faith and independence. This meant that Algerian troops must not fight in the French army against Moroccan insurgents. It meant too that Algerians had to reject assimilation. Sending a few middle-class representatives to the French Assembly would not right the grave injustice done to the Algerian majority. The only answer was national independence. This alone would allow Muslim Algeria to expunge the shame of colonialism.

Surviving in a semi-clandestine way the ENA was reconstituted as the 'Glorious North African Star' ('Glorieuse Étoile Nord-Africaine') in May 1933. By adding the 'Glorious' Messali got round the political ban and was able to engage in more open militant activity. Going from meeting to meeting in the poorer suburbs of Paris, Lyon, Saint-Étienne, and Lille, Messali articulated Muslim pain through simple, well-chosen phrases, particularly important because so many in the audience could not read or write. Stressing social egalitarianism and the recovery of honour (nif), Messali made the comparison with the Irish struggle against British imperialism.[29] Like the Irish, he argued, Algerians were involved in struggle over land and religious freedom, a national perspective that was reflected in slogans, songs, and the creation of a green-and-white flag with a star and crescent.

The significance of Islam was further strengthened when Messali, forced to flee France after a further wave of police repression, made his way to meet Emir Shakib Arslan in Geneva at the end of 1935. In conversation, Arslan underlined the importance of pan-Islamic and pan-Arab solidarity. He also emphasized the need to resist French attempts at a policy of divide and rule across North Africa. In foregrounding Berber difference from the Arabs, Arslan warned, the French were trying to weaken both Algerian and Moroccan nationalism.[30] Undoubtedly such advice from Arslan reinforced Messali's convictions. More firmly than ever, Algeria was linked to the wider Muslim world. Through religion, language, and culture Algerians were Arabs—an article of faith which promoted support for other Arab struggles, notably the Palestinian revolt against the British Mandate, and rejected any talk of a separate Berber identity.

Messali's meeting with Arslan was another example of the ENA's independence from the PCF. Yet, the link would always be used by the settler press as a slur against Algerian nationalism. For them communism and anti-colonial nationalism were allies in a plot against French power, a suspicion that was also prominent amongst the Socialist Party which had boycotted the Anti-Imperialist Congress in Belgium on the grounds that it was a

Soviet-controlled front.[31] In truth the relationship between Messali and the PCF was now marked by suspicion and hostility which in turn was further complicated by the emergence of the Algerian Communist Party (PCA) as an independent political party.

Like the PCF the origins of the PCA are to be found in the 1920 Congress of Tours when the three socialist federations in Algeria split into two parts. Those, however, who sided with the Third International stopped well short of Lenin's call for the unconditional support for anti-colonial nationalism, stating, in the famous Sidi Bel-Abbès motion on 22 April 1921, that:

> The liberation of the native proletariat in North Africa will only be the fruit of a revolution in the metropole . . . The best way to aid all liberation movements in our colony is not to abandon this colony, as is said in the eighth condition of adherence to the Third International, but on the contrary to remain there, under the Communist Party . . . in order to multiply propaganda in favour of trade unionism, communism and cooperativism.[32]

Citing as evidence Muslim refusal to educate women, 'native' ignorance of communist doctrine, as well as the exploitative role of the Arab bourgeoisie, the communist role was to bring political and social liberation.[33] Roundly condemned by Leon Trotsky in December 1922, the three federations eventually embraced, by a narrow margin, the Third International's doctrine in March 1926.[34] With a few hundred members, mostly drawn from working-class settlers, the three federations opposed French imperialism, denouncing the 1930 centenary with tracts addressed specifically to the Muslim population: 'On 1 May, your brothers, the French workers, will demonstrate against their bourgeoisie; fraternize with them; demonstrate against the centenary, against your enslavement, against French colonization.'[35]

Such language meant that activists remained on the margins of French Algeria. Nevertheless, in a bid to give fresh organizational impetus, the French Communist Party decided, at its national conference in Villeurbanne in France in January 1936, to establish the Algerian federations as a separate party.

The Ulema, the Élus, the Étoile Nord-Africaine, and the Algerian Communist Party: these were the four groups that expressed opposition to French Algeria in the 1930s. Yet, if the Ulema and the Élus were more elitist, if the Étoile Nord-Africaine was the most proletarian, and if the

Algerian Communist Party was the only party that attracted both European and Algerian members, all four were male dominated in terms of recruitment and leadership. Similarly, all four enjoyed an upsurge of support between 1933 and 1936 as the impact of the global depression created a radical atmosphere in Algeria.

Economic crisis

The economic crisis in the 1930s was the product of a demographic increase. By 1936 the Muslim population stood at 6 million and this increase stretched the country's resources to breaking point. Algeria could not cope with the fall-out from the 1929 Wall Street Crash which, once it hit, was longer and more protracted than elsewhere. Exports fell from 10.6 thousand million francs in 1930 to 8 thousand million two years later, producing a generalized collapse that, given the level of discrimination, struck the Muslim population much harder. Small craft workshops, a feature of the Muslim *quartier* in the major towns and cities, closed en masse. Earnings from emigration, which had kept some of the poorest regions alive, dried up. Muslims farmers were unable to pay debts. Unemployment, already bad, became endemic. The word *kríz* (crisis) entered the Arabic language to become a constant topic of daily conversation. This misery was reflected in popular music, much like Woody Guthrie's dustbowl ballads in the USA. One 1935 song by Mouhad Ahmed, entitled 'The Unemployed Worker' and accompanied by a single mandolin, painted a bleak portrait of devastated lives.[36] For everyone—Arab, French, and Italian—each day was a struggle for survival:

> Allow me to recite the poem of unemployment.
> The crisis reigns from Paris to Tunis amongst the Arabs, the Italians
>   and even the French.
> I will only tell you the truth.
> The unemployed are as numerous as pins.
> You can find them everywhere.
> The cafés are full of them.

This crisis produced a rural exodus. Desperate for any kind of employment, thousands flocked to the coast and in the major towns and cities this produced a tinderbox atmosphere.[37] Gathering on street corners, young

Algerians felt angry and humiliated. Forced to live on their wits, confronted with settler and police racism on a daily basis, lacking educational opportunities afforded to Europeans, many found it difficult to maintain their self-control. Hemmed in on all sides, the slightest incident could provoke violence and in 1933 and 1934 Algeria witnessed a spate of urban rioting. On 12 February 1934 a 10,000-strong demonstration in Algiers organized by the Communist and Socialist Parties against fascism, as a response to right-wing rioting outside the National Assembly in Paris on 6 February, included a large number of Muslims. When the demonstration was blocked by the police, more young Muslims descended from the Casbah, brandishing Muslim placards and ransacking rich shops in the European *quartier*: an act of aggressive bravura that produced widespread fear in the settler population.

Rioting was repeated on an even grander scale on 5 August 1934 in Constantine. In this case Muslim anger expressed itself through attacks on Jewish property and Jews themselves who, through assimilation, were seen to have rejected Algeria and embraced France, in effect becoming part of the system that was strangling Muslims. Allied to this, the close proximity of the Jewish *quartier* made them into an easier target for Muslims, with scuffles on 3 August erupting into full-scale violence two days later.[38] In all, twenty-three Jews and four Muslims were killed as the authorities blamed the communists, Élus, and the Ulema for stirring up trouble. They in turn talked about an imperialist plot, while in France Messali warned against colonial agents provocateurs who were setting Jew against Muslim.[39]

Anger manifested itself in aggression on the football field. Reports to the French authorities regularly report how matches between settler and Muslim teams ended in violence on the pitch. Some were even abandoned as Algeria witnessed an explosion of Muslim football clubs in the 1920s and early 1930s, all clamouring to participate in the North African championship established in 1927. One letter, on 15 May 1936 from the mayor of Djidjelli to the local prefect in Bougie in eastern Algeria, warned that if there was a fixture between a Muslim and European team then racial confrontation was certain: 'If a team essentially composed of natives should meet with one made up in large part of Europeans, it is beyond doubt that sporting antagonism, pushed to fever pitch, will add to the racial antagonism and at this moment the repercussions would be especially dangerous.'[40]

These teams were particularly important to young men who found in them a collective identity denied by the centenary. Invariably linked to the

Ulema, these clubs, like similar ones for cycling, basketball, swimming, tennis, shooting, boules, and rugby, expressed nationalism through their names, their symbols, and their shirt strips. The name Mouloudia Club, for instance, founded in the Casbah of Algiers in August 1921, was taken from Mouloud, the festival celebrating the birth of the prophet Mohammed, while their team colours were the red and green of Islam.[41]

Suspicious that these clubs were fronts for anti-French activity, the 'Native Affairs' unit compiled regular reports on their activities on and off the field which would be sent upwards through the system to the three prefects in Oran, Algiers, and Constantine, before ending up on the desk of the Governor-General in Algiers.[42] Columns carefully tabulated who played for these teams, who was financing them, and what were their links with political groups and parties. These reports caused alarm because the authorities did not want sport to become organized along racial lines and in regard to football, far and away the most popular sporting pastime for young Muslim men, the Governor-General introduced a circular in January 1928 stating that all teams must have at least three European footballers; a ratio that was increased to five in October 1934. These rules were very unpopular amongst the Algerian teams and their supporters. Crowds chanted against it and teams tried to get round the quota, either by playing naturalized Muslims or claiming that it was impossible to recruit European members—a measure of how nothing was more important than football in solidifying a sense of 'us' and 'them'. Through it, young Muslim men were able to conquer public space and impose themselves physically.

The Popular Front

By 1935 these tensions framed all political statements and were central to a defining moment in Algerian history: the Popular Front.[43] In France the impetus for the Popular Front stemmed from two events that symbolized the rise of fascism: Hitler coming to power on 30 January 1933 and the right-wing riots in Paris on 6 February 1934. These twin threats led to a grass-roots anti-fascist movement which organized a general strike in defence of the Third Republic on 12 February 1934. In bringing together communists with socialists and even radicals this was a moment of unity that was solidified by a major turning point from above, namely the Comintern's abandonment of a class–against–class strategy in June 1934 in favour of a popular front that aimed to build the broadest possible coalition against fascism. In one stroke the PCF abandoned sectarianism whereby the Socialist Party, supposedly diverting the working class away from revolution, was attacked as the main enemy, replacing this with a new line championing patriotism, anti-fascism, and national defence. Class hatred gave way to the outstretched hand, as the PCF sought unity, not only with the Socialist Party, but the Radical Party as well, where younger activists, disenchanted with the old guard and led by Pierre Mendès France, pushed for cooperation.

Symbolically the three parties cemented this alliance with a celebratory demonstration in Paris on 14 July 1935 when marchers, many dressed in Phrygian bonnets and with clenched fists held high, chanted the Popular Front slogans of 'bread, peace, and work' and 'down with fascism'. Thousands of Algerians, Moroccans, and Tunisians participated, too, who, in identifying with the Popular Front, also wanted to publicly assert their separate national identities on the streets of the French capital. The Étoile Nord-Africaine in particular did not want to compromise its independence. In standing full-square behind Messali Hadj, waving Algerian flags and shouting calls for the liberation of North Africa and the Arab world, the Algerian cortège reflected a rising mood of hope. As part of the Popular Front family, united with communists, socialists, and radicals and caught up in the atmosphere of fraternity and solidarity, these Algerians expected a future left-wing government to satisfy their aspirations.

Such politicization was not just limited to immigrants in France. Back in Algeria the PCA's membership rose from 600 in 1935 to 3,500 in 1936, including 700 Muslim members, while sales of the communist daily, *La Lutte Sociale*, shot up from 3,000 to 8,000. The PCA's principal enemy was Gabriel Lambert, ex-priest and mayor of Oran since 1934. Strongly anti-Semitic, Lambert was to become a loud supporter of General Franco during the Spanish Civil War between 1936 and 1939. Like Franco, Lambert wished to cleanse Algeria of 'undesirables' such as Jews, communists, socialists, freemasons, and Algerian nationalists—attitudes that won him wide support amongst the settlers and were also reflected in the rise of the right-wing Croix-de-Feu. By 1935 the membership of the latter stood at 15,000 in Algeria and when their leader, Colonel de la Rocque, visited Algiers on 7 June 1935 thousands of Europeans and Muslims protested, clashing with police and Croix-de-Feu supporters.[44]

On 12 January 1936 the Communist, Socialist, and Radical Parties formalized an electoral pact for the national elections on 26 April. Each called on their supporters to vote for the best-placed second-round candidate, inscribing an electoral discipline which carried the day at the second ballot on 3 May. So, although the Popular Front won a moderate swing overall, the results were startling because the Communists doubled their vote to 1,500,000, while the Socialists lost 2 per cent and the Radicals, punished for their participation in power, lost 15 per cent. In the second round this translated into 72 seats for the PCF, 146 for the SFIO—now the largest party—and 116 for the Radical Party, down from 159 in 1932. Overall the Popular Front had 376 seats against 222 on the right and with this mandate Blum, the first Socialist prime minister in the history of France, formed a government of Radicals and Socialists. Tactically the PCF supported from the backbenches calculating that Communist Party ministers would frighten off middle-class voters.

In Algeria the elections went against the trend. There they represented a victory for the right which, supported by the Croix-de-Feu, won six seats, while the left returned two Radicals, a Socialist and a Radical Socialist. Crucially, although these four campaigned on anti-fascism, they were lukewarm about change in Algeria itself. In this sense the election was different from the mainland where two Frances now confronted each other in a civil-war atmosphere. In Algeria the 1936 election was a statement about the political exclusion of the Muslim majority which now stood at 6 million.

The victory of the Popular Front was immediately followed by a huge wave of strikes and factory occupations in May and June that were larger than any previous ones in French history. Involving close to 2 million workers, the strikers revelled in the collective atmosphere. Momentarily everything seemed possible as singing and dancing went hand in hand with mock trials of employers. Petrified by this militancy, employers met with trade union representatives in the presence of Blum and on the night of 7–8 June signed the Matignon Agreements which accepted a forty-hour week, annual paid holidays, the recognition of trade union rights, and a 15–17 per cent increase in wages. It was a major victory that instilled hope in Messali Hadj who, granted an amnesty by the Popular Front, returned to Paris to press the Algerian case. In *El-Ouma*, now openly sold for the first time, he appealed to the French revolutionary tradition and called for the establishment of an Algerian parliament:

Only at that moment can we say that justice has been rendered to us; for in that way, we can effectively participate in the affairs of our country, and that day we will say that the democratic France of 89, of 48 . . . will have realized a work of civilization in emancipating the Algerian people from exploitation, servitude, and injustice.[45]

On 20 June Messali met with Raoul Aubaud, secretary of state at the Ministry of the Interior; on 26 June he spoke at a huge anti-colonial rally with the Tunisian nationalist leader Habib Bourguiba; and on the Popular Front Bastille Day march he led 30,000 North Africans who reiterated their demands for independence.[46]

In the wake of the Matignon Agreements the Blum government enacted an ambitious series of reforms outlined in the Popular Front's common programme. The school leaving age was raised to fourteen, the Bank of France made more accountable, and the armaments industry was nationalized. The paramilitary leagues, including the Croix-de-Feu, were dissolved. In the empire Blum appointed a commission to investigate living conditions in the colonies, amnestied Indochinese nationalists, and signed a treaty with Syria, accorded to France as a mandate in 1919 after the break-up of the Ottoman Empire, that opened the way, in theory at least, to some form of self-government. On Algeria, Blum, in conjunction with Maurice Viollette, introduced proposals to extend voting rights to 25,000 Muslims.

Resuscitating reforms Viollette had originally outlined to coincide with the centenary in 1930, the Popular Front blueprint produced a wide debate within Algeria about assimilation. The most famous exchange was between Ferhat Abbas and Ben Badis. Writing in February 1936, this was the moment Abbas had been waiting for. Now '1789 France' was poised to open the door to Muslims.[47] To back up this conclusion Abbas argued that the Algerian nation was a myth. He had looked in the history books. He had questioned the living and the dead. He had visited the cemeteries. Nobody, he claimed, had spoken of it. Yet, in embracing assimilation Abbas was nuanced, warning:

Without the emancipation of the natives, there will be no enduring French Algeria. I am France because, me, I am the majority, I am the soldier, I am the worker, I am the artisan, I am the consumer . . . The interests of France become our interests the instant that our interests become those of France.[48]

Replying to Abbas two months later Ben Badis was unequivocal. He, too, had looked in the history books. Unlike Abbas, however, he had found the Algerian nation:

> We, we have scrutinized the pages of history and the contemporary situation. And we have found the Algerian and Muslim nation ... She has her own culture, her own habits and customs, good or bad, like every nation of this world. What is more, this Algerian and Muslim nation is not France.[49]

Importantly, this debate was not limited to the political elite. Large numbers of ordinary Algerians were drawn into the argument through the press, petitions, and meetings. All the police documents testify to the depth of this political discussion, much of which looked to the Blum government as an ally in the struggle against colonialism. One report related how on 30 May 1937 Muslim footballers from the Djidjelli team, well known for their nationalist sympathies and travelling to Constantine for a match, sang the following to the tune of the International in Arabic with clenched fists:

> We do not want war
> We want to live on our land
> We are with the working class
> With us comrade Blum
> Long live Blum!
> Leave de la Rocque and his friends
> Like the dogs who bark
> With us comrade Blum
> Long live Blum[50]

The Algerian Muslim Congress

Despite the differences between the Federation and the Ulema this did not prevent a common platform. Together with the PCA and the ENA they launched an Algerian Muslim Congress to articulate grass-roots grievances, modelling it on the estates-general from the 1789 French Revolution. Four thousand delegates, sent from across Algeria by local committees, met in the Majestic cinema in Algiers on 7 June 1936 to draw up a charter of demands which, after much negotiation and compromise, called for integration into France, the abolition of the Governor-General, a single electoral college, universal manhood suffrage, and representation in the National Assembly.[51]

These were then presented in person to Blum and Viollette in Paris on 24 July by a small group of nominated representatives led by Dr Bendjelloul from the Fédération.

On 2 August a huge rally in the municipal stadium in Algiers, attended by 10,000, was organized to acclaim the returning delegates. However, the delegation had nothing to offer. Blum and Viollette had told them that the time was not right and that their demands went too far; disappointment that was compounded still further by Messali who, himself rebuffed by the Popular Front government, made a late and dramatic intervention at the mass meeting. Returning that morning for the first time in thirteen years, this was an emotional moment for Messali, still largely unknown in Algeria. Speaking briefly in Arabic, he then switched to French for the bulk of his brief speech, deploying all his oratorical skills to devastating affect. Tracing the long march of the Étoile Nord-Africaine, Messali acknowledged the work of the Congress, but underlined that the ENA could never accept Algeria's integration into France because this was the result of 'a brutal conquest, followed by a military occupation'.[52] Messali was also opposed to representation in the National Assembly. Instead he proposed the establishment of 'an Algerian parliament, elected on universal suffrage, without distinction of race or religion'.[53] In conclusion Messali underlined that sending a delegation to Paris was not enough. The people had to be vigilant:

> My brothers, you must not now sleep and become deaf believing that all activity is now finished, because it has only begun. You must organize yourselves, unite yourselves within your organizations, to be strong, to be respected and in order that your powerful voice can be heard on the other side of the Mediterranean. For the freedom and renaissance of Algeria, rally yourselves en masse around your national organization, the Étoile Nord-Africaine, which knows how to defend you and will lead you towards the path of emancipation.[54]

Then, after climaxing with the cry 'down with the *indigénat* . . . long live the Algerian people, long live the fraternity of peoples and long live the Étoile Nord-Africaine', Messali pulled up a piece of earth and brandished it to the ecstatic crowd, telling them that 'this land is not for sale'.[55] It was an electrifying moment. As political theatre it could not be bettered. Nothing summed up so succinctly Algerian grievances and this left the others on the podium ill at ease. They knew that they had been outflanked by Messali. The Étoile Nord-Africaine had crossed the Mediterranean, a major shift away from immigrants in France to Algeria itself, and in the following three months he was acclaimed wherever he went, particularly by the militant, dispossessed young.[56]

Support for Messali was strengthened by the failure of the Blum–Viollette Bill which was put before the National Assembly in December 1936. Blocked by the colonial lobby, the bill limped on during 1937, bolstered by reassuring noises from the government, before being finally buried by the Senate in 1938—the final death knell for the Congress. As such it was the victim of rapidly changing circumstances. On 22 June 1937 Blum, unable to cope with a deepening financial crisis and confronted with the outbreak of the Spanish Civil War, resigned and, although he stayed on as deputy prime minister, the Popular Front experiment was over. Government paralysis then continued until April 1938 when President Lebrun turned to the 54-year-old middle-of-the-road Radical Édouard Daladier, veteran of fifteen cabinets and three times prime minister. Faced with the threat of Nazi Germany, Daladier moved sharply to the right through a blend of anti-communism, authoritarianism, imperialism, and rearmament. Law and order became the order of the day. Algeria had to be secured from foreign and internal subversion, producing a process of anti-nationalist repression mirrored in Morocco, Syria, and Tunisia.

Repression

This repression had begun in January 1937 when the Blum government had banned the ENA on 26 January, using the same law that had suppressed the right-wing leagues. The major difference, though, was that the ENA had been part of the original Popular Front coalition. For the ENA this was the Blum government turning on its own and *El Ouma* proclaimed: 'They have betrayed us! The Popular Front is traitorous! The Popular Front has sacrificed one of its members with the support of the communists!'[57]

Shocked but defiant, Messali and other leading ENA activists, Embarek Filali, Mouauya Abdelkrom, Kehal Arezki, Amar Khider, and Belkacem Radjef, founded the Parti du Peuple Algérien (PPA) in Paris in March. In June Messali returned definitively to Algeria where the PPA now emerged as the rising political force. On the Bastille Day March in Algiers the PPA contingent, led by Messali himself, unfurled the Algerian flag and chanted 'independence', 'Algerian parliament', and 'long live Islam'.

This language emphasized just how far Algerian politics had moved on during the 1920s and 1930s. Without doubt this was a hugely creative moment when nationalists drew upon their interaction with French Left culture to invent their own traditions. PPA activists had their own party hymn composed by the nationalist poet Zakariyya Mufdi; they had their own sign in the form of the index finger on the right hand pointing skywards to God; and their own symbols, which usually involved images of Messali embellished with quotes from the Qu'ran. In each case they represented an outpouring of nationalist feeling which underlined pan-Arab solidarity with Morocco, Syria, and Tunisia, as well as the Palestinian revolt against the British. Inevitably, however, Messali was quickly confronted with renewed repression. The French, unnerved by the way in which Messali had stirred up popular grievances, were fearful that this mood could be exploited by German and Italian spies. On these grounds Messali and several other PPA leaders were arrested on 27 August 1937 and then condemned to two years' imprisonment as common criminals. Unbowed, Messali launched a hunger strike, the first in Algerian history, for political-prisoner status.

Radical atmosphere

If the surge in support for Messali was a consequence of disillusion with the Popular Front, it was also the product of renewed economic hardship. 1937 was known popularly throughout North Africa as the 'year of the great hunger'. In Kabylia families tried to survive on wild roots and rotting animal remains. These famine conditions created an aggressive atmosphere in the countryside that witnessed a spate of attacks on European farms.[58] They also produced a renewed flood of thousands of Algerians into the towns and cities, desperate for food and work. Painfully aware of how political radicalism could feed off social tensions, the 'Native Affairs Unit' monitored Muslim parties and associations for an expression of nationalist feeling.

Music, for example, was closely surveyed as in the case of the Bachtarzi Mahieddine Orchestra. Born in 1897 and a student at a religious school, Bachtarzi Mahieddine was blessed with an exceptional voice. In 1925 he had been acclaimed by the French press as the North Africa equivalent of Caruso, the world famous Italian-American tenor, and in 1926 it was he who inaugurated the new Paris Mosque with the first call to prayer.[59] By the early 1930s he had established his own musical troupe that specialized in mixing North African music with popular theatre. With a cheeky face and smoothed-back hair, Bachtarzi sang in a language that the populace could understand. Effortlessly blending French with spoken Arabic, his songs had explicit political overtones which led one collection to be banned in 1937 for anti-French sentiment.

All the songs encapsulated the mood of disenchantment with the Popular Front. One was an ironic lament on France's failure to remain true to the qualities of liberty, equality, fraternity, while another—'We Do Not Know which Path to Take'—explained how, after one hundred years of being treated like donkeys and kept in ignorance, the Popular Front government had at last promised reform. Yet, once in power Blum kept telling Algerians to wait until finally they had lost all patience:

Figure 3.3a–b Front and back cover of a song booklet, banned by the French in 1937, by Bachtarzi Mahieddine.

Figure 3.3a–b (continued)

> For one hundred years they utter
> That the Arabs are donkeys and understand nothing
> And at the moment when we want to understand
> By force they want to keep us blind . . .
>
> Over the past year we have known a big hope
> At the moment when the Popular Front was formed
> You will have rights, you will have lots of things
> Opprobrium will be finished, unhappiness will be finished
>
> For more than a year we have waited
> And our enemies still repeat to us: wait

The song was a clear warning about the French Left. It was telling Algerians that the Popular Front was in truth an enemy because the promise of reform was just another ploy to maintain the status quo.

Between 22 September 1936 and 31 March 1937 the Bachtarzi Mahieddine Orchestra toured the country performing in twenty-four venues to audiences, almost all of whom were Muslim, ranging from 100 to 2,000.[60] This was then followed by a similar tour in 1938. Such numbers underline how these evenings, made up of theatre followed by music both classical and popular, were major public events. This notoriety brought Bachtarzi Mahieddine into a constant battle with authority. Police reports, noting what was said and sung, painted the picture of a man forever testing the limits of censorship. As master of ceremonies Bachtarzi Mahieddine, full of wit and aplomb, engaged with the audience under the guise of entertainment. In asides interspersed between the songs he told them 'do not let yourselves be exploited'[61] and: 'The delegations sent by you have come back with nothing gained. Unite. Forget the quarrels that divide you. There must be no more distinctions between Kabyles and Arabs.'[62] He also warned against falling into the trap of anti-Semitism and called on the audience to 'take control of their own lives'.[63]

Frequently Bachtarzi Mahieddine outwitted the authorities through subterfuge. In April 1937 the mayor of the Inkerman commune complained to the prefect of Oran that he had been duped. Prior to the performance Mahieddine's description of the plot of the play *Marriage by Telephone* had seemed acceptable. But in reality it had a strong anti-French content, as the actors departed from the agreed script through a series of carefully rehearsed improvisations:

> Amongst other things, one passage, where one of the actors violently criticizes a marabout...a second actor leaps to his defence saying 'this one is a poor wretch with one foot in the grave, he is an adversary of the third order. Those who we should hate are those who have robbed us of control of this country, who have taken our land, who have taken our children.'[64]

The Bachtarzi Mahieddine Orchestra was a measure of the radical atmosphere between 1937 and 1939. This atmosphere was also evident in the popularity amongst Algerians of Egyptian films and music, a statement about Algeria's link with the wider Arab world, and the regular outbreaks of anti-French feeling within cinemas.[65] On 27 February 1938 in the Casino Novelty Cinema in Algiers young Algerians watching the film *The Men without a Name* (*Les homes sans nom*), glorifying the Foreign Legion, used the cover of the darkened cinema to cheer when a French colonel was shot by a Moroccan.[66] Deliberately going against the message of the film to antagonize settlers in the audience, who themselves cheered when the same Moroccan was killed minutes later, these adolescent Algerians also jeered the raising of the tricolore at the end of the film.

Such incidents reflected the all-pervading sense of conflict. By 1938 the political landscape was more embattled than ever. With Messali in prison the PPA had to contend, not only with the Daladier government's energetic repression, but also intensified communist hostility. Accusing the PPA of being sectarian, communist slurs also made much of the fact that the party's name closely resembled that of the explicitly fascist party Parti Populaire Français (PPF), founded in June 1936. This hostility became definitive, when Maurice Thorez, speaking in Algiers in March 1939, described Algeria not as a nation, but as 'a nation in the process of formation'.[67] According to this formula Algeria was a melting pot of some twenty races which, given the international fight against fascism, needed to remain under the protective wing of the Third Republic.

Not surprisingly Messali was aghast. Thorez's analysis was a denial of the Algerian nation that exemplified the gulf with the left. Like the Socialists, loyal custodians of the empire who had baulked at even timid reform in the face of the colonial lobby, the Communists were now unambiguously upholding French sovereignty. Neither understood how Algerian politics had been completely altered by the 1930s. Assimilation was dead. National-ism had emerged and by the simple law of numbers this was now impossible to ignore.

The impact of World War Two

On 23 August 1939 Nazi Germany and the Soviet Union signed a non-aggression pact which opened the way for the partition of Poland. Three days later the Algerian and French Communist Parties were banned as well as the PPA, accused of being defeatist. Messali, who had just been released, was thrown back in prison, and there was a wave of PPA arrests in Algeria and France. This repression intensified under the Vichy regime that emerged from defeat in the summer of 1940 under the leadership of the 84-year-old World War One hero Marshal Pétain. The PPA ban remained in place and Messali himself was sentenced to sixteen years hard labour in March 1941.

Such measures were welcomed with open arms by the majority of settlers. The repression of communist and nationalists was a return to the colonial status quo. It was an authoritarianism that made them feel safe after the uncertainties of the Popular Front years. Reflecting their own conservative, right-wing values, most Europeans embraced Vichy's National Revolution which sought to instil values that idealized family and peasant life, called for discipline and obedience, and revered the Roman Catholic Church as a model for moral leadership. They embraced Vichy's anti-republicanism, anti-socialism and anti-communism. And, most of all, they embraced Vichy's Jewish Statute in October 1940, which revoked the Crémieux Decrees and stripped Jews of their status as French citizens.[68] Amongst Algerians the Vichy period provoked mixed feelings. Abbas made overtures to Pétain in April 1941. A minority of PPA activists even looked to Nazi Germany as a possible ally against the French. Most PPA activists, though, remained true to Messali's anti-fascist line, fighting hard to maintain the organization intact in the face of Vichy repression.

What transformed this situation was 'Operation Torch': the American and British landings in Algeria and Morocco on 8 November 1942.[69] Made up of an armada of 290 ships, the American and British forces attacked Oran and Algiers, vastly outnumbering the Vichy forces who concluded a ceasefire that night. Algerians, in particular, were impressed by the swagger of the US troops. With their brand-new uniforms, netted helmets, and open-top cars known as jeeps, they had the air of victors and American phrases like 'OK' and 'chewing gum' became part of everyday conversation. By way of contrast the arrival of American and British troops made the French look defeated. 1940 had already destroyed the aura of colonial invincibility, but, as the Allied forces quickly brushed aside Vichy resistance, Algerians saw French humiliation for themselves and this image left a deep impression.

In Algiers the 12-year-old Jacques Derrida, who would later become one of France's most significant academic philosophers, had been excluded from his school as an Algerian Jew under Vichy's anti-Semitic laws. For him the arrival of the Allies was an immensely significant moment:

> At dawn, we began to hear heavy gunfire ... And then, in the afternoon ... we saw in front of our house soldiers with helmets that we had never seen. They were not French helmets. We said to ourselves: they are Germans. And it was the Americans. We had never seen an American helmet either. And that evening, the Americans arrived en masse, as always distributing cigarettes,

chewing gum, chocolate, kids starting going up to them . . . That was called the liberation.[70]

It was a political earthquake that, by ending the Vichy regime, would allow Algerian Jews to retrieve their citizenship and in the case of school children like Derrida go back to school, although this would not happen until Vichy's Jewish Statute was revoked in October 1943.[71]

In Tizi-Ouzou in Kabylia the 16-year-old PPA member Hocine Aït Ahmed, one of the future FLN leaders, like most of his Algerian compatriots, also experienced the Allied landing as a political earthquake: 'One can say that opinion, as a whole, moved on to the Allied side . . . the population sympathized with the American Army. There was a democratic side to the way in which the officers and soldiers behaved.'[72]

Specifically, Aït Ahmed underlined, the Americans brought with them the new ideas of the Atlantic Charter signed by Franklin Roosevelt and Winston Churchill in August 1941, which had a huge impact on Algerian political opinion. In asserting a set of democratic ideals directly opposed to Nazism, the Charter emphasized the rights of all peoples to choose their own form of government. Churchill, sensing the implicit threat to the British Empire, underlined that these rights were restricted to Nazi-occupied Europe, but Roosevelt was clear that they should be applied everywhere, to European and non-European alike. Already, during the initial November 1942 landing US planes had dropped thousands of leaflets, adorned with the American flag and Roosevelt's picture, addressed to the people of French North Africa which stated: 'We come to your country to free you from the grip of conquerors who seek to deprive you of your sovereign rights, your religious freedom and the right to lead your way of life in peace.'[73]

Roosevelt reiterated this point in person on 22 January 1943 in Casablanca during a private meeting with the Moroccan sultan, Mohammed V, much to the consternation of the French authorities. He was adamant that Morocco should belong to Moroccans, telling the sultan:

Why does Morocco, inhabited by Moroccans, belong to France? Anything must be better than to live under French colonial rule. Should a land belong to France? By what logic and by what custom and by what historical rule? . . . When we've won the war, I will work with all my might and main to see that the United States is not wheedled into the position of accepting any plan that will further France's imperialistic ambitions.[74]

Although Roosevelt made no public commitment to end French rule in North Africa, nationalists in Algeria, Morocco, and Tunisia quickly made his language of self-determination into their own. When, in early 1944, the Moroccan Istiqlal Movement and the Tunisian Front demanded independence, they both did so in terms of the Atlantic Charter.

In the same way, in Algeria, Abbas—who prominently displayed a picture of Roosevelt in his shop in Sétif—met with the USA president's personal envoy, Robert Murphy, at the end of 1942. Encouraged by the sympathetic response he drew up a list of demands that were presented to the American, British, and French authorities, thereby drawing attention to the relative weakness of the colonial power. This was then followed up by a nine-page 'Manifesto of the Algerian People', signed by fifty members of the Fédération on 31 March 1943, that catalogued their demands. In no position to ignore them the French authorities asked for a clear programme of reform, which Abbas unveiled on 11 June 1943. Within this platform he called for a new beginning. Invoking the 1789 precedent, Abbas underlined that the world was undergoing a revolution. Democracy was no longer the preserve of Europe. Imperialism was finished. Algerians, like other colonial subjects, wanted to be treated as equals. Conscious of their recruitment into the Free French Army, they wanted to know that their fight to liberate Nazi Europe would lead to their own liberation through self-government.[75]

These political demands caused consternation amongst large numbers of Europeans. They hated the disappearance of the Vichy regime and the arrival of the Allies. They sensed that the status quo, re-established under Pétain's National Revolution, was slipping away, principally because the USA was encouraging Algerian nationalism, but also as a result of what, in their view, was the dangerous liberalism of de Gaulle's new Provisional Government in Algiers. They were angered by the way in which representatives from the Provisional Government were talking to Abbas, seemingly conferring legitimacy on his 'Manifesto'—anger magnified even further when, on 7 March 1944, de Gaulle unveiled reforms granting citizenship to 65,000 Muslims.

Through this initiative de Gaulle hoped to win over Algerian opinion, especially since large numbers of Algerians were fighting alongside the Allies in the Free French Army in Italy, invaded in 1943. But his reforms were also a statement about French sovereignty in Algeria. Like so many of the Europeans, de Gaulle hated the presence of the Americans and the British. He hated the fact that Roosevelt had fervently backed his political rival, the more senior General Henri Giraud, in their battle for leadership of the Conseil National de la Résistance in May 1943, a confrontation that de Gaulle won because he secured the support of all the political parties connected to the French Resistance, including the Communists. He hated the way in which Roosevelt was stirring up anti-French nationalism in Algeria and Morocco. He hated the manner in which American and British control of North Africa had underlined France's own loss of political, economic, and strategic power. The March 1944 reforms, like the Brazzaville Conference, were about wresting back the initiative from the British and the USA. They were an attempt to impose French-designed solutions which would crush the rumours, widely circulating in Algerian society, that France would be divested of Algeria and the empire after the defeat of Nazi Germany. The other side of de Gaulle's policy was force. When he departed for the Liberation of Paris at the end of August 1944, he left orders to the army and police that Algerian nationalism must be closely monitored and any threat to French rule repressed. Looking forward to the post-war world, he wished to project the image of a strong, unified nation that would bury the humiliation of 1940 and ensure France's equal place at the victors' table with the UK, USA, and USSR.

For Abbas the 7 March 1944 reforms were too little, too late and on 14 March he, along with the Ulema and the banned PPA, although not the PCA, formed the Association des Amis du Manifeste et de la Liberté (AML). The goal was 'an autonomous Republic federated with a renewed, anti-colonialist and anti-imperialist French Republic', a future that was outlined in the AML's newspaper, Equality (Égalité), as well as numerous tracts, speeches, and public meetings.[76] In one ten-page pamphlet, entitled 'I Accuse Europe', Abbas denounced the network of spies and informers put in place by the French, before calling on the authorities in Algiers to accept the liberation of colonized peoples in general and Algeria in particular. Across the political spectrum, he argued, from Messali to the Ulema, everybody believed that a union was possible with 'sincerely democratic France'.[77] But 'for that it is necessary, it is indispensable that colonization puts its sword in the scabbard and declares peace to peoples that it has never stopped for an instant to oppress and exploit, under the pretext of assimilating and civilizing them'.[78]

During the spring and summer the AML mushroomed into the first mass movement in Algerian political history. Soon it had over 100,000 members but, from the outset, the organization's grass roots were effectively infiltrated and taken over by the PPA which, much more radical than the AML leadership, looked to prepare a climactic event that would end French rule. In Tizi-Ouzou, Aït-Ahmed and his fellow pupils at lycée Ben-Aknou intensified their political activism. They produce a typed paper, *Student Patriot* (*L'Étudiant Patriote*), composed popular patriotic songs in Berber calling on Berbers to rise up, and established links with university students and the local Ulema.[79]

Infused with the religious imagery of rural Islam, this discourse was millenarian in tone. Again and again it talked about the final reckoning that was moving ever closer and was now within the Algerian people's grasp. On the night of 13 May 1944, for example, in Biskra, in the east of the country, graffiti painted in green enamel called for readiness in the following terms: 'Muslim Brothers, Prepare Yourselves', 'Muslim Brothers, prepare yourselves for H. Hour', 'Prepare for the Revolution'.[80]

The sense of an impending revolt was evident in the way in which grass-roots members, particularly in the eastern part of the country, picked up and hid weapons still strewn across North Africa in the wake of 'Operation Torch' and the battles between the Allied and Axis forces in the Tunisian campaign.[81] It was reflected in hostility towards the settlers. One police report from Biskra related how, on 14 May 1944, a European shopkeeper had found on his counter a typed text, 'Manifesto of the Algerian People', folded in four, which stated: 'Allies, you want to liberate those peoples subjugated since 1940 and you forget those who have been subjugated for more than a century. The Algerian People categorically refuse French citizenship and want Algerian citizenship and an Algerian parliament.'[82]

It was also fuelled by the shortage of food which, after a poor harvest and a long winter, led to famine conditions in early 1945. This hunger put people on edge and led to accusations that rationing was not only being organized in favour of the settlers, but was worse than in occupied Europe. Already at a public meeting in Biskra on Monday 9 April 1944, attended by 1,000 people, Sidi Moussa, a chemist in Sétif and PCA member, had claimed that: 'Hitler gives 250 grams of wheat a day and we who are free, we only receive 200 grams. All this must be done away.'[83]

Such language underlines how, by this point, the majority of Muslims and settlers had grown accustomed to fearing and hating the other side. The country was primed for conflict and throughout 1944 and early 1945 there were daily instances of tension and confrontation whether it be stones thrown at French schoolchildren, insults on public transport and in the marketplace, or groups forbidding Muslims to frequent French cafés.[84] These incidents were particularly pronounced in the Constantine department and led to a febrile climate awash with all types of rumour. There was speculation that the Anglo-Saxons were ready to replace French rule with a Muslim government. There was speculation about the impact of the formation of the Arab League in March 1945. There was even speculation about a maquis organized by the Germans. Certainly the French were seen to be vulnerable and at the AML conference in Algiers on 2 April the overwhelming number of delegates, conscious of the impending establishment of the United Nations in San Francisco, voted for the immediate creation of a separate Algerian parliament rather than an autonomous republic federated to France.

Writing regular despatches to the British Embassy in Paris and the Foreign Office in London, John Cavell, the British Consul in Algiers, testified to this rising militancy throughout 1945. Already on 9 February 1945 he was predicting violence when British and US troops left Algeria because of the rise of nationalism, fuelled by the huge food shortages brought on by the ongoing war, and the 'exploitation and discrimination' suffered by the 'Arabs' who, he wrote, were seen by the French as 'an inferior race'.[85] In early May he met two young Algerian PPA members in the British Consulate. In talking to Cavell they made it very clear that, on the basis of the Atlantic Charter, they had high hopes that during the San Francisco Conference 'the status of all colonies and dependencies would be considered and modified'.[86] But, disappointed that the 'native populations of North Africa were not going to be represented', they were asking Cavell if he could pass on a message to the British government calling on them to support the participation of Algerian nationalist parties at the Conference.[87] From the beginning Cavell had made it clear that he could not, underlining that, in his understanding, 'only independent states were to be represented':

> They then said that Algerian Arabs had lost all hope of obtaining satisfaction from the French Government of their national aspirations and that life under French dominion had become intolerable and for many was not worth living. Their party was determined to insist that the status of Moslems in North Africa should be covered by international guarantees which would oblige the French Government to modify the regime in Algeria.[88]

Cavell was similarly non-committal when they asked him about Britain's stance over the colonial issue, which, he argued, would probably not be discussed at San Francisco because the priority was the establishment of a general framework rather than specific issues. Describing the two PPA members as 'young hotheads', he concluded the meeting with a call for 'patience' and 'moderation', emphasizing that the social hardships were 'the direct effects of the war now happily drawing to an end'.[89]

Cavell's communiqués showed just how fragile French rule was, which is why, in an effort to maintain control, the authorities deported Messali Hadj to Brazzaville on 23 April 1945. Yet, this only served to ratchet up the tension still further and on 1 May across Algeria there were major clashes and demonstrations that resulted in six Muslims dead. On 7 May the authorities announced that an armistice had been signed and that the war in Europe was at an end. In Sétif, victory was signalled by the peeling church bells and wailing sirens and on the streets Europeans expressed joy and relief. However, it immediately became clear that Muslims did not share the same sentiments. They did not join in with the celebrations. Only a handful of Muslim ex-servicemen participated in the veterans march-past and when one shouted 'Long live de Gaulle! Long live Messali!' the on-looking Muslim crowd responded in unison 'Long live Messali!' For Muslims 7 May was not the end. It was the beginning. This was the final trigger they had been waiting for.

PART II

Undeclared war
1945–59

4
Sliding into War
Tuesday, 8 May 1945

Across Algeria towns and cities witnessed crowds brandishing British, American, Soviet, French, and Algerian flags and placards with the slogans 'Long live Messali!', 'For the liberation of peoples, long live free and independent Algeria!', 'Down with colonialism', and 'Long live the Atlantic Charter'. Chanting the Algerian national anthem and with the index finger on the right hand pointed towards the sky, women and young men, in particular scouts, were at the forefront of these demonstrations. In occupying public space the crowds represented a direct challenge to French sovereignty. Anticipating the formation of the United Nations in San Francisco, they wanted to show that Algerians existed and were ready to take their place amongst the nation states of the world. Inevitably this produced a tense atmosphere, but for the most part there were no major confrontations largely because, in the absence of a general order, the local police were pragmatic. Most chose to look on and let the demonstrators carry banners rather than intervene.

However, in the town of Sétif in eastern Algeria it was different. Here hatred over the land issue ran deep. Local Algerians were enraged by the fact that since 1853 the Swiss-owned Compagnie Genevoise had owned 15,000 hectares of the best land in the area which was used for export crops. Forced to cope with hunger and deprivation—there had been no rain since January—they felt that they were starving in a land of plenty. On top of this, Sétif, through the prominence of local politicians such as Ferhat Abbas, had assumed the status of the capital of Muslim Algeria. Nationalism was widespread, leading, as we have seen, to a mood of confrontation during the 'Victory in Europe' celebrations on 7 May. For many this was the sign they had been waiting for and on the following day, a market day which swelled the numbers still further, thousands poured into the town armed with knives, axes, sabres, even pistols.

Assembling outside the main mosque at 9.15 a.m., the 8,000 demonstrators were determined to march down Avenue Clemenceau to the war monument and lay down a wreath. Negotiations with the waiting police, just twenty in total, had led to an agreement on no nationalist banners, but this was immediately ignored once the demonstration, filmed by British troops stationed nearby, got under way. Ten minutes later, gendarmes, observing from 'Café de France', waded into the crowd to seize the offending flags. Scuffles broke out. The police were attacked on all sides. Suddenly shots rang out killing a 20-year-old scout, Bouziz Salah, followed by further exchanges of gunfire that produced a general panic. Fleeing into the side streets and towards the market, some demonstrators set upon Europeans, killing twenty-one, including the socialist mayor Édouard Deluca, and wounding a further forty-nine, notably the local Communist Party leader, Albert Denier, whose hands were cut off.[1]

By late morning the violence had petered out, but the news quickly spread to the surrounding countryside. This ignited an uprising throughout the western part of the Constantine department, including Bougie, the Babor mountains in Kabylia, Kherrata, and the outskirts of Bône on the coast.

Chanting 'Holy War in the name of Allah' and 'Allauh Akbar', racial and religious hatreds, fuelled by hunger, produced indiscriminate anti-settler violence. Chouche Abderrahmane, for example, was twenty at the time. On hearing about Sétif, 2,000 men from his mountain village, Oued-El-Bared, just 18 km from Sétif, attacked the settlers in nearby Kherrata. Although they were AML activists, this was not a coordinated uprising. It was a spontaneous act of revenge:

> We were armed with knives and rifles. It was my father who killed the baker because he was French. We broke down the doors, burning down the houses with the oil and petrol that we found...Around midday reinforcements arrived. We believed that it was the Americans who had come to help us. The reinforcements, in lorries, fired with machine guns. We lost one man, Lakdimi Saïd.[2]

The men took to the mountains along with their women, children, and animals. Over the following three days 102 Europeans were killed. Much of it was crude face-to-face violence, followed up by ritualistic dismemberment where genitals were cut off and placed in the mouths of corpses, breasts slashed,

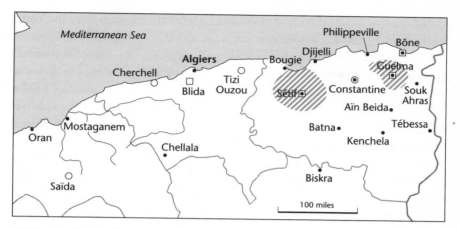

• Algerian nationalist demonstration on 1st May   ☐ Violent Algerian demonstrations on 8th May
▨▨ Rebel zones   ○ Attempted Algerian insurrection after 8th May

Map 4.1 May 1945: Algerian demonstrations and insurrection.

throats slit, and bellies disembowelled. In Chevreul, 40 km to the north–east of Sétif, settlers, all modest farmers whose largest holding was just 200 hectares, were forced to take refuge in the local police station for thirty hours. What shocked them was that they knew their assailants. They were their labourers and servants, some of whom had worked on their farms for thirty years.

The response was swift and brutal. That evening, Governor-General Yves Chataigneau, appointed by de Gaulle the previous September, proclaimed a state of siege in Constantine department that was extended to the rest of Algeria on the following day. He also ordered General Duval and the local prefect, André Lestrade-Carbonnel, to quell the uprising, unleashing a 10,000-man military operation comprising Moroccan, West African, and Foreign Legion units. Significantly, however, this was a solely French operation. After the RAF initially helped to airlift seventy-five legionaries, the British, like the USA, carefully avoided giving further logistical support because, as John Cavell, the British Consul, underlined, they realized that, if this French repression was excessive, such aid could risk 'embarrassing repercussions in the world'.[3]

As these units combed the countryside Duval was determined to make an example. This was an integral part of France and in the ensuing weeks Duval's men flushed out all the insurgents in a pitiless fashion. Burning down houses and carrying out summary executions, their actions were backed up by the navy and air force which shelled the coast and bombed whole villages with, the British Consulate noted, nearly 300 aerial sorties.[4] Chouche Abderrahmane, involved in the attack on Kherrata, was arrested with two uncles and six other people from his village: '1,000 to 2,000 of the arrondissement were arrested on information from the qaïds. Others were killed a bit further on. My father had taken to the maquis. His mother was arrested as a hostage. He gave himself up because of her and was immediately shot. He was a AML member.'[5]

Within the Sétif region, this repression, lasting until 24 May, was characterized by the systematic humiliation of prisoners. French soldiers wanted to ram home who had won and who had lost. In the Babors mountain villages 5,000 peasants were herded together and forced on their knees in front of the tricolore to beg forgiveness. Elsewhere others had to prostrate themselves on the floor and chant: 'We are dogs and Ferhat Abbas is a dog.'[6] Soldiers also made rings out of fingers mutilated from the dead, war trophies that would be bragged about for years to come as legitimate forms of revenge.[7]

Guelma

If Sétif was the first epicentre of violence, the other was the town of Guelma 320 km to the north near the Tunisian border.[8] There, the repression was led not by the army but by settler militias at the behest of the local sub-prefect André Achiary. A Gaullist resister who had played a clandestine role during the November 1942 landings, Achiary, also close to the local SFIO, had the look of a man of action in his military uniform and sunglasses. With the chain of command running up to Algiers and Paris weak, Achiary took control of the situation, distributing arms to settlers in late April.

On 8 May itself 2,500 Algerians with flags and placards converged on the war monument in the late afternoon. Immediately their route was barred by Achiary and the police who, shooting in the air, called on the demonstrators to disperse. In the resultant confusion, the crowd ran in all directions fired on by militia stationed in the overlooking houses. At this point Achiary imposed a curfew, arresting local AML leaders, organizing armed patrols and positioning machine guns on each street corner. Egged on by his immediate superior, the prefect for the Constantine department, André

Lestrade-Carbonnel, Achiary established a 'committee of public safety' and 'emergency courts'.

Within this process, legal niceties were cast aside as Achiary's militia, explicitly using the metaphor of the hunt, rounded on the local Muslim population. Particular savagery was reserved for assimilated Muslims. As a local politician close to Ferhat Abbas and the owner of the largest café in Guelma, le Grand Hôtel d'Orient, at the intersection of the Arab *quartier* and the European *quartier*, Mohammed Reggui was a symbol of 'native' advancement. By murdering him and then leaving his body in the street in front of his café, the militia was making a statement. They wanted to re-establish hierarchies after the uncertainties of the war years. Threatened by both the assertiveness of the Muslim population and de Gaulle's March 1944 reforms, Guelma's 4,000 settlers wanted to stand up to the town's 16,500 Muslims. Throughout the rest of May, although there were no casualties amongst the army, police, or militia, a quarter of the Muslim adult population aged between twenty-five and forty-five, 1,500 in all, were killed, mostly traders, craftsmen, and minor officials, and buried in mass graves. Fearful of an inquiry, these bodies were then dug up by Achiary's militia at the end of May and incinerated in lime kilns. The nature of this bloodshed means that Guelma must be understood not as a nationalist uprising, but as a settler insurrection. Fitting into a tradition established by the Algiers Commune and the 1898 riots, this was another example of settlers acting on their own initiative and imposing their rule through violence.

As news of Sétif and Guelma spread to the rest of Algeria, the PPA base, believing that the final reckoning had arrived and spurred on by hope of an Anglo-Saxon intervention, pushed the leadership to call for a general uprising. This leadership though, still disorientated by Messali's deportation on 23 April, was ill prepared.[9] Responding to events, it set 23 May as the date for insurrection but in truth this was impossible to actualize. Plagued by poor communication, the response was uneven which led the leadership to issue a counter-order calling for an end to the insurrection. In large part, too, this decision was conditioned by the very strength of the French response. To have continued would have been suicide as, following on from an immediate ban on the AML, hundreds of PPA activists were arrested, along with the Ulema leader, Bachir al-Ibrahimi, and Abbas himself who, despite being in Algiers at the time, was blamed as the chief instigator of revolt.[10]

Climate of fear

In the wake of May 1945 a climate of fear descended on the country. This is evident from despatches to the British Foreign Office from the Consulate in Algiers. On 12 June 1945 John Cavell, the British Consul, described the situation in the following terms:

> There was no doubt that very great anxiety existed in official circles who feared that something of the nature of a holy war was about to start. The Europeans who have been prey of the wildest rumours have been in a state of nervousness bordering on panic. Those living in the country fortified their houses and spent many sleepless nights. A certain French journalist who has lived many years in England made discreet enquiries as to whether I would receive his wife and daughter into my house. The British Vice-Consul at Bône who visited the Guelma district on May 30th reported that he found the situation very threatening. As an instance of the general nervousness prevailing he related to me that a quarrel between two market women at Bône, where no Europeans had been killed, was sufficient a few days ago to cause the inhabitants to run panic stricken to their houses.[11]

The climate of fear is evident in the letters opened by the French police. Settler families wrote continually about 'tension' and 'anxiety'.[12] And it is evident from families with relatives who had disappeared. In El-Arrouch the adolescent Mohammed Harbi was anxious because two of his relatives had been picked up by Achiary's militia in Guelma.[13] Attentive to any news about their fate, they were eventually forced to accept that both were dead. In the same way Marcel Reggui returned to his native Guelma in the summer of 1945. A Muslim convert to Catholicism, close to the left-wing Catholic journal *Esprit* and a Socialist Party member, he was determined to establish the truth about his two brothers and sister, all of whom had been killed in May.[14]

With so many questions hanging in the air, the government had quickly set up an inquiry on 19 May under the auspices of General Paul Tubert, Resistance veteran, close to the communists, and a leading member of the League of the Rights of Man.[15] However, this inquiry was cut short, partly because the ongoing violence prevented the inquiry from visiting Guelma, but mainly because the Socialist Minister of the Interior, Adrien Tixier, himself under enormous pressure from de Gaulle, wanted to bury the whole affair.[16] Speaking in the Provisional Assembly on 18 July, Tixier, who had gone in person to Algeria, including Guelma, at the end of June to assess the situation on the ground, claimed that the violence had been exaggerated by the British and Americans.[17] While the *New York Times* had talked of between 7,000 and 20,000 dead, the truth, Tixier claimed, was 1,500.

Just how many died has remained an unresolved controversy. At the time British army sources put the figure at 6,000, three years later the nationalist press would talk of 15,000 to 20,000, while since independence Algerian estimates have never been less than 45,000. Whichever is the real number, what cannot be denied is the long-term significance of Sétif. Certainly General Duval was under no illusions, commenting bluntly: 'If France does nothing in ten years, it will start again worse and in an irremediable fashion.'[18]

This conclusion was echoed by John Cavell in his despatch to the British Foreign Office on 12 June 1945:

> It is probably safe to assume that the Algerian nationalist movement has been checked but it would be unwise to assume that it has been killed. The ruthless destruction of villages and the indiscriminate slaughter of women and children will never be forgotten. The movement will of necessity go underground for the time being and will come to the surface in another form.[19]

Such comments recognized the way in which Sétif signalled the political awakening of rural Algeria. May 1945 was not a peasant *jacquerie*. Yes, hunger played a role. Yes, religion and place had been reignited within the tradition of armed revolt. Now, however, these motivations, central to resistance in the nineteenth century, were articulated within the language of militant nationalism. Islam stood side by side with ideas of the right to self-determination, testament to the manner in which Algerian symbols and traditions, invented over the past twenty years, had taken root in the popular imagination. Furthermore, this popular imagination understood the repression as the product of a left-wing government based on anti-Nazi Resistance values. It remembered the role of Tixier as the SFIO Minister of the Interior who, even if he was ill at ease with some aspects of the repression, was in no doubt about the urgent need to restore French sovereignty, laying the blame for the violence on the PPA and AML.[20] It remembered, too, the fact that the Communist Minister of Air, Charles Tillon, did not resign, while the communist press described the PPA as pro-Hitler.[21]

Settlers triumphant

The May 1945 violence was the result of a triangular dynamic made up of Algerian nationalism, settlers acting on their own initiative, and a French state eager to reassert national sovereignty over the empire. In this way Sétif was linked to wider insecurities. Fearful about the country's place in the post-1945 world, de Gaulle was determined to hold on to French geopolitical influence. For de Gaulle, anger at the manner in which the Anglo-Saxon presence had undermined French sovereignty in Algeria, Morocco, and Tunisia had been magnified by French exclusion from the Yalta Conference in February 1945, the formation of the Arab League in March 1945, and rumours that large parts of the French Empire were about to be put under a United Nations trusteeship. All of this was interpreted as an Anglo-Saxon plot to push France out of the Middle East and North Africa.[22] For this reason Sétif was inseparable from other events in the empire. Along with the repression of nationalist demonstrations in Syria on 8 May and the dispatching of troops to Indochina, it sent a clear signal to Britain, the Soviet Union, and the USA about France's recovery of great-power status.

In this climate of muscular imperialism the settlers felt protected. Backed up by the provisional government, they felt that May 1945 had restored them to a position of supreme strength. Yet, in reality nothing could be the same again. Rural Algeria had confronted European Algeria, producing a society more polarized than ever. Unable to cope with the drip-drip of violence which Sétif had brought to a head, settlers in the Constantine department departed the countryside in ever increasing numbers. Some left for what they saw as the safety of the towns and coast; others even countenanced leaving Algeria altogether, accelerating a process, in place since World War One, which in the east of the country brought an end to a world, however unequal, of contact and personal interaction.[23] This rural-settler exodus solidified an urban, coastal European Algeria that underwent a shift in self-perception in the late 1940s and early 1950s. Faced with Muslim Algeria, settlers retreated from the idea of being Algerian in the sense articulated at the end of the nineteenth century. Now Algeria was equated with Muslim nationalism. In opposition to this settlers began to forge a new identity, still strongly separatist, still strongly anti-Semitic, still strongly anti-Arab, that talked about themselves as the *pieds-noirs* (black feet); a phrase of uncertain origin that, in encapsulating the settler specificity, would be finally cemented during the war of liberation itself.[24]

Not all settlers though were like this. A minority wanted to address Algerian demands. One was the writer Albert Camus, born into a poor background with a mother of Spanish descent. In the 1930s he had flirted briefly with the PCA, writing articles on the Kabyle famine in the communist-supporting press in 1939.[25] Wishing to alert settlers to the plight of the Muslim population, Camus preached not domination but harmony.[26] Calling for a more inclusive Algeria, he wanted settler and Muslim alike to embrace the Mediterranean as a place of shared cultural unity. Emerging from the Liberation as rising star of the intellectual left—he had edited the clandestine Resistance paper *Combat* in Paris—Camus wrote a series of eye-witness accounts for the paper on the aftermath of Sétif.[27] Within them he movingly described famine conditions. He also tried to go beyond stereotypes. 'The Arab people' were not, he emphasized, an amorphous, apathetic mass.[28] They were fully engaged with contemporary debates as evidenced by the rise of Ferhat Abbas and the AML, the most significant political phenomenon since the conquest. However, in analysing the AML, Camus stopped well short of supporting independence. The solution for him was to be found in finally bringing French democracy to Algeria. By extending the March 1944 reforms, France had to win over the 'Arab masses' through practical action.[29]

Another voice for change was the Radical politician Jacques Chevallier. Born in 1911 in Bordeaux, Chevallier, closely supported by the tycoon Georges Blachette, owner of the daily *Journal d'Alger* whose extensive alfalfa holding had earned him the nickname 'king of alfalfa', sought to include nationalists in the political process in the late 1940s and early 1950s. As deputy for Algiers from 1946 onwards, he espoused a liberal position that seemed far removed from hard-line settler sentiment. Calling for an end to racial prejudice, Chevallier wanted to disarm extremism by enacting a liberal compromise that would bring French and Muslim together, albeit within a French framework.

One person who went further was André Mandouze. Unusually tall and imposing, Mandouze had been a leading member of the Catholic Resistance in Lyon.[30] In 1946 he had crossed the Mediterranean to take up a history lectureship at Algiers University. There he was shocked to find what he had fought against. Writing three articles in the Catholic review *Esprit*, Mandouze, trying to convey the violent atmosphere all around him, warned that Algeria was primed for war. Resolved to act, Mandouze sought to establish a dialogue between a small group of nationalists and liberal-minded settlers through the journal *Consciences Maghrebiennes*, a process that politicized a tiny minority of left-wing Catholics, notably brother and sister Pierre and Anne-Marie Chaulet, who would subsequently fight for Algerian independence.

But these were the exceptions rather than the rule. In general traditional settler attitudes became more entrenched than ever. They could not countenance the smallest change because it was viewed as a stepping stone to their worst nightmare, nationalist rule; a conservative mindset that was a major factor in the rising climate of violence in the late 1940s. This mindset explains the continuing anti-Semitism. The by now 130,000-strong Jewish community was identified with reform since large numbers either voted for the Communist and Socialist Parties or at the very least supported greater equality for Muslims, even if they did not envisage an end to French rule. This mindset also explains the opposition to the Governor-General, Yves Chataigneau. Accused of being too socialist, too liberal, Chataigneau was stigmatized as 'Chataigneau ben Mohammed, the gravedigger of Algeria'. By attempting to improve Muslim living and working conditions, he was seen to be letting the nationalists in by the back door.[31] Settler leaders like Amédée Froger, mayor of Boufarik and president of the Federation of Algerian Mayors, and Alain de Sérigny, editor of the hard-line *Écho d'Alger*, became very good at saying no, playing on the prejudices of their supporters. But in doing so they made full-scale conflict all the more inevitable because the result of their intransigence was a blocked society, bristling with hatred and resentments on all sides.

Recreating nationalist politics

Sétif and Guelma continued to reverberate in Muslim Algeria throughout 1945 and 1946. One effect was to politicize a new generation. Zina Haraigue, an 11-year-old resident from Sétif, witnessed the 8 May demonstration at first hand. She saw the police firing into the crowd. She suffered, too, as Algerians in the town were confined to their houses, unable to go out for food or water—a formative experience that drew her into nationalist politics, leading ultimately to imprisonment in La Roquette in Paris in the late 1950s.[32] Equally for the writer Kateb Yacine, as a 16-year-old imprisoned for his participation in the Sétif demonstration, May 1945 was a defining moment. 'Bodies everywhere in all the streets, the repression was blind'; this was his dominant memory of the day and in the wake of this brutality, compounded by the fact that his parents were forced to flee their home in Guelma, his nationalism would take on a precise form.[33]

News of May 1945 also impacted on demobilized Muslim soldiers. Some 136,000 had fought in Europe and on returning to Algeria they were greeted by a country reeling from repression, famine, and typhus. The disjunction between the ideal of anti-Nazi liberation and the reality of French Algeria could not have been more startling. Angered by the double standards, a number of war veterans like Mostefa Ben Boulaïd, Mohammed Boudiaf, and Ahmed Ben Bella, all later to become prominent figures in the war against the French, began to look towards violent action as the only way forward, enacting a process that would lead ultimately to the foundation of the Front de Libération Nationale (FLN) in November 1954.

The fact that May 1945 became such a rallying cry, both for a new generation and for disgruntled war veterans, underlined just how far Algerian nationalism had travelled since the 1920s. Whereas the Shawiya revolt in 1916 had remained at the level of an oral memory, Sétif became embedded within a wider and more sophisticated political culture. Quickly postcards with an Algerian flag and pictures of martyrs, including the first victim of 8 May, Bouzid Salah, circulated with the inscriptions 'Honour and Glory to the Martyrs of National Liberation' and 'The Algerian People will never forget you'. In Tlemcen on 23 February 1946, a theatre production in spoken Arabic, *The Other Muslim*, recreated Sétif, calling on the Muslim audience to learn the lessons of the repression.[34] Likewise all the nationalist parties and affiliated organizations commemorated Sétif through songs, ceremonies, and press articles; while in Guelma in September 1945 the end of Ramadan was not marked by the traditional outpouring of joy. It became a day of mourning for those killed during the repression.

The resilience of Algerian politics was exemplified by the return of Ferhat Abbas, freed under the amnesty law approved by the National Assembly on 9 March 1946, and Messali Hadj, pardoned on 30 October the same year. Undeterred by Sétif, both were more determined than ever to press their respective causes. Wanting to show that May 1945 had not killed off Algerian nationalism, they created, along with the Algerian Communist

Party, a political culture, based on meetings, party organizations, and a nationalist press which presented Algerians with a series of alternatives.

In the case of Abbas, he established a political party in April 1946, along with Ahmed Boumendjel, Ahmed Francis, and Abdelkader Mahdad: the Union Démocratique du Manifeste Algérien (UDMA).[35] Drawn from the Francophone middle classes, UDMA pinned its hopes not on violence, but the power of argument. The aim was to convince the fledgling Fourth Republic that the only practicable solution was an Algerian state federated to France. Losing no time Abbas set out his perspectives on 1 May in an impassioned tract entitled 'Appeal to Algerian youth'.[36] Tracing his own political journey, Abbas explained the origins of the AML. Stating categorically that the AML was not responsible for Sétif, Abbas pointed the finger at settler agents provocateurs within the French administration, citing the prefect for Constantine, Lestrande-Carbonnel, and Achiary. By stirring up hatred and violence, he argued, they had unleashed 'a truly Hitlerian terror' intended to quash Algerian aspirations and open the way to hard-line colonialism.[37] In spite of this repression, however, the AML's ideals remained intact: 'Not assimilation, not new masters, not separatism. A young people, completing its democratic and social education, realizing its industrial and scientific facilities, pursuing its intellectual and moral renewal, linked to a great liberal nation: a young nascent democracy guided by the great French democracy.'[38]

In appealing to the 'France of 1789', Abbas offered up the image of a pluralistic society, based upon the principle of equality and democracy, which would bring together Christians, Muslims, and Jews. Armed with these arguments Abbas sought to forge links with the SFIO and insert himself into the electoral process, while carefully distancing the UDMA from the PPA whose violence, he maintained, had been so disastrous.[39]

Abbas also reached out to the Algerian Communist Party whose position evolved during late 1945 and early 1946. Thus, although the PCA had denounced the PPA at the time of Sétif, this stance was always tempered by a much greater condemnation of settler extremism, which led directly into a campaign for the release of prisoners and an amnesty. Benefiting from the prestige of the Soviet Union, the PCA enjoyed a surge of support in the national elections to the Constituent Assembly in Paris in October 1945, the first mass Muslim participation in the political process, capturing a quarter of the European College vote and a fifth in the Muslim College. Even given the fact that over half the voters in the Muslim College

Figure 4.1 Ferhat Abbas with his brother-in-law Ahmed Francis in front of the French National Assembly in 1948.

abstained, following the call for a boycott by both the PPA and AML, the result gave the party electoral legitimacy and on 24 March 1946 the Algerian Communists set out a blueprint for political change.[40] Addressing the concrete issues of hunger and unemployment, the party called for the establishment of an Algerian Assembly that would unite all Algerians, women as well as men, regardless of race or religion. Like Abbas's proposal, the document, even if it did not utter the word independence, seemed to lay the basis for some form of autonomy. The implication was there although, remaining true to the French Communist Party General-Secretary Maurice Thorez's doctrine of 'nation in formation', the PCA also underlined the need to ally Algeria with the new France, as well as solidarity with French

Communists who now had six members in the government. The nationalist tone was undeniable, reflecting a growing Muslim membership, principally in the towns and cities, as well as the increasing influence of prominent Muslim members, such as Larbi Bouhali, Sadek Hadjeres, and Abdelhamid Benzine. The tone was also evident in the communist paper *Alger-République* which reflected the day-to-day economic and social struggles of Algerians in a way that the European press never did. Moreover, the paper's offices in central Algiers were a remarkable crossroads where nationalists of all colours, from the singer Bachtarzi Mahieddine, the writer Kateb Yacine, through to UDMA members like the lawyer Ali Boumendjel, met and discussed their ideas, often then writing in *Alger-Républicain* itself.[41]

Although the UDMA and the PCA won adherents in 1946, the undisputed star of Algerian nationalism continued to be Messali Hadj. Such support was a reflection of the demographic dynamic. By 1946 there were over 7 million Muslims who, poor and dispossessed, saw Messali as their saviour figure: 'the great one' (*el-zaim*). They identified with the way in which he underlined the need to recover their land and culture. They identified, too, with the way in which he, unlike either Abbas or the Communists, unambiguously rejected the link with France and placed Algeria in the Arab world.

Messali, determined not to be marginalized by the UDMA's ballot-box strategy, immediately pressed for participation in elections. Despite the overwhelming opposition, others on the PPA central committee reluctantly gave in to Messali, bowing to his prestige, and this led to the formation of the Mouvement pour le Triomphe des Libertés Démocratiques (MTLD) in October 1946. The argument over strategy, though, remained unresolved. Many new members, profoundly marked by May 1945, were worried by what they saw as a descent into reformism. In an effort to hold the party together a clandestine congress was held in Algiers on 15 February 1947 where leaders engaged in a series of bitter and far-ranging arguments on what was to be done.[42] Hocine Aït Ahmed, by now twenty-one and later one of the FLN founders, put the case for armed action. For him war with France was inevitable and he called for the establishment of a paramilitary organization. At the end, however, no one current won a definitive victory. Instead a compromise was brokered that gave the party three structures: the MTLD to contest elections, the paramilitary Organisation Spéciale (OS) to prepare the armed struggle, and the clandestine PPA to safeguard the party's revolutionary soul. Within this schema Messali, from the outset, was determined to keep the OS—a concession to keep the younger generation in check—on the sidelines. He distrusted their veneration of guerrilla warfare, preferring to emphasize mass action and political engagement.[43]

Elections

In 1946 in France three parties dominated politics: the Communist Party, the Socialist Party, and a new grouping, the Christian Democrat Mouvement Républicain Populaire (MRP), launched in November 1944. All three were closely identified with the Resistance. All three presented themselves as the custodians of true republican values. All three were involved in introducing wide-ranging social changes, including the establishment of the welfare state and the first steps towards economic planning. All three, too, were involved in a flurry of referenda and elections that sought to establish the principles of the new Fourth Republic. On mainland France this process, leading to four consultations in 1946, produced increasing apathy. The intricate issues seemed increasingly irrelevant to a population struggling with food shortages and galloping inflation. In Algeria these perceptions were compounded by the continuing backdrop of Sétif, and for the Constituent Assembly elections in October 1945 the supporters of the still imprisoned Abbas and Messali called for a boycott. Then in the elections to the second Constituent Assembly on 2 June 1946, the newly formed UDMA participated while the PPA did not, a state of affairs that led Abbas's party to win eleven seats out of thirteen for the second college, although half the electorate abstained.

With this electoral legitimacy Abbas now had the opportunity he had been waiting for. Travelling to Paris he was propelled to the centre of the debates on the most complex issue facing the second Constituent Assembly: the French Union. Encapsulating a reformed relationship between France and the empire, the roots of the French Union can be traced back to the conference of colonial governors at Brazzaville organized by the then Provisional Government in late January 1944.[44] Rejecting the notion of self-government, Brazzaville nonetheless set out ideas for decentralization and the wider participation of indigenous populations, talking in general terms about a French Federation. This phrase then became the French Union, first uttered in respect of Indochina in March 1945 when the

Provisional Government, reacting to the Japanese takeover on 9 March, issued the following Declaration

> The Indochinese Federation will join with France and the other parts of the French community to form a "French Union", whose external interests will be represented by France. Indochina will enjoy its proper freedom within this Union.[45]

During the first Constituent Assembly the constitutional blueprint for the French Union was introduced by Marius Moutet, the Socialist Party Minister for Overseas France and former Minister for Colonies under the Blum Popular Front Government. Underlining just how far the emerging republic was being defined by socialist ideas, his speech accepted that the impact of World War Two, the Atlantic Charter, as well as past errors in French colonial policy meant that the status quo was not tenable.[46] Now, however, France had an opportunity to establish a liberal policy that would be an example to the world. Moutet admitted that this policy contained dangers. Too much liberalism risked stirring up nationalism and ultimately separatism. However, to do nothing would be even worse. France had to act or be dominated by events. In practice this meant recognizing that inhabitants in the overseas territories and the metropole had the same rights. Racism had to be done away with and a new climate established. Thereafter the debate was steeped in left-leaning reformist thinking derived from the 1920s and 1930s as Assembly members talked in grand terms about a French Union based on principles of 'humanism', 'civilization', and the 'rights of man'.

Fear of a communist-dominated National Assembly led to the rejection of the draft constitution in the referendum of 5 May 1946, which is why under the auspices of the second Constituent Assembly Abbas was able to revisit the criteria for the French Union. As with the first Constituent Assembly, this was the longest debate because it hinged on three complex legal issues: how the diverse territories related to the French Union, how delegates would be elected to the French Union Assembly, and what would be its relationship to the National Assembly.[47] Time and time again Abbas intervened, even presenting a counter-proposal for the French Union. Stressing that force was not an option, he called on France to listen to the colonies and accept a federal solution:

> We need France; we are, in effect, only apprentices in the matter of democracy. Only, it is necessary to break the vicious circle: if you keep us under direct administration, how do you want us to progress. If, today, there is

nobody amongst us who is capable of holding the devolved posts of men of State, it is simply because you have done nothing to teach us how to do it.

In not listening to us, you will signal your desire to maintain the native in the condition of the native, and by that your refusal to see in him a man like others.[48]

Abbas's pleas were ignored, however. Desperate to put the new constitution to the country, Moutet intervened to hurry the debate to a conclusion whose final preamble in October 1946 defined the French Union as an entity 'formed by France and overseas countries and based on equality of rights and obligations without distinction of race or religion'. Under this scheme no concession was given to the rising tide of independence. French sovereignty was maintained, while discrimination, in the form of the hated *indigénat*, was ended and the local populations empowered through a series of local assemblies, as well as various levels of representation in parliament and the French Union Assembly.

The 1947 Statute

By abolishing the special assembly established in 1900, the Vichy regime had left Algeria without formal political structures. The urgent need to end this uncertainty was recognized throughout French Union debate. Indeed Abbas himself introduced proposals at the end of proceedings, outlining an autonomous republic within the French Union.[49] This long and difficult political argument continued during the remainder of 1946 and early 1947 and centred on four competing blueprints. The government project, piloted by the Socialist Minister of the Interior, Édouard Depreux, set out a Governor-General to represent Paris and an Assembly to deal with local affairs while guarding the country's status as three French departments. A different proposal emanating from Joseph Begarra, the leading figure in the Socialist Party in Oran, and supported by the three SFIO Federations in Algeria, envisaged giving more say to the Assembly and replacing the Governor-General with a minister resident in Algiers.[50] The Communist project gave Algeria membership of the French Union, but decentralized more power to the Assembly than those outlined by either Depreux or Begarra.[51] Lastly, Abbas's UDMA continued to press for a sovereign Assembly within the French Union, while the five PPA–MTLD deputies, elected to the French parliament in November 1946, categorically rejected this formula, calling for a constituent assembly to let the Algerian people decide.[52]

Within this clash of ideas, the situation was complicated still further by developments in national politics. On the one hand de Gaulle, who resigned as head of state in January 1946, launched the Rassemblement du Peuple Français (RPF) in April which, in mixing anti-Soviet rhetoric and opposition to the Fourth Republic, also went back on his own March 1944 reforms, angering Algerians but winning support amongst settlers. On the other, in May 1947 the ejection of Communist ministers from government brought an end to tripartite government. What then emerged was a 'Third Force' government stretching from the Socialist Party to the moderate right that was united by anti-communism, anti-Gaullism and defence of the French Union. By definition 'Third Force' politics was based on negotiation as the interests of various coalition parties, now including the Radicals, the Union Démocratique et Socialiste de la Résistance (UDSR), and the Independents, had to be accommodated to preserve government unity. Over Algeria this meant that to guide the reforms through parliament Depreux, the Interior Minister, had to agree to a watering down by the MRP and the end result, the Statute finally adopted by the National Assembly on 27 August, was a compromise.

Within this Statute Algeria remained as three departments under the authority of a Governor-General who was directly responsible to the Minister of the Interior in Paris. To support this structure an Algerian Assembly was established whose role was to apply legislation and administer limited budgetary powers. Voting for this Assembly was conducted on the basis of two separate electoral colleges each electing sixty members; the first by 460,000 Europeans, plus 58,000 assimilated Muslims; the second by 1,400,000 unassimilated Muslims. Thus, unequal political weighting continued to be built into the system. In tandem with this arrangement the Statute also proposed five flagship reforms that would abolish the *communes mixtes*, end the military government of the Saharan territories, enshrine Arabic as an official language alongside French, separate religion and the State, and give the vote to Muslim women.

Writing on 2 August in the Socialist Party daily, *Le Populaire*, the former prime minister Léon Blum defended the reforms as a positive step forward, even if they stopped short of what the Socialists had wanted. Not to vote for them, he argued, would be interpreted as a sign of 'indifference or weakness' on the part of the metropole, an error that parliament and public opinion must guard against: 'One must not imagine that with the vote on the Statute everything will be finished and that all aspects of Algeria's problems will be solved in one go. The application of the Statute will be delicate: the Muslims must feel themselves to be a free people without the settlers feeling like a minority people.'[53]

Amongst Algerian nationalists the Statute met opposition across the board. This hostility had already been voiced during a government fact-finding mission in March which had provoked nationalist protests and it returned again in a final, heated National Assembly debate on 12 September 1947. There the five MTLD deputies refused to recognize the Assembly's right to legislate on Algeria, denouncing the Statute as an imposed solution. The UDMA group meanwhile called, again, for an autonomous republic which, allied with Morocco and Tunisia, would constitute a North African Federation within the French Union. On the colonial lobby's side the leading settler deputies, principally Lucien Borgeaud and René Mayer, brandished the spectre of a Muslim dominated, pro-communist Algerian Assembly that would threaten national security. They also used every opportunity to jeer the UDMA arguments, mocking Abbas's French accent as well as his claim to speak in the name of true French values to justify an Algerian republic. Finally voted through on 20 September with 322 for, 86 against, and 184 abstentions, the colonial lobby managed to extract a last-minute amendment whereby the flagship reforms had to be approved by the Algerian Assembly. In practice this meant that in Algeria the Statute re-mained a dead letter, hated by nationalists and settler conservatives alike. In contrast in Paris the 1947 Statute came to stand for a reformist consensus. Seen from this perspective, the promise of the Statute was seen to be the best hope; an incremental solution that, in the face of extremists on both sides, would eventually bring Muslim and settler together into a common entity under French rule.

'French Socialism: our enemy number one'

Despite the success of the colonial lobby's rearguard action, the prospect of elections for an Algerian Assembly inspired fear amongst the settlers. This fear was the product of a generalized surge in nationalist militancy which was reflected not only in the campaign against the Statute but in the continuing importance of the Ulema and its religious schools, the boycott of pro-French imams, the regular defacing of official posters portraying Europeans and Muslims coming together through sport and healthy activity, and pro-independence graffiti.[54] But it was also the consequence of the elections to municipal and village councils in October and November 1947 which were a major triumph for the MTLD. The prospect of an equally crushing victory at the elections to the Assembly caused panic amongst the settlers because, they reasoned, it would open the way to independence.

Certainly within rural, eastern Algeria there was a return to the mood of early 1945. Police reports testified to a millenarian atmosphere where the elections were presented by PPA-MTLD activists as the grand event that would end colonialism and bring them to immediate power. MTLD activists were reported to have told other Algerians that after the elections 'France will no longer exist' and that:

> The force shown by the civil and military authorities is only ephemeral. The prisoners are going to be freed shortly, after the intervention of foreign powers—America in particular whose battle ships have dropped anchor in the main ports of Algeria. Algeria will be freed with little fighting from the occupier.[55]

Equally as a young nationalist in El-Arrouch, Mohammed Harbi has a very clear memory of a meeting of the town's major families in the run-up to the election. The subject of their discussion: how the land was to be redistributed once the PPA-MTLD had won.[56] As in 1945 this climate was fuelled by rumours about outside intervention, this time by the United Nations or by the North African Liberation Committee, formed in Cairo in January 1948 by Abd el-Krim, legendary leader of the Rif uprising in the 1920s, and Habib Bourguiba, the leader of Tunisian nationalism. This tension was stretched even further by the impact of the cold war. A wave of communist-inspired strikes in the winter of 1947 in mainland France, uncompromisingly repressed by the Socialist Minister of the Interior, Jules Moch, stoked up anti-communist sentiment amongst the settlers. Appeals were even made to Washington as the conservative press portrayed the Communist Party and Algerian nationalist as allies in the same plot to subvert France from within.

In this febrile atmosphere, René Mayer, the Radical Party deputy for Constantine since 1946, threatened to resign from the Third Force government unless the Governor-General Chataigneau, judged as 'pro-Arab', was removed. Faced with this blackmail, the Socialist Minister of the Interior, Jules Moch, grappling with the communist strike movement, replaced him as Governor-General with another Socialist Party stalwart: Marcel-Edmond Naegelen, Minister of Education and deputy for the Lower-Rhine. Born in Belfort in 1892 into an Alsace family who had left after the Franco-Prussian War, Governor-General Naegelen was, like so many Alsace exiles, a fervent left-wing patriot. For Naegelen, the true France was the France of 'liberty, equality, fraternity' whose personal history made him sensitive to one issue above all others: the need to defend the republic's frontiers. An SFIO member since 1910, decorated World War One hero, World War Two Resister, Naegelen was, in common with so many Socialists, a fierce anti-communist who, proud of Alsace-Lorraine's reincorporation into the Third Republic, had opposed the autonomist movements there during the 1930s.

With no in-depth knowledge of the country (he visited once as Minister of Education in 1946), Naegelen underlined the need to apply the values of France's revolutionary tradition, especially given the hundredth anniversary of the 1848 Revolution:

> I assume the heavy responsibility that has been given to me at the moment when France and the entire world celebrate the hundredth anniversary of the Revolution of 1848 which, once again, is ringing out across the world the French message of liberty and human fraternity that, across the oceans, has emancipated millions of human beings.

In approaching Algerian nationalism, Naegelen used the prism of anti-communism and anti-separatism, stating categorically in his first speech on 24 February: 'I will stand up with the greatest vigour against all attempts at separatism. I leave with the firm will, not to resolve all the problems immediately, but determined to make them lose their acuteness and best serve the interest of France.'

First of all this meant putting back the date of the two-round elections to 4 and 11 April 1948. This gave the police time to put pressure on the MTLD, raiding party offices, arresting MTLD candidates, and banning the party paper El-Maghreb El-Arabi—all of which were backed up by military manoeuvres in Kabylia designed to intimidate the local population. Then, on the day of the first round itself, the authorities fired upon nationalist voters, killing ten and wounding many more.

Despite this violence, the first round still produced overwhelming support for the MTLD in the second college. Expectations reached fever pitch, leading the authorities to resort to fraud to cheat the MTLD of final victory. Ballot-rigging, the arrest of electoral officials suspected of pro-nationalist sentiment, and the non–issue of registration cards ensured that only nine MTLD deputies and eight UDMA deputies were elected in the second round on 11 April. Angry and dispirited nationalists sent telegrams of protest directly to the Governor-General's office charting the irregularities.[57] In response Naegelen denied electoral wrong-doing. For him any action was a necessary riposte to intimidation by MTLD activists of which, it is true, there was also widespread evidence.[58] To Algerian nationalists, however, this was a defining moment. April 1948 was a mockery of democracy and in the UDMA press there was a blanket condemnation. On 23 April in *La République Algérienne*, the UDMA newspaper, Abbas described it as the electoral equivalent to Sétif, telling readers that the 'Pétain regime' had effectively been resuscitated, while another front-page article described Algeria as one 'immense prison'.[59] For Abbas it showed beyond doubt that the Socialist Party could not be trusted and within the UDMA there was a turning away from the French left because, it seemed to them, for all the talk of 'liberty' and 'fraternity', the true purpose of elections was to produce pliable collaborators to do French bidding. Within the MTLD the reaction was even more extreme. In the words of Mohammed Harbi, April 1948 enshrined the Socialist Party as 'our enemy number one' in the eyes of MTLD activists.[60]

With nationalists shouting 'give us arms' in the face of the repression and fraud, it was inevitable that April 1948 provided a vanguard of young recruits to the party's paramilitary organization, the OS.[61] Still starved of funds and party support, this was the moment when the OS really took off, stockpiling arms and establishing training camps. Tightly organized and following strict security, the OS numbered about 1,000 by the end of the year.[62] Mostly in their twenties, mostly formed by the scouts and the nationalist sporting organizations, all men, including two future Algerian presidents, Ahmed Ben Bella and Mohammed Boudiaf, the OS was committed to the violent overthrow of colonialism. Mounting a number of operations, notably a raid on the Oran Post Office in April 1949 to procure funds, the OS began to prepare in earnest for a guerrilla war which was deemed inevitable.

Naegelen's third way

In contrast, Naegelen and the settlers breathed a collective sigh of relief. The worst, it seemed, had been averted. Force had maintained French rule, mirroring developments elsewhere in the French Union with the crackdown in French West Africa, repression in Madagascar in March 1947, and the intensification of the war in Indochina.[63] Thereafter, Naegelen was continually vigilant about threats to French sovereignty, not just about communism and nationalism but also rival British and US imperialisms which he accused of courting Abbas in the quest for geopolitical influence.[64]

Although Naegelen felt an affinity with the settlers, in particular those from Alsace, he always underlined the case for reform which he envisaged as a three-pronged battle against racism, the ignorance of the metropolitan opinion, and nationalist intransigence. The defeat of communism and nationalism had to be accompanied by socialism, defined as greater social equality. Algeria's problems were understood as social, rather than political, and in practical terms this meant improving the Muslim lot through greater educational opportunities and the modernizing of 'native' agricultural practices. France, as he stated in his speech at the opening of the Algerian Assembly on 21 May 1948, had to reach out to Muslims who were equal citizens: 'For myself... I will not betray my mission. I have not come to Algeria to keep guard over a muzzled people, but on the contrary to raise it to a full consciousness of itself and to adhere at last to the promises of democracy.'[65]

In this respect he was very blunt about the depth of anti-Muslim prejudice. This, he recognized, manifested itself every day, whether in the form of making Algerians wait until the last in the queue or simply denigrating language. As one Algerian, a teacher, said in explaining to Naegelen the cumulative effect of these incidents: 'Muslims, we all carry a scar. And, every now and then, this returns to give us a more or less burning sensation.'[66] But in wishing to make such racism a thing of the past, Naegelen recognized that transforming attitudes took time. Ultimately prejudice could only be undone by long-term education. Here, though, his continual complaint was the lack of resources. After 1948 Algeria, Naegelen claimed, was ignored because as Governor-General he did not have a place at the cabinet table. Likewise he felt unsupported by Socialist

Party members of the Third Force government. Consequently, he argued, the progress of reform was severely hampered.

In the meantime there was no let-up in the repression of Algerian nationalists. Primarily this effort was directed against the OS. Involving the establishment of a Muslim anti-OS militia, this operation, lasting from March to May 1950, led to the arrest of 400 OS activists, including Ahmed Ben Bella. This was a major coup for Naegelen, effectively dismantling the OS, who stood down as Governor-General in April 1951 to be replaced by Roger Léonard. By this point electoral fraud had become a fine art and at the national elections on 17 June 1951 neither the MTLD nor UDMA won a single seat, although parts of the press in France, principally Claude Bourdet in the left-wing magazine *France-Observateur*, talked about massive human rights abuses, describing what was taking place as a 'Gestapo' style system.

Crisis of Algerian nationalism 1948–51

In cutting the ground from under Abbas, Naegelen's tactics ensured that nationalist moderates were marginalized. Their arguments seemed less and less credible. This in turn led the UDMA to sink their differences with the other parties and seek a closer alliance with the more extreme Messali through the establishment of the 'Algerian Front' in August 1951. Bringing together the Ulema, the Communist Party, UDMA, and the MTLD for the first time on a common platform, the 'Algerian Front' demanded the cancellation of the elections, the freeing of political prisoners, and the ending of personal restrictions on Messali Hadj.

The other aspect of Naegelen's strategy was the decision *not* to ban the MTLD. As a result the party, struggling to survive continual repression, imploded from the inside through a series of internal crises, the first of which was the 'Berber Crisis' of 1949. The spark for this was a booklet, signed by the intellectuals Yahia Henine, Mabrouk Belhocine, and Sadek Hadjeres, which took issue with the assertion that Algeria was exclusively Arab, arguing that nationalism needed to incorporate the country's Turkish and Berber components.[67] Messali was furious. This was much too close to the Communist Party concept of Algeria as a 'nation in formation'. Even worse, by evoking a separate Berber identity, it played into the colonial divide-and-rule strategy. What followed were a series of bruising purges which left a bitter taste, particularly within the party's organization in

France where, given the pattern of immigration, there had always been a preponderance of Berber Kabyles. As a result, the centrality of an Arab and Muslim within Algerian nationalism was reaffirmed and any possibility of a different nationalism, more pluralistic and less attached to religion and Arab ethnicity, effectively quashed.[68]

Then one year later there was the fallout from the dismantling of the OS. Messali had always wanted to keep them on the fringes and at the subsequent trials in 1951 they were instructed, as a matter of party discipline, to hide their links with the MTLD.[69] Unsurprisingly many felt badly let down, intensifying their hostility to Messali. Criticism of Messali came from others within the party, too, in the guise of the central committee, led by a group of predominantly middle-class militants, exemplified by Benyoucef Ben Khedda, son of a magistrate and a chemist from Blida. Known as the centralists, their clash with Messali was over the party's internal structures. In their opinion Messali might still be the hero of the masses but his omnipresence was crippling the organization. Too dictatorial, they disliked the fact that every decision had to go through him, a situation made even worse in May 1952 when Messali was deported to France. Placed under house arrest, he continued to maintain control, telephoning orders on a daily basis. From then on, relations rapidly deteriorated and over the next eighteen months the party effectively split into two. To make matters worse the infighting was further exacerbated by the conflict over strategy. So, Messali still adhered to mass action, the OS remnants to armed insurrection, while another current within the MTLD entered into a working alliance with Jacques Chevallier, elected mayor of Algiers in May 1953 on a platform that called for an end to racism and the application of the Statute. Seeing the practical benefits in his plan to construct public housing for Muslims, five MTLD municipal councillors, led by the lawyer Abderrahmane Kiouane, accepted posts in his administration.

With the UDMA rebuffed by the successive governments and the MTLD at war with itself, Algerian nationalism seemed to be a spent force. Yet, paradoxically, the international context offered enormous hope. Indian independence from Britain in 1947 and Indonesian independence from the Dutch in 1949 seemed to symbolize that the idea of empire was on the retreat. In Egypt in 1954 Colonel Nasser was a beacon of pan-Arab nationalism, having emerged as the unquestioned leader of the army officers who overthrew the pro-British monarchy two years previously. Added to this there was also the undeniable fact that by 1954 the French Union was in a bad way. A succession of short-lived governments talked in general terms about the defence of the West, the

Figure 4.2 Messali Hadj, the leader of the MTLD, in Niort, France in 1952 after being expelled from Algeria and put under house arrest by the French authorities.

civilizing mission, and the economic importance of the Union, but in practice policy was being overwhelmed by events. In Indochina in June 1949 the Fourth Republic, in an attempt to separate nationalists from Ho Chi Minh's communist Vietminh, had recognized the new state of Vietnam on condition that the country, along with Laos and Cambodia, should remain within the French Union. However, although the Annamite emperor Bao-Dai was installed as head of state, the war against the Vietminh continued unabated as the French looked to the US government to shoulder the military cost of the cold war front. In Morocco *Istiqlal*, the independence party formed in 1943, had mushroomed into a mass party of 100,000 members by 1951. Rioting in Casablanca in December 1952 led to the banning of *Istiqlal*. Further, the settlers, constituting 200,000 out of a population of 9 million, were dismayed by the nationalist sentiments of Sultan Mohammed Ben Youssef and on 20 August 1953 he was deported to Madagascar and replaced by the more compliant Moulay

Arafa. Nationalists were outraged and in the following two years the country became locked into a spiral of violence and counter-violence. In Tunisia the same pattern of repression existed, where the settler population, amounting to 150,000 out of a total of 3 million, had pressured the government into cracking down on the nationalist *Neo-Detour* party, arresting their leader Habib Bourguiba. Then, in December 1952, Ferhat Hached, a leading pro-independence trade unionist, was gunned down by the 'Red Hand', a shadowy group of settler terrorists.

Algeria: 1954

At the beginning of 1954 Algeria was on the margins of government thinking. Official eyes were elsewhere. They were preoccupied by the Fourth Republic's chronic instability as the Assembly elected in 1951 proved incapable of producing a stable coalition. Indeed at one point in the summer of 1953 the country was without a government for thirty-six days. They were preoccupied by the unresolved issue of West German rearmament as successive governments were unable to garner enough votes to ratify the May 1952 European Defence Treaty. And finally they were preoccupied with the ongoing violence in Indochina, Morocco, and Tunisia.

In his New Year message for 1954 the Governor-General, Roger Léonard, painted an optimistic picture.[70] While recognizing the enormous work to be done, he was reassured by the way in which the country had avoided the 'tearing apart' seen elsewhere, a veiled allusion to Morocco and Tunisia. In contrast, Algeria was constructing a diverse society where each person, Christian, Muslim, Jew, free-thinker, had a place. Such a viewpoint, however, missed the signs of tension that were everywhere. There was a cultural militancy. To read the novels and plays of Mohammed Dib, Mouloud Mammeri, Mouloud Feraoun, and Kateb Yacine, all published in French in the early 1950s, was to journey into a place ignored by settler society.[71] Articulating the emotions and aspirations of Muslim Algeria, they portrayed their interior world in a way which even liberal writers like Albert Camus never had. There was the continued militancy of Algerian immigration in France. On the Bastille demonstration in 1953 in Paris Algerian demonstrators, tightly disciplined within their own cortège and their own flags, were violently attacked by the police, leading to the deaths of six nationalists. There were also the endemic social inequalities in Algeria itself.

On the coast Europeans might have been benefiting from the early stages of France's long post-1945 economic boom, but in the interior, where three-quarters of the 8.4 million Muslim population lived, crushing poverty was the norm. One million were totally or partially unemployed, and a further 2 million totally unemployed. On average an agricultural labourer worked no more than sixty-five days a year. Educational exclusion was another enormous problem. Amongst Algerians there was an 85 per cent illiteracy rate. Only one Algerian boy in every five went to primary school, dropping to one in sixteen for girls.

This rural Algeria was still overwhelmingly hostile to French Algeria. The ethnographer Jean Servier, for example, travelled extensively in the remote mountains of Kabylia in the summer of 1953 doing fieldwork for a research project into Berber customs. Trying to establish contact with local tribes he encountered a world bristling with hatred. At one point he heard mountain villagers still using the old Arabic term for Christian, *el-Roumi*, as they warned others to offer no help to Servier. Equally, when examining Berber inscriptions, he was menaced by a crowd of young Algerians who told Servier that they were 'Arabs'. This polarization was also reflected in a continuing climate of violence in the east of the country. During the first ten months of 1954 there was one terrorist attack a week.[72] In the Aurès and on the Tunisian frontier police reports testified to the existence of armed groups.

All of these signs point to a country slipping into conflict. Is it right, though, to draw a straight line from May 1945 to November 1954? Certainly neither Abbas nor Messali envisaged a long-drawn-out war of liberation. The problem, however, was that Naegelen's fraud and repression gave nationalism no space to express itself democratically and then evolve. If the Fourth Republic, epitomized by the Socialist Party, had chosen to negotiate with Abbas or Messali, a more peaceful transition could have emerged, producing a different Algeria and a different France. But the gap was too great. The Fourth Republic did not want to relinquish sovereignty. Algeria was too important for the recovery of national self-esteem after occupation. It did not want to apply anything other than a French-designed solution. Moreover, such wider strategic concerns meant that the Fourth Republic always hung back from reform lest this provoked a show-down with the settlers. As a result, the Naegelen period was a tipping point. By choosing not to engage with Abbas or Messali, he allowed the ground to be occupied by those who wanted a violent confrontation with French rule.

5

'Algeria is France' 1954–6

Monday, All Saints' Day, 1 November 1954

Algeria is France. From Flanders to the Congo, there is the law, one single nation, one sole Parliament.

François Mitterrand, Minister of the Interior,
the National Assembly, 12 November 1954.

I n the early hours of the morning small armed groups carried out a series of attacks across Algeria. In the Oran department two farms were targeted, crops burned and telephone wires cut. In Algiers three bombs exploded at the radio station, the gasworks, and a petrol depot. On the Mitidja plain separate operations tried, and failed, to procure arms from the barracks in Boufarik and Blida. In Kabylia, cork and tobacco storehouses were set alight and a Muslim policeman killed at Dra el-Mizan.

The largest number of incidents took place in the Constantine department, the area most resistant to French rule. There the violence was concentrated in the mountainous Aurès region in the south-east. On the afternoon of Sunday 31 October in Khenchela the local football team gave its usual battling performance. After the game all the players met secretly at Fontaine-Chaude, the old Roman thermal baths, where they changed into their uniforms and checked their weapons before spreading out over the surrounding countryside. That night they attacked the barracks, killing two soldiers, and stole firearms from the police station. Elsewhere French troops and police came under fire in Batna and Condé-Semendou, while Arris, the main administrative centre, was subjected to an all-out assault. Cut off for several hours, Jean Servier, still researching in the area, had to assume command and organize the town's defence.

The most notorious incident took place in the gorge of Tighanimine when the bus travelling from Biskra to Arris was stopped by a makeshift roadblock between 7.00 and 7.30 a.m. Hadj Sadok, a loyal *qaïd* returning to warn the authorities of the uprising, and the Monnerots, a married couple in their early twenties just appointed as teachers at the nearby village school in Tiffelfel, were ordered to dismount. Calling the men criminals Sadok made a reach for his pistol whereupon he was mown down by a burst of gunfire that also wounded Guy Monnerot, and his wife. The bus driver was then told to drive to Arris with Sadok's body, a warning of the power of the revolt, while the Monnerots were abandoned on the roadside, Mr Monnerot eventually bleeding to death.[1]

In Algiers, Roger Léonard, flooded with telephone calls and messages, convened an emergency meeting with Jean Vaujour, head of the DST, commissioner Benhamou, in charge of the police in Algiers, and General Cherrière. Surveying the reports, all four agreed that this was a synchronized operation. In places amateurish, in places highly disciplined, seventy separate incidents had left nine dead, four wounded and a significant amount of material damage, totalling 200 million francs.[2] All four agreed too that this was a serious threat to law and order, even if they had little idea who the instigators were.

Pamphlets found scattered on the roads in Kabylia revealed the authors of the violence to be an unknown entity: the Front de Libération Nationale which easily lent itself to the acronym FLN.[3] Taking the form of a political tract, the 1 November declaration was uncompromising. Referring to splits within the nationalist movement without naming the protagonists, the declaration emphasized that these were in the past. All must now rally behind the FLN, the new embodiment of the Algerian nation.

To the Algerian people,
To the militants of the National Cause!
... After decades of struggle, the National Movement has reached its final phase of fulfilment.
... a group of responsible young people and dedicated militants, gathering about it the majority of wholesome and resolute elements, has judged that the moment has come to take the National Movement out of the impasse into which it has been forced by the conflicts of persons and influence, and to launch itself into the true revolutionary struggle at the side of Moroccan and Tunisian brothers ...

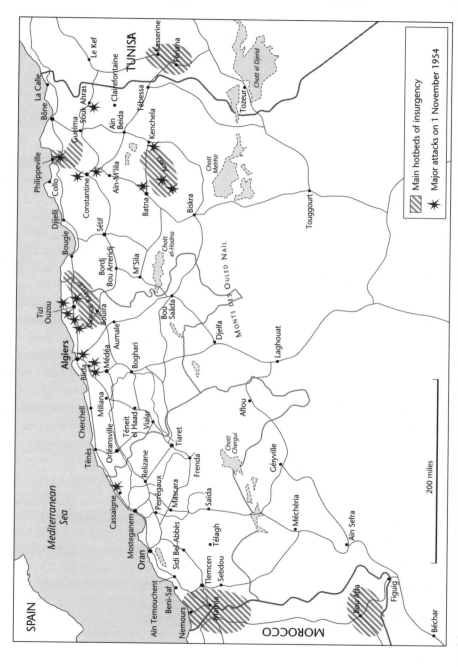

Map 5.1 1 November 1954: The FLN insurrection.

Our movement of regeneration presents itself under the label of:

NATIONAL LIBERATION FRONT

thus freeing itself from any possible compromise and offering to all Algerian compatriots of every social position and of all parties . . . the goal of joining in the national struggle.

GOAL

National independence through:

1. restoration of the Algerian state, sovereign, democratic, and social, within the framework of the principles of Islam;

2. preservation of all fundamental freedoms, without distinction of race or religion.

INTERNAL OBJECTIVES

1. Internationalization of the Algerian problem.

2. Pursuit of North African unity in its national Arab-Islamic context.

3. Assertion, through the United Nations Charter, of our active sympathy towards all nations that may support our liberating action.

MEANS OF STRUGGLE

. . . by every means until the realization of our goal . . . action abroad to make the Algerian problem a reality for the entire world, with the support of our natural allies . . . the struggle will be long, but the outcome is certain . . . in order to limit bloodshed we propose an honourable platform for discussion with the French authorities . . .

1. recognition of Algerian nationhood by an official declaration;

2. opening of negotiation . . . on a basis of recognition of Algerian sovereignty, one and indivisible;

3. liberation of all political prisoners . . .

IN RETURN FOR WHICH

1. French cultural and economic interests will be respected, as well as persons and families;

2. all French citizens desiring to remain in Algeria will be allowed to opt for their original nationality, in which case they will be considered foreigners, or for Algerian nationality, in which case they will be considered as Algerians both in rights and duties;

3. the ties between France and Algeria will be defined by agreement between the two powers, on a basis of equality and mutual respect!

Algerians! We ask you to reflect on our Charter set out above. It is your duty to associate yourselves with it to save our country and give it back its liberty. The NATIONAL LIBERATION FRONT is your front, its victory is yours.[4]

In demanding the restoration of an independent Algerian state based upon Arab and Muslim values the document was reiterating the classic tenets of Messali Hadj. Where it departed was in the absence of any reference to an elected assembly. To Messali the ballot box had always been the route to independence. Elections would give nationalists the legitimacy with which to negotiate with the French. The role of violence was to pressurize the French into accepting this transition process as Bourguiba had done in Tunisia. In contrast the 1 November declaration placed armed struggle at the centre of the liberation struggle. There was no need for elections. Guns alone gave the FLN the right to speak for the nation. Violence was the essence of the revolution and those who had placed their hopes into a gradualist solution were denounced as 'reformists' and 'traitors'. This violence was keyed into absolutes. There was no third way. People could only be for or against the FLN.

Couched in this language of force and authority, the 1 November declaration intended to light a fuse of violent revolt. This did not happen. Despite mass support for independence the Muslim population waited on events, partly because they had no idea what the FLN was and partly because they remembered the repression after May 1945. Only over the ensuing months did the FLN's existence filter through to a growing audience, either by word of mouth, further clandestine tracts, or the propaganda impact of growing FLN violence.

These basic facts are a reminder of the gulf between 1 November and its subsequent mythologization.[5] Although within post-independence Algeria the image of a single Algerian people responding as one to the FLN's call became the cornerstone of the new country's national identity, at the time it was a confused event, overshadowed by the much greater violence in Morocco and Tunisia. In Arris, Jean Servier believed that the attack was violence spilling over from the Tunisian frontier.[6] On the FLN side some activists even thought that they were fighting for Messali.[7] Nor was there any sense of dramatic beginning for the vast majority of Algerians. It was only in retrospect, as the bloodshed deepened during the next two years, that 1 November 1954 was elevated into *the* starting point for the war of liberation. At first the conflict was a disaggregated phenomenon begun by a tiny vanguard minority. When and how it started differed from region to region, even from village to village, and for the initial ten months the conflict was restricted to rural eastern Algeria.

For French people, too, there was no sense that a conflict had begun. There was no announcement that the country was in a state of war mirroring August 1914 or September 1939. In legal terms this remained an undeclared war because Algeria was an integral part of France. France was not fighting a separate nation state but preserving internal sovereignty and on these grounds the word war was banned from the official lexicon. Instead the unfolding violence was described as the 'maintenance of law and order', 'pacification', or just simply 'events'. Moreover, such words served to minimize the conflict and render it more acceptable to the general public. Only gradually over the following eighteen months, when the war touched individuals in a direct manner as with the recall of metropolitan reservists in autumn 1955, did Algeria assume the status of a national crisis.

What was the FLN?

Believing that Algerian nationalism was racked by terminal conflict, the French authorities were caught off guard by the insurrection. This ignorance was underlined by the way in which the authorities targeted the MTLD, banning the party, seizing its documents, and arresting 2,000 members during November and December.

In actual fact the FLN came from the fringes of the MTLD and its chief architect was Mohammed Boudiaf. A leading figure in the OS, Boudiaf had escaped the net in 1950, finally ending up in Paris as the head of the MTLD in France in June 1953.[8] Depressed by the way in which the MTLD was tearing itself apart Boudiaf came to the conclusion that only a totally new organization, committed to armed insurrection, could save Algerian nationalism. It was a conviction based on three interconnected arguments. First, Boudiaf was motivated by anger at Messali who, determined to keep the OS remnants on the sidelines, had done nothing to aid those in prison or on the run. The drive to by-pass old structures, therefore, was about overcoming exclusion and marginalizing Messali—a determination deepened when Boudiaf was attacked in Algiers by Messali supporters on 9 May 1954.[9] Secondly, and allied to this, Boudiaf was bewildered by the split within the MTLD between the centralists and Messali which by 1954 had become definitive.[10] For him the time had come to cut through this internecine war, achieve unity and take the fight to the real enemy: France. Thirdly, there was the threat of reformism. Boudiaf was worried by the way in which the twenty-five MTLD representatives elected to the Algiers municipal council in May 1953 had entered into a working partnership with the new mayor Jacques Chevallier.[11] He was worried too by the investiture of the Radical Party's Pierre Mendès France as prime minister on 17 June 1954. He knew that Mendès France's dramatic ending of the Indochina war, combined with his declaration to transfer sovereignty back to the Tunisian people, had nurtured hopes that perhaps a peaceful solution could be found for Algeria as well. But to Boudiaf dialogue with liberals like Chevallier and Mendès France was a trap which redoubled his efforts to move to armed liberation. Through spectacular action Boudiaf wanted to seize centre stage and sabotage the middle ground.

Drawing upon the old OS networks, Boudiaf was at the hub of conspiratorial meetings that led to the formation of the 'Committee of the Twenty-Two' in Algiers in June 1954.[12] Calling for a boycott of the separate conferences organized by the centralists and Messalists, this meeting affirmed the need to achieve unity through armed struggle, designating a five-man Council of the Revolution to coordinate the insurrection. Comprising Boudiaf, Rabah Bitat, Mostefa Ben Boulaïd, Larbi Ben M'hidi, and Mourad Didouche, it was expanded to six in the late summer with the addition of Belkacem Krim who, pursued by the police since 1947, brought with him a nucleus of 500 armed men in the Kabyle mountains. In the meantime the Council linked up with the MTLD delegation in Cairo, Ahmed Ben Bella, Hocine Aït Ahmed, and Mohammed Khider, who were immediately receptive to its ideas and strategy.[13] Rankled by the way in which exiled Moroccan and Tunisian nationalists looked down on them, they too were desperate for armed confrontation.

These then were the nine historic leaders. Generationally all were young. Mostly in their thirties, their political beliefs had been moulded by participation in the scouts and nationalist sporting clubs as well as their experiences of World War Two and May 1945. Geographically all, apart from Ben Bella, were from the eastern part of the country. Sociologically all came from a rural elite impoverished by colonialism.[14] Aït Ahmed, Krim, and Ben Boulaïd were Berberphone and the others Arabaphone, but only Aït Ahmed and Khider possessed a knowledge of written Arabic. Boudiaf and Aït Ahmed were the more secular in their outlook and the most widely read.[15] All had gone to primary school, which set them apart from the mass of Muslims, while Ben M'hidi, Ben Bella, and Aït Ahmed had attended secondary school. Ben Bella, Boudiaf, and Krim had fought in the French army.

Unlike Messali they had had no prolonged interaction with the French working-class movement. Their world was rural Algeria. Close enough to understand the long hatreds of the Algerian dispossessed, they were sufficiently distinct to feel that they had the right to lead them. Convinced that the peasant masses were primed for conflict, the FLN's purpose was to act as a trigger and assume the leadership of this struggle.[16]

So, although in French-language documents the FLN might talk about revolution, in Arabic the preferred term was *thawra* meaning uprising rather than overturning structures. Such language illustrated the way in which the FLN of 1954 was an expression of the conservative interior. There was no vision of making society anew. It was a return to Arab and Islamic values. Reflecting a mixture of millenarianism, virility, and pride, the FLN was going to cleanse the country of the stain of humiliation through violence. In Kabylia, Ali Zamoum, for example, remembered the joy amongst his fellow FLN combatants when they learnt that the uprising was set for midnight on 1 November:

> A silence following this sentence and smiles of joy broke out on the faces of my companions. At last! The 1 of November cured us of all our wounds, of all our humiliations. Torture and prison, all our suffering had not been in vain. We were going to hold up our heads and put ourselves on the wavelength of History.[17]

No less importantly this FLN mindset was forged by the memory of Naegelen.[18] To the FLN, Naegelen's fraud and repression showed that socialists and radicals could not be trusted. Under no circumstances would they lay down their arms. The French state had to accept unconditional independence.

Such an uncompromising stance, spurred on too by Indochina, Morocco, Tunisia, as well as the Mau-Mau uprising against British rule in Kenya in 1952, underlined how violence was central to FLN culture. With the 1 November Declaration a new hierarchy was imposed onto Algerian politics. Henceforth the ballot-box strategy was destroyed. Only those with guns could deliver opinions and orders. The role of the populace was to follow because, as the progenitor of violent revolt, it was the FLN, and the FLN alone, which had the right to represent the Algerian nation at the negotiating table. It was without doubt an authoritarian model of action. Yet, it was also one which, by lionizing the Algerian people as the heroes of the war of independence, rejected the cult of personality and thus marked a further break with Messali-style politics.

Figure 5.1 Bitat, Ben Boulaïd, Didouche, Boudiaf, Krim, and Ben M'hidi—FLN leaders, 24 October 1954.

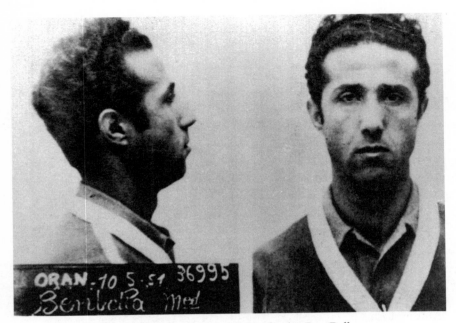

Figure 5.2 French custody photograph of FLN leader Ben Bella.

Despite the shared beliefs, there were personality clashes over power. In large part this stemmed from the lack of precise structures. Unlike the MTLD, the FLN never existed as an independent political party. It had no real programme beyond independence. It was the product of war. Operating in clandestine conditions the FLN, and its military wing the ALN, had to improvise from the start and this meant that, in terms of strategy and leadership, the organization was dominated from its inception by the people with the guns on the ground. Moreover, it was a situation further complicated by tensions between the interior and the Cairo delegation which, playing on its personal contacts with Nasser, was determined not to be excluded from the final decision-making process.

In the face of these tensions, Boudiaf worked tirelessly to maintain the momentum, liaising between Cairo and Morocco. The final meetings took place on 10 and 24 October in Algiers. Endowing the new movement with its final name—Front de Libération Nationale—these meetings divided the country into six zones, each with precise objectives. Psychologically this was crucial. The aim was to attack symbols of French rule in all three departments. In contrast to 1916 and 1945 where just one region had been concerned, this would mark out 1 November 1954 as a *national* insurrection.

In making these final plans, nobody was under any illusions about the enormity of the challenge. Even with the defeat in Indochina, France still had the fourth most powerful army in the world. In comparison, the FLN had no finance, little military equipment, and 1,000 men at most. To make matters worse, unlike Mohammed V in Morocco and Bourguiba in Tunisia, it was led by unknown leaders. However, the FLN was determined to make up for this inequality by deploying what have been called 'weapons of the weak': silence, sabotage, subterfuge.[19] Through terrorism the FLN wanted to bring the climate of insecurity—already deeply embedded within the European psyche—to a new level. This strategy, it was reasoned, would eventually force France to accept independence.

Reactions

Amongst Europeans there was total surprise at 1 November. Such surprise, however, did not stop the settler press from automatically branding the authors as a pathological minority with no legitimacy. They wanted the immediate restoration of law and order.

In a succinct radio address on 5 November Léonard underlined French resolve.[20] Carefully measuring his language, he made no mention of the FLN. Instead Léonard denounced the attacks as a foreign plot, pointing the finger at Nasser without explicitly naming him, before going on to outline the military and police measures that would bring the Tunisian frontier and the Aurès under control. Nothing, he concluded, must be allowed to harm the French policy of progress and reform.

In metropolitan France reaction was slower. On the following day Algeria registered a column in *Le Monde*, in *Le Figaro*, and in *France-Soir*.[21] Then, in the following weeks and months a consensus from the right through to the socialists denied any political motivation behind the insurrection. The perpetrators were criminalized. They were attacked as the outstretched tentacles of an Egyptian orchestrated plot. Alain Savary, born in Algeria and a leading SFIO expert on North Africa, characterized 1 November as bloodletting between rival MTLD fractions.[22] The left-leaning National Teachers Union (*Syndicat National des Instituteurs*—SNI), shocked by the death of Monnerot, interpreted the violence in the Aurès as the product of a tribal society that had always romanticized arms and outlaws.

The PCF was the only major party to see 1 November as a political act. Condemning repression, it called on 8 November for the setting up of a round table to bring all those concerned together.[23] But, by linking Algeria to the establishment of German imperialism on African soil, and by warning that terrorist methods could play into the hands of colonialism, the declaration underlined a problem common to all the parties: an ignorance about Algerian politics that prevented French politicians from grasping the full scale of the problem.[24]

Within the government itself Mendès France was adamant that secession from the metropole was unthinkable. Speaking to the National Assembly on 12 November Mendès France explained why Algeria was different from Indochina and the rest of French North Africa. Decolonization was not an option because the people there were French citizens.[25] This was an integral part of France and sovereignty was not negotiable; a muscular language backed up by his Minister of the Interior, François Mitterrand, who, invoking a republican patriotism, told the Assembly: 'Algeria is France. And who amongst you, *Mesdames* and *messieurs*, would hesitate to employ all methods to preserve France?'[26]

If this was the stance of the French political class, what was the reaction amongst the other nationalist parties? Privately Messali Hadj, still under house arrest in Niort, was angry. For him the FLN was a *coup d'état* by OS extremists who wished to challenge his status as the symbol of the Algerian nation. Publicly, however, he underlined 1 November's legitimacy. Comparing Algeria to Morocco and Tunisia, he called for the end of colonialism, even letting the rumour run that his supporters were behind it.[27] What followed were two months of negotiation, but these broke down because neither he nor the FLN were willing to compromise. Both wanted to monopolize the future of the nationalist movement and in December 1954 Messali formed the rival Mouvement National Algérien (MNA), opening the way to a brutal fratricidal conflict within the Algerian cause.

Like Messali the other parties were caught off guard. But, unlike Messali, they made no attempt to claim 1 November for themselves. Uneasy with action that was not their own, the communists, centralists, and UDMA were prudent. For them the FLN's strategy was certain political suicide. The French army's strength meant that it could not possibly endure. Some even advanced the thesis of a colonial plot to allow another May 1945. Instead

UDMA and the PCA used the fallout from 1 November to press their own solutions. In the case of UDMA Ferhat Abbas restated his call for an independent Algerian state federated to France, while the PCA demanded a democratic framework that would take into account all the inhabitants in Algeria without race or religious distinction as well as the interests of France.[28] Scepticism, incredulity and the elucidation of alternative scenarios were the norm which in turn intensified the FLN leader's hostility to the established politicians. More than ever, they were determined to impose their will on the other parties.

Climate of fear

This logic led to 178 attacks in November 1954 and 201 in December. These receded during the winter months of January and February before taking off again in March. Then, the upward spiral of FLN violence was relentless with 196 incidents in April, 455 in May, 501 in June, and 441 in July.[29] Nevertheless this was not, it must be stressed again, a total war affecting the whole country. In the beginning fighting was contained in eastern Algeria, but even then it is vital not to impose an undifferentiated chronology. In 1955 this was a creeping conflict. The manner in which it insinuated itself into people's lives varied from place to place and from individual to individual, often shaped by the importance of a local event, family connection, or the religious calendar rather than 1 November 1954 as a significant date. In the case of Ferroudja Amarouche, the war began in 1955, the day that the French soldiers arrived in her village, Bouzeguen, in the region of Azazga, Kabylia, a memory framed by the fact that this was during Ramadan and that her father-in-law died shortly after:

> It was the day that the French soldiers came to the village of Bouzeguen, in 1955, it was the month of Ramadan. The *maquisards* had burnt down the cork firm, to show their rejection of the French. My father-in-law had fought in the war with France (the First World War), and when they announced this fire, he said 'It's a declaration of war.' My father-in-law died just after, at Azazga, he had a café there.[30]

For rural women, most of whom had little formal education, they were drawn into the conflict as the maquis, at first a mysterious and elusive presence, began to impose itself, killing Algerians deemed to be pro-French.

Then, once a village or area was considered safe, the ALN made itself visible, looking to local women to provide the practical support, water, food, and clothing, which the maquis needed to survive.[31]

Despite these geographical limitations, the violence produced a climate of fear throughout the country. This stemmed from the army's inability to destroy the ALN. In part this failure was a classic example of over-stretch. With so many forces in Indochina, Morocco, and Tunisia, the French army in Algeria had only 50,000 troops and of these just 12,000 were combat effective. But it was also due to clumsy tactics. The deployment of jeeps, personnel carriers, and tanks was totally unsuited for the mountainous terrains of the Aurès and Kabylia. Drawing on their knowledge of the local terrain, the small pockets of ALN maquis fighters were able to evade the French columns and by February Cherrière was forced to admit failure.

By demonstrating their capacity to endure, this in itself was a major victory for the ALN and FLN. No longer could the FLN be dismissed as a ragbag of terrorists and during the first six months of 1955 these acronyms entered the everyday vocabulary, defining the political landscape in a way which the French found increasingly difficult to counter. The numbers fighting remained very small; a mere 500 in Aurès and 300 in Kabylia, 1 or 2 per cent of the local population at the most. The ALN was not a traditional army in which anyone could enlist, even if the ALN was to decree that all men between eighteen and forty should be ready to be mobilized.[32] The ALN was a clandestine organization where recruitment depended on knowledge, contacts, and the principles of basic security. The local ALN leaders, fearful of police infiltration, had to be sure of any recruit. Similarly there were severe logistical constraints. The ALN was lacking in everything—medicine, food, and above all weapons—and this lack meant careful vetting about numbers. They did not want to overwhelm the makeshift mountain camps with people who could not be fed, clothed, or armed.

Collectively the ALN was able to survive because it drew upon a deeply embedded culture of mountain resistance to outside authority.[33] For Ben Boulaïd's forces in the Aurès and Krim's in Kabylia these were two worlds of natural fortresses, a dissident landscape passed orally down the centuries. They knew the perfect vantage points from which to attack. They knew perfect places where to hide. They knew too how to procure food and shelter, particularly important given the especially harsh winter weather in January 1955 when, in places, temperatures dropped to below zero, and this made it impossible to isolate and finish off the ALN.

Survival was also sustained by Islam. This was the basis of daily life in the maquis. The soldiers were *moudjahid*. They were fighters for *jihad*. If they died in combat they had the status of *chahid* (martyr). There was no smoking or alcohol. Homosexuality and sexual relations outside of marriage were forbidden. Everybody prayed five times a day and followed Ramadan.[34] This discipline instilled a sense of solidarity. The ALN were brothers in arms, a male image reinforced by the way in which the small minority of women in the maquis were kept away from bearing weapons. Instead they were allotted roles involving nursing, cooking, and working as agents de liaison.

Like the 'historic leaders', most of the maquis were in their thirties, some even in their twenties. Like the 'historic leaders' too most, such as Lakhdar Ben Tobbal and Amar Mostefa Benaouda, had a background in the OS and MTLD.[35] It fell to these people on the ground to maintain the momentum of revolt and during the winter and spring they were confronted with two problems. First, there was poor communication between the six zones. Without central direction all were virtually cut off from each other and inevitably this produced a fragmented strategy that weakened the FLN from the inside. Secondly, the FLN was continually reeling from the repression. Of the top and secondary leadership Mourad Didouche was killed in combat in January 1955, while Rabah Bitiat and Ali Zamoum were arrested. The result was an organization always in flux where, in the face of death and imprisonment, new faces were obliged to come forward and assume command. This brought a new generation to the fore with no background in the previous political parties. The FLN was all they knew and it was the FLN which made them, propelling these young men to power and influence.

Determined to stave off defeat the local ALN leaders steadily raised the level of violence. Under the cover of night, vines were vandalized, livestock disembowelled, and telegraph polls blown up. There were also spectacular ambushes of French soldiers and in May the first bomb exploded in Constantine on the tenth anniversary of Sétif. Europeans in remote rural farms were targeted and by August 1955 twenty had been killed. Most violence, however, was directed against the Muslim population in the Aurès and Kabylia. Partly this was motivated by the need to control them. In a guerrilla war where intelligence was the key the ALN had to ensure the silence of the population. Partly, too, it was motivated by the desire for polarization. By murdering Muslim police and administrators, eighty-eight alone in April, the ALN was destroying all points of contact between European and Muslim. It was dividing society into two warring factions.

These methods explain the range of emotions within the local Muslim population. Even if there was an instinctive hatred of the French, and even if there was a sense of proprietorial claim in some villages, 'our young men out there', there was also fear, confusion, and ambivalence. The middle classes in particular were perturbed by the FLN's violent methods, while at a popular level reticence was fuelled by the knowledge that the rival MNA under Messali Hadj had formed its own maquis by March 1955. Trying to capture this complex mood *Le Monde* journalist André Leveuf wrote a series of eye-witness reports from Kabylia in January. Within them he portrayed a society on the brink. Wherever he looked there was fear. Everywhere people were weighing up the stark choice imposed by the ALN violence.[36] In the wake of an attack on the village of Tizi N'Djemaa one Muslim official told Leveuf:

> When I try to calculate those inhabitants in this commune in which I can have entire confidence, I perceive that they amount to ten per cent of the masses. Alongside this faithful, I calculate at eighty per cent those who live in what I will call prudent expectation. Careful above all not to run any risk, neither on one side nor the other, they observe in silence the unfolding facts, waiting to discern the sense in which the wind will blow.[37]

Such comments led Leveuf to a pessimistic conclusion. In the absence of anything other than a military solution, the aura of maquis, combined with endemic poverty and the impact of French repression, carried out by young soldiers who had little understanding of the local inhabitants, could only mean one thing: the ALN would find plentiful recruits in the months to come.

The coming of Abbane Ramdane

In January 1955 Abbane Ramdane was released from prison. Thirty-five years old, he had been the local MTLD leader in Sétif, arrested and sentenced as part of the 1950 sweep against the OS. Crucially this meant that he had missed out on the whole MTLD crisis. Berberphone, secular in outlook, the recipient of a secondary education, he was strong willed with razor-sharp political instincts. These qualities led him to be immediately recruited by Omar Oumrane, an old friend and Krim's chief lieutenant. Abbane quickly assumed the leadership of the interior FLN in Algeria over and against the external FLN in Cairo.

With Abbane came a new level of sophistication. He had the vision to see what the FLN had to do to win. He understood the need for symbols—a national anthem and a clandestine press—that would galvanize the population to identify with the FLN. He saw too that the FLN had to break out of its narrow OS origins. Violence on its own was not enough. If the FLN was to be transformed into a genuine national resistance front, physical intimidation had to be combined with negotiation. But in accepting the need for dialogue, Abbane was clear that this could only be conducted on the FLN's terms. Political pluralism was rejected. Each party had to disband and allow their members to join the FLN on an individual basis.

Abbane's first achievement was the 1 April 1955 Declaration. Much more widely read and diffused than the 1 November Declaration, the words were masterfully crisp and to the point. Calling on all Algerians to unite behind the FLN, the proclamation ended with a warning to the other political parties that the ALN would be 'pitiless towards traitors and enemies of the country'.[38] These verbal threats continued with a further tract in June when Abbane, accusing Abbas and Messali of entering into secret contacts with the French government, reiterated that it was the FLN alone which had the right to speak on behalf of the ALN.

What motivated Abbane's war of words was continuing fear of a compromise solution. Abbane was worried that if the FLN remained isolated, this would leave the way open for the French to construct a third-force alternative. Because of this Abbane put out secret feelers to the other political parties and during the summer he met centralists like Benyoucef Ben Khedda, who had been imprisoned in December and then released in March 1955; Abbas; the Ulemas; as well as the Communists. The MNA, though, remained the exception to this strategy. There Abbane remained unflinching. The MNA was vilified for sowing confusion and on this basis, Abbane eventually concluded, all suspected Messali supporters must be 'shot without a trial'.[39]

The rise of Abbane created tensions with Cairo where the exterior delegation had now been joined by Boudiaf. They disliked his assertion of the primacy of the interior over exterior. They disliked the manner in which he was bringing on board old political leaders. But most of all, they disliked the fact that he had usurped the legitimacy of the original progenitors of 1 November. Abbane in turn denounced them for behaving like a government in exile.[40] In a series of letters that grew more barbed by the day, he accused Ben Bella of wanting to be Nasser. Living in Cairo, far from the harsh realities of war, they had no right to give orders.

It was a telling exchange. The letters showed that the FLN was not a unified structure. Already looking forward to post-independence competing groups, Abbane in Algiers, the exterior delegation in Cairo, and the individual maquis leaders were engaged in a bitter struggle for power. The miracle was that despite these tensions the FLN's forward march to political dominance could not be halted.

The fall of Mendès France

Although Pierre Mendès France had met force with force, instructing the army to extinguish the rebellion as quickly as possible, this was one side of a double-pronged strategy. Repression had to be accompanied by reform whose aim was to find a third way between conservative settlers and extremist nationalists and construct a Franco-Muslim community based on equality. By taking this line Mendès France was merely reflecting the consensus established by the 1947 Statute and the reforms undertaken by Chataigneau, Naegelen, and Léonard. What was different was his sense of urgency. No longer could the colonial lobby be allowed to sabotage change. The reformist agenda had to be sped through without delay.

Belief in the application of the Statute was inseparable from a continued belief in the French Union. For Mendès France and Mitterrand the French Union was not a lost cause. After the loss of Indochina following the defeat at Dien Bien Phu they envisaged a remodelled French Union focused upon Africa. Stretching from Paris to Brazzaville in the French Congo, the lynchpin of this reformed entity was to be a reformed Algeria. Making good the 1947 Statute, therefore, always had a wider significance. For Mendès France and Mitterrand it was the foundation stone of a new relationship with the African territories based on equality, cooperation, and decentralization, albeit one whose evolution was to be controlled by France. The third way was about maintaining French global power in the face of the Soviet Union, the USA, and pan-Arab nationalism. Without a reformed Algeria and French Union France's great-power status would be gone for ever, a view that was stated in categorical terms by Naegelen in a series of articles in the socialist daily *Le Populaire* in December 1954: 'To lose North Africa... would be to lose in quick succession all of Africa, then the French Union, it would make France fall to the level of a second-rate power and even a vassal power. It is not only our prestige that is at stake, but also our national independence.'[41]

This assumption became the driving principle for a tightly knit set of politicians drawn from the Socialists, the Radicals, and the UDSR who, backed up by a continuity of civil-service personnel, became the key decision-makers in successive governments. So, the Radical Maurice Bourgès-Maunoury was Minister of Defence from January 1956 to May 1957 before becoming premier himself in June 1957. The UDSR member François Mitterrand was Minister of the Interior in the Mendès government and Justice Minister in the Mollet government. Indeed he took the lead in January 1955 by announcing ambitious plans for greater employment and educational opportunities for Muslims in combination with a programme of public works to bring roads, post offices, and town-hall offices to even the remote parts of Algeria. He also proclaimed that voting rights would be accorded to Algerian women and *communes mixtes* abolished as he prepared to apply the 1947 Statute. No less importantly, he outlined plans to properly integrate the police force in Algeria into its mainland equivalent—a statement, in Mitterrand's view, that as regards police procedures and their adherence to the law Algeria *was* France.[42]

This determination to press through with reform was backed up still further by the appointment of Jacques Soustelle as Governor-General on 25 January. Born of Protestant working-class stock in Montpellier, he had carved out a career for himself during the 1930s as a lecturer in ethnology at the prestigious Musée de l'Homme in Paris, specializing in Aztec and Mayan civilizations. Politically speaking, Soustelle was part of the non-communist anti-fascist left who had rallied to the Free French cause in June 1940. After the Liberation he was elected as deputy for Lyon as a social republican where, styling himself as a left-wing Gaullist, Soustelle rose to become a senior figure in de Gaulle's Rassemblement du Peuple Français (RPF). By choosing Soustelle, Mendès France had hoped that his anti-fascist patriotic credentials would secure a wide spectrum of support for his Algeria policy. In reality they raised the ire of the colonial lobby who interpreted Soustelle's appointment as a dangerous threat. By broadening the Mendès France government's appeal, argued René Mayer, the Radical deputy for Constantine in Algeria, it was going to ensure the continuation of the left-of-centre non-communist experiment that, after Indochina and Tunisia, was preparing the ground for a similar sell-out in Algeria.

Convinced of the need to kill off the Mendès France government, Mayer led the charge in the National Assembly on 5 February.[43] Within the debate on North Africa, Mayer and his supporters saw conspiracies on all sides.

Liberal solutions, they reasoned, were not going to rescue French power. They were going to liquidate it, leaving Algeria, Morocco, and Tunisia open to either Anglo-Saxon or communist domination and that evening the government was defeated by 319 votes to 273, with 22 abstentions. Those voting for Mendès France were the Socialists, the UDSR, two-thirds of the Radicals and Gaullists, and a few Moderates; while those voting against were made up of the MRP, the right, seventeen Gaullists, and twenty Radicals, as well as, crucially, the Communists.

Jacques Soustelle

Although Soustelle had been the trigger for Mendès France's fall, he was kept on by the new government established by the Radical Edgar Faure on 23 February. But in trying to fashion a common North African policy, Faure was absorbed by the seemingly much greater crises in Morocco and Tunisia. In April he had to overcome the final stumbling blocks to an agreement with Bourguiba, notably over the rights of the European community in Tunisia. In June, Morocco was shaken by renewed violence when over 800 incidents included the assassination of the liberal industrialist Lemaigre-Dubreuil.. Thus Algeria was left in Soustelle's hands.

Soustelle had no illusions about the scale of the task. He knew that he was distrusted by the settler lobby as Mendès France's man.[44] But he knew too that this hostility must not detract him from accelerating reform that would win over the Muslim majority. To see for himself, Soustelle immediately went on a fact-finding tour of the Aurès mountains. His assessment was that the strength of the revolt, rooted in extreme poverty and a lack of day-to-day governance, had been underestimated.[45] This was going to be a long war. But, Soustelle maintained, the population had not yet thrown its lot in with the FLN. Based on this conclusion his task was to convince Muslims that France was going to stay, defeat the FLN, and significantly improve their basic conditions of existence.

If the people were the prize, Soustelle reasoned, a radically new strategy was needed: one which recognized that winning 'hearts and minds' was just as important as winning ground. Soustelle's answer was the establishment of the Sections Adminstratives Spécialisées (SAS). Wearing distinctive blue kepis, the SAS could be traced back to the *Bureaux Arabes* in the 1830s, and more recently Marshal Lyautey's strategy in Morocco in the 1920s, where special units endowed with a knowledge of local languages and customs had worked amongst the population to convince them of the benefits of French rule. Trained by the military but under the orders of the local prefect, the SAS officers' brief, summed up in the word 'pacification', was to build bridges between France and poor Muslims through the construction of schools, roads, and clinics. In this way, as Soustelle underlined in a telegram to the prefects in Algiers, Oran, Constantine, and Bône on 15 December, areas would not be won and then lost.[46] They would be made permanently secure, thereby depriving the FLN of the local infrastructures of support crucial to its survival.

In tandem with the SAS, Soustelle advanced the concept of integration as a practical way forward.[47] For Soustelle this was a formula rooted in reality. In contrast to assimilation, integration recognized the linguistic, cultural, and religious specificity of the different communities, while anchoring the three departments into a process that would progressively introduce a French administrative framework.[48] Soustelle's hope was that integration would become the basis of a dialogue and during spring and early summer he put out feelers to Algerian political leaders through his two most knowledgeable emissaries, Germaine Tillion and Vincent Monteil. Tillion was one of the earliest anti-Nazi Resisters in 1940 and had survived deportation to Ravensbrück. During the 1930s she had conducted extensive fieldwork as an ethnographer in the Aurès to which she had returned in 1955.[49] Monteil was a veteran of the Free French as well as Indochina and Korea. He was also a noted expert on Islam and fluent in Arabic. Together they formed the liberal wing of the Soustelle cabinet and both were responsible for developing contacts with all shades of opinion, even the FLN. Monteil talked at length with Mostefa Ben Boulaïd after the latter was arrested on the Tunisian border, succeeded in getting Ben Khedda released, and on 28 March arranged a secret meeting between Soustelle and five leading Algerians, including Ahmad Tawfiq al-Madani from the Ulemas and Ahmed Francis from the UDMA. These efforts explain why the country was awash with rumours about compromise. They explain too why the FLN racheted up its campaign of violence and intimidation.

The French army

In elucidating the precepts of counter-insurgency warfare, Soustelle's thinking dovetailed with the vision of the French army which, during the course of 1955, emerged to become—alongside the settlers, the Algerian population, the FLN, and Fourth Republic reformism—one of the key factors in the unfolding dynamic. This vision was the product of a generation of officers whose outlook had been forged by the colonial repression in Morocco in the 1930s, engagement in the Free French, the cold war and finally defeat in Indochina. Collectively they were imbued with patriotism, anti-communism, and an abiding feeling of shame at the fall of France in 1940. But collectively too there was also a sense of detachment from the nation. Nurtured by their struggles in support of de Gaulle and then deepened by their experience in the Far East, it was an esprit de corps that felt bitter at the way in which their sacrifices in Indochina had been betrayed by Fourth Republic politicians.

Understood from this perspective the army's mission in Algeria was redemptive. It was about restoring military greatness and expunging shame—a common perspective amongst senior officers like Paul Cherrière, Henri Lorillot, Jacques Massu, and Marcel Bigeard who, determined to learn the lessons of Indochina, drew upon the chief theoretician of counter-revolutionary warfare: Colonel Lacheroy. Steeped in the writings of Ho Chi Minh and Chairman Mao, Lacheroy, himself a veteran of Indochina, believed that international communism was engaged in a long war of stealth and cunning. Carefully avoiding a frontal confrontation in Europe, Communism was now busy enlisting anti-colonial nationalism in Africa and Asia. To win this war the French army, Lacheroy argued, had to adopt the methods of their adversaries. Like them they had to be 'fish in water' amongst the population. Like them they had to be utterly ruthless. And like them they had to be fighting for political objectives that the people could identify with.

On this basis the army adopted new and far-reaching techniques. It emptied rural areas, relocating whole villages in order to cut the ALN off from the population. It raised the first anti-FLN Algerian militias drawing upon the advice of anthropologists like Jean Servier. It also engaged in psychological warfare. A raft of anti-FLN pamphlets, cartoons, and films were produced in Arabic and French which dehumanized the FLN as locusts while calling on the population to denounce them. For the army, the significance of these images was the fact that they disproved the lie that it was defending colonialism. The army, it claimed, was engaged in a heroic mission to defend the French Union and save the people from communism and pan-Arabism, an argument that converged perfectly with the reformist blueprint sketched out by the likes of Naegelen, Mitterrand, and Mendès France.

Figure 5.3b 'Voici l'image du fellaga': French army anti–FLN poster (Arab version).

Figure 5.3a 'Voici l'image du fellaga': French army anti–FLN poster (French version).

Figure 5.4 'Everybody talks—the rebel surrenders'.

Figure 5.5 'The accomplices of the rebels they also will be punished: Talk!'

State of emergency

With the situation on the ground slipping out of control, Edgar Faure's government introduced state-of-emergency legislation on 3 April 1955 in the Aurès and Grande Kabylia. Based on the logic that exceptional circumstances required exceptional laws, this legislation gave the army the new legal apparatus to prosecute the war against the FLN.[50] Ironically it also became the measure of revolt as the state of emergency was steadily extended to other regions throughout 1955.

Alongside the state of emergency, the Faure government also covered the use of collective reprisals against villages suspected of supporting the FLN and summary executions, defining the rules of engagement by a special decree on 1 July 1955 in the following terms: 'In the fighting on the ground, there must be no hesitation on the conduct to follow. Every rebel using weapons or seen carrying weapons or in the middle of carrying out an exaction must be immediately shot ... every suspect who tries to escape must be opened fire upon.'[51]

Backed up by these draconian laws, Faure bolstered army numbers by the recall of the first reservists on 19 May 1955. Since they were mostly Europeans, there was no protest at being asked to give up their jobs and family although Soustelle did receive some requests for exemption on the grounds of necessity for the local economy in Algeria.[52] The overwhelming majority, however, were only too willing to defend their territory. As the settler Bernard Coll remembered:

> In every pied-noir family, there were ex-servicemen, one in four had fought in a war, whether 14–18, whether 39–45 ... There was therefore a permanent immersion in the army. The pieds-noirs were focused on these notions of France, the army, patriotism, war. We were deeply patriotic.[53]

The reservists' lot was the daily control of the population. They had to comb villages, establish roadblocks, check identity papers, and guard internment camps, the first of which was set in Kenchela in the Aurès. Mostly, this was tense and difficult work for which they were ill prepared. In theory they were supposed to differentiate between the 'terrorists' and the people. In practice the repression was too indiscriminate and the resentment it generated pushed large numbers onto the FLN's side. Then, in a significant FLN propaganda victory, there were the first revelations about human rights abuses published by Claude Bourdet in *France-Observateur* and François Mauriac in *L'Express* in January 1955, claims that were further substantiated by the resignation of Monteil on 24 June over torture by the police.[54] Yet, people in metropolitan France were ignorant of these details. Algeria still seemed far away. The communist press, for example, was dominated by the polemic between the PCF General-Secretary Maurice Thorez and Mendès France over whether or not working-class living standards were increasing or decreasing. Thorez's argument that the working class was becoming impoverished was widely diffused within the PCF press, principally because this debate was seen to tap into the day-to-day lives of the communist electorate.

FLN victory at the Bandung Conference

The Bandung Conference opened in Indonesia on 18 April 1955. Lasting eight days, the Conference, attended by twenty-three countries which accounted for half the world's population, was marked by belief, confidence, and idealism.[55] Within the proceedings Egypt's President Nasser, China's foreign minister Chou En-lai and Yugoslavia's President Tito loomed large, although Jawaharlal Nehru, prime minister of India, was the acknowledged elder statesman. Veteran of the Congress of Oppressed Nations in Brussels in 1927, where Messali had first uttered the call for Algerian independence, his doctrine of non-alignment shaped the whole conference. No longer pawns in the 'Great Game', Nehru argued, these countries had to become a force for good in international relations and the final communiqué called for a new global politics based on the recognition of the equality of races enshrined in the United Nations Charter. Making an explicit link between Nazism and colonialism, the Bandung Conference declared its support for the rights of the peoples of Algeria, Morocco, and Tunisia to self-determination.

This was a major coup for the FLN whose delegation, comprising Hocine Aït Ahmed and M'hamed Yazid, were present as observers. It ensured the FLN's pre-eminence over the MNA. It also opened the way for the internationalization of the Algerian question at the United Nations and shortly afterwards Yazid arrived in New York to open an FLN office at 150, East 56th Street. A centralist who had rallied to the FLN in Cairo in autumn 1954, Yazid was well known for his pro-US sympathies. Married to an American, Olivia La Guardia, and speaking English with a strong New York accent, Yazid became the most effective exponent of the FLN cause, a tireless lobbyist who cultivated links not just with the countries of Africa, Asia, and Latin America, but also US politicians, like the rising star of the Democrat Party, John F. Kennedy. Recognizing that words were the equal of military might, he sought to isolate France and on 30 September, as a result of the combined pressure of the Bandung countries, time was set aside for Algeria to be discussed for the first time at the UN, the first shot in a complex diplomatic duel. Thus, Algeria's supporters invoked the right to self-determination, while the French delegation, boycotting the debate in protest, replied that the UN had no right to intervene in a domestic problem.

20 August: The Philippeville massacres

Despite the diplomatic victory at Bandung, on the ground the ALN was hard-pressed on all sides. This produced a mood of desperation amongst the two leaders of the North Constantine region, Zighoud Youcef and Lakhdar Ben Tobbal. Fearing that the struggle was losing momentum, they decided, on their own initiative, to launch a new uprising in and around the coastal town of Philippeville on 20 August, the second anniversary of the deposing of the sultan of Morocco by French army. Through spectacular action Youcef and Ben Tobbal wanted to relieve pressure on the encircled Aurès, reply to collective reprisals practised by the French army, and put pressure on the moderates who had still not thrown in their lot with the FLN. To underline the last point, tracts were distributed in advance describing UDMA members, like Allaoua Abbas, Fernat Abbas's nephew and the deputy for Constantine, as traitors to be executed.[56] No less importantly, Youcef and Ben Tobbal wanted to bring Algeria to the attention of the world. By an uprising they wanted to show that the FLN was not a fringe group but the expression of the Algerian people.

Throughout mid-August the atmosphere in the region was tense, fuelled by rumours of an Egyptian invasion on the coast. Then, at midday on Saturday 20 August thousands of peasants, egged on by ALN maquisards, descended on thirty towns and villages stretching from Collo and Philippeville on the coast to Guelma and Oued-Zénati in North Constantine.[57] Chanting 'jihad', 'the Egyptian army has landed', and 'the Americans are with us' and armed with knives, clubs, sticks, axes, and pitchforks, the attackers were merciless. Many were motivated by hopes of revenge for Sétif ten years earlier and the result was crude face-to-face violence where civilians were hunted down in the streets and clubbed to death. Lasting three days, the peak of horror was reached at El-Halia, a small pyrite mining centre near to Philippeville. There thirty-seven Europeans were killed, including ten children, by Algerian workers they had known for years. Overall 123 died, made up of seventy-one Europeans, thirty-one soldiers and police officers, and twenty-one Algerians, including Allaoua Abbas.

As with Sétif, the response was ferocious. Whole villages were subjected to collective reprisal. At El-Halia eighty Algerians were shot on the spot.[58] In Philippeville hundreds were herded into the local football stadium and executed.[59] Then, on the day the Philippeville victims were buried, European mourners rounded up and lynched seven Muslims. Quickly it was possible to talk about thousands killed by the counter-repression with the FLN putting the figure as high as 12,000, a moment of violent intensity that made August 1955 into one of the defining events of the conflict. This was the point when a low-level war became an all-out war.

On the European side, a pamphlet about the massacres was sent to all the mayors in mainland France.[60] The photographs did not hang back. They catalogued in explicit detail how the victims—'French Algeria's martyrs'— had been hacked to pieces even after death, men emasculated, mothers disembowelled, children mutilated. Consolidating the image of FLN savagery, the photographs' message was simple: to negotiate would be a betrayal of those who had suffered such horrific deaths.[61]

On the Algerian side, August 1955 represented a huge psychological victory for the FLN. The strategy of tension had paid off and in the following months the FLN assumed the dimensions of a genuinely popular movement, easily overshadowing the MNA. Within the Constantine region the flood of MTLD members to the FLN now became irreversible. Meanwhile in the west the first serious maquis groups took to the mountains on the Moroccan border around Tlemcen.

No to integration

For Governor-General Soustelle, too, the Philippeville massacres were a decisive event. After 20 August, repression overshadowed the liberal dimension but measures, including banning the PCA on 21 September 1955, played into the FLN's hands. In polarizing the situation still further, it swung the moderates behind the FLN. On 3 September Mohammed Bendjelloul, the old champion of assimilation, headed a delegation to Paris which told Faure that nobody on the Algerian side believed in Soustelle's policy.[62] It was a major turning point. Three weeks later a group of sixty-one moderates, drawn from the second college of the Algerian Assembly, the National Assembly, the Assembly for the French Union, and the Council of the Republic and including Bendjelloul and Abbas, signed a declaration 'condemning the blind repression', describing Soustelle's policy of integration as a failure and stating that the immense majority of Algerians supported nationalism (*idée nationale algérienne*).[63]

Engineered by Abbane, this was a major coup for the FLN and a major blow for Soustelle. The moderates had chosen and with them the third force disappeared, further isolating France in the run-up to the United Nations vote on 30 September. Thereafter the FLN did not let up, calling in December on all elected representatives to resign. With only settler deputies now remaining, the Algerian Assembly was dead.

Reactions in France

On 15 September 1955 *France-Observateur* carried the first interview with the FLN leaders by the journalist Robert Barrat, a left-wing Catholic well known for his anti-colonial views.[64] Travelling to Palestro in Kabylia, Barrat met not just Abbane and Amar Ouamrane, but ordinary maquis fighters. In talking to Barrat they stressed that Messali no longer had any authority in Algeria. They stressed the FLN's anti-communism. They also stressed the significance of 1 November 1954. As one young soldier explained: 'What happened on 1 November is something new in Algeria. It is not a revolt, it is a war. We will fight for a year, five years, ten years if necessary. If we fall, the young will replace us in the struggle.'[65]

Yet, such determination was tempered by language seemingly more moderate than the original November 1954 Declaration. Presenting themselves as realists, they understood that 'independence must be achieved by stages and democratically', proposing free elections that would lead to an Algerian government which would negotiate with the Fourth Republic.[66]

In the wake of the interview *France-Observateur* was immediately seized, Barrat was arrested, while the Minister of the Interior, Bourgès-Maunoury, stated categorically that Abbane Ramdane was not an authentic spokesman for the Algerian people.[67] Such official intransigence was a measure of the government's response to the Philippeville massacre. Having recalled 60,000 reservists in August, bolstered by orders that 180,000 conscripts had to remain with their units, the government was in no mood for dissent, particularly since on 1 September in Paris 2,000 reservists had refused to board their train shouting 'Morocco for Moroccans' and 'No war in Algeria', followed by similar incidents in Lyon, Brive, Perpignan, Bordeaux, and Rouen. The war had finally come to France, a fact reflected in the formation on 7 November of the 'Committee of Intellectuals against the Continuation of the War in North Africa'. Bringing together a wide range of intellectuals identified with the World War Two Resistance, including Jean-Paul Sartre, André Mandouze, and Robert Barrat, the Committee called for the opening of negotiations, warning: 'This war is shameful. We have no right to impose on our soldiers methods that we ourselves condemned ten years ago, and which risks transforming each one of them into a war criminal.'[68]

Elections 2 January 1956

Looking for a fresh mandate to strengthen his position over Algeria, Faure decided in November to bring forward the French legislative elections by six months to 2 January 1956. In Soustelle's opinion the timing was a disaster. By introducing uncertainty it handed the initiative over to the FLN, just when his strategy of coordinated military and social action was achieving results.[69] Soustelle was not surprised, therefore, when December witnessed a fresh surge in violence. Both the FLN and MNA threatened to kill any Algerian who stood as a candidate and, in this climate, elections in Algeria were impossible. For the settlers, however, this annulment created a crisis of representation. They felt unheard, fearful that a Paris solution was going to be imposed on them.

In France the political landscape continued to be as complex as ever. The Communist Party, with 160,000 members, remained a powerful entity but, conscious of isolation, it now reached out to the Socialist Party with the prospect of a new Popular Front. This was rejected by the SFIO whose 110,000 members saw the Communist Party as a Soviet vassal. Yet, not powerful enough to emulate the strength of the Social Democrats in West Germany or the Labour Party in Britain, the Socialist Party could not govern alone. The Christian Democrat Mouvement Républican Populaire (MRP) meanwhile was a pale shadow of its 1946 self, membership having dwindled to 50,000. Elsewhere the RPF had imploded when de Gaulle, disgusted with the Fourth Republic, had dissolved its parliamentary wing and retired from politics in May 1953. The Radical Party had split into two factions: one supporting Edgar Faure and the other Mendès France. The right meanwhile was grouped together in the Union des Indépendants et Paysans. Given the relative strengths of the parties and given the ideological conflicts, it was difficult to see how the election was going to deliver a stable government—a situation made even harder by the emergence of the extreme-right Union de Défense des Commerçants et Artisans (UDCA), led by Pierre Poujade, a stationer from the Lot.

As the campaign unfolded, intensive negotiations took place between the Socialist Party, François Mitterrand's Union Démocratique et Socialiste de la Résistance, supporters of Mendès France, and a rump of left-wing Gaullists. Supported by the radical weekly *L'Express*, this coalition known as the Republican Front was officially unveiled on 8 December. Taking as its symbol the Phrygian cap, this was a non-communist left-of-centre alliance which came together on a common programme of social reform, modernization and 'peace in Algeria'. Careful to distinguish itself from the Popular Front twenty years before, the Republican Front cast itself as a third way, rejecting the Communist Party on the extreme left and the Faure government on the right.

Within the Republican Front coalition two dominant figures emerged. The first was Mendès France who fought an exhausting campaign. Seeing Algeria as the crucial issue, he gave a speech in Marseille on 26 December 1955 where he saw Tunisia, accorded internal autonomy by his government, as the model:

> At any price we must find a solution to the Algerian conflict before March, as otherwise the war will take on tragic proportions. The Algerian Assembly no longer represents anything, and must be dissolved. After a number of stages— but within six months—honest and controlled elections must be held in Algeria. We can then freely discuss the future Statute of Algeria with the legitimate representatives of Algeria, so as to find a solution on Tunisian lines.[70]

The other key figure was Guy Mollet, general secretary of the Socialist Party since 1946. With his slicked-back hair and black-rimmed glasses Mollet was a pillar of the party. A deputy for the socialist bastion of Arras in northern France whose fiftieth birthday coincided with the elections on 2 January

1956, Mollet was a Resistance veteran, fiercely anti-Soviet, and a fervent Anglophile—as a prisoner of war in Germany he wrote a study of English grammar later published by Hachette—who prided himself on being a Marxist. Campaigning, like Mendès, on the theme of 'peace in Algeria', in practice his words were vague and ambiguous. So he talked consistently of this 'stupid war with no way out', stating in *L'Express* on 19 December:

> Will we know how to respond to the national demand of people to whom Europe has taught the freedom of the rights of man and who now demand that she herself put these lessons in practice? Will we know how to make these people associates and friends? The French will respond on 2 January. They will say, without doubt, what is their choice between this future of reconciliation and peace and, on the other hand, a stupid war with no way out.[71]

But in his final electoral address 'peace' was envisaged as the need to re-establish law and order, implying a continuation of the war against the FLN and MNA, which, once achieved, would lay the basis of a reformed Algeria.[72]

Amongst the people, opinion polls revealed Algeria to be one, albeit the most important, amongst a number of problems with 25 per cent seeing it as the major issue, followed by 15 per cent citing wages, 9 per cent an improvement in East–West relations, 5 per cent better housing, and 5 per cent monetary stability. Similarly on the hustings the parties foregrounded a range of issues. Thus, the Communist Party, too, talked about 'peace in Algeria', but this was also balanced by the significance of bread-and-butter issues of work and food prices, as well as a concerted campaign to woo socialist supporters away from the Republican Front and into a reformed Popular Front. Equally Poujade's UDCA combined defence of French Algeria with hatred of the traditional parties and opposition to 'Jewish capitalism'.

After a month of campaigning the voters went to the polls on 2 January 1956. What rapidly became clear was that no clear majority had emerged. The Communist Party was still the biggest party with 5.5 million votes, followed by the Socialist Party (3.3 million), the Radicals (3 million), the Christian Democrat MRP (2.4 million), the Independents (3.5 million), the Poujadists (2.5 million), and the Gaullists (900,000). It was a confused landscape and over the next four weeks the politicians entered into a tortuous cycle of political manoeuvring, the backdrop to which was freezing conditions. By the beginning of February, this weather saw temperatures plummet to -20 °C in Paris, accompanied by blocks of ice on the Loire and over a metre of snow in Normandy.

Within the unfolding scenario, a Republican Front government seemed the most likely as the Socialist Party, given that it was the largest party in the alliance, decided on the best course of action. At a meeting of the ruling committee of the SFIO, Mollet expressed reluctance at becoming prime minister, arguing that, since this would not be a solely socialist government, Mendès France would be better placed to lead any coalition administration.[73] Then, at a specially convened party conference at Puteaux on 14 and 15 January, the Socialist Party set forth its political agenda for government, outlining Algeria as the major issue, along with disarmament, European economic integration, and pension increases for retired people.[74]

During a further meeting of the SFIO ruling committee on 25 January, Gaston Defferre and Pierre Commin expressed their exasperation at Mendès France's actions who, in their view, was not only patently ill at ease with the SFIO's social agenda, but also unwilling to commit himself to a precise post in the government, including the possibility of being prime minister.[75] At this point Mollet intervened, stating that although he had supported the idea of Mendès France as prime minister, the latter's evasiveness, not least over economic policy, had led him to the conclusion that he himself, as leader of the Socialist Party, would have to be prime minister, a position unanimously supported within the committee. Recognizing the political risks, Mollet stated:

> We must go forward without the slightest moderation on the programme outlined in the Congress. That will carry the others or else they will leave. Without provocation, in a measured declaration, we will put the accent on two points:
>   Algeria
>   Old People.[76]

On 26 January President Coty invited Guy Mollet to form a government and within his administration key posts went to Socialist Party deputies: Christian Pineau at Foreign Affairs, Albert Gazier at Social Affairs, Max Lejeune for the Army. Beyond the SFIO, François Mitterrand became Justice Minister, Bourgès-Maunoury Minister of Defence, and Pierre Mendès France a Minister without Portfolio. Marcel Champeix, another Socialist Party stalwart, was named Secretary of State for Algerian Affairs, while General Catroux was made Governor-General, now renamed Minister-Resident and given cabinet status. Formerly Governor-General in 1943–4 and identified with the recent policy of reconciliation in Morocco, Catroux seemed to embody the Republican Front's conciliatory approach. All men, all left of centre, the government was composed of thirty-six ministers, secretaries of state, and under-secretaries of state, comprised of eighteen from the SFIO, of which fourteen were from the Radical Party, two from the Rassemblement Démocratique Africain, and one from UDSR. On the following day they posed together for the official government photograph, one that had to be taken in the Élysée itself rather than on the steps because of the sub-zero temperatures.[77]

On 31 January Mollet's investiture speech spelt out the Republican Front's programme underlining support for European unity, international disarmament, decentralization of powers in the French Union, as well as the completion of independence in Morocco and Tunisia. Over Algeria, he preached a solution that would accord equality and maintain the 'indissoluble union between Algeria and France' while recognizing the distinctiveness of the former.[78] In the short term: 'The objectives of France, the will of the government, is, before everything, to re-establish peace, free fear from the minds of everyone and, for that, to obtain the cessation of terrorism and blind repression.'[79]

Once peace was achieved elections would then take place through a single electoral college. After a long and wide-ranging debate the Mollet administration was voted into office in the National Assembly on 5 February by 420 deputies to 71 with 83 abstentions, with support not just from the Republican Front coalition, but the Communist Party, still seeking a rerun of the Popular Front, and a majority of the Christian Democrat MRP and the Gaullists, the latter reassured by his talk of the unbreakable bonds between Algeria and France. Armed with this mandate Mollet immediately travelled to Algiers.[80] His purpose: to defuse the violence by establishing confidence in the government's reforms.

6

Guy Mollet's War 1956

Monday, 6 February 1956

In flying to Algiers Mollet hoped to emulate Mendès France's dramatic visit to Tunis in July 1954 which had rescued a violent situation and opened the way to internal autonomy. But, from the moment his plane touched down at 2.30 p.m., Mollet's shuttle diplomacy was greeted with silent protest. As the official cavalcade made its way from the airport to central Algiers in the cold weather, shutters were drawn en masse, no crowds cheered and in the European parts of the city there was a general strike.

Mollet was in the eye of the storm. Fuelled by the uncertainty flowing from the election result, January had witnessed ceaseless polarization. On the FLN's side, Abbane's politics continued to pay off handsomely, with both the Ulema and Abbas publicly rallying behind the FLN.[1] Messali meanwhile had proposed round-table discussions to pave the way to independence. On the settler side, the unending stream of attacks against Europeans in the countryside, graphically reported by the *Écho d'Alger*, produced a violent atmosphere—a mood made worse by nationalist graffiti giving them the choice of 'the suitcase or the coffin'.[2] In concrete terms this anxiety expressed itself not just in hatred of the FLN, but also through hostility to the Republican Front. Any government including Mendès France was automatically suspect, his presence leading them to one conclusion, namely that Mollet was about to force through a Tunisian-style solution and abandon French Algeria.

Deprived of deputies the European leaders looked to the street. By direct action they wanted to impose their wishes on Paris and throughout January an ex-servicemen's organization, made up principally of ordinary European veterans from both world wars, created an insurrectionary climate, stoked up still further by the *Écho d'Alger's* threats of secession. The influential leaders, a mixture of old and new faces, were Amédée Froger, mayor of Boufarik and mainstay of the colonial lobby; André Achiary, leader of the May 1945 violence in Guelma; Jean-Baptiste Biaggi, Gaullist Resistance veteran with links to Soustelle; Joseph Ortiz, café owner and local Poujadist leader; and Pierre Lagaillarde, a firebrand student leader from Algiers University. Forming a 'Committee for the Defence of French Algeria', their watchword, encapsulating the settlers' deepest fears, was 'resistance to abandonment'.[3]

   This confrontational stance led settler activists to break up a meeting on 22 January organized by Albert Camus calling for a truce because for them his liberal compromise, searching for people of goodwill on both sides who would stop the circle of violence, smacked of defeatism.[4] It led to a triumphant sending off for the departing Soustelle on 2 February, a clear warning to the incoming Catroux. And finally it led to preparations for a violent coup to intimidate Mollet. On 5 February 20,000 ex-servicemen paraded through Algiers and that night Biaggi whipped up a public meeting into a frenzy, telling them: 'To arms citizens!'[5]

   At the airport Mollet, in a succinct address, appealed for calm. Stating that he brought with him no 'miracle remedy', Mollet's prime concern was to stop the flow of bloodshed, both French and Muslim. With this thought uppermost, Mollet underlined his own patriotic bond with Algeria: 'I am a man from the North, I have spent all my life there and yet I feel fraternal links with all the inhabitants of Algeria. I believe that I have proved this as a veteran of the war, of the Resistance and of the Liberation.'[6] Then, sensitive to settler feelings, Mollet's first port of call at 3.00 p.m. was the main war monument situated on the plateau de Glières, part of the vast space, known as the Forum, opposite the Governor-General's office. Suitably solemn, he laid a wreath honouring those from Algeria who had given their lives for France in the two world wars. Suddenly though, a well-prepared crowd broke through the police cordon to pelt the prime minister with tomatoes and clods of earth. Shouting 'Mollet to the stake', 'Mollet resign', and 'throw Catroux into the sea', the settler anxieties—fear of terrorism, fear of being disenfranchised, fear of being sold out—surged forward in one climactic moment, leaving Mollet, surrounded on all sides, in real physical danger. As Biaggi later explained, the demonstrators were acting on cue:

> Mollet coming without Catroux, the orders, given by us . . . were rigorously followed: nobody on the route, all the city around the war monument, silence

first of all, then unleashing of hostile shouting: a van of tomatoes hanging around near to the plateau de Glières: in the morning, a tract edited by secondary school students had said: 'The national tomato will be our weapon; in Algeria, it comes in every season.'[7]

Saved by volleys of tear gas and baton-wielding riot police, Mollet made his way to the governmental residence at the Palais d'Été. Barracked in and badly shaken, he tried to take stock of the situation surrounded by Max Lejuene, Minister for the Army, Albert Gazier, Joseph Begarra, and Pierre Lambert, prefect for Oran. Talking by telephone with President Coty, Mollet learnt that Catroux, himself informed by telephone of the unfolding drama, had already handed in his resignation from the post of Minister-Resident.[8] In this heated atmosphere Mollet was in no position to refuse. On hearing the news the settler crowd were delirious. Paris had given way to Algiers and that evening, to mark their victory, a small number tore up the Palais d'Été gardens.

Figure 6.1 6 February 1956, the 'Day of the Tomatoes': protesting French settlers recoiling from tear gas.

Over the following days Mollet sought to rebuild confidence. He met settler delegations and then travelled to Constantine to get a measure of the military situation in the east of the country, still deep in snow. At the same time he cast around for a new Minister-Resident, eventually choosing Robert Lacoste, Finance Minister and Socialist Party deputy, after others, including Pierre Mendès France, refused. Finally, after three days of consultation he traced out the government proposals in a special radio broadcast from Algiers on 9 February. Warning the Europeans against extremists he also attacked the FLN, without explicitly naming them, as a 'handful of maniacs and criminals who take their orders from outside Algeria', before outlining his model for a reformed Algeria, modern, industrialized, democratic, that would unite French and Muslim within one equal community.[9] To realize this vision Mollet could not have been firmer about the government's military intentions even if he avoided use of the word war, stating unambiguously: 'The Government will fight, France will fight to remain in Algeria, and she will remain there. There is no future for Algeria without France.'[10]

On Friday 10 February the prime minister returned to Paris to explain the train of events to the National Assembly and government. Conscious that the arguments had not been aired in cabinet, Mollet set out what he, as a socialist and patriot who identified with popular aspirations, saw to be the legitimate aspect of 6 February. Speaking forcefully in the first person, Mollet underlined that he readily assumed total responsibility for his response:

> This harrowing demonstration was meanwhile, for a good number, the expression of profound and highly respectable feelings: attachment to France, anguish of being abandoned. I said so in Algiers, I want to repeat it here. There was in the demonstration a certain part which was sane, whatever exploitation some extremist organizations wanted to make of it.
>
> I took account of these feelings when I took my decisions. Under the terms of the Constitution, it is my responsibility to do so, me alone, and I assume it totally.[11]

Reactions

In terms of reactions to 6 February the settlers were ecstatic. Now they felt protected and in the *Écho d'Alger* the editor, Alain de Sérigny, held up Naegelen's tenure as Governor-General between 1948 and 1951 as the model to follow.[12] Naegelen's socialism was the type of socialism Sérigny wanted because:

Figure 6.2 *L'Écho d'Alger* of 7 February 1956. The ecstatic headlines reflect the way in which the European press saw the 'Day of the Tomatoes' as a huge victory for French Algeria.

> M. Naegelen, equally a member of the Socialist Party ... had affirmed from village to village the French character of the Algerian soil and reduced to nothing the separatist pretentions ...[13]

In contrast, within the government and the Socialist Party there was disquiet, not least caused by the impression that 6 February 1956 had altered policy, smacking of a *coup d'état* and evoking the right-wing riots in front of the Paris National Assembly exactly twenty-two years before. These concerns, tempered by the need to maintain unity and support Mollet, were aired at the SFIO's ruling committee on 22 February. Marceau Pivert was perturbed by the fact that the party's 'worst adversaries' supported the government's policies and he called on Mollet to make an unambiguous statement in favour of 'peace' and 'free elections'.[14] Paul Rimbert pondered whether there could be a round table with all the concerned parties, analogous to the way in which the Moroccan crisis had been resolved.[15] Mollet identified three strands to the 'rebellion': the first was made up of youngsters, similar in mentality to the French Resistance, who felt deceived by France and with whom it would be possible to negotiate; a second was dependent on Cairo and responsible for the worst atrocities, with whom no discussion was possible; a third was simply made up of criminals.[16] The Communist Party meanwhile denounced 6 February as a 'fascist conspiracy' while, still holding out for a Popular Front Alliance, restrained its condemnation of Mollet.

On the Algerian side there was nothing but anger. For the young Mohammed Harbi, now a student activist in Paris, this solidified hatred of the Socialist Party: 'We expected nothing from the socialists. It was a capitulation. They had sided with the settlers.'[17] In his diary the writer Mouloud Feraoun noted how an Algerian friend posed the question: what if 6 February had involved young Algerian nationalists?[18] 'If there had been young natives from the Casbah, from Belcourt, or Maison-Carrée instead of all those French people, what would the CRS, the police officers, or later France have done? Yes, what would France have done?'[19] The implication of his question: without doubt the French reaction would have been ferocious.

In this sense what was striking about 6 February was the absence of any Algerian participation. It accelerated a process of separation. The last remnants of any Muslim third force withdrew from the political scene. On 19 March Abdelkader Sayah, president of the Algerian Assembly, resigned and on 11 April the Assembly, deemed unworkable, was dissolved.[20]

Amongst the foreign journalists covering Algeria Edward Behr, the *Time* correspondent, was one who, in the ensuing years, came to see 6 February as the defining event in the conflict. The manner in which Mollet gave in to the crowd, strengthened by the fact that no European activists were arrested, meant that henceforth the 'European demonstrators felt that there was nothing that street violence could not achieve'.[21] Was it, though,

Avant le 2 janvier   Avant le 6 février   Après le 6 février

Figure 6.3 Anti-Mollet cartoon from the weekly satirical paper *Le Canard Enchaîné*, which portrayed him as the painter Guimollo, who promised peace but brought conflict and torture to Algeria: 'In the style of Picasso: The Guimollo mystery', 30 May 1956.

a betrayal for those who voted for the Republican Front's 'Peace in Algeria'? Certainly a younger voter like Georges Mattéi thought so.[22] He had voted communist on the grounds that it was going to stop the war and was subsequently incredulous that this vote led him to being sent to Algeria as a reservist. And certainly the satirical political magazine *Le Canard Enchaîné* thought so too, caricaturing Guy Mollet as a hapless painter, Guimollo, whose policy had swung from one of reconciliation to one of conflict (Figure 6.3).

Mollet did not agree, however. For him there was continuity. In his address to the National Assembly on 10 February Mollet went out of his way to stress that his policy was *not* an about-turn.[23] He was remaining faithful to his electoral promises within which he had always envisaged a new institutional structure that would recognize both Algeria's specificity and the indissoluble bond with France. In this way the phrase 'peace in Algeria' was stripped of its ambiguity. Representing the re-establishment of law and order, it stood for the continuation of France's undeclared war against 'rebels' described by Mollet as an 'extremist minority'.[24]

Special powers

In appointing Robert Lacoste as Minister-Resident Mollet was handing power to a bullish, no-nonsense politician. Patriot, socialist, prominent trade unionist during the 1920s and 1930s, Lacoste, born in the Dordogne in 1898, was a man with impressive Resistance credentials whose father, a Resister too, was shot by the Germans in March 1944. Fiercely opposed to appeasement in 1938, strongly anti-communist, committed to European unity, though an opponent of German rearmament, Lacoste, with little prior knowledge of Algeria, followed the line prescribed by Mollet.

Lacoste immediately demanded sweeping special powers to apply the government's programme. Mixing reform with repression, the first four articles outlined ambitious measures to promote economic expansion, social equality and administrative reorganization, while the fifth authorized Lacoste to rule by decree, in effect giving him the right to take any measures he considered necessary to restore order. On 12 March Mollet made the vote on these special powers into a vote of confidence in his government, thus ensuring they were passed by 455 deputies. Even the Communist Party supported him, their reservations outweighed by the continuing hope of a Popular Front with the Socialist Party.

Backed up by the full force of the law, the special powers, signed off by Mitterrand as Justice Minister, gave the Republican Front government carte blanche in Algeria and on the following day police powers were devolved to the army. Now it had the right to arrest, detain, and interrogate suspects—a measure of how, on the ground, military authority was replacing civil authority.

Armed with these powers Mollet hoped to quickly defeat the FLN, win Muslim 'hearts and minds', and lay the basis for his oft-repeated triptych: ceasefire, elections, and negotiations with the democratic representatives that emerged. In practice huge numbers of Algerians recoiled in horror because the repression was directed solely against the FLN, MNA, and PCA. A curfew in Algiers, censorship of dissent, sweeping arrests and internment—in the light of the special powers, it was difficult to see how the country was going to step back from all-out conflict. This was a final turning point because, as Mohammed Harbi remembered: 'Now all of France, even the communists, was against us.'[25]

Noble ideals

The Republican Front government did not see it like that. For Mollet, he was not plunging France into an ignoble war. In his view the government was not defending an unacceptable colonial system. On the contrary, the government, made up of Resistance veterans committed to left-of-centre, progressive values, claimed to be upholding the very highest principles of the French republican tradition.

Over the following months Mollet, in tandem with Lacoste, Pineau, Lejeune, and Champeix, endeavoured to get this message across in parliament, in the press, on radio and television, and through short information films and specially produced easy-to-read pamphlets and posters.[26] Calling on public opinion to study the facts, they drew upon a range of arguments. The idea of a separate Algerian state was categorically denied. French sovereignty was strenuously upheld. The rights of the settler minority were stressed. The role, too, of the 200,000 Algerians working in France, their wage packets essential to the functioning of regions like Kabylia, was given a new emphasis.[27]

Looked at through this lens, the government contended, the problem was not one of Algerian self-determination. Rather it was balance and mediation. The government's role was to prevent one ethnic group subjugating the other. It was about creating a shared Franco-Muslim community based on toleration, respect, and equal political rights. In holding up this ideal the government evoked the 1571 St Bartholomew's Day Massacre in Paris when Catholics slaughtered Protestants. The army's mission was to prevent a modern-day equivalent. By re-establishing 'peace in Algeria', the government argued, it was laying the ground for political harmony.

To win over Muslim opinion the Republican Front unveiled a raft of social rights. The welfare reforms introduced by Albert Gazier, Minister of Social Affairs, notably the extensions of holiday leave to three weeks and greater pensions, were, it was announced, to be extended to Algeria.[28] Allied to this, on 21 February Lacoste outlined ambitious proposals to address what he saw as the root cause of rebellion: Muslim unemployment.[29] By encouraging immigration to France, much needed in the construction industry—agrarian reform; industrialization; as well as expanding educational opportunities and promotion within the civil service—Lacoste wanted to dramatically improve Muslim wages and so bolster the case for French rule. Why, he argued, would Algerians want independence when France could offer very much better living standards than, say, Egypt?

During 1956 the government returned again and again to this economic argument, claiming that France was not engaged in exploitation. Through huge investment France was modernizing the country, overcoming poverty and under-development in a way which no independent Algeria could hope to match. As one government leaflet put it in a series of succinct bullet points:

- The Algerian economy only survives thanks to rich artificial injections made by French investment
- French aid reached 150 billion francs in 1956, not taking into account military expenditure
- The increase in social investment, destined only to raise the living standards of the population and realized at a loss, reaches a third of total investment, which exceeds, by far, the financial possibilities of an Algeria given over to its own resources.[30]

The symbol of this economic development was the Sahara. Seen by the Mollet government as the new frontier for the new generation, French technical expertise had transformed the desert since 1946 through the discovery of oil and gas, so making France into a potential energy power on the world stage. In 1956 the crowning achievement of this process was the opening of the Hassi Messaoud complex from which pipelines flowed all the way to the coast. The key now, however, was cooperation. The local populations had to be involved so that the Sahara's riches could be exploited for the common good.

Conceiving the French role so, the Republican Front saw its adversaries as neither the Muslim majority nor ordinary settlers. They were a minority of hardliners: the FLN terrorizing the population on one side, the cabal of rich settlers blocking reform on the other. This meant that the Republican Front was engaged in a double-edged struggle. It was striking outwards against these two extremes in defence of a Franco-Muslim community in the centre. Furthermore, this strategy analysed Algeria in terms of the traditional socialist terrain of class war. This was a struggle of rich against poor that crossed racial divides.

In striving to bring together poor settlers and Muslims, the Republican Front invoked the concept of the 'third way': the classic reformist perspective going back to the 1920s. In 1956 the 'third way' was embodied by the 54-year-old Marcel Champeix: Resistance veteran deported to Mathausen Concentration Camp during the Occupation, Socialist Party senator for the Corrèze in south central France since 1946, and, within the Mollet government, Secretary of State for Algerian Affairs in the Ministry of the Interior. The conundrum for him was how to devise the appropriate structures.[31] He wanted to empower the local populations. He wanted to promote pluralism. But this had to be done without opening the back door to independence. With this end in mind his suggestions included doing away with the Minister-Resident, the status of Algiers as the capital, and the Algerian

Figure 6.4 Robert Lacoste, Minister-Resident for Algeria from February 1956 to April 1958 at Hassi Massoud in February 1957 where the French had been exploring for oil since 1946. © ECPAD.

Assembly, and replacing them with three regions, thus developing grass-roots democracy while preventing the emergence of an embryonic nation state. Throughout 1956 and 1957 he worked tirelessly on blueprints for reform which, by charting a middle course between colonialism and the FLN, became the justification for what the Mollet government, still denying the word war, called 'pacification'. As Champeix told the Oran General Council on 4 May 1956:

> In committing to its policy of pacification and the re-establishment of order, the Government...will go right to the end of its resolution and modify

profoundly the conditions themselves of the administrative, economic and social order of our Algerian departments, so that this order is made up truly of social and human progress, of justice and of liberty.

Pacification will not lead to a consolidation of the status quo: it will only find its true justification in the way it will know how to substitute a bygone past by a new Franco-Muslim community made by the free adherence of the populations to respecting the rights of each other and according to the laws of democracy.[32]

International context

As calculated vagueness gave way to hard-edged choices, one theme became central to the government's argument: the need to place Algeria within the wider international context. Throughout 1956 Algeria was linked to Morocco and Tunisia, both accorded independence in March, as Alain Savary, the Minister for Moroccan and Tunisian Affairs, strove to build a new post-colonial relationship with North Africa that would maintain French influence. At the same time Algeria was also closely connected to the reform policy in Black Africa and Madagascar. Steered through the National Assembly in June 1956 by Gaston Defferre, Minister for Overseas Territories and the Socialist mayor of Marseille, and brought into force in April 1957, the Defferre law introduced self-government, enfranchising all citizens in the French Union and granting budgetary control to local assemblies.[33] In establishing such liberal structures, the Republican Front government cited the Defferre reforms as evidence of their good intentions in Algeria. As in Black Africa, Mollet in Algeria was searching for a solution based on democratic participation. He wanted to give ordinary Muslims a voice in their own affairs.

By transforming Black Africa, Defferre wished to create a bloc stretching from Paris to the Congo that, duly insulated from nationalist extremism and international communism, would maintain French standing in the world. In this way, reform, both in Algeria and Black Africa, dovetailed with another absolute priority in international relations: opposition to Colonel Nasser's regime in Egypt. Right from the beginning, French governments had attacked Nasser as the soul behind the FLN revolt, a theme restated in no uncertain terms on 11 March 1956 by Mollet in a meeting at Chequers with the British prime minister, Anthony Eden. Seeing pan-Arab nationalism through the prism of 1930s appeasement, Mollet conjured up Nasser as a Hitler-type figure, telling Eden: 'All this (is) in the works of Nasser, just as Hitler's policy (was) written down in *Mein Kampf*. Nasser has the ambition to recreate the conquests of Islam. But his present position is largely due to the policy of the West in building him up and flattering him.'[34]

Amongst his government colleagues this was the widely held view, although Pineau, as Minister of Foreign Affairs, visiting Nasser on his own initiative in February, believed that he could be weaned away from the FLN through diplomatic engagement. Mollet, however, was not impressed. Like Bourgès-Maunoury, Lacoste, and Lejeune, he dismissed Nasser as a 'monument of duplicity' who was the mastermind behind the Algerian rebellion, an anti-Semite and a neo-Nazi.[35] Moreover, behind Nasser the Republican Front government saw the hidden hand of the Soviet Union.

Such a conclusion underlined a further dimension of the Mollet policy: international anti-communism. All the cabinet were strongly marked by an anti-Soviet perspective and within Algeria they saw another cold-war front. Even if the FLN was not communist, it was being manipulated by the Algerian Communist Party. Even if Nasser was not a communist, he was being infiltrated and controlled by the Soviet Union as evidenced by Egypt's major arms deal with Czechoslovakia in September 1955. On this basis, the Republican Front made the case for the transfer of French troops from Europe to Algeria, telling NATO that it was fighting a proxy war. For what else was pan-Arabism, asserted Alexandre Parodi, the French NATO representative on 7 March, other than a Soviet plot to encircle the West via the Mediterranean, a claim stated as an incontrovertible truth although, as he admitted, the French possessed no concrete intelligence to substantiate this perspective:

> I explained in detail the danger that the Algerian situation posed to the security of Europe . . . I indicated that we did not have evidence of direct Soviet intervention, but nonetheless Algeria was without doubt the continuation, through Arab nationalism, of Soviet action on certain countries such as Egypt.[36]

Algeria was part of the Atlantic zone, a point made by Mollet in an interview circulated in the US press in March, and again by Pineau at the NATO council meeting in Paris on 5 May 1956, and in the face of this pressure the other NATO allies bowed to French demands, even if Washington was unconvinced, fearing that Algeria was in fact doing the opposite, namely stirring up anti-Western feeling in the Arab world and playing into the hands of the Soviet Union.[37]

The identification of Nasser as enemy number one on the international scene was inseparable from support for Israel.[38] Within the Republican Front government this support was partly out of realpolitik (it wanted to use Israel as a stick to beat the Egyptian leader) but also because, with so many in the cabinet personally marked by the Resistance and the memories of the concentration camps, there was a strong feeling of solidarity for the fledgling Jewish state headed by David Ben-Gurion, socialist, Zionist, and leading figure in the Israeli Labour Party (Mapai). Championed by the SFIO as an example of socialism in practice, the kibbutz movement in particular was seen to embody a democratic society that stood as an alternative to Stalinism. Israel's cause was that of socialist internationalism since both countries were involved in the same struggle: the defence of a progressive, left-of-centre ideology against a pan-Arab nationalism, characterized as reactionary, racist, and religiously fanatical.

Close political and military cooperation had begun under the Faure government in October 1955 through the supply of two dozen fighter planes, thus breaking the international ban on the supply of arms to Israel. These deepened under the Mollet government and at the end of June 1956 senior military officials from both sides met in secret in a château in Vermars, south of Paris.[39] There the Israeli delegation, in a carefully prepared resumé, deliberately talked up the danger Nasser posed to the West. His goal, it was claimed, was to get rid of all French influence in North Africa and the Middle East and transform Egypt into a forward base for Soviet power. To stop this Israel was prepared for joint action which, directly or indirectly, would bring Nasser down. Such a perspective, repeatedly stressing Nasser's support for the FLN, pandered to France's worst fears, intensifying the government's belligerent stance. The assumption that if Nasser was destroyed the FLN would collapse became an official mantra, and for this reason the Vermars conference ended with an agreement on intelligence cooperation in return for Israel receiving 72 Mystère fighters and 200 tanks.

The Israeli alliance was symptomatic of the manner in which Mollet's government connected Algeria to the broader context of French Africa, the cold war and the Middle East. This connection was paradoxical. While doing everything to prevent internationalization of the Algerian problem at the United Nations, the French government was presenting the conflict in international terms. It was also psychological. Through a mixture of moral argument and military strength the Republican Front wanted to recover the great-power status lost in defeat and occupation during World War Two, the great unspoken backdrop to 1956.[40] In Algeria, like in Black Africa, in the Middle East, and in the creation of the European Economic Community, Mollet wished to project the sense of a world mission. He wanted to demonstrate that France was not in terminal decline. Instead the country was still a beacon of civilized values which stood in polar opposition to the two most pressing global threats: communism and Arab nationalism.

Operation Valmy

For a patriot like Max Lejeune, Minister for the Armed Forces, the battle of Valmy stood for the very best in the republican tradition, namely the victory of liberty over tyranny, when on 22 September 1792 a citizen army defeated the Prussian invaders and saved the French Revolution.[41] The desire to invoke this revolutionary past, given a renewed meaning by the French Resistance, was why he chose to baptize the recall of the remaining reservists 'Operation Valmy'. Lasting from April to June 1956, this was the largest deployment of troops outside mainland France since the original 1830 invasion which, by also extending military service to twenty-seven months, doubled troop numbers to 400,000, rising to 450,000 in July 1957. By any measure it was a momentous decision. The war had finally come to France. Now Algeria would touch ordinary French people in a way that Indochina, restricted to volunteers and professionals, never did.

In taking this step Lejeune, unanimously supported in cabinet, was responding to the demands of the military. If 'pacification' was going to succeed, they argued, the army needed more soldiers on the ground. At the same time Lejeune recognized the political need for immediate results. Time was of the essence. The army must not get bogged down in a long and drawn-out counter-insurgency campaign as in Indochina. Through Operation Valmy's dramatic 'surge', Lejeune wished to deliver a swift and absolute victory. He wanted to force the FLN to surrender and so open the path to a ceasefire, elections, and negotiations.

In galvanizing the conscripts and reservists, Lejeune continued to draw upon the language of revolutionary patriotism. Their mission, he explained, was not oppression. It was not occupation. It was an act of generosity. By protecting their vulnerable fellow citizens from terrorism, they were the embodiment of liberty, equality, and fraternity:

> We want the men in Algeria to be more free, more fraternal, more equal, that is to say more French. We must guarantee their political liberties and their social emancipation in the face of a few thousand rebels inspired by unemployment, the absence of hope, religious fanaticism, and not least the fit of nationalists who aspire to an unrealisable independence.[42]

Recalling the messianic tone of the first French Republic in 1793, Lejeune's rhetoric displayed certainty in victory. Through the sheer weight of numbers Lejeune expected the nation in arms to win, a belief forcefully reiterated by President René Coty in a speech at the World War One battlefield of Verdun on 17 June:

> Down there, the nation is in danger, the nation is fighting. One's duty is simple and clear. To those not accustomed to military discipline, it means the minimum of civic discipline which forbids all acts that trouble the children of the nation that the Republic has called to arms to vanquish this terrible violence. French strength being inseparable from French generosity.

The reservists revolt

On 29 March Claude Bourdet, Resistance intellectual and left-wing journalist, published an impassioned plea in *France-Observateur*.[43] In it he warned about the consequences of a policy that was about to propel a whole generation into a conflict they did not want to fight. Bourdet's words led him to be arrested and *France-Observateur* to be seized, ironically on the orders of his erstwhile Resistance comrade, Defence Minister Bourgès-Maunoury, but they testified to the mood of disquiet in the country. This was evident, too, in the article in *Le Monde* on 5 April by Henri Marrou, Professor of History at the Sorbonne and another Resistance intellectual, who expressed his shame at the Republican Front's intensification of the conflict.[44] But most of all it was reflected in opposition amongst the reservists. Recalled to fight for six months, they were in no mood to go, not out of any identification with Algerian nationalism but because of the impact on their lives. Aged twenty-three, twenty-four, even twenty-five, many men had established family and career ties which they did not want to disrupt. In the case of Noël Trouillourd, eventually escorted to his unit by a gendarme, his first instinct was refusal because of the needs of the family farm at Beaucroissant in the mountainous Isère region near Grenoble: 'I refused to leave. I did not want to go there. There was work on the farm... We needed to make the hay, my brother was still at school and my father was all alone.'[45]

Once in uniform this rebellious atmosphere continued, largely because the reservists were shocked at the poor organization and conditions within the barracks and draft centres. Joining up with his regiment at Dreux to the west of Paris, Georges Mattéi, a tough, strong-willed individual, politically to the left of the Communist Party, witnessed complete disorder.[46] Discipline was non-existent. Men went absent without leave. They refused to salute or saluted sloppily. Officers were insulted.

The most serious acts of opposition took place in and around railway stations when the trains transporting soldiers to the Mediterranean tried to depart. Troops shouting 'down with Mollet', 'down with Lacoste', 'demobilization', 'peace in Algeria'; vandalism; violent confrontations with the police—these incidents were widespread. Recalled from his native Lyon, Jean Masson remembers his train just inching forward over many hours as reservists repeatedly pulled the brake cordon.[47] Rapidly the Ministry of the Interior was flooded with telegrams and telephone messages from local prefects charting reservist protests in Albi, Bourg, Chartres, Le Mans, Laon, Rouen, Toulouse, Versailles, and Montpellier.[48] One report, dated 18 May, even talked of stories circulating about the existence of a maquis for deserters in the departments of the Creuse, Haute-Vienne, Corrèze, Dordogne, and Indre-et-Loire, a rumour fuelled further by the appearance of a tract in Limoges signed simply 'The Will of the People' and calling on reservists 'to join the maquis... Contact reliable comrades... From now on, prepare with your comrades the sabotage of railway lines and the transporting of material, the organization of the maquis, the general strike.'[49]

The biggest protest took place in Grenoble in the Alps on 18 May in the early evening. Already the region in and around the city had witnessed the blocking of troop trains since mid-April organized by communists and new leftists, some operating under the banner of 'The Committee of Young People for a Peaceful Solution to the Problems of North Africa'. It was this group, supported by the local Communist Party, which called for a demonstration at 6.30 p.m. in front of the Grenoble station to stop a train that they believed contained departing soldiers, but was in actual fact the daily Grenoble to Chambéry stopping service. Two thousand protestors converged on the station and when they found this cordoned off by riot police there were violent clashes which lasted until midnight.[50] One of the organizers was Ezio Goy, a French communist of Italian parents whose father had fled the Fascist regime. Interviewed thirty-five years later, he remembered a confrontational atmosphere:

> I was near a barrier in front of two riot policemen, and one of them, just in front of me, hit the head of a worker who was cycling past with his carbine. Blood spurted out. That revolted me and, with a certain number of young people—I was twenty-four at the time—we ran onto the railway track. A train which had just left the station was coming towards us and it stopped in front of the demonstrators who were on the track.[51]

Across France these protests continued throughout May with further clashes at Angers, Antibes, Port-de-Bouc, Brive, Le Havre, and Voiron. Involving not just soldiers but ordinary civilians, in particular women, usually from the Communist Party-affiliated organization the Union des Femmes Françaises (UFF), the 'reservists' movement' produced seventy-six incidents in total, arguably the largest French anti-war protest throughout the eight-year conflict.[52] Why did it dissipate? One factor was logistical forethought. Trains ran at night. After Lyon they avoided the major towns of the Rhône Valley. At Marseille troops disembarked not at the main station, Saint Charles, but one away from the city centre, Arenc. These measures, backed up by the presence of riot police, made protest more difficult. They also ensured that they took place away from public view, a cover-up reinforced by the lack of coverage within the national newspapers. During April and May, only *Le Monde* and *L'Humanité* devoted in-depth articles to the 'reservists' movement'.[53] In the rest of the press it was ignored, principally out of patriotic support for the government.

Another factor was the absence of any organized political support. The Communist Party did not countenance desertion for fear that this would expose it to the threat of dissolution. Instead activists had to press for a ceasefire and negotiations. As Alfred Malleret-Joinville, a member of the central committee, explained in a party meeting in Tours in early May, when asked by a militant what should a party member say to reservists leaving for Algeria: 'This is a complicated question . . . After all we do not want Algeria to fall into the hands of a pro-American government.'[54] The party line was opposed to desertion, citing Lenin's dictum from World War One that all communists must go and fight, pursuing the class struggle from within the army. And in applying this line the PCF was very severe. In the case of Louis Orhant who deserted in Algeria in September 1956, the Communist Party expelled him. After returning incognito to explain his motivations, he was denounced to the police by his father, an old Communist Party member, and forced to flee France.[55]

The Communist Party line in 1956 left the reservists with no clear alternative to Lejeune's revolutionary patriotism. Consequently only a handful deserted, such as Jacques Berthelet, inspired by his father's anti-militarism as well as the example of the pacifist Romain Rolland who had denounced World War One with his 1914 pamphlet *Above the Melee* (*Au-dessus de la mêlée*).[56] Most went to Algeria, but without much enthusiasm. Anxious about what was awaiting them, they walked off gangplanks in Algiers and Oran still shouting 'Lynch Guy Mollet!', 'Lynch Lacoste!', 'Algerians to work!', and 'Vive la quille' (demobilization).[57] Of course some did feel a sense of mission. Some did feel a duty to live up to the preceding generations who had fought in the two world wars. In Georges Mattéi's case, conscious of having been too young for the Resistance, he wanted to test his manhood in battle. But for the most part the prevailing attitude was one of confusion, apathy, and resignation.[58]

Ultimately what diluted the rebellious mood was the war itself. Confronted with life-or-death situations, minds became focused, not least because in many cases the perpetrators of the reservists' revolt, earmarked by military intelligence, were sent to the fiercest combat zones. Indeed Jean Manin, a reservist at the forefront of protests, remembered one officer saying of the soldiers that refused to present arms or who let off the fire alarms in the barracks: 'Let them do that. When one of theirs has been killed, at that moment they will get down to making war.'[59]

In this respect the single most important event was the ambush of twenty-one young soldiers, all from Paris, at the Palestro gorge, 80 km south-east from Algiers on 18 May—the biggest single loss of life suffered by the French army since the conflict began and the same day as the anti-war protest in Grenoble. Palestro produced a sea-change in attitudes because of the defilement of the reservists' bodies which included castration, disembowelment, and the stuffing of ventral cavities with stones, facts seized upon by Lacoste who, helicoptered to Palestro, argued that the ambush and its aftermath showed 'what side was practising extermination'.[60] This violence—and its impact on the parents, wives, and fiancées of the dead men—was graphically reported in the French press.[61] It was also stressed in the localities back in France from which the men came, with the municipal council of Saint-Germain-en-Laye, just outside of Paris and home to three of the fallen soldiers, marking their memory with several minutes of silence. In underlining how they died 'in atrocious conditions', the council was emblematic of a wider emotional response which, in reinforcing the image of patriotic duty in the face of the 'FLN barbarism', effectively effaced the reservists' revolt.[62] On a more basic level, in the minds of some reservists the stories of mutilation instilled a basic desire for revenge, while those still harbouring anti-war sentiments knew that, if they were going to survive, they would have to be disciplined and fight like soldiers.

Just as importantly, Palestro solidified the traditional divide between home front and battle front. Families, mothers, fathers, brothers, sisters, but in particular newly married wives and first-time parents became anxious about the fate of their loved ones fighting in Algeria.[63] They felt protective of 'our men' over there. They listened to the news and scoured newspapers for clues to where they might be. They waited for letters that gave them hard news not speculation or rumour.

These emotional bonds were symbolized officially by the 'day of the soldier' on 26 September. They were obvious, too, in the visits organized by the *Écho d'Alger* so that a small number of wives could visit their husbands on duty in Algeria. Inevitably these bonds created a sense of 'us' and 'them', making those their men were fighting against, the FLN, into a clear and recognizable enemy. Spring 1956 was the point when the Algerian conflict became ingrained in French social consciousness. Algeria was no longer far away. Its names and places were part of everyday conversation. Even if the word was still withheld, France was a society at war.

The face of battle

Within the government and the Socialist Party, Mollet's intensification of the conflict produced great strains. Mendès France resigned as Minister without Portfolio on 23 May because, in his opinion, change was too slow.[64] Although he had supported the use of force, this was only one side of the equation. Equality was not being implemented:

> Now any policy which ignores the sentiments and the miseries of the native population leads, step by step, from the loss of the Algerian people to that of Algeria, and then, inevitably, to the loss of all of our Africa . . . In Algeria, if we want to save the French presence, we must bring onto our side the elements of

the population that for so long have shown confidence in France in order to ensure their gradual emancipation.[65]

Anger at 'pacification first' was also voiced at the SFIO party conference in Lille from 29 June to 3 July. Daniel Mayer and André Philip called for a ceasefire and the opening of negotiations, while the final resolution on Algeria, a compromise designed to preserve unity, stressed that pacification was war on two fronts: against terrorism *and* colonial privilege.

This opposition was directed at Lacoste and Lejeune who, in the search for military success, were ensuring that repression took precedence over reform. Lejeune in particular continually castigated the generals. He wanted them to turn the situation on its head, transforming the FLN from the hunters into the hunted.[66] This desire to tighten the chase and to deprive the guerrillas of any safe havens was the logic behind the recall of the reservists. In protecting the population and guarding key strategic points, Lejeune reasoned, they would free up the paratroopers who could then pursue and finish off the ALN, measures backed up by the deployment of tracker dogs and the raising of Muslim anti-FLN militias who, through their local knowledge, would be the eyes and ears of the counter-insurgency.

Following on from 'Operation Valmy', the first huge pacification sweep, covered in detail by the French press, was entitled 'Hope'.[67] In theory, the aim was to defeat the ALN by winning the allegiance of the population. In practice, this subtle strategy was harder to carry out. The situation was complicated. The army was not just fighting the ALN, but also the MNA and a communist maquis in the Ouarsenis in the west entitled the Combattants de la Libération (CDL), bolstered by the desertion on 4 April 1956 of a 28-year-old settler, communist Henri Maillot, who brought with him grenades, ammunition, and over 200 automatic weapons.[68] Unlike World War One, there was no vivid distinction between home and battle fronts. The fighting was everywhere, the enemy invisible and elusive. In this context, nerves frayed by thirst and physical exhaustion, it was all too easy to forget the finer points of 'pacification' and see all Algerians as one amorphous mass, actively or complicitly supporting the insurgency—a conclusion undoubtedly bolstered by reservist ignorance. Most of the reservists had little knowledge of Algeria beyond the basic information booklets they had been given on arrival.[69] Few could speak Arabic or Berber and this communication problem created an inevitable gulf. Moreover, as one reservist, Robert Bonnaud, remembered, the other men in his unit found it hard to identify with a Muslim way of life that forbade alcohol and the eating of ham.[70]

Certainly reservist and conscript letters testified to this brutal 'us' and 'them' truth. Written to their loved ones during the long bouts of lassitude and boredom which punctuated the fighting, these letters did not hold back. In the case of a set of letters sent to Roman Catholic priests, subsequently published in early 1957, the words took the form of a confession.[71] Ignoring army strictures to tone down their language, these letters confided in detail the horror of the war.[72] There was fear and anxiety. As one soldier explained: 'The nights on guard duty are hard: apprehension, cold, fatigue. The worried men distrust any sound and often fire indiscriminately on a shadow, a cow or a donkey.'[73]

Then there was the disgust at what they were being ordered to do. Burning down villages, summary executions, torture: these methods were systemic. One letter quoted a corporal from the Foreign Legion who, explicitly seeing the parallel with Oradour-sur-Glane when, on 10 June 1944, the SS 'Das Reich' division killed all 643 villagers as revenge for Resistance in the region, admitted: 'If one day there was a new Nuremberg trial, we will all be guilty: Oradours, we are carrying them out every day.'[74]

A further letter described the different types of torture used to make people talk.[75] One technique, the 'swimming pool', involved four soldiers in the pool with a prisoner who would be forced to drink cups of water before being put in a refrigerator at -10 °C. Another, the 'country tele-phone', consisted of fixing electrodes to the captives and then winding up the dynamo until volts of electricity shot through their body. Another, still, consisted of beating the prisoner's feet raw and then placing them in cold water. Theoretically these practices were forbidden, but, as one reservist explained, the army developed elaborate strategies of concealment.[76] Sol-diers took care to ensure that torture did not leave too many visible traces. Alternatively reports of the enemy killed in combat were inflated so that prisoners could be tortured and then shot on the following day.

In the Kabyle mountains, Georges Mattéi's war experience was framed by his personal memory of the Resistance. Growing up in Burgundy with his uncle, a communist Resister, he had witnessed villages being burnt down by the Nazis. Now, to his horror, he and his unit were doing exactly the same. One day he was policing a roadblock on the outskirts of a village with two other soldiers:

> We had taken some prisoners that day. There were some women we penned up to the right of the village, and then some men on the left because the previous day, there'd been an ambush outside the village. So there was the standard clamp-down on the village so that the Resistance—note that I use the word 'Resistance'—would lose popular support. This old bloke came up to me and our lads started bawling abuse at him. I leapt to the old bloke's defence out of simple respect for old folk, and because he looked like my grandfather . . . And the old bloke said to me: 'Come on, see if you can see my son.' I had a look and then said: 'He's not there.' And we had killed him. There had been some executions and some attempts to escape. The old bloke said to me: 'Here you are, I brought this for him.' I felt sick, really sick. The bloke had given me two eggs and a little round loaf. Bloody hell, that knocked me sideways.[77]

Within the reservist letters and Mattéi's testimony there is one overriding emotion: shame. Others took pleasure in killing, however. In Jean Martin's letters, peppered with racism and anti-communism, he described his visceral excitement at war.[78] Fighting on the Moroccan border, he felt an adrenalin rush during close hand-to-hand combat, even if these moments of intensity were interspersed with long lulls of inactivity. He has no moral qualms about the methods being used to fight the FLN: 'We never bury their dead . . . We leave the bodies as an example to the local inhabitants.'[79]

If Martin's violent machismo was one face of battle, other reservists did endeavour to carry out a humanitarian mission. They took pride in what they did. They did not torture. They were not racist. They did connect with the Muslim population, building roads, providing medical care, and teaching in schools. Jean-Claude Kerspern, for instance, was a sergeant with the colonial infantry in Kabylia:

> In the village where our unit was stationed, I know numerous examples of comrades who gave the best of themselves in the service of Muslims. There was not on our part any pitying condescension, but a feeling of equality in the face of the human qualities of the Kabyles and the intuition of accomplishing a social service. I am convinced that all those amongst us who carried out the work of pacification . . . acquired a more complete notion of their social duties. On their return, many continued to have a great interest in Algeria.[80]

Such perspectives were a reality. They must balance those of contrition and guilt. However, the longer the war went on, the more impossible it became to disentangle these images from those of violent repression which, in the

last analysis, played into the guerrillas' hands because it united the population behind the FLN.

Throughout the summer and autumn of 1956 and into spring 1957 the
ALN offensive in the rural interior intensified, climaxing with 1,000 operations a week in February 1957.[81] Part of the reservist force was deployed to
roll back this offensive and became involved in heavy fighting in Kabylia
and around Souk-Ahras near to the Tunisian border. Others were used to
protect train lines and stations which were subjected to 957 FLN attacks in
the three years after 1 November 1954, while the rest were dispersed across
the country to man rural checkpoints, carry out 'stop and search' operations,
and build links with the Muslim population.

Away from military operations these French troops lived in barracks, life
on a collective scale that was documented by the soldiers themselves with
their cheap Kodak cameras. In this tightly controlled environment the men,
sleeping in tents or makeshift huts, had little privacy. It was a very macho
culture. Walls and lockers were adorned with sexually suggestive pictures of
young women. Relief from the stress and boredom was to be found in hard
drinking, masturbation, and visits to specially organized military brothels.[82]
This atmosphere gave rise to a specific war culture where Arab words, like
mektoub (fate), *kif-kif* (same old thing), and *fissa* (quick), intermingled with
anti-Algerian prejudice and resentment at military authority. In this context
the cult object par excellence was the wooden skittle (*quille*) on which
soldiers notched where and when they fought as a method of counting
down the time to their demobilization. These skittles were a measure of
apathy. Many reservists and conscripts did not feel any identification with
Mollet's 'pacification'. They just wanted to get back to France alive which is
why many reservists felt that they had been betrayed, and then exploited, by
the Republican Front government—an anti-politician resentment that was
also prevalent in letters.[83] On hearing in June 1957 that Mollet's extension
of military service to two years was to be kept in place, one conscript sent an
angry letter to the editor of *Le Bled*, the army newspaper:

> [All my comrades] have done the duty that was theirs to do by the nation.
> Sometimes they may have grumbled a bit, but THEY HAVE NEVER
> SHIRKED. They were full of hope that, finally, they'd be able to return to
> their homes in order to enjoy a well-earned rest. Only now I find, and I am
> not the only one to find this, that we are being TREATED LIKE FOOLS a
> little more every day.[84]

It was a telling letter, one not published by *Le Bled*, whose emotional content revealed a decisive factor in the unfolding conflict: the feelings of ordinary reservists and conscripts who, like their families, could only wonder how long French politicians expected them to fight in Algeria.

FLN response

The socialist government of Guy MOLLET has just been granted 'The Special Powers' from the French Parliament to carry out a total war on Algerians. Let us note in passing that the friends of MAURICE THOREZ gave their support to 'Comrade' MOLLET. Also, the slogan, dear to Algerian Communists, of their solidarity of the working class with peoples fighting for independence has been exposed, once again, as being a myth . . .

Reports are coming in to us from all corners of Algeria signalling that a ferocious and blind repression is raining down on our people (lynchings, rapes, summary executions of men, old people, women and children . . .).

It is in these conditions that Monsieur Guy MOLLET asks us to lay down our arms. He promises on the other hand 'free elections' in three months.

The FLN, the mouthpiece of the ALN, responds to the head of the French Government that we have not taken up arms in order for free elections in Algeria, but in order that our Country recovers it independence and liberty.

[Tract distributed in the Chélif Valley in the days following the special powers vote on 12 March 1956][85]

This dismissal of Mollet's proposed elections was the legacy of twenty years of disappointments. Once again, the disjuncture between promise and reality showed that neither the Socialists nor the Communists could be trusted. Their principles might have a noble ring, but in practice, the FLN argued, the issuing of the special powers was a declaration of total war.

For Abbane and the internal leadership it was imperative that the FLN responded in kind. It had to initiate its own mass mobilization that would both withstand the troop surge and further confirm the FLN as the sole representative of the Algerian people. In April Muslims were ordered to stop buying cigarettes and alcohol in order to hurt the colonial economy. They were also instructed to shun the cinema or theatre.[86] In May 1956 tracts called on students and secondary-school pupils to strike, while others ordered Muslim men to ignore the reservist draft. Algerian football teams were also told to withdraw from all cup and league fixtures. Then, in September, the FLN told Muslim families to boycott the return to school.

Collectively these measures made absence into a statement. They demonstrated that Muslim loyalties lay with the FLN and not the Republican Front's nation in arms. But in galvanizing the people in this manner the FLN used intimidation as well as appeals to patriotism, Islam, and the enduring sense of humiliation. Those Muslims who rejected the FLN's authority became the targets of horrendous violence, as on the night of 13–14 April 1956 when Colonel Amirouche, leader of Wilaya 3, ordered the destruction of a reticent population in Ihadjadjen in the Lower Soummam in Kabylia, slitting the throats of several hundred as a warning to others.

Whatever the morality of the FLN's methods, what could not be denied was their success. In numerical terms this was the ALN's high point on the ground. 'To take to the maquis' became a common phrase and by the end of 1956 there were 20,000 armed guerrillas supported by approximately 40,000 auxiliaries. Whole swathes of the country, in Kabylia and in the north of the Constantine department, fell under the ALN's control, a counter-society that was strengthened still further by the establishment of a radio station, Voice of Combatant Algeria; a clandestine newspaper, El-Moudjahid; and independent trade union and student organizations.[87]

The flow of new recruits produced tensions within the ALN. Many were students and there was a good deal of suspicion between them—urban, educated, more middle class—and the older guerrillas—rural, conservative and, in many cases, illiterate. This was particularly acute in respect to the influx of women such as Nefissa Hamoud, the first female doctor in the maquis. By bringing women into the public realm, her presence, along with others like Mériem Belmihoub and Mimi Ben Mohand, challenged the established norms within Algerian society.[88] For this reason these women maquisardes, 1,744 according to official Algerian statistics after the conflict, were kept away from bearing arms, nor were they given any senior positions of command.[89] They were allotted clearly defined roles that reflected the traditional gender divides. Some, who were qualified, worked as doctors and nurses; others acted as liaison agents or transported messages and mail.

In 1957 and 1958 a series of directives ordered these women to be taken out of the maquis and transferred to bases in Morocco and Tunisia—a measure of the way in which some male maquis leaders, anxious to avoid sexual contact between young men and women in their ranks, were unhappy at a female presence.[90] In January 1957 Wilaya 2 in north-eastern Algeria decreed that it was 'forbidden for women nurses to frequent and sleep in the middle of male fighters. They must only mix with civilians and

Figure 6.5 FLN officer talking to a small boy in a secret FLN hiding place in 1957; the boy has the Qu'ran written on a wooden board.

Figure 6.6 Algerian women in the maquis.

then only women.'[91] This segregation was taken to an even more extreme level by Wilaya 2 on 17 December 1958:

> We reiterate once again that it is forbidden for all women to join our ranks; if they join our ranks, they must be sent back to the start of their destination even if the enemy apprehends them. Those men who accompany these women must be punished with the death penalty.[92]

These orders were echoed by Commander Si Allal in Wilaya 5 on 2 November 1960:

> I tell you one last time that it is forbidden to recruit female fighters [djoundiates] and nurses without the Zone's authorization. In independent Algeria, the freedom of Muslim women stops at the step of the door. A woman will never be the equal of a man.[93]

However, it is important to stress that these directives were not always put into practice. Women did remain in the maquis, unaware of the orders to remove them.[94] As a combatant with Wilaya 2, Farida Belguembour fought in the maquis right until the end of the war where, she underlined, she was always treated as an equal by the men, while the French army files list Malika Hamdani and Fatima Naimi, both from Wilaya 2, as being killed in action at the end 1961—three years after the Wilaya 2 ban on women. Furthermore, as one of the officers in Wilaya 2, Colonel Ali Kafi made a distinction between 'educated women' and 'rural women'.[95] For him the former, as nurses or combatants, were few in number, while the latter played an 'essential role'.[96] Rural women, according to Kafi, provided the basic structures—food, cooking, clothing—which were the lifeblood of the maquis: 'Without them, the revolution would not have endured. They occupied themselves with the moudjahidines night and day. They washed clothing, cooked and constantly worked to cover up any trace of their presence.'[97]

The rules governing women show how maquis life was very strict. All guerrillas had to obey orders without hesitation. They could be executed for murder, desertion, defeatism, dissent, betrayal, disobedience, rape, and negligence.[98] Through such strictures the different zones sought to maintain purpose and momentum because they knew that set-piece battles had to be avoided. Rather, the ALN had to make up for the asymmetry of forces through secrecy, speed, and surprise. By being like a 'mosquito in the night' the ALN had to continue to wear down their adversaries through destruction and harassment.[99]

Secret contacts

In public the language of the Republican Front and the FLN was bellicose. Both called the other intransigent. Both blamed the other for the bloodshed. But in secret there were contacts. These resulted from the Foreign Minister Christian Pineau's visit to Nasser in March when feelers were put out to the FLN external delegation in Cairo.

What followed was an initial meeting in Cairo on 12 April 1956 between Joseph Begarra, the leading Socialist Party figure in Oran, and Mohammed Khider, one of the leaders of the exterior delegation. On the FLN side Khider immediately reported back to Ben Bella and Lamine Debaghine, while Guy Mollet was kept informed via Georges Gorse, former ambassador to Egypt. We must be absolutely clear, therefore, that these contacts never had the status of official negotiations. They were discussions about discussions between the higher echelons of the Socialist Party and the FLN.

Right from the start there was ample scope for confusion, misunderstanding, and breakdown because each was teasing out the other's limits of what was acceptable. Initially the gap seemed too great. Begarra restated the triptych of ceasefire, elections, and negotiations, while Khider reiterated Algeria's right to independence. The next day, though, Khider seemed to shift. He wanted Begarra to be more precise about what Mollet meant by recognizing the 'Algerian personality'. Begarra explained that this would involve a large measure of internal autonomy. Khider's response, implying that there was some flexibility on the FLN's part, led Begarra to become momentarily excited. On 20 April Begarra believed that he was close to an agreement, leading Mollet to even announce publicly the possibility of a ceasefire. However, on 24 April Khider retracted, saying that this was him speaking in a personal capacity. He then broached the idea that the external delegation should come to Algeria under French protection for negotiations, a scenario Begarra was willing to discuss but which Mollet rejected because he did not want to endow the exterior delegation with political legitimacy.

The fact that no agreement was reached demonstrated how delicate the whole process was. Begarra himself was bitterly disappointed. It made him cynical about the exterior delegation's motives for dialogue. In his view this was not about peace but the power struggle within the FLN. They wanted to ensure that the externals won over the internals as the representatives of the FLN. Nonetheless the channels of communication continued. This time the baton was taken up by Pierre Commin, the Socialist Party general secretary, in July in Belgrade, followed by September in Rome and then Belgrade again in October.

That these contacts should continue as the war intensified was not contradictory. From Ireland to South Africa recent history is full of governments who opened channels of communication with organizations they publicly vilified as 'terrorists'. In the specific case of the Republican Front, policy was always premised on the fact that eventually the conflict would end and round-table discussions begin. However, Mollet always wanted to negotiate from a position of strength, a political logic which all subsequent governments would adhere to right up to the end of the conflict in 1962.

Soummam Conference

On 19 September a special edition of *El-Moudjahid* reported on a meeting of the FLN internal leadership in the valley of the Soummam, not far from Akbou in Kabylia, on 20 August, one year exactly after the Constantine uprising. Bringing together leading figures such as Larbi Ben M'Hidi, Omar Ouamrane, Belkacem Krim, Zighoud Youssef, Ben Tobbal, and Abbane Ramdane, the fact that this took place in Algeria under the noses of the French army was a major statement in itself about the FLN's strength on the ground.

Abbane had first broached the need for such a meeting in a secret letter to the Cairo delegation on 3 April.[100] Describing the magnitude of the Republican Front's war effort, Abbane said that the threat of defeat was real. Confronted with French reinforcements and their adaptation to counter-insurgency, some guerrillas, starved of ammunition, were putting down their weapons and returning to their homes. Even more alarmingly in certain regions the people were turning against the maquis and asking for army protection. Given this dire situation, Abbane argued, there was no alternative but to organize a conference that would establish, in a final and definitive manner, the FLN's political dominance. Furthermore, this conference had to take place inside the country, even if the risk of capture was enormous, because this would demonstrate the FLN's legitimacy within Algerian society. It would prove that the organization was neither controlled by Nasser nor reliant on Tunisia or Morocco, but rooted in the people.

The preparation was done by Abbane who played on the political and personal networks that he had built up over the preceding eighteen months. Working in conjunction with Larbi Ben M'Hidi, he skilfully exploited the maquis leaders' resentments towards the exterior delegation. By accusing them of being out of touch with the reality on the ground, Abbane ensured Cairo's marginalization within the Soummam proceedings. Thus dominant, he was able to enshrine two basic organizational principles: the primacy of the civil over the military and the interior over the exterior.[101]

After twenty days of heated discussions the resultant document, stretching to a formidable forty pages, dealt with all aspects of the FLN struggle.[102] First and foremost, the platform projected the image of a people united behind the FLN in the battle for national independence—a model of a centralized power analogous to the Jacobin state pioneered by the French Revolution. All aspects of society were covered, from the specific role of the peasantry through to that of women and students. In this respect the image was much more secular. Less accent was placed on Islam and the nation was not defined in terms of ethnicity or religion. The Algeria of the future, it was stressed, had a place for Jews and Europeans. No less significantly, Nasser's role was downplayed in favour of an unashamedly Algerian perspective.

Such a tone revealed the influence of Amar Ouzegane who, although expelled from the PCA in 1948, had retained a more secular and more Marxist outlook. Specifically, Ouzegane endowed the FLN with precise political structures, the outlines of an embryonic nation state. At the summit was the Comité de Coordination et d'Exécution (CCE), a clandestine government, which, residing in Algiers, was composed of Abbane, Ben M'Hidi, and Krim along with two ex-centralists, Benyoucef Ben Khedda and Saad Dahlalb. Eclipsing the original 1 November 1954 progenitors as a decision-making body this was complemented by a nascent parliament, the Conseil National de la Révolution Algérienne (CNRA). Made up of thirty-four members, including Ben Bella, Boudiaf, Khider, and Debahine from the Cairo delegation; Abbas from UDMA; and Tawfiq El Madani from the Ulema, the CNRA had the power to open negotiations and announce a ceasefire on the basis of three clearly enunciated conditions: recognition of the existence of the Algerian nation, acceptance of independence, and the release of all political prisoners.

In terms of the armed struggle, Soummam established the civil structures that would govern the military, appointing political commissaries to organize the population, advising on military strategy, and putting in place people's assemblies: a counter-state replacing French law and authority. The army itself was then divided into six zones (*wilayas*), themselves each made up of sub-zones (*mintaqa*), regions (*nahia*), and sectors (*kism*). Algiers meanwhile was made into an autonomous zone. In terms of fighting units the ALN was based on the principles of a strict military hierarchy comprising battalions of 350 men (*failek*) followed by companies of 100 men (*katiba*), sections of 35 men (*ferka*), and groups of 11 men (*fawj*). Officer grades, replicating those of the French army, went from lieutenant, through to captain and commander, before stopping at colonel, the ALN's most senior post.

Soummam also defined the rules of engagement. Guerrillas were ordered not to cut throats or mutilate bodies. Instead in the future those sentenced to death would be shot. Nor were they to execute prisoners. Finally, and most importantly, Soummam produced a clear set of war aims: recognition of Algerian independence and the FLN as sole representative of the nation. In contrast, the Republican Front's third way never had this clarity. It could never find a solution to match the FLN's uncomplicated call for the right to national self-determination.

Although the Soummam Platform was transmitted down through the FLN via tracts and the clandestine press, it was immediately contested by Ben Bella. Frustrated by the fact that he had been unable to attend in person, he challenged the whole basis of the document. He wanted to hold on to the legitimacy of the architects of the 1 November Declaration. He wished to reassert the power of the exterior delegation and the military over the political arrivistes who, he claimed, in a bid to further their personal ambitions had deliberately marginalized Islam and the role of Nasser in favour of a greater place for Europeans and Jews.

Such anger was testament to the inescapable fact that Soumman was a crowning achievement for Abbane. The climax of the previous eighteen months, Soummam united all the major political parties—a feat not achieved in the years 1946 to 1954. This unification was done on the FLN's terms. The structures established by Soummam did not conceive of the FLN as a federation of political parties. Thus, in respect to the Algerian Communist Party a secret agreement led to the dissolution of the communist maquis on 1 July. Under this communist guerrillas were allowed to join the FLN on an individual basis, with the Communist Party, although continuing to exist as a separate organization, accepting the FLN's dominance of the political and military field. The major exception continued to

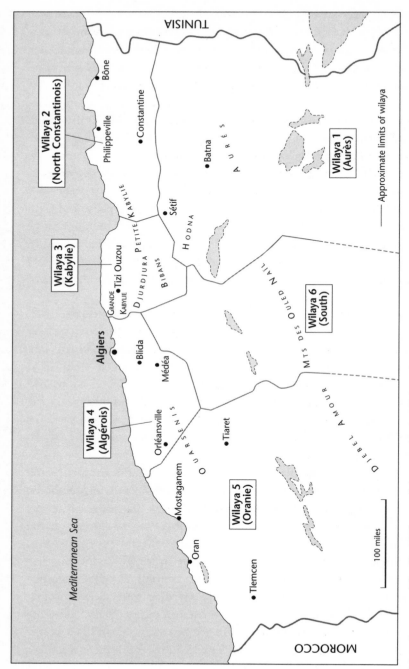

Map 6.1 1956: The Six Wilayas of the Armée de Libération Nationale (ALN).

be Messali's MNA, which the Soummam Platform now vowed to liquidate in the coming months, leading to the deaths of thousands in Kabylia.

Urban violence and counter-violence

Throughout the summer of 1956 the Minister-Resident Lacoste was upbeat. The revolt, he continually claimed, was on its last legs. Yet, such optimism flew in the face of reality. Algeria became locked into a cycle of violence and counter-violence that now extended from the rural interior to Algiers itself.

It was an ugly spiral where one issue dominated all others: whether the government should guillotine the 253 FLN prisoners on death row. The settler press had been clamouring for this all spring. Accusing Paris of weakness, they wanted revenge. At government level the issue had already been discussed in a cabinet meeting on 15 February, giving rise to tensions that were documented by Champeix in a seven-page hand-written note that now resides in the Socialist Party Archive.[103] Within the exchanges Defferre, Mendès France, and Savary were against any executions, while Lacoste, Lejeune, Bourgès-Maunoury, and Mitterrand were in favour, their argument being that the army could not understand why the death sentences, having gone through a court process, were not being carried out. Mollet himself was much more reluctant. He did not want to transform the FLN prisoners into martyrs. But in the end he gave way, partly because he wanted to send a strong message after the failure of the secret contacts.

On 19 June the first FLN prisoners, Ahmed Zabana and Abdelkader Ferradj, were guillotined in the early hours of the morning at Barberousse prison in Algiers and Abdelkader Ben Moussa on 19 June. For the FLN this was a declaration of war. FLN operatives were already primed to respond to the executions with immediate reprisals with orders to 'Kill any European between the age of 18 and 54 years. No women, no children, no old people.'[104] On each corpse they were instructed to leave a noting stating 'Brother Zabana you have been avenged' and between 20 and 24 June the FLN carried out twenty-one attacks in Algiers, leaving ten dead.

Law and order had broken down in the capital. Angry at this FLN violence, shadowy elements in the police, linked to the underground organizations created by André Achiary in the run-up to the 6 February demonstration, took matters into their own hands. On the night of 10 August they planted a bomb in the middle of the densely populated Casbah at rue de Thèbes. The

Figure 6.7 Guy Mollet, the head of the Republican Front government, flanked on his right by François Mitterrand, the Justice Minister, and on his left by Maurice Bourgès-Maunoury, the Defence Minister, September 1956.

explosion demolished several residential buildings and killed up to seventy people, creating a climate of violence which was fuelled by daily rumours of an imminent 'committee of public safety' to defend French Algeria.

In retaliation the FLN, wishing to demonstrate to the world its hold over the population, launched its own campaign of indiscriminate, urban violence, transforming Algiers into a major point of confrontation. On 30 September the FLN, using women operatives, who passed themselves off as French women to get through the army checkpoints, exploded bombs at two crowded cafés in the city centre, the Milk Bar and the Cafeteria, killing four and wounding fifty-two. It was a major propaganda victory. The fact that the FLN was able to strike with such impunity seemed to demonstrate to the world's media that the FLN was winning.

Suez and Hungary

On 26 July 1956 Nasser proclaimed the nationalization of the Suez Canal to an ecstatic crowd in Alexandria. Coming seven days after the US, displeased by Nasser's increasingly anti-Western tone, had broken off talks about the financing of the Aswan High Dam on the Nile, this action symbolized Egypt's independence from the West and was supported by India and Yugoslavia.[105] Henceforth, he explained, the Canal would no longer be administered from Paris by the Suez Canal Company. It would be run by Egyptians and the revenues used to finance the country's modernization, a provocative snub to Britain and France that enhanced his status as the beacon for Arab nationalism in the region.

Within the Mollet government this was seen as a further act of aggression which tilted Egypt towards the Soviet camp. It confirmed their belief that pan-Arab nationalism and communism were ideological allies in a global struggle against French, and, ultimately, Western civilization, making the appeasement analogy more relevant than ever. There must be no repeat of Munich 1938. Within Marcel Champeix's notes, scribbled during cabinet meetings in July and August, the hardening of perspectives was unmistakeable. Mitterrand talked of the need to 'liquidate Nasser'.[106] Lacoste meanwhile claimed that 'one division in Egypt is worth four in Algeria'.

Outwardly Mollet and the British Conservative Prime Minister Eden said they wished to resolve the crisis through peaceful channels. With the US they agreed to put a plan to Nasser, duly rejected, but also tried to work through the United Nations. In private neither wanted a diplomatic solution. Impatient for military action, they saw the UN's structures as too cumbersome. Consequently, as the talking went on, the British and French military drew up a plan of attack, 'Operation Musketeer', while France increased arms supplies to Israel.

From the French point of view the operation was given a final and conclusive logic by the discovery on 16 October of a cargo ship from Egypt with weapons destined for the FLN. Five days later the timetable for war was finalized at top-secret negotiations at Sèvres just south of Paris. There it was agreed that on 29 October Israel would attack the Egyptian army in Sinai, pressing forward to occupy the whole of the peninsula up to the western edge of the Canal. On the 30th the British and French, presenting themselves as the voice of the international community, would then issue an ultimatum to *both* sides calling on them to withdraw from the Canal zone to their original positions. This would then give the waiting Anglo-French force the pretext to attack Egypt, seize back control of the Canal and fatally damage Nasser.

It was organized mendacity on a grand scale which initially went according to plan. The Israelis attacked, ignoring a UN call for a ceasefire, and by 5 November the first British and French troops had landed in Egypt. At this point, however, the threads began to unravel. In the White House the newly re-elected President Dwight Eisenhower was furious at the deception. By running counter to his plan to construct an anti-communist alliance within the Middle East and North Africa, they had put their own national interests above those of the NATO alliance. In reply, Eisenhower refused to guarantee the supply of US petrol to replenish that of the Gulf, lost through the Canal's closure, and allowed a run on sterling to develop—two economic batons that forced Eden to give way on 6 November, followed by Mollet shortly after.

Britain and France withdrew from the Canal Zone in December in humiliation, while on the 'Arab street', including most significantly of all in Algeria, the words 'Nasser' and 'Egypt' gleamed and soared. Moreover, in cold-war terms Suez handed a propaganda victory to the Soviet Union who, in delivering an ultimatum to Paris and London on 5 November, cast itself as a defender of Arab rights. Worse still, with the world's attention momentarily diverted, Suez provided the Soviet Union with a unique opportunity to crush the Hungarian revolution and reimpose a pro-Moscow regime in Budapest.

The sight of the Red Army on the streets of Budapest was a powerful reassertion of cold war which, unleashing a wave of anti-communist demonstrations in France, continued to be fundamental to the Republican Front's perception of the Algerian War. For Mollet's government, Algeria and Hungary were intertwined. Communist repression in Budapest was mirrored by what was seen as communist-controlled terrorism in Algiers, a conclusion confirmed by the arrest of an Algerian Communist Party member, Fernand Iveton, for planting a bomb in a factory in November.[107]

Figure 6.8 'The Communists throw away the mask': a government poster portraying Soviet repression in Hungary and the FLN struggle as two faces of the same international communist plot against France.

22 October

In the midst of the build-up to Suez, secret talks continued between the Socialist Party and the FLN. There were meetings in Belgrade followed by a further one in Rome. Added to this, another channel developed via Alain Savary, Minister of Moroccan and Tunisian Affairs, and his personal contacts with Bourguiba and King Mohammed V of Morocco who, desperate to stem the bloodshed, hoped to resolve the Algerian question within a broader North African framework. With this end in mind they organized a round-table conference in Tunis. Inviting the FLN's external leadership, both wished to explore the possibility of a Maghreb Commonwealth which, in bringing together Algeria, Tunisia, Morocco, and the Sahara, would be the basis of a new cooperative, post-colonial relationship with France.

On 22 October Ben Bella, Boudiaf, Aït Ahmed, Khider, and the Algerian intellectual Mostefa Lacheraf, after lengthy discussions with Mohammed V, took a DC 3 Air Atlas flight from Rabat to Tunis for the conference. However, the same morning, Air Marshal Frandon, head of the French Air Force in North Africa, learnt from French intelligence that the DC 3 would be flying over Algerian air space. At this point Frandon, acting on his own initiative and without prior government approval, took an audacious step. He decided to intercept the plane, thus presenting the cabinet with a fait accompli which, he believed, would decapitate the FLN rebellion.

The first minister to be informed of the plan was Lejeune who, willing to cover the military, told General Lorillot, the French Commander-in-Chief in Algeria, by telephone: 'It must be forced to land in Algeria . . . It is passing through French air space, for the sky of Algeria, it is the sky of France.'[108]

Contacting the plane's French pilot, Air Marshal Frandon convinced him of the necessity to change destination. Thus, at 4.00 p.m. the DC 3 landed not in Tunis but in Algiers where the five FLN passengers were immediately arrested, the first airline hijack in history.

When Mollet was told what had happened that evening he was furious that the military had deliberately ignored the government. However, with the Suez operation about to be launched, he had little option but to back the army. Within the cabinet Savary resigned, while Bourgès-Maunoury and Lacoste defended the action on legal grounds, even if they were not party to it. As a fugitive from justice, they argued, the army had a duty to arrest Ben Bella.

For this reason 22 October pleased the hardliners on both sides. Within the government, the hawks—Bourgès-Maunoury, Lacoste, and Lejeune—knew that this would finally destroy the contacts between the FLN and the Socialist Party. Within the FLN, the guerrillas, in particular in Wilaya 2, were gleeful because by eliminating the external delegation from the internal power struggle, and by burying the possibility of a compromise within a wider North African context, the hijacking left the internal resistance dominant.

Consequently, 22 October poses an intriguing counter-factual scenario. What if the contacts had continued and what if the Tunis Conference had gone ahead? Could a peaceful solution have been found? To envisage this scenario ignores three other fundamental factors in the equation. First, these contacts never had the status of official negotiations and anyway, as Lejeune's actions showed, there were deep divisions within the government over them. Secondly, there was no unanimity on the FLN side since these contacts were a major point of contention in the power struggle between Abbane and the Cairo delegation. Thirdly, it is unlikely that the army, already resentful at being 'sold out' over Indochina, let alone the settlers, would have accepted such a proposal, thereby raising the spectre of a another 6 February revolt except this time one supported by the military.

The balance sheet of 1956

Reaching back to the comic tradition of the seventeenth century, Ray Ventura's 1932 'Tout va très bien, Madame la Marquise' was one of the great popular songs of the early days of gramophone and radio. Like Molière, the humour was to be found in the voice of the servants. Speaking down the telephone, they tell the horrified Marquise of the ever-escalating disasters that include the death of her husband and destruction of the chateau, punctuating each event with the ironic refrain: 'Apart from that, everything is fine.'

In portraying Robert Lacoste playing 'Tout va très bien, Monsieur le Président' down the telephone to Mollet, the cartoon in L'Express was a wry satirical comment on 1956 (Figure 6.9). The song was shorthand for the contrast between the Republican Front's rolling rhetoric and the cruel reality because, whatever Lacoste might say, Algeria was not fine. In the wake of 6 February Mollet had promised a new Algeria based on reconcili-

Figure 6.9 Cartoon from the weekly political magazine *L'Express*, which has Robert Lacoste playing 'Tout va très bien, Monsieur le Prèsident' down the telephone to Mollet, satirizing Lacoste's claim that the conflict in Algeria was nearly won, 12 October 1956.

ation. He had justified the special powers and the recall of the reservists as necessary methods that would re-establish peace in the space of months. In actual fact neither reconciliation nor peace had been achieved. By the end of 1956, they seemed further away than ever as war, with all its attendant pain and suffering, became entrenched.

7

The 'Battle of Algiers' and its Aftermath: January 1957 to May 1958

Monday, 7 January 1957

A t exactly 7.00 a.m. Robert Lacoste handed over police powers to General Massu. His mission: to restore law and order to the capital. The fact that Lacoste had to resort to the army was a measure of just how far Algiers was out of control by the end of 1956. At regular intervals between October and December FLN bombs exploded in the European parts of the city along the rue d'Isly and the rue Michelet. Fuelled by an anger at the continual guillotining of nationalists, these bombs produced a volatile atmosphere. Tension was everywhere. Europeans felt afraid. They avoided public places. They began to see all Muslims as automatically suspect. On 7 January alone six attacks across Algiers, including one on an army check-point, resulted in eight deaths.[1]

At any moment this fear could tip over into anti-Algerian violence and, when on 28 December 1956 Amédée Froger, mayor of Boufarik and a living symbol of French Algeria, was assassinated in broad daylight by an FLN gunman, European rage was palpable. At the funeral on the next day groups of young Europeans, some armed with revolvers and machine guns, broke off from the procession to vent their anger on any passing Algerians, leaving eight dead and forty-eight injured. In front of the Majestic cinema one Muslim, who supposedly made an obscene gesture towards the mourners, was chased through the streets and beaten to death.

Faced with these scenes of unending violence, stretching police resources to the limit, Lacoste told his approving government colleagues at the cabinet

Figure 7.1 General Jacques Massu, commander of the 10th Parachute Division.

meeting on 4 January that he had no choice. He had to transfer their powers
to Massu because, with Algeria tabled to be discussed at the UN in early
1957, the FLN was, more than ever, determined to present itself to the
world as the sole and legitimate spokesperson for the Algerian people. This
explained the relentless surge in FLN attacks during 1956 which rose from
60 in July to 122 in December.[2] It also explained why Radio Free Algeria
and FLN tracts were talking of a general strike in January that would put
Algeria in the world's spotlight. In short, Lacoste continued, the final
moment of truth had arrived. This was not a time to be weak, he argued.
The government had to be even stronger. If it was to prevent defeat, it had

to be every bit as ruthless as the FLN, which is why Lacoste and his colleagues had no qualms about giving away further power to the military, even if it represented a further ebbing away of civil authority.

In giving this task to Massu, the army was entering a complex terrain where it confronted not just the FLN and the MNA, but also an insurrectionary mood amongst hard-line Europeans in Algiers such as Lagaillarde, Ortiz, and Achiary. They opposed Lacoste's reforms on 11 December 1956 that dissolved the existing local councils and opened the way to equal Muslim representation. They opposed his crack-down on European extremism that led to the banning of the ORAF, the moving force behind the 6 February demonstration. They were also at the forefront of the Froger funeral that had ended with the crowds shouting 'Lynch Mollet', 'Lynch Lacoste' and, in an effort to make common cause with the military, 'army in power'. Then finally it was murky elements within the ORAF that tried to kill the new commander-in-chief General Raoul Salan.

Joining the army at the age of seventeen when he fought in the final battles of World War One, the now robust, white-haired Salan arrived in December 1956 with a long military career behind him. Serving throughout the French Empire during the 1920s and 1930s, he adroitly navigated the political and military complexities of World War Two, fighting in June 1940, remaining loyal to the Vichy regime while stationed in French West Africa, before leading the 6th Senegalese Regiment with distinction in 1944 and 1945 in France and Germany. At the end of the war in Europe he was immediately despatched to Indochina where he stayed for ten years, eventually rising to commander-in-chief there in 1952. Without doubt this last fact was the one that counted more than any other against Salan amongst European extremists. Although ironically he would end up as a die-hard supporter of French Algeria, they saw him as a liberal and a defeatist who, as in Indochina, was preparing the ground for a sell-out in Algeria. On 16 January 1957 at 7.00 p.m., an ORAF militant, Philippe Castille, fired a bazooka at Salan's office, killing one of his officers. Thereafter the 'bazooka affair' would remain a murky episode, linked not just to extremist circles in Algiers but to Gaullist politicians in Paris plotting to overthrow the Fourth Republic regime, which nevertheless underlined one of the key factors in the Algerian drama: the ceaseless radicalization of Europeans who, still intoxicated by the victory of 6 February, believed that France's destiny belonged to the streets of Algiers.

Mollet's 9 January 1957 Declaration

As Massu's paratroopers began their first operations, a sweep of the Casbah in the early hours of 8 January, the Republican Front government was completely isolated on the international scene. In a show of solidarity with Egypt, all Arab countries with the exception of Lebanon had broken diplomatic relations with France. Within the International Socialist movement, established in Frankfurt in 1951 and bringing together all of the left-of-centre social democratic parties, the French Socialist Party was roundly condemned over Suez, most notably by the British Labour Party.[3] There was, too, the continuing anger of the Eisenhower administration in Washington which saw French foreign policy as one wrecking their hopes of a broad anti-communist alliance in the Arab world.

Nevertheless Mollet himself remained unrepentant. Bolstered by a vote of confidence on 20 December 1956, won by 325 to 210, he produced a long and detailed declaration on all aspects of the Algerian question. Backed up by robust articles in the socialist press which explained that 'peace in Algeria' never meant peace at any price, but the defeat of terrorism and the establishment of a Franco–Muslim community, this declaration, unveiled to journalists on 9 January 1957 and subsequently broadcast on the radio, was a definitive statement of the French case.[4]

Agreement on the final text was made at the 4 January cabinet meeting which, although delivered by Mollet, was a collective statement, one that gave political backing to the army's operations in Algiers while looking ahead to the decisive UN vote tabled for the end of January. Totalling just over ten pages the declaration reiterated the classic tenets of the third-way, reformist position. Underlining that France would never abandon Algeria, Mollet explained that his government's approach was based upon the principles of equality, coexistence, and a recognition of Algeria's distinctiveness. To talk of 'colonialism and 'anti-colonialism', Mollet argued, was to 'grossly misunderstand' both the problem and its solutions.[5] Algerian society had to be analysed as an ethnically diverse entity composed of Europeans, Berbers, Arabs, and Jews which had become solidified into two communities, both of whom saw Algeria as 'their country'.[6] The government's mission was to bring about reconciliation:

The problem of Algeria is to ensure the coexistence of these two communities without either one being able to oppress the other. The Muslim community has numbers in its favour. The community of European origin, by its knowledge, and technical expertise, has been responsible for the economic expansion of Algeria, has made it a modern country, and stills controls a large part of its economy today. In our eyes, it is out of the question that either of these communities should impose its law on the other, whether it be the law of numbers or the law of economic power. Algeria can live and prosper only through active cooperation between the two communities in equality, liberty and justice.[7]

The government's mission was also to raise the living standards of all Algerians through a vast plan of economic and social reforms that would include 'agrarian reform and land distribution, large-scale increases in school enrolment and vocational training, wage rises, the extension of old age retirement benefits to all Algerians, and the guarantee to the Muslims of broader access to the Civil Service'.[8] These increased living standards would, Mollet stressed, lay the basis for the complete liberation of each Algerian man and woman which he then contrasted with the FLN's pseudo-liberation:

There are some who criticize us for not granting Algeria independence, pure and simple, 'national liberation'. An independence which would result in inevitable economic and social regression as well as political regression towards dictatorship or the quasi-feudal regime of certain Arab states—would this be progress?[9]

In marshalling the French case, Mollet drew upon other familiar arguments. France had a sovereign right to be in Algeria because in 1830 it had brought order to a 'chaotic assemblage of Kabyle republics and Arab kingdoms', opening up the way to over a century of achievements composed of 'modernization of the economy, protection of public health, population growth'.[10] The UN had no right to intervene in what was an internal problem. The rebellion was the work of Egypt. The FLN was merely trying to impose its will through 'fanaticism and violence'.[11] The only genuinely democratic solution, Mollet argued, was the government's famous triptych: an unconditional ceasefire, followed by free elections based on a single electoral college, and then free discussions with the elected representatives of the Algerian population.

While searching for this democratic solution Mollet admitted that he had had contacts with the FLN. But here he was clear that these discussions were

about how to achieve a ceasefire. Nothing more. He did not recognize the
FLN as representative—that would be decided by the ballot box—and
anyway these contacts had revealed the FLN to be riven with in-fighting,
the major reason why they broke down. In the meantime the government
was proceeding with far-reaching administrative reforms that were doing
away with the old 'communes mixtes', where the local administrator was a
French uniformed official, and replacing them with hundreds of new
elected communes with mayors that would empower the Muslim population—the best training for 'the responsibilities of direct administration' and
'the habits of democracy'.[12]

In presenting these arguments Mollet was clear that he was stating
nothing new. Ever since February 1956, these ideas had driven forward
his policy. However, at the same time two interconnected themes were
given a new urgency one year on, namely the manner in which a reformed
Algeria was inseparable from the devolution of power in French Africa and
the movement towards European unity. These two ideas, seen as absolute
priorities in the international field, were summed up in the concept of
'Eurafrica'. With Algeria as the keystone this new 'Eurafrican' community
would be based upon values of cooperation and mutual independence:

> France is negotiating at this time with her European partners for the organi-
> zation of a vast common market, to which the Overseas Territories will be
> associated. All of Europe will be called upon to help in the development of
> Africa, and tomorrow Eurafrica may become one of the principal factors in
> world policy.
>
> Isolated nations can no longer keep pace with the world. What would
> Algeria amount to by itself? On the other hand, what future might it have, as
> one of the foundations of the Eurafrican community now taking shape?

France's mission, Mollet argued, was to enable Algerians to bypass 'the stage
of narrow nationalism'. Based on the principles of democracy and internationalism, his government had to ensure 'personal liberation' for all the
country's inhabitants; coexistence between the populations; and Algeria's
participation in the new emerging 'Eurafrica' that, given the increasing
powerlessness of the nation state in the modern world, represented 'the
only independence which is real in the twentieth century'.[13]

By concluding with Algeria's potential place within 'Eurafrica', Mollet
was signalling the significance of this concept at the beginning of 1957. For
him this was a vision of the future where France would be the bridgehead

between Africa and the other five members of the new European Economic Community: Belgium, West Germany, Italy, and Luxembourg. Running counter to Anglo-Saxon and communist influences, 'Eurafrica' would maintain France's pre-eminence as a global power. It would ensure that, unlike at the Yalta Conference in 1945, France was not frozen out of world affairs by the big three: Britain, the US, and the Soviet Union.

This importance explains why, in the run-up to the signing of the Treaty of Rome, formally establishing the EEC in 1957, no theme was more insistent than 'Eurafrica' in justifying government action in Algeria. Mollet returned to it in detail on 25 January, in a speech in Paris at a luncheon organized by the 'Republican Circle' and the 'Society of Economic Studies'.[14] Citing Togo in French West Africa, which had chosen self-government within the French Republic rather than outright independence, Mollet emphasized how this example was the guiding model for policy in Europe, Black Africa, and Algeria. Why? Because voters there had understood the limitations of independence in the mid-1950s. They realized that, in contrast, the Republican Front reforms would allow Togo to manage their own affairs while benefiting from the economic support of the wider Franco-African whole. In the same way, Mollet contended, Algeria would have infinitely greater opportunities within the Eurafrican community than within a Muslim state which, although calling itself sovereign, would be 'doomed to political anarchy and social regression'.[15]

No less importantly, by tracing out a common future that answered demands for emancipation, 'Eurafrica' would insulate Africa from 'fanatical nationalist movements' which the Soviet Union had always sought to infiltrate and control.[16] The symbol par excellence of this new relationship was the Sahara, which on 10 January was transformed into a separate autonomous region—Organisation Commune des Régions Sahariennes (OCRS)—under the authority of Max Lejeune. Throughout 1957 both Lejeune and Champeix insisted that the Sahara's wealth would be exploited not by international capitalism but in tandem with Morocco and Tunisia for the good of the local populations: an example of the vast revolution that the Republican Front was now undertaking throughout Africa in the name of anti-communism. In *Le Populaire* on 14 January Darrius Le Core took up this anti-communist theme, stating that the vision of a new Algeria sitting within a 'Eurafrican' entity would be a blow to the 'dictatorships in Cairo and the Kremlin' who threatened 'Western democracy' just as Hitler and Stalin had in 1939.[17] In the same vein Mollet told US journalists at the end of February:

France is proceeding at the same time with revolutionary transformations in the overseas territories. In the face of limited nationalism and communism, so often complicit with one another, we propose the only remedy, that of forming between Europe and Africa a vast ensemble of free people aiding each other in their mutual profit and their common prosperity.[18]

The '9 January Declaration' was Mollet's most comprehensive public document about Algeria. Trying to seize back the initiative after Suez, it set out the convictions that, he believed, would win the argument at the UN. In equal measure the '9 January Declaration' sought to construct a consensus amongst the mainstream parties. Deliberately excluding the Communists and the Poujadists, both considered beyond the pale, Mollet wrote to all the other political groupings as well as leading figures in both the Assembly and the Senate, including all the former Fourth Republic prime ministers. His ambition: to reach agreement on a basic set of principles that would operate above party politics and that all subsequent governments would follow, counteracting instability in the parliamentary system which the FLN could exploit. What followed was a flurry of letters that provided a telling snapshot of the Fourth Republic's political class. So, whether it was the Radical Party, François Mitterrand's UDSR, the Christian Democrat MRP, Jacques Chaban-Delmas's Gaullists, or indeed the Socialist Party itself: all were adamant that France must not abandon Algeria, that the UN had no right to intervene, that the FLN was manipulated by Moscow's hidden hand, and that the essence of the problem was the coexistence of the differing communities, even if there were differences about the extent to which Algeria should be accorded internal autonomy or the necessity of contacts with the FLN.[19] In this respect Joseph Perrin, speaking for the UDSR parliamentary group, was representative of the general tone. Like Mollet, the UDSR saw the new Algeria and the new Africa in terms of the renunciation of privilege and the promotion of political and social equality:

It would be in vain in effect to believe that the Franco-African community will be created and will endure without a loyal renouncement of all political, economic and social privileges and the inequalities that lead from them. For too long some have been able to think that the considerable contribution of the Nation to maintaining the indissoluble links between Algeria and the Metropole would only be a new way of maintaining a state of things that democrats have always opposed.[20]

But although there was general support for Mollet, there were also warnings. Replying on behalf of the Radical-Socialist Party, André Morice and

Henri Queuille, the first shortly to become Minister of Defence and the other a former prime minister, advanced the notion of blood sacrifice.[21] More contacts with the FLN, they wrote, would be an insult to the young soldiers and to the innocent European Muslim victims of terrorism. Under no circumstances would negotiations be permissible—a political calculus that was mirrored by hardliners on the FLN side. Like their French adversaries, they invoked their own dead in the name of intransigence. Furthermore, in the case of arch Gaullist and senator Michel Debré, his response, written in a passionate style, was one long warning about the incurable malaise at the heart of the Fourth Republic.[22] Without a far-reaching reform of the state, he contended, there would be no end to the Algeria drama and here the only possible solution was 'a government of national salvation' led by General de Gaulle.[23]

Mollet's diplomatic international offensive

Strengthened by the cross-party support, the 9 January Declaration became the basis of a major diplomatic offensive. In anticipation of the UN vote, between 15 and 24 of January Mollet met with the ambassadors of Uruguay, Mexico, Canada, Pakistan, Turkey, Japan, Belgium, Colombia, Costa Rica, Guatemala, Honduras, Panama, San Salvador, Switzerland, Peru, and the USA, in each case taking time and effort to convince them of the French argument. In New York the Foreign Minister Christian Pineau worked the UN corridors tirelessly, backed up by a special delegation at the French Embassy that included Marcel Champeix; Jacques Soustelle; Ali Chekkal, vice-president of the old Algerian Assembly; and leading French Muslims from the world of sport, notably the Davis Cup tennis player Abdessalam and the long-distance runner Alain Mimoun, winner of gold in the 10,000 metres at the 1956 Melbourne Olympics.

Departing from the previous stance which had boycotted discussion of the Algerian question, Pineau opened the UN session on Algeria on 4 February with a three-hour speech restating the key themes of the 9 January Declaration. Faced with unremitting hostility from a pro-Algerian Afro-Asian caucus made up of Syria, Iraq, Morocco, Tunisia, Saudi Arabia, and Indonesia, the French delegation produced a stream of facts and figures to counter the FLN office, ably led by the ever articulate Mohammed Yazid, a permanent fixture on the Manhattan diplomatic scene. And it was politicking that produced results. The French delegation successfully headed off the Afro-Asian resolution calling for the recognition of Algerian self-determination and immediate negotiations, in favour of an anodyne outcome that talked in general terms of the hope for a peaceful, democratic, and just solution in conformity with the UN Charter.[24] In stopping so far short of FLN demands, Mollet claimed the vote to be a French victory. By neutralizing the Afro-Asian lobby, he believed, he had won the Republican Front government breathing space. Now the government could press ahead with the far-reaching reforms that would ultimately defeat the FLN.

Determined to capitalize on the UN vote, Mollet went in person to Washington on 25 February with Christian Pineau and Louis Joxe, French ambassador to the UN. Welcomed at the airport by Vice-President Richard Nixon and Secretary of State Foster Dulles, he and his entourage then followed a gruelling five-day schedule which included talks with Eisenhower in the White House, radio interviews, and a major press conference with 500 journalists at the National Press Club before departing on 28 February for the United Nations in New York. In each case, Mollet's pronouncements, widely reported in the international media, sought to repair the damage done to Franco-American relations after Suez.

But if outwardly the trip was one of smiles and warm words, in private there were sharp divergences between Washington and Paris. These tensions became obvious when, one week after Mollet's visit, Eisenhower made a major statement about US policy in the Middle East. Eisenhower had studiously avoided discussing this imminent initiative with Mollet because he knew that, by calling for a broad US-led anti-communist alliance across the Muslim world, the Declaration was taking the lessons of Suez to their logical conclusion: the replacement of the old colonial powers in the Middle East by the USA.[25] In particular Eisenhower wanted to support moderate nationalists like Bourguiba and Mohammed V against radical ones who could be drawn into the Soviet camp, a strategy which, in his eyes, was being made so much harder by the anti-Western sentiment stirred up over Algeria.[26] Conversely, the Eisenhower Declaration reinforced insecurities within the Republican Front about France's standing in the world. As Britain assiduously rebuilt the special relationship with the US during 1957, France felt frozen out by the 'Anglo-Saxon powers'—a psychological complex that reinforced the conviction that France had to create a new independent bloc centred on the European Economic Community, Algeria, and 'Eurafrica'.

Dissenting Voices

While Mollet received overwhelming backing from the mainstream parties, dissenting voices did exist. Within the Socialist Party one of its towering figures—the Popular Front deputy and Resistance hero André Philip— publicly disavowed Mollet's policy in the letters pages of Le Monde in November 1956, before formally resigning in January 1957. Although he supported the special powers and although he favoured firm action against Nasser, over in Algeria, Philip argued, Mollet had become disengaged from reality. His government's actions were the negation of socialism and in a book published shortly afterwards Philip wrote belligerently about Mollet's betrayal.[27] Other members who broke ranks included the youth-wing leader and rising star Michel Rocard, the former minister Alain Savary, the historian Charles André-Julien, and the National Council member Marceau Pivert. Savary expressed his dismay directly to Mollet; André-Julien, incensed by the way his expertise on Algeria had been deliberately ignored during 1956, openly asserted the reality of nationalism; while Pivert accused the party leadership of taking up the ideological themes of 'Order, Authority, Nation': the hallmark of those 'neo-socialists' like Marcel Déat who split with the SFIO in 1933 and then drifted ever rightwards until they embraced fascism and collaboration during the Occupation.[28] At the regional level the SFIO in Ardennes on the border with Luxembourg became a hub of anti-government opposition led by the redoubtable Andrée Vienot, resistance veteran and mayor of Rocroi. She was absolutely clear that Mollet's Algerian policy was a betrayal of the promises made during the 2 January 1956 election, telling Pierre Commin, SFIO general secretary, on 13 March 1956: 'Do not be mistaken. It is . . . for peace, for the return of the soldiers that the country has voted socialist in a proportion that has surprised us.'[29]

Elsewhere the Communist Party continued to denounce the repression, even if it preferred to talk of peace rather than independence. There was also vocal opposition from the familiar figures of Claude Bourdet in France-Observateur and Jean-Paul Sartre in Les Temps Modernes. In Algeria disappointment in the Republican Front led two municipal councillors in Algiers, Paul Houdard and André Gallice, to found a monthly journal L'Espoir in June 1956. Drawing in the secondary-school history teacher, Charles-Robert Ageron and the Muslim intellectuals Mahfoud Kaddache and Mouloud Mammeri,

L'Espoir professed no ideology except that of dialogue. It was a voice of moderation that wanted to stop the escalation of repression and terrorism.

Criticism of Mollet's policies did not just come from the left, however. In the glossy weekly magazine, *Paris Match*, its influential editor Raymond Cartier had already questioned the rationale of Mollet's Africa policy in August 1956. Why, he asked, was the Republican Front government investing in these overseas territories when it could be spending this money on the metropole, modernizing the economy and making France more competitive on the international markets?[30] After all, argued Cartier:

> The richest and most stable country in Europe, Switzerland, has never had a square metre overseas. Sweden, another phenomenon of prosperity, has been the same case for two centuries. Germany lost, in 1918, the few colonies that Wilhelm II had acquired and it has achieved in two cases a striking industrial resurrection.[31]

As professor of sociology at the Sorbonne and a regular contributor to the right-wing daily *Le Figaro*, Raymond Aron asked, too, whether, in objective economic terms, Mollet's policy in Algeria made sense.[32] Even on the Sahara, Aron's response was no. Potential revenues from oil might look enticing. But ultimately, he concluded, they could never provide a financial solution to the problems of underdevelopment and demographic explosion. Like the rest of Algeria, the cost of the Sahara was too great a burden for the French economy. It would be much better, therefore, to prepare the way for an independent state.

By subjecting Mollet's claims to a rational calculus, Cartier and Aron were returning to an argument that had been there right from 1830: did Algeria represent a profit or a loss? In late 1956 and early 1957, though, this question was brushed aside. Within the mainstream parties there was a momentary unity behind Mollet. His policies were seen to make military, political, and economic sense, producing a consensus which the British journalist Alexander Werth called 'national Molletism'.[33]

But if this consensus was clear within the National Assembly, it was not so in the country at large. In the opinion polls those confident in Mollet were always in a minority, falling from 37% satisfied in March 1956 to 30% in July before rising again to 39% in March 1957.[34] Nor was there unanimous support for the government's expansion of the war effort. In spring 1956, 48% opposed the sending of conscripts and 49% the recall of the reservists. In July 1956, 51% rejected the idea of increased taxation to finance the cost of Algeria. Moreover, from July 1956 onwards a small majority, 45% against 23%, favoured negotiations over the use of force, while those who supported the maintenance of French Algeria dropped steadily from 49% in February 1956, to 40% in April and 34% in March 1957.

None of these figures was a ringing endorsement of Mollet's policies. He might have been convinced that this was a just conflict in defence of the national interest, but public opinion was much less sure. Successive polls never reflected his certainties, underlining a separation between the populace and the political class that would deepen throughout 1957 and early 1958.

The first 'Battle of Algiers': strategy and thinking

During January, February, and March 1957 'national Molletism' provided the political context for the 'Battle of Algiers': the most famous event during the whole Algerian War, subsequently immortalized in Gillo Pontecorvo's 1966 film. To call it a battle, however, is a misnomer. This was not urban warfare on a grand scale like Stalingrad in 1942 or even the Irish Easter uprising in 1916. There was no sustained street-to-street combat. Instead the confrontation took the form of short bursts of fighting at close quarters, interspersed with bombs on the one side and mass round-ups and torture on the other, as the FLN and the French army fought for the control of the capital's Muslim population.

On the FLN side the strategy behind the 'Battle of Algiers' reflected Abbane Ramdane's high hopes at the beginning of 1957. With the crucial UN vote imminent, he, more than anyone, believed that victory was within their grasp. He was convinced that France, isolated after Suez and 'six months' away from bankruptcy, had lost the political and economic will to fight on.[35] All that was needed, he argued, was one final surge to force the French into negotiations: the 'Algerian Dien Bien Phu' which, Abbane promised, would take place on the streets of Algiers.[36] This was the thinking behind the eight-day general strike, timed in advance of the UN vote.[37] It was also the thinking behind the campaign of urban terrorism. No longer would the war be hidden away in the countryside. Continuous violence on the streets of Algiers, the centre of French power, would demonstrate to the world that the FLN struggle was not just pockets of resistance in the mountains but a mass movement supported by the towns and cities, the urban equivalent of the 20 August 1955 Constantinois insurrection.[38]

At the same time the FLN's urban terrorism—brutal, direct, and completely indiscriminate—showed a hardening of tone. Hitherto Abbane and Ben Khedda had underlined the need to spare the lives of European civilians.[39] Now both men's views changed. Seeing the widespread European support for military repression transformed civilians, in the FLN's eyes, into legitimate targets. Moreover, it was a question of political honour. By striking back at Europeans, the FLN wanted to present itself as the defender of the Muslim community, simultaneously creating a climate of panic that would sap the French capacity to stay in Algeria. As one FLN directive stated: 'A bomb causing the death of ten people and wounding fifty others is the equivalent on a psychological level to the loss of a French battalion.'[40]

Finally, in launching the 'Battle of Algiers', the FLN wanted to show that they, and not the MNA, were the true representatives of the Algerian nation. Abbane wished to ensure that the conflict ended not as in Morocco, a round table between all the parties at Aix-les-Bains, but like in Indochina: one-to-one negotiations between equals that would win power for him and the FLN's internal leadership. As Ben Khedda later explained, the strike's aim was to confer definitive legitimacy on the FLN:

> On this point, there was a conflict between the MNA and the FLN, notably in France where lots of Algerians misled by MNA propaganda believed that the war was led by the latter. The event opened their eyes, and it is following this strike that practically all of the Algerian emigration in France moved over to the FLN camp.[41]

The mastermind behind the bombing campaign was Saadi Yacef.[42] Born in 1928, Yacef was a true son of the Casbah. A baker by trade, he was a keen footballer who knew the Muslim *quartier* winding, tiny trap-like streets by heart. Drawn into the clandestine PPA in 1944, he was a member of the OS who managed to escape the crack-down in 1949 and make his way to France. Returning to Algiers as a baker in 1952, he was contacted after 1 November 1954 and subsequently hid two of the original FLN leaders, Rabah Bitat and Belkacem Krim. Arrested in France in Orly in May 1955 he was incarcerated in the Barberousse prison in Algiers and then freed after four months, leading to rumours that he had been recruited by the French secret services. At this point Yacef headed back to France whereupon he was ordered by the FLN to return to Algiers under pain of death. Reeling from arrests of leaders in Algiers, Yacef was quickly pushed into a leadership role under Ben M'Hidi.

From the outset Yacef knew that an offensive in the capital was always going to be difficult. This was not eastern Algeria where the FLN could disappear into a Muslim sea. Algiers was the centre of French military and political power where 300,000 Europeans lived uneasily with Muslims. Yacef's initial strategy, therefore, was to transform the Casbah into an FLN fortress. Using strong-arm tactics, he cleansed it of criminals and the MNA. He made sure that nothing moved without his knowledge. He transformed the topography of the Casbah, creating an elaborate under-ground world of secret passages, safe houses, concealed rooms, and hidden bomb-making factories. To the end, his right-hand man was Ali Ammar, alias Ali la Pointe, who like so many of the Casbah's illiterate youth lived by his wits. A street-wise tough, Ali la Pointe had been a shoe-shine boy, boxer, and draft-dodger. Recruited during a spell in Barberousse prison in 1955, he was to become one of the FLN's deadliest operatives whose capacity to evade the French army made him into a legendary figure.

Numerically speaking, Yacef was able to call upon 1,500 fighters organized into small, independent cells.[43] In sealing off his operatives from each other in this manner Yacef knew that he was making the FLN a difficult entity to eradicate. Deprived of the knowledge of the other operatives, captured prisoners would only ever have the tiniest amount of information to divulge. They could never threaten the overall survival of the organization. In tandem with watertight security the other two aspects of Yacef's strategy were the amassing of a deadly armoury of timers and explosives—using the bomb-making expertise of Abderrahmane Taleb, Giorgio Daniel, and Gabriel Timsit, all three Algerian communists—and the deployment of a number of younger, educated, middle-class Muslim women: Hassiba Ben Bouali, Djamila Bouazza, Djamila Bouhired, Zohra Drif, and Samia Lakhdari. Already used to devastating effect in the 30 September 1956 attacks on the crowded European cafés, these women would continue to disguise themselves as French in order to pass bombs unnoticed through the checkpoints. Thus, even if they were not in posi-tions of command, they represented the entry of women into public, political space at a time when women in parts of the rural ALN were being obliged to leave the front-line maquis. Exhilarating and empowering, their actions were statements about their personal independence, as Zohra Drif subsequently underlined:

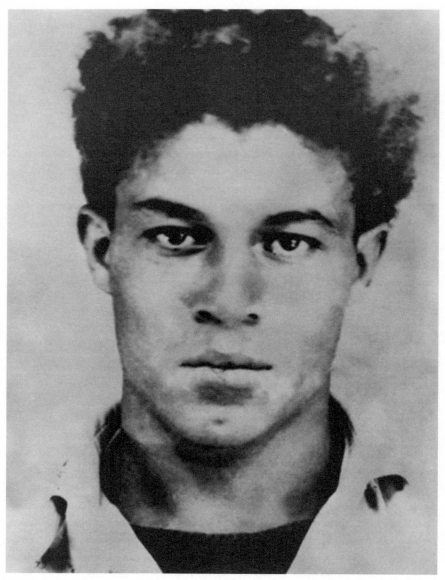

Figure 7.2 Ali Ammar, alias Ali la Pointe, one of the FLN's deadliest operatives during the 'Battle of Algiers'.

They suggested that I work with the families of prisoners, but I wanted to participate directly in armed conflict. I thought I would only be used as a nurse or a secretary in the maquis; I wanted to work with a terrorist group, here in Algiers.[44]

On the French side, Massu was under no doubt about the task facing him and his men. This was police work. But while the police had become constrained and predictable, the army had to be *un*restrained and *un*predictable. It had to operate at night and in total secrecy. It had to go where the police had previously never gone. It had to anticipate the FLN strategy. In short, the army had to treat the Casbah like the Aurès and Kabylia. It had to take the lessons learnt in rural anti-guerrilla warfare and apply them to an urban context.

In the first instance this meant intelligence. Information, gathered through photographs taken on the ground and from above by helicopter, was all. Armed with this knowledge, Bigeard built up a picture of the FLN's command structure that was transposed in diagrammatic form to a large information board, an outline regularly updated to the waiting press to become a measure of the army's success. It also meant control of the Muslim population. Here Colonel Trinquier—born of Alpine peasant stock and another Indochina veteran—developed an intricate system of surveillance and protection. Under the Trinquier system each street in the Casbah had an army informer. Nobody could move in or out of Algiers without the army's knowledge: the basis of a comprehensive card–index system listing whom the authorities should arrest and interrogate.

Finally, this meant that the army had to be ruthless. If the mission was to stop terrorism then officers and their men had to ignore legal niceties: the army had to employ torture and intimidation. In the case of the 44–year–old Colonel Argoud, already in Kabylia throughout the summer of 1956 his troops had destroyed pro–nationalist villages, executed prisoners, and left FLN corpses on the streets.[45] Now they did the same in Algiers. Speaking in December 1960 he recalled:

> I was commanding the Arba sector during the battle of Algiers in 1957; although I had full legal powers I did not wish to have recourse to them because I was responsible for the lives both of the troops and civilians; so, after an exhaustive and detailed inquiry carried out with the assistance of Inspectors of the criminal police, I gave orders that those who had committed murder or were leaders of the insurrection should be publicly executed by firing squad in the square.[46]

Such systematic repression gave certain buildings a terrifying reputation. In the villas of Susini, Tourelles, and Rose, a network of detention centres dotted across Algiers, Massu's men tortured thousands before disposing of the bodies, either by incineration or dumping them by helicopter into the sea.[47] In effect the bay of Algiers became a watery grave with many of the corpses being washed up on the local beaches, a fact that led paratroopers to talk with macabre humour of 'Bigeard's prawns'.[48]

Crucially, it must be reiterated that these methods did not operate in a political vacuum. Although there was no written order sanctioning torture, the army was verbally encouraged to use it by Lacoste, Lejeune, and Bourgès-Maunoury. These three wanted the army to liquidate the FLN leadership in Algiers, while calling for care to avoid any 'mistakes' which might embarrass the Mollet administration—a euphemism which reminded officers that these methods must be kept away from the public eye. As General Allard explained four years later:

> I was personally present during a number of visits made in the different sector headquarters by Mrs Bourgès-Maunoury, Lacoste, Lejeune etc., and, on each occasion, these authorities gave orders that the war should be pursued with the utmost possible vigour. I remember in particular a visit to the headquarters of Colonel Bigeard during which he produced statistics to show that he had destroyed nearly three-quarters of the rebel organization in his sector. One of the ministers present congratulated him and encouraged him to carry on and finish the job. I cannot now remember which minister this was; I think that it was M. Lejeune but I cannot be sure of this. I can, however, still see Colonel Bigeard replying to him: 'Mr Minister, do you think that we arrive at such results with the procedures of a choir boy?' The only reply was that he should be careful that too much mud did not stick.[49]

The General Strike and its aftermath

On Saturday 26 January the FLN planted three bombs along the crowded rue Michelet in the Otomatic, Cafétaria, and Coq Hardi cafés. All going off in the early evening, they left four dead and thirty-four wounded, including two young children: a deadly prelude to the eight-day strike timed to start forty eight hours later. In the wake of this violence the streets began to empty. Shops shut. Muslim workers, many prudently taking sick leave, hurried home. There was panic buying of food and provisions. By evening of the 27th the 'Arab' *quartier* was silent.

The following day even Lacoste was forced to admit that the strike had near total support in Algiers and the larger towns across the country. The issue for the French army was how to react. At first Massu tried persuasion. Helicopters dropped tracts telling the Muslim population to 'have confidence in the forces of order'. In the Casbah soldiers handed out sweets to children and tried to convince them to go back to school. When these tactics had no impact Massu deployed force. Paratroopers forced owners to open their shops, rounding people up in the streets, and shunting them into lorries to take them to work.

Confronted with this repression the strike became difficult to sustain. Caught between the army and the FLN, support wavered and this in turn provoked FLN reprisals. On 29 January near Boghni in Kabylia a dead Muslim woman was found hanging from a tree with the placard 'traitor to the sister patrie'; on 30 January in Médéa a local butcher, Benimane Bennaceur, had his hair and eyebrows shaved with a cross shaved on his skull; while on 2 February in Constantine, Lemadi Tahar, president of the taxi union, was attacked in broad daylight for not following the strike.[50] Likewise, once the eight days had passed, the FLN returned to terrorism. Desperate to show that it had not been defeated, Yacef's operatives mounted a fresh wave of attacks. This included two bombs on 10 February at densely crowded football matches in Belcourt and El-Biar.[51] Placed under the terraces, both explosions caused horrendous carnage, leaving ten dead and thirty-four injured. Having arrived in Algiers the day before, Bourgès-Maunoury was taken aback by the indiscriminate cruelty of such violence. Scarcely able to control his anger, he told Massu in no uncertain terms: 'We must finish these people off.'[52]

Bolstered by France's victory at the UN on 15 February, the army continued to tighten the hunt for the FLN. By the middle of the month the army had made 448 arrests and captured 87 bombs, 5,429 detonators, and 70 kilos of explosives. Then, on 23 February, a major coup: in rue Claude-Debussy a patrol stumbled on Ben M'Hidi's safe house by accident. Arrested in his pyjamas, Ben M'Hidi was immediately interrogated by Bigeard before being paraded to the world press. Eleven days later, however, it was announced by Pierre Gorlin, Lacoste's press officer, that Ben M'Hidi had 'committed suicide by hanging himself in his cell with the help of strips torn from his shirt'.[53] In reality a special counter-insurgency unit detailed to

Figure 7.3 'Battle of Algiers'—handcuffed Larbi Ben M'Hidi, 28 February 1957.

kill the FLN leadership, put in place by Massu, covered by Lejeune and commanded by Colonel Aussaresses, had whisked away Ben M'Hidi to an isolated farm 18 kilometres to the south of Algiers.[54] In such seclusion this unit had even more freedom to operate beyond the law and there Ben M'Hidi was handcuffed and then hung in a manner that, Aussaresses hoped, would suggest suicide.[55] Afterwards Ben M'Hidi's body was taken back to an Algiers hospital.

These details about Ben M'Hidi's death would not surface until over forty years later with Aussaresses's personal account of the 'Battle of Algiers', but even at the time they were contested.[56] Elements of the left-of-centre press, notably *France-Observateur*, were sceptical about the official version, a scepticism that intensified with the death of Ali Boumendjel, a well-known Algerian lawyer and FLN member, on 23 March.[57] Arrested on 9 February, Boumendjel, so the authorities claimed, had thrown himself out of a window of a building used by paratroopers for interrogation on avenue Georges-Clemenceau in El-Biar. In contrast to the vast majority who had disappeared or died in custody, Boumendjel was middle class and a rising star of the Algiers law circuit. These connections meant that his 'suicide' produced a public reaction. *Le Monde* reported that his brother, Ahmed Boumendjel, also a lawyer, had sent a letter directly to the President of the Republic; the President of the Bar in Paris condemned the army practices as contrary to French law; while René Capitant, professor of law at Algiers University, suspended his teaching in protest, writing to the Education Minister, René Billières, that:

> Ali Boumendjel was my student at the law faculty in Algiers at the moment when I was heading the Combat resistance movement in North Africa. The news of his death in these conditions overwhelms me ... while such practices—which even in a full war we never inflicted on German prisoners—will be prescribed and tolerated against Algerians by the government of my country, I feel myself unable to teach in a French law faculty.[58]

Such misgivings did not stop the repression. On the contrary the government continued to give the army its full backing. Mollet and his ministers wanted to decapitate the FLN and in the face of this repression the CCE was forced to flee Algiers at the end of February. Carefully disguising themselves as Europeans, Abbane, Krim, Ben Khedda, and Saad Dahlab were driven in two cars to the maquis in the Atlas mountains, above the town of Blida just south of Algiers. From there Abbane and Dahlab went to Morocco while Ben Khedda and Krim headed to Tunisia.

Back in Algiers, Yacef was disgusted by their flight. As a son of the Casbah there had always been a tension between him and the more middle-class leadership and for this reason his anger was above all directed against Abbane and Dahlab. In his eyes, by abandoning the capital they were cowards. They had done untold damage to the FLN's prestige. They had handed victory to the Mollet government.

Whatever the truth of Yacef's views, there can be no doubt about the historical significance of the CCE's departure, a significance which would deepen the longer the conflict went on.[59] Henceforth the FLN's leadership would reside in exile. Cut off from the population and the realities of the war, its power structures would develop outside of the country—a fact filled with momentous consequences for the independent Algeria to come.[60]

Torture

At the end of March the bombing had receded and amongst the government and European population there was a palpable feeling of relief. The worst, it seemed, was over. But in talking about military success, the argument about ends and means refused to go away.[61] Accusations about torture were not new. Writing in *France-Observateur*, the left-wing Resistance veteran Claude Bourdet had denounced Gestapo-style methods in Algeria ever since 1951. The Nazi analogy was also taken up by the Catholic intellectual François Mauriac in *L'Express* in January 1955. Then in December 1955 Jean Daniel, again in *L'Express*, launched a controversy over footage of a gendarme executing a prisoner on 20 August 1955.[62] But until now none of these revelations had made a lasting impact. They became lost, partly because of the unending cycle of government instability and partly because the press held back. Editors Hubert Beuve-Méry at *Le Monde* and Jean-Marie Domenach at *Esprit* were reluctant to criticize for fear of exacerbating this instability.[63]

By spring 1957 the situation had changed. Mollet's government had been in power for fourteen months and this durability ensured that sections of the press broke their silence. Moreover, this was the point when the reservists recalled in April 1956 were demobilized, an event which led a tiny minority of soldiers to speak out publicly about their war experiences. The conjuncture of these factors meant that 1957 saw a stream of revelations about torture and what gave these revelations authenticity was the power of personal testimony. By underlining what they had seen with their own eyes, these witnesses challenged the official version at every level.

This was the case with Robert Bonnaud. Returning to his native Marseille, Bonnaud, a history teacher and Communist Party member, was encouraged by his close friend Pierre Vidal-Naquet to write down his experiences of fighting in the Nementchas mountains in eastern Algeria.[64] Vidal-Naquet, a history lecturer at Caen University, then contacted Domenach at *Esprit* who, frustrated at the failure of his earlier attempts to privately alert the government about abuses, saw Bonnaud's article as way of going public over torture in April 1957. Written in a simple and precise style, the

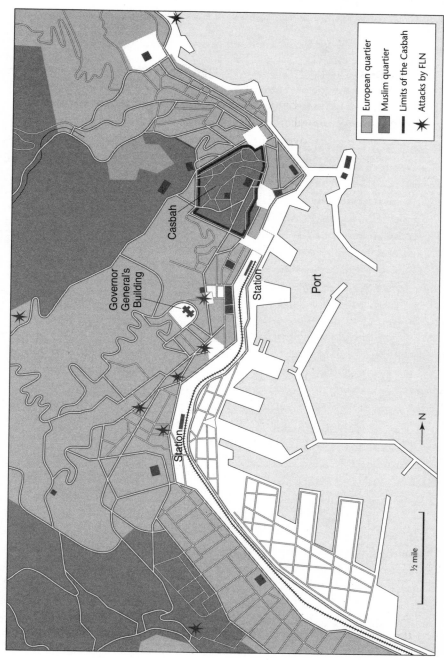

Map 7.1 January–March 1957: The first 'Battle of Algiers'.

resultant piece set out to communicate the 'intangible' horror of the conflict. It conveyed what he had witnessed at first hand:

> The suspect is lashed to the table with chains in wet rags that are attached to the
> electrodes. A gendarme turns the handle on the field telephone; the strength of
> the electric charge varies according to the rate at which he turns the handle; he
> knows that variations in the current are especially painful . . . The electrodes are
> fixed to the temples, to the underside of the tongue, to the genitals as well as to
> any other sensitive part of the body . . . Such torture leaves hardly any marks.[65]

The other first-hand accounts were a series of anonymous letters published
by a group of Roman Catholic priests, as well as articles by Jean Müller in
Témoignage Chrétien in February, Jean-Jacques Servan-Schreiber in *L'Express* in March, and Georges Mattéi in *Les Temps Modernes* in July.[66] Muller
was a former lorry driver who had been killed in action, Servan-Schreiber a
lieutenant and editor of *L'Express*, while Georges Mattéi was a reservist in
Kabylia and in each case, they, like Bonnaud and the letters, wanted to bring
the realities of war back to metropolitan France. They wanted to shake their
compatriots out of apathy and indifference.

The force of these returning reservists' accounts was compounded by
the impact of three further voices of public protest, the first of which was
the liberal Catholic author Pierre-Henri Simon. Although no supporter of
Algerian independence, his book *Contre la torture*, published by Seuil on 13
March 1957, was a humanist rejection of torture. Such practices, he contended, were sullying France's moral authority in the world—an argument
seized upon by the *Le Monde* editor Hubert Beuve-Méry. Like Domenach
he had been fobbed off when he confronted Mollet with reservists' letters
about torture in the previous autumn.[67] Now, Beuve-Méry used the Simon
book to write a dramatic editorial on 13 March 1957. Entitled 'Are we the
winners over Hitler?', it stated: 'From now on, the French must know that
they no longer quite have the right to condemn in the same terms as ten
years ago the destroyers of Oradour and the torturers of the Gestapo.'[68]

The second voice of protest was the Archbishop of Algiers, Léon Étienne
Duval. Appointed in February 1954, Duval had denounced torture in
January 1955.[69] He did so again in early 1957: a stance which led Europeans
to attack him as 'Mohammed Duval'. Challenging priests in the French
army who had sanctioned it on the grounds that terrorism was the greater
evil, Duval's weekly sermons were unambiguous. Torture was contrary to

the teachings of Christ and could not be justified in any context. On 15 February he wrote to Lacoste:

> Massive arrests of 'suspects' have taken place and continue to take place in the city of Algiers. It is undeniable that amongst these 'suspects' there is a good number who are innocent of any crime . . . These men grouped into diverse centres (Ben Aknoun, Baïnem, villa Susini, municipal stadium) find themselves in conditions incompatible with respect for the human person; their families are kept in ignorance of what has become of them.[70]

The third voice of protest was that of a serving officer, Jacques Pâris de la Bollardière. A devout Catholic born in Brittany, the son of an officer killed in World War One, de la Bollardière was a Gaullist Resister from the first hour who had then risen to become one of the most decorated soldiers in the army. A veteran of Indochina, he arrived in Algeria in July 1956. Promoted to general in November he was put in command of the eastern sector of the Atlas mountains around Blida. Initially, de la Bollardière believed in 'pacification'. He wanted to stem the violence and preserve coexistence between the two communities. In action, though, he became disillusioned. He was shocked by how his reservists had been thrown into Algeria without the slightest moral or physical preparation.[71] He was shocked, too, by the way in which torture had become routine. Eventually on 7 March 1957 he wrote to Salan asking to be transferred to France because he could not accept the methods being used to achieve victory.[72] Then on 28 March Bollardière allowed *L'Express* to publish an open letter. In it he supported Servan-Schreiber, a former lieutenant under his command in 1956, against the government, who were trying to censor extracts from his book which were being published in *L'Express*:

> I think that it is highly desirable that having carried out your action and shared our efforts, you carry out your job as a journalist underlining to public opinion the dramatic aspects of the revolutionary war that we are confronted with, and the incredible danger that there would be for us to lose sight, under the fallacious pretext of immediate efficiency, of the moral values that alone have until now made the greatness of our civilization and of our army.[73]

Ministers were furious. Hauled up in front of Bourgès–Maunoury and Lejeune, both threatened to throw him out of the army. Condemned to sixty days solitary confinement, he was then punished with an obscure posting to Equatorial Africa.

Bollardière's revulsion at torture was mirrored in private by Paul Teitgen, Secretary-General to the Algiers prefecture since August 1956. A former Resister in Nancy, deported to Dachau Concentration Camp for nine months, Teitgen wrote to Lacoste on 24 March. There he made an explicit comparison with his own horrors at the hands of the Gestapo:

> I would never make such a claim if I had not, during recent visits to the internment camps in Paul-Cazelles and Beni Messous, recognized on certain internees the profound traces of physical cruelty and torture that...I was personally subjected to in the basements of the Gestapo in Nancy.[74]

In the letter Teitgen talked about signing paperwork that, in effect, retrospectively sanctioned the prolonged detention and torture of nearly 2,000 individuals. Later he would give the figure of 3,024 disappeared prisoners between 28 January and 2 April who have never been accounted for to this day.

Teitgen finally resigned on 8 October, although his letter would not be made public until 1960: a journey, like that of Bollardière, from private angst to public protest. This protest was not uniform, however. Condemnation of torture did not mean support for independence let alone the FLN. Bonnaud might support Algerian nationalism, but Simon and Bollardière were motivated by patriotism. By disavowing torture they believed that they were defending the true French values of democracy and human rights. Nevertheless when added to the high-profile deaths of Ben M'Hidi and Boumendjel, the cumulative effect of the torture debate was too big to ignore. The government had a case to answer and it replied in a robust manner. On 14 April Mollet told party members in the Marne region:

> Let us be clear. Without doubt some acts of violence, extremely rare, are to be deplored. But they have been...the result of terrorist atrocities. As to acts of premeditated torture...I say that if that was the case, it would be intolerable. The methods of the French army have been compared to that of the Gestapo. That comparison is a scandal. Hitler gave orders that advocated these barbaric methods, while Lacoste and I have always given orders in a sense that is completely contrary. Enquiries have anyway been set up...But these, I repeat, could almost be counted on the fingers of a hand.[75]

He poured doubt on the eye-witness accounts, while press articles denigrating the army were censored. On 27 March in *Le Populaire*, Party loyalist Claude Fuzier called the attacks on French methods an odious diversion from the real issue: FLN barbarity.[76] At the same time, while denying the collective use of torture, the government was clear that if individual cases did exist they would be punished, and to this end it established on 5 April a Commission to safeguard rights and individual liberties. Including Robert Delvignette, former Governor-General in the colonies, and André François-Poncet, former ambassador and president of the Red Cross, the Commission, Mollet underlined, was not window dressing. In producing a comprehensive report on torture, it would have the freedom to investigate all aspects of the army's role in Algeria.[77]

The fall of Mollet's government

Bitter though the torture controversy was, it did not engulf Mollet's government, which survived a vote of confidence with ease on 27 March.[78] Momentarily bolstered, welcome relief was provided by news of Algerian-born Alphonse Halimi, 'the terror from Constantine', winning the world featherweight title on 1 April after a fifteen-round contest against defending champion Mario d'Agata. This was then followed by Queen Elizabeth II's official four-day visit to Paris beginning on 8 April—a carefully choreographed event drawing thousands of onlookers and widely covered in the press.[79]

Despite these diversions, however, Algeria refused to go away. In particular the financial consequences of Mollet's policy began to loom large. Here the most pressing problem was military spending which had mushroomed to 300 billion francs. Severely constraining the government's ability to finance its ambitious economic and social programme, expenditure on Algeria became the root cause of a budget deficit which spiralled out of control from 650 billion francs in 1955 to 925 billion in 1956, and 1,100 billion in 1957. This in turn created a balance-of-payments crisis where the more the franc plummeted on the international markets, the more the government looked economically beleaguered. Working long hours under incredible stress, Mollet himself looked increasingly exhausted and on 21 May 1957 the Republican Front was overturned in a vote of no confidence by a disparate coalition of Communists, Poujadists, and seventy-one Moderates and Radicals, all ostensibly opposed to the government's financial policies. Stony faced, Mollet went to the Élysée very late on 22 May to hand in his government's resignation to President Coty. It was the longest-lasting government of the Fourth Republic which during fourteen months had taken many momentous decisions including the decentralization of power in Black Africa, the Suez Affair, the signing of the Treaty of Rome, the development of atomic research and the dramatic expansion of the military and civilian effort in Algeria: all part of a generalized plan to maintain French standing in the world.

Although Mollet stood down, he remained the kingmaker. Without Mollet and the Socialist Party nothing was possible and it was he who recommended that President Coty approach Bourgès-Maunoury to be prime minister. This Coty duly did and on 11 June Bourgès-Maunoury formed a new government, invested by 240 to 194 votes, with 150 abstentions. Retaining the same Socialist and Radical colouring as the Republican Front, Lacoste, Lejeune, Pineau, Gazier, and Jacquet continued as ministers, while those perceived as too moderate over Algeria, Defferre and the UDSR's Mitterrand, were jettisoned. Undoubtedly this made the new government into a war cabinet. With Socialists still holding the key positions, continuity over Algeria was assured, a point underlined in the socialist press and by Bourgès-Maunoury himself who, in his investiture speech, stressed the country's personal debt to Mollet: 'I was for sixteen months in total solidarity with…Mollet. If, during this period, the country has overcome hard tests with a resolution ceaselessly reinforced, it is due to his firmness, to his tenacity, to his courage that we owe it.'[80]

Mélouza

Beni Ilmane is a small village in the Melouza region on the high plateau overlooking the town of M'Sila on the borders of Kabylia and the Constantinois in eastern Algeria. A strategically important area, the ALN had tried to win over the population with little success. Staunchly pro-MNA, in March 1957 the villagers had killed a number of ALN maquisards.[81] In response, FLN tracts accused them of being 'spies' and 'Messali traitors' who were giving intelligence on ALN positions to the French.[82] Angry at their allegiance to Messali, Mohammed Saïd, head of Wilaya 3, ordered the destruction of the village and its inhabitants. Arriving on the morning of 29 May the ALN, led by a Captain Arab, rounded up the 300 or so villagers in front of the mosque where they were exhorted to rally to the FLN. When they refused the ALN butchered them to death with axes, knives, and pick axes. Leaving the mutilated bodies in the open air—some with their eyes torn out, others with their hands cut off—the carnage was discovered two days later by the French army. Internationally the FLN would always lay the blame for the massacres on the French, while across the Mélouza region itself ALN tracts told another story. There they warned others to take heed of the Beni Ilmane example: 'These executions rid our region of traitors and bring relief to all Algerians worthy of this name. They also clearly show our determination to finish off those who do not want to march with the Glorious ALN.'[83]

The French military immediately seized upon what became known as the 'Mélouza massacre' as the FLN equivalent of 'Oradour'. The editorial of *Le Bled*, the army newspaper, proclaimed: 'Worse than Oradour: Mechta-Kasba: the butchery of the FLN.'[84]

In the socialist press it was seen as irrefutable evidence of the FLN's pathological intentions. For *Le Populaire* the massacre showed once and for all that the FLN could not be equated with the French Resistance.[85] Instead it was motivated by the thirst for violence and dictatorship. However, in simplifying the Mélouza story into one of 'loyal Muslims' against the 'totalitarian FLN', *Le Populaire* was forgetting that Beni Ilmane was not pro-French. It was pro-Messali, which meant that the massacres were the result of a civil war between rival nationalists, both groups of whom wanted independence.

The 'Mélouza massacre' was the climax of a process present right from the FLN's beginning in 1954: the violent imposition of the FLN as the sole representative of the Algerian people. In the spring and summer of 1957 this violence continued to be visited upon Muslim officials in the colonial administration and pro-French Muslims, such as Ali Chekkal, former vice-president of the Algerian Assembly, assassinated at the French Football Cup Final on 26 May in Paris just a few yards from President Coty.[86] But most of all, it continued to be visited upon the MNA. This involved an offensive against those areas still under MNA control, notably the high plains in southern Kabylia where the Mélouza region was situated. It also involved ferocious violence against the MNA in France where the 'war within a war' led to 4,000 deaths.[87] Pro-MNA cafés were strafed and leading figures assassinated, including in Paris on 7 October Filali Abdallah, Messali's constant companion since 1933. As with so many fratricidal conflicts, the bloodshed on both sides was unforgiving but by the end of 1957 the FLN was the victor. The MNA had been destroyed as the last serious political rival, even if pockets of pro-Messali support continued in northern France right until 1962.

Figure 7.4 'The jackals devour each other': a French poster characterizing the war between the FLN and the MNA as wanton bloodlust.

Within the French left, even those who supported independence were revolted by the anti-MNA violence. A petition condemning this violence was signed by prominent left intellectuals like the surrealists André Breton, Michel Leiris, and Maurice Nadeau.[88] Marceau Pivert, a long-time supporter of Messali Hadj in the process of leaving the Socialist Party over Algeria, likened the FLN's strategy to Stalinism. For him it was liquidating the MNA just as the Communists had liquidated the Anarchists and the Trotskyists during the Spanish Civil War. Meanwhile, in the *France-Observateur* on 7 November 1957 Claude Bourdet looked forward in anguish. What, he asked, did this violence mean for the future of Algeria?:

> The anti-messalist attacks have now a systematic character and this liquidation of political rivals augurs badly for the spirit of justice that the leadership of the Front will show tomorrow at the head of an Algerian government, as much as regards their compatriots as the Europeans.[89]

The second 'Battle of Algiers'

Early Sunday evening of 9 June an FLN bomb went off in the Casino, a well-known European music hall and gambling establishment perched on the rocky Corniche promontory some 9 km out on the western fringes of Algiers. Placed under the orchestra platform the device, exploding as people danced, caused maximum carnage. With nine dead, eighty-five wounded and bits of bodies strewn across the floor, the result was a sickening sight. So thought Massu, so too thought Pierre Maisonneuve, the man in charge of coordinating relations between Lacoste and the military.[90] For him the aftermath of the Casino justified torture, however regrettable this was, because the authorities had to protect the population:

> Whoever saw the dozens of young people, victims of the explosion at the Casino de la Corniche, crippled at seventeen, eighteen years for the rest of their days, will not be able to forget it. And these were not—to use the phraseology of the time—horrible capitalist exploiters; they were poor kids, typists, sellers, junior clerks who were spending a tranquil Sunday after a working week...So we have to choose between the consequences. It is terrible but that is the lot of political men in charge during moments of crisis. It is easy to criticize afterwards.[91]

The second 'Battle of Algiers' had begun and the reaction of Europeans was angry. They wanted Arab blood and during the funeral on 11 June young Europeans ransacked Muslim shops and set upon bystanders leaving five dead, some gaffed by meathooks. In surveying these ghastly scenes in *L'Express* on 14 June, François Mauriac was adamant about the FLN methods. By pulling the trigger it wanted to provoke revenge violence that would produce yet more polarization: 'Horror calls horror. The FLN knows this, it looks for it, it will hesitate at nothing that will produce blind reprisals. Whatever happens on the streets of Algiers, let us say it very clearly, the FLN will have wanted it.'[92]

For the military the return of violence in the capital was a shock. It had underestimated Yacef's capacity to rebuild his networks. But in embarking on this fresh wave of terrorism it would be wrong to portray Yacef as an unthinking psychopath. On 4 July, during a remarkable four-hour secret meeting with Germaine Tillion, the former Soustelle Cabinet member, who had returned to Algeria to investigate torture under the auspices of the 'Commission Internationale contre Le Régime Concentrationnaire', he would admit to grave doubts about his actions.[93] The problem, he claimed, was that colonialism had made Algerians into 'assassins' because 'it's the only way we can express ourselves'.[94]

In the midst of this fresh violence, the 49th annual Socialist Party conference took place in Toulouse between 27 June and 1 July 1957. The Mélouza atrocity had undoubtedly reinforced the hardliners and both Lejeune and Lacoste arrived in a bullish mood. Heartened by the way in which the SFIO had held together during 1957—party membership had actually increased during this period—Lejeune made it clear that he did not want to be lectured on socialism by Aneurin Bevan.[95] Attending on behalf of the Labour Party, Bevan was arguing for Algerian self-determination by drawing a parallel with Clement Attlee's decolonization policy in India ten years earlier. Equally, in a National Council meeting on 12 May Lacoste had already belittled Charles-André Julien's protests about rape by paratroopers. Exuding a patriotic machismo, he told the assembled members that, although the allegations were probably true, he was certain paratroopers would not have to resort to these methods to register 'such a success' with women.[96] Now, within the conference, Lacoste went on to the offensive, donning the mantle of the progressive left against reaction. He attacked those who were sceptical about reform as being guilty of 'parliamentary cretinism': a Marxist term. Similarly he proclaimed his revolution to be a genuine revolution as opposed to the false one proposed by the FLN, telling delegates:

> If I am optimistic . . . it is because I believe in this other revolution . . . The work that we have done, we must follow it through and go forward. That is why we will be demanding in the coming months the outlining of a blueprint [*loi-cadre*]. This blueprint will not be an artificial gesture. It will be rooted in the reality that we have created . . . I do not say that it will resolve everything. But I say that if we show our will to create new institutions, conforming to democracy and to our duties towards the two communities, European and Muslim, we will have arrived at 'pacification'.[97]

This was fighting language which knew how to appeal to the conference floor. Unsurprisingly, therefore, the Lacoste motion, backed to the hilt by Mollet, won handsomely with 2,547 for. Against it a second solution put forward by Defferre and the Bouches-du-Rhône federation and devolving more autonomy to Algeria garnered 779, while the third motion talking about independence mustered a mere 498. In this way Mollet maintained control of the party, sending a clear message that the Socialist Party and the Socialist ministers were right behind the government, which itself renewed and extended the special powers on 16 July 1957.

Figure 7.5 Zohra Drif, one of the FLN's female operatives, in custody.

Back in Algiers, there was no let-up on the army's part. Indeed, it began to implement new techniques of infiltration. The paratroopers worked on prisoners who, demoralized by defeat, were converted to the French cause and then sent back to penetrate the FLN. Through these methods the paratroopers chalked up success after success. On 26 August two of Yacef's key operatives, Mourad and Kamel, were pinned down and killed. This opened the way to Yacef who, along with Zohra Drif, was captured alive on 24 September. Finally, on 7 October Ali la Pointe was cornered in a safe house on 5 Rue des Abderames near the top of the Casbah. Refusing to surrender, he, along with Hassiba Ben Bouali and the 12-year-old Petit Omar, was blown up—an explosion whose strength killed a further seventeen Algerian civilians. Within the rubble the paratroopers dug furiously until they exhumed Ali la Pointe's corpse: for Massu the physical proof of his men's final victory. The 'Battle of Algiers' was over.

Figure 7.6 Digging for Ali la Pointe's body after he was blown up in an FLN safe house on 7 October 1957.

The loi-cadre

On 17 September 1957 the government at last presented the proposed *loi-cadre* for Algeria to the National Assembly. This was the revolution that Lacoste had been fighting for ever since February 1956: one that affirmed Algeria's status as an integral part of France, while simultaneously empowering the local population in the running of their own affairs. In truth, the revolution had been watered down during the countless amendments in committee. Contentious questions, notably whether elections would be based on a single college, had been put to one side and this meant that Lacoste's proposals could never match the clarity of the FLN's call for independence.

Moreover, European opposition was primed. Soustelle and his supporters led the charge and on 30 September, knowing that they could count on the entrenched opposition of the Communists and Poujadists, the loi-cadre was rejected by 279 votes to 253. Thus began the eighteenth government crisis since the beginning of the Fourth Republic. France was without a government for thirty-five days until 6 November 1957 when the 38-year-old Radical Félix Gaillard managed to construct an administration drawing support from the Socialists through to the right. With Lacoste and Lejeune still at the helm in Algeria and the Sahara, continuity was once again guaranteed and on 28 January 1958 the loi-cadre was voted through, albeit in a truncated form. For Mollet, though, there was no doubt that this still represented the best future for Algeria.[98] After the elections following a ceasefire, the loi-cadre would be the basis of a debate with the country's representatives who themselves would be free to suggest their own proposals. This dialogue, he contended, would then feed into a definitive solution to be sanctioned by the French Parliament.

Away from the political establishment it was possible to discern a shift in public opinion. The public was still confused and divided. In September 1957 only 17% supported the integration of Algeria with France, as opposed to 21% who wanted a gradual progression to economic and financial independence, and 23% who supported independence.[99] Then in January 1958 51% expressed the view that Algeria would no longer be French in ten years' time. Clearly, a possible majority in favour of negotiations was crystallizing, one that wanted a way out based on peace with honour.

La Question

On 28 February 1958 the publishers Éditions de Minuit brought out *La Question*, Henri Alleg's eye-witness account of torture. Journalist and Algerian Communist Party member, Alleg had been picked up on 12 June 1957 and taken to the outskirts of Algiers, where he was subjected to electric shocks and ducked until he was half drowned. Since Éditions de Minuit, founded clandestinely during the Nazi Occupation, was an icon of

Resistance values, La Question had an enormous impact. The commissioning editor, Jérôme Lindon, wished to show that the conflict was implicating his compatriots in the same way that Nazism implicated all Germans. Through the power of testimony he wanted to confront French people with a question: were they prepared to let torture be carried out in their name?

La Question sold 66,000 before being banned by the government on 27 March when the police raided the Éditions de Minuit offices to seize the remaining 7,000 copies. Thereafter the book circulated in a semi-clandestine fashion selling a further 90,000 copies. One survey of forty-six bookshops in fifteen French towns, taken in April 1958, revealed that La Question was second only in popularity to Anne Frank's Diary. The book was translated into numerous foreign languages with the English version containing a preface by Jean-Paul Sartre, the existentialist philosopher and political activist, then France's most famous intellectual. Given his international stature Sartre's words carried a huge moral authority:

> We know now that it is not a question of punishing or re-educating certain individuals, and that the Algerian War cannot be humanized. Torture was imposed here by circumstances and demanded by racial hatred. In some ways it is the essence of the conflict and expresses its deepest truth.[100]

La Question provoked a major international scandal about torture which throughout 1957 had refused to go away. In November 1957 Pierre Vidal-Naquet had been instrumental in establishing the Maurice Audin Committee. This sought to establish the truth about the fate of Maurice Audin, communist and lecturer at Algiers University, who had 'disappeared' after being arrested by Massu's paratroopers on 11 June. Likewise by the end of 1957 the Commission to safeguard rights and individual liberties set up by Mollet had become mired in controversy. Given the task of investigating allegations of torture, the publication of their final report was delayed by both the Bourgès-Maunoury and Galliard governments because it was too critical. Rather than exonerating the army, the conclusion substantiated many of the torture accusations. In protest two members, Garçon and Delavignette, resigned. Then on 14 December extracts of the report, cataloguing a range of human rights abuses, were published in Le Monde.

Amongst Algerians there is no doubt that torture and internment strengthened support for the FLN. Out of the Casbah's total population of 80,000 between thirty and forty per cent of its active male population was arrested, at one stage or another, and in truth this had always been part of the FLN strategy. By pulling the trigger and letting the French react, it was unleashing a process of violence that would ultimately force the Algerian population full-square behind the FLN. This was why by 1957 the writer Mouloud Feraoun recorded gloomily in his diary that 'there is no room left for discussion, only fighting and destruction. More and more there seems to be no way out except death.'[101] It was why in Algiers Algerians cheered as ambulances took away the European dead and wounded. It was also why in June, when a group of thirty-two Algerian schoolboys from the Algiers Casbah aged between ten and fourteen were asked by their teacher what they would do if they were invisible, sixteen replied steal weapons, eleven said they would kill paratroopers, ten kill soldiers, seven kill all French people, three kill Lacoste, and two kill Mollet.[102] When pushed to go into more detail the following response was typical:

> If I was invisible I will go into a barracks and kill all the soldiers who are in the barracks and I will throw a bomb into the barracks. And after I will go into the parachutists' homes and I will kill them like dogs . . . Long live the Arabs and long live the FLN.[103]

Such answers explain why the 'Battle of Algiers' was a pyrrhic victory. The methods of victory had definitively alienated Muslim hearts and minds.

8

Complex Violence: December 1957 to September 1959

Thursday, 29 May 1958

O n the front page *El-Moudjahid* carried a heavily black-rimmed obituary bearing the caption: 'Abbane Ramdane has died in action.'[1] Explaining that he had crossed back into Algeria in December 1957, the article underlined Abbane's selfless heroism. Moving undetected through the length and breadth of the country, the article applauded Abbane's dedication to his important liaison mission which had inspired 'affection' and 'admiration' all around him.[2] Then in mid-April tragedy struck. Abbane and his men were caught up in a prolonged firefight with the French army during which he was seriously wounded, dying several hours later. Describing Abbane as a 'beautiful' and 'noble' figure whose 'courage' and 'willpower' had marked the essential phases of the Algerian people's struggle, the obituary traced his political career before concluding that with his death:

> The National Liberation Front loses one of its best organizers. Combatant Algeria one of its most valued children.
> We cry for a brother in combat whose memory will know how to guide us.[3]

It was a lie. Abbane had been killed five months earlier on 27 December 1957. Lured to Morocco for a conference with Mohammed V, Abbane was accompanied from Tunis by Belkacem Krim and Mahmoud Chérif, chief of Wilaya 1 in the Aurès. On landing at Tétouan on the 26th, the three men were whisked away to a remote farmhouse by Abdelhafid Boussouf, the head of Wilaya 5.[4] There Boussouf's men took Abbane into a back room and strangled him—ironically the same death that Ben M'Hidi had suffered at the hands of the French paratroopers ten months earlier. He was thirty-eight.

The killing of Abbane was the outcome of the ongoing power struggle within the FLN. Within this struggle Abbane's standing had been at its height at the beginning of 1957. Emboldened by his triumph at the Soummam Conference, Abbane believed that with the general strike the victory of the interior resistance was imminent. Consequently defeat did Abbane untold harm and throughout 1957 his prestige ebbed away. One after another of the military leaders lined up to attack him, and none more so than Boussouf, the black-haired former teacher who at thirty-one was the youngest of the Wilaya commanders. This particular clash flowed from Abbane's experience of Wilaya 5. Forced to take refuge there after the leadership fled Algiers in February 1957, Abbane was shocked by the structures and practices already put in place in Wilaya 5 in Morocco by Boussouf. In his eyes Boussouf was not engaging in action against the French. He was building up a military power base for his personal ambitions. Why, Abbane asked acerbically, was Boussouf staying in Morocco, enjoying the luxuries of personal body guards, cars and villas when he should be fighting with his troops in Algeria?

The spine of the 'Boussouf system' was the secret police. Handpicked training for this secret police—long and hard—inculcated strict allegiance to Boussouf, indifference to human suffering and expertise in manipulation and disinformation. Known as 'Boussouf's boys', they were a caste apart who imposed terror in the name of order, discipline and, above all, unquestioning obedience.[5] Nothing happened without their knowledge. Summary executions, torture, and disappearances became the norm.[6] Fear and uncertainty became the daily lot because Boussouf's impressive signals and intelligence system was not just about monitoring the French army. It also surveyed the every movement of the Algerian population in Morocco.

'Boussouf's boys' were the Algerian equivalent of the Soviet KGB, a security apparatus which became the hub of a system based on control, patronage, and corruption. Promotion within the 'Boussouf system' was never about talent or merit. It was about rewarding loyalty and conformity. It was about the establishment of a bureaucracy armed with a strong sense of clan solidarity. It was about the recreation of a traditional entity deeply embedded within the collective Algerian imaginary, namely a community organized on principles of mutual surveillance, submission, and loyalty.[7]

All of these practices were geared to one aim: the strengthening of Boussouf's power base. This explains why Abbane was so angry about the rise of Boussouf's right-hand man, the equally ambitious Houari Boumediène.

Why, Abbane also asked, had the 25-year-old Boumediène been made the number two in Wilaya 5 when men of his age and combat experience would be barely captains in Wilaya 4 or 2?[8] This hostility, deepened by the suspicion that Boussouf supported Abbane's hated political rival Ben Bella, led Abbane to denounce the state of affairs in Morocco in stinging terms. Speaking in August 1957 at Guentis, near to Tunis, Abbane raged against the 'feudal spirit' existing in Wilaya 5.[9] Here, he warned, was a man who was trying to overturn the Soummam Conference principles and subject civil power to military control.

In launching such a generalized attack on the militarization of the FLN, Abbane alienated his erstwhile ally Belkacem Krim. So, whereas in the previous year Krim had sided with Abbane against the exterior, now Krim felt outnumbered by the politicians within the FLN leadership. In large part, this hostility was derived from his sense of personal destiny. As the one 'historic leader' from November 1954 still at liberty, Krim felt that he alone was the rightful custodian of the revolution. But equally as a military man he did not want to be relegated by Abbane to a secondary role. This antipathy, overriding any sense of Kabyle solidarity, led Krim to seek an anti-Abbane alliance with Ben Tobbal, leader of Wilaya 2, and Boussouf. Unsurprisingly the two men, both born in Milia near Constantine, both close friends, both members of the 22 June 1954 Committee that led directly to the FLN, needed no prompting. The threat to Boussouf was self-evident, while Ben Tobbal, always unhappy at the place accorded to politicians by Soummam, was inherently suspicious. He saw Abbane as a late-comer who was preparing to sell out the revolution to the French and on these grounds the three men formed an anti-Abbane alliance.

The three men exacted their revenge on Abbane at the meeting of the FLN's governing body, the Conseil National de la Révolution Algérienne (CNRA), in Cairo on 27 August 1957. There Abbane was hopelessly isolated. Nobody but he stood up to the three colonels and the principles of the Soummam Conference were reversed. Henceforth the exterior would dominate over the interior and the military over the political. Equally, echoing Ben Bella's criticism concerning the omission of Islam at Soummam, the Cairo meeting reaffirmed that the aim of the revolution was the creation of a democratic and social republic based on Muslim principles.[10]

This new balance of power was reflected in the FLN leadership where the executive was stripped of Abbane's two closest allies, Ben Khedda and

Saad Dahlab, and then expanded to nine, composed of five colonels—Krim, Boussouf, Ben Tobbal, Ouamrane, and Mahmoud Chérif—to four politicians—Ferhat Abbas, Lamine Debaghine, Abdelhamid Mehri, and Abbane Ramdane. Likewise the new CNRA grew from thirty-four to fifty-four members, two-thirds of whom were military officers.[11] It was nothing short of a '*coup d'état*'.[12] Through it the 'three B's'—Belkacem Krim, Ben Tobbal, and Boussouf—had installed a military despotism at the summit of the power structure, justifying it as a return to the FLN's original spirit. From now on the army men would determine political choices. The role of politicians was to provide a facade. They were to be ready to negotiate, while the three B's built up an imposing military machine which already looked forward to post-independence.

In practical terms this meant the creation of two Comités Opérationnels Militaires (COM) to oversee internal resistance from the Tunisian and Moroccan frontiers. In Tunisia at Ghardimaou, Mohammedi Saïd took command of Wilayas 1, 2, and 3, while at Oujda in Morocco, the headquarters of Wilaya 5, Boumediène, the man Boussouf chose to replace himself, now directed Wilayas 4, 5, and 6. Taciturn, efficient, and ruthless, Boumediène came from a peasant family in Guelma, where he had attended Qu'ranic school before going to study at the Zeytouna mosque in Tunis and Al-Azhar University in Egypt. Returning to fight in Oranie in 1955 Boumediène spent a few months in the maquis before rising to become Boussouf's lieutenant. Installed at Oujda he saw his mission as a waiting game. Under his command it was a question of conserving strength. He had no wish to engage in wasteful attacks. He wanted to build up a professional fighting force, using many officers who had defected from the French army.

Completely marginalized during autumn 1957 Abbane threatened to return to Algeria: his intention to appeal directly to the people and the maquis over the heads of the three B's.[13] This more than anything sealed Abbane's fate because the three B's feared his continued support in Wilaya 4 under Colonel Sadek. All three wanted him silenced though Belkacem Krim would always claim that it was Boussouf alone who decided to murder Abbane.[14] The other colonels wanted to imprison him. As such, the wider significance of August 1957 would become apparent the more the conflict went on and then over into independence. This was the moment when the military took control: the unwritten law of Algerian politics to this day.[15]

And the war carries on

Inevitably this last outcome begs a series of counter-factual scenarios. What if the Soummam principles had endured? What if the 'Battle of Algiers' had produced an FLN victory? And what if Abbane had won out in the FLN's internal struggle? But in each case the answer takes us back to the FLN's founding context. This was an entity based on the cult of the strong warrior: an image with long roots in Algeria's rural society, deeply hostile to politicians, and highly dictatorial. Given these constraints, Abbane's room for manoeuvre was limited.[16] He was always going to come into conflict with the military hard men. But in considering the Abbane alternative we must avoid hagiography and myth-making about futures lost. Abbane was no pluralist. In pursuing the war against the MNA, he too enhanced the FLN's authoritarian culture. Likewise we must not forget the other crucial factor in this scenario: the Mollet government. This could never countenance defeat and the longer the war continued the longer Boussouf and then Boumediène had time to fashion the Wilaya 5 machine, ensuring the final marginalization of politicians and the domination of the military.

On another level Abbane's murder underlined how by 1957 the war was a complex and multilayered conflict. It was not just French against Algerian, even if this was the defining aspect of the conflict. It was also FLN against FLN. It was FLN against other Algerians. It was French against French. It was a war of the cities. It was a war of the countryside. It was a war of image and propaganda. It was a war of international diplomacy that transcended national boundaries and linked Algeria to metropolitan France, the French Union, the European Economic Community, the Arab World, and the cold war. In military terms the initiative was now passing to the French army by the autumn of 1957. With Algiers lost the ALN was pushed back into its rural bastions. The reasons for this success were twofold. First, there was the recruitment of Muslim anti-FLN units because, as Mohammed Harbi later admitted, ALN massacres like the one at Mélouza had made many willing to fight on the French side, hand over intelligence, or at the very least seek French protection.[17] Secondly, there was the construction of the Morice Line in June 1957, named after the then Minister of Defence André Morice. Stretching 300 km along the road from Bône to Tebessa on the Tunisian border, the Morice Line was a forbidding edifice made up of electric and barbed wire fences, mines, searchlights, and watch towers, all backed up by radar and air and naval surveillance. Behind it five paratrooper regiments stood ready to repel any incursion.

Matched by an equivalent along the Moroccan frontier, the Morice Line cut the maquis off from outside arms and provisions. Provoking a 'Battle of the Frontiers' along the Tunisian border, the lack of weapons and ammunition made it harder and harder for the internal resistance to carry on fighting. Yet, bleak as war looked on the ground, the diplomatic revolution continued. On 2 July 1957, a young and ambitious US senator, John F. Kennedy, made a speech in favour of Algerian independence. On 26 December 1957 the Afro-Asian Conference in Cairo gave a ringing endorsement of the FLN. Then on 15 April 1958 a major propaganda coup: the best Algerian footballers in the French League left for Tunis to form a national FLN team.[18] Two men—Rachid Mekhloufi from Saint Étienne and Mustapha Zitouni from AS Monaco—were certainties for the French squad heading for the World Cup in Sweden. By defecting they dealt a major blow to French chances and in their first game, widely covered across the Arab World, the FLN team beat Tunisia 5-1, before going on to register a string of similar results against Yugoslavia, Hungary, Czechoslovakia, and China.

Sakiet

On 8 February 1958 French planes pursued the ALN over the Tunisian border and bombed the frontier village of Sidi Youssef Sakiet, killing 70 and wounding 150, including children. As the images of civilian distress shot round the world, the opprobrium was instant and overwhelming. Even countries like Sweden and Norway, hitherto discreetly silent, expressed their disapproval at the UN.[19] Now the French were more isolated than ever on the international scene. For the Arab and Muslim countries this was a war crime, the colonial equivalent of the Nazi bombing of Guernica in 1937 during the Spanish Civil War.

The primary cause of Sakiet was French army frustration. In the 'Battle of the Frontiers' they came to regard President Bourguiba of Tunisia as an ally of the FLN. He was providing the FLN with safe havens. He was allowing them to build up their army and between July 1957 and February 1958 the French government made twenty-three protests delivered to Tunis. The immediate trigger, however, was Bourguiba himself. He was worried by the way in which Algerian presence on Tunisian soil and the growing influence of Nasser throughout North Africa were destabilizing his own government. For this reason Bourguiba wanted an end to the conflict and again he sought to act as go-between between the FLN and France in January 1958. The FLN response, though, was immediately hostile. It wanted to assert its independence from Bourguiba. It wanted to show that Tunisians did not dominate Algerians and two days later this led to renewed fighting near Sakiet. This left the French army straining at the leash. It saw Sakiet as an Algerian town and on 29 January 1958 the Gaillard government sanctioned an attack.[20]

Sakiet provoked an immediate crisis in Franco-Tunisian relations with Bourguiba blockading the French naval base at Bizerte and closing the French consulates. It also led directly to harsh exchanges between the US and France. For US President Eisenhower the French action was a nightmare scenario. It was isolating moderates like Bourguiba and encouraging radicals, potentially pushing the whole of the Arab world into the hands of the Soviets. On these grounds Eisenhower warned that unless Gaillard accepted the proposal of 'good offices' from the United States and Britain then American loans to France would be jeopardized.[21] Confronted with this pressure Gaillard had no alternative but to give in and receive two US envoys: Robert Murphy, former Consul to Algiers during World War Two, and Harold Beeley, Under-Secretary of State at the Foreign Office.

In France there was outrage from all sides. Murphy in particular was badly seen. As the man who had forged relations with Abbas in 1943 he was the example par excellence of Anglo-Saxon meddling. Critics warned about a 'new Munich'. On 15 April the Gaillard government was overthrown by 321 to 225. It was the twentieth ministerial crisis of the Fourth Republic and for the rest of April France was without a government until eventually President Coty, again advised by Mollet, called upon Pierre Pflimlin to form an administration on 8 May. An MRP stalwart, Pierre Pflimlin made known his willingness to open negotiations with the FLN for a ceasefire.

By this point France and Algeria were awash with plot and counter-plot, threatening the Fourth Republic on all sides. There were plots amongst European hardliners like Biaggi, Lagaillarde, and Ortiz. Organized within a Committee of Vigilance they wanted a re-run of 6 February 1956. There were plots within the army. Indeed, on 9 May Salan sent a telegram to the Minister of Defence, Jacques Chaban-Delmas, stating that the army could not countenance the abandonment of Algeria. He added ominously that he could not predict how his officers would react to such a proposal.[22] There were plots amongst Gaullists, who saw in the crisis the moment they had been waiting for: the return of de Gaulle. Thus, the Gaullist Chaban-Delmas arranged the sending of Gaullist agents to Algiers, notably Léon Delbecque, who contacted activists and military men on the ground.

In this conspiratorial atmosphere Lacoste left Algiers on 10 May, talking in dark terms of 'a diplomatic Dien Bien Phu'. He omitted to mention that on the previous day he had met in secret with members of the Committee of Vigilance on 9 May. Through mass street protest they wanted to make sure that any new government kept on Lacoste as Minister-Resident. In return Lacoste promised that in the event of any such demonstrations the police would not intervene. In effect he was giving a green light to the European activists who were incensed to learn on 10 May that the FLN had executed three French soldiers, prisoners since 1956 for torture, rape, and killing. How, Europeans asked, could the government contemplate talking to such people?[23]

May 1958 crisis and the return of de Gaulle

In Paris the date set for Pflimlin's investiture was 13 May 1958. In Algiers, General Salan chose the same day to lay flowers on the war monument at plateau Glières in memory of the three executed French prisoners. It was an explicit warning to the incoming administration and as Salan carried out the ceremony a demonstration of 100,000 Europeans converged on the Forum as well. Egged on by Lagaillarde and Ortiz, this crowd vented their anger on the American Cultural Centre, underlining the strong anti-US feelings of May 1958, before going on to ransack the government offices, throwing documents and typewriters from the windows.

Such vandalism was an attack on the Fourth Republic's authority. But neither the police nor the army intervened to uphold this authority. They let the events happen before Colonel Trinquier, aided by Lagaillarde, hastily formed a Committee of Public Safety; a title which, in referencing the most perilous phase of the French Revolution, evoked the image of the 'Republic in danger'. Arriving later, Massu was horrified by the chaos and immediately took control of the Committee of Public Safety, announcing from the balcony of the Minister-Resident's Office at 8.45 p.m. that: 'I, General Massu, have just formed a committee of public safety . . . so that in France a

government of public safety may be formed, presided over by General de
Gaulle.'[24] Back in Paris the freshly invested Pflimlin was resolute. He
condemned the military leaders and called for a union of Republican
Defence, naming Mollet as vice-premier and making Jules Moch, another
Socialist Party stalwart, Minister of the Interior.

Initially few picked up on Massu's reference to de Gaulle, but on 15 May
Salan again shouted his name from the balcony, this time to huge acclaim.
The de Gaulle genie was out of the bottle, a fact reiterated by the arrival in
Algiers of Soustelle on 17 May who too pronounced from the Minister-
Resident's Office 'Vive de Gaulle!', 'Vive French Algeria!', and 'Vive the
Republic!' Yet, the 67-year-old de Gaulle was very careful in his public
statements. He did not go to Algiers to assume the leadership of the
Committee of Public Safety. Nor did he openly back Massu and Salan.
Instead he remained at his home in Colombey-les-Deux-Églises. From
there he foregrounded his personal legitimacy as the leader of the World
War Two Resistance, met leading political figures like the former prime-
minister Antoine Pinay, and courted Mollet's support at a press conference
on 19 May.

While de Gaulle waited on events, on 16–18 May Algiers witnessed what
seemed to be remarkable scenes of fraternization between Algerians and
Europeans. In the Forum Algerian women burned their veils and Europeans
acclaimed their Muslim brothers and sisters, linking arms to the chant 'from
Dunkirk to Tamanrasset there is only one nation'.[25] The arrival of the
Algerians was the work of Colonels Godard and Trinquier, using their
system of control established during the 'Battle of Algiers', and for them it
was a major victory. In their view this was the equivalent of 4 August 1789
when the French Revolution abolished feudal privileges. This was the
moment of reconciliation when the Franco-Muslim community became a
reality. Was it genuine or was it stage managed? Certainly the FLN would
always denounce the images as a fraud. This was not an expression of
Franco-Algerian harmony because, *El-Moudjahid* and the FLN radio stations
claimed, the Algerians had been forced to participate at gunpoint.[26]

The intensity with which *El-Moudjahid* attacked the 16 May fraternization
underlined how such scenes represented the FLN's worst nightmare: the loss
of Algerian 'hearts and minds' to the French army. The control of the
population was still the prize and throughout May 1958 the momentum
seemed to be pulling in an anti-FLN direction. Across Algeria other
Committees of Public Safety sprang up, federated into one large Committee

·of Public Safety Algeria–Sahara, and within this federation there was a significant Algerian participation. It was not just an expression of European hope. The Committee of Public Safety was headed by both Massu and Chérif Sidi Cara and of the seventy-two members thirteen were Muslim. Even more significantly, pro-French Algerian voices were pushed to the fore within all the public demonstrations. So, on 28 May at Blida a 15-year-old girl by the name of Malika, subsequently adopted by Massu, told a crowd of 30,000 people that: 'I, I love the French . . . We are all united behind the Army and have sworn to fight to the end for Algeria and France to live together. I hope with all my heart that Algeria remains French and the *fellagha* must know that no foreign hand will be laid on Algeria.'[27]

Hovering over these events was the threat of paratroopers dropping on Paris to install de Gaulle in power: 'Operation Resurrection'. Salan called off the operation on 19 May, but then pressed ahead on 24–5 May, successfully establishing a Committee of Public Safety in Corsica. The country appeared to be on the brink of a *coup d'état* at which point an exhausted Pflimlin met with de Gaulle on the night of 26 May. The following day de Gaulle carried out his master stroke: at midday he announced that he had begun to form a Republican government that would ensure national unity. Pflimlin was aghast. This possibility had never been discussed at their meeting but in the face of this fait accompli he had no other option than to resign on 28 May. With the possibility of the paratroopers still looming large, several hundred thousand people, including Pierre Mendès France, André Philip, François Mitterrand, and Jean-Paul Sartre, marched in Paris in protest but in truth there was little they could do. On 29 May Coty asked de Gaulle to form a government and on 30 de Gaulle met with Guy Mollet, still the arbiter in the National Assembly. Mollet wanted assurances that de Gaulle would keep France in NATO and abide by the Assembly. Convinced of his sincerity, Mollet then carried the Socialist parliamentary group, albeit by the tiny majority of 77 to 74, arguing that only de Gaulle's moral authority could save the country from a military coup.

The last obstacle to power had been removed and on 1 June de Gaulle appeared before the National Assembly. Demanding full powers for his government and promising to introduce a new constitution, his government was invested by 329 to 224 votes in the face of opposition from the Communists, Mendès France supporters, and about half the Socialists. It was an emphatic victory for change, although de Gaulle's first administration displayed considerable continuity with the old system. Mollet was deputy prime minister, Lejeune Minister of the Sahara, Pflimlin and Jacquinot Ministers of State, while Michel Debré and André Malraux were the only prominent Gaullists included.

Such an outcome underlines de Gaulle's razor-sharp political skills. Throughout May 1958 he judged the public mood perfectly. Sensing that the majority wanted to end the Fourth Republic, he channelled the crisis to his own advantage. In particular he played upon the threat of the putsch, knowing that his major advantage was his legitimacy as the man of the French Resistance. Unlike the Fourth Republic he alone could command the personal allegiance of the armed forces and police in Algeria and this ultimately was the decisive factor in his return.

This explains why both the US and Britain stood aside and let the Fourth Republic fall.[28] This explains, too, the absence of any major opposition within France itself. By May 1958 the majority of French people were disenchanted with the system. They were exasperated by its inherent instability. They had no faith in its ability to bring an end to the Algerian crisis. In contrast de Gaulle was seen as the one figure able to save the country from civil war, bring about national unity, and find a palatable solution in Algeria.

'I have understood you'

What was de Gaulle's position on Algeria in 1958? The past pointed in different directions. He was the man who had sanctioned the May 1945 repression, condemned the 1947 Statute and underlined the need to maintain French sovereignty in the late 1940s. But he was also the man who remembered the settlers' pro-Vichy sentiments during World War Two. Equally he was a man whose position seemed to have evolved by the mid-1950s. At a press conference on 30 June 1955 de Gaulle had talked about the need to integrate Algeria 'into a community larger than France' and 'replace domination with association', an echo of Mollet's subsequent 'Eurafrica' vision.[29] Nevertheless, within any such larger entity de Gaulle underlined the importance of protecting France's energy interests in the Sahara, a place he had visited in March 1957 and which, like Mollet, he saw as a key geo-strategic asset.

On 4 June 1958 de Gaulle was given an ecstatic welcome as his cavalcade made its way from the airport in Algiers. It was a complete contrast to the hostile reception accorded to Mollet two years earlier. Standing aloft in an open-top Citroën the six foot seven de Gaulle, dressed in the uniform of a brigadier-general, acknowledged the flag-waving crowds who lined the streets and balconies. Laying a wreath at the main war monument, he visited a battleship in Algiers harbour, before going to address the waiting multitude in the Forum at 7.00 p.m. Introduced by Salan, all hinged on de Gaulle's ability to deliver a speech that would capture the mood of the moment. Arriving on the balcony arms aloft in a huge V-sign, the sight of the general produced a deafening sound. For three minutes de Gaulle could not make himself heard and then he pronounced:

I have understood you.[30]

It was a brilliant phrase. With these four words he established an immediate rapport with the huge crowd. He had won them over, continuing:

I know what has occurred here. I see what you have sought to accomplish.
I see that the road you have opened in Algeria is that of renewal and fraternity.
   I say renewal in every respect. But, very rightly, you wanted to begin at the beginning; that is, with our institutions; and that is why I am here.
   I say fraternity, for you will provide the magnificent example of men . . . who share in the same ardour and live hand in hand.[31]

In reaching out to the crowd de Gaulle hung back from any mention of French Algeria. Instead he talked in terms of political equality and fraternity, imposing his own specific meaning on the events of May 1958. For France, de Gaulle underlined, there was just one category of inhabitant: French people with 'the same rights and the same duties'.[32] His mission, therefore, was to 'open the doors that have been shut for many' and give them 'dignity' and a 'patrie'.[33] In this respect de Gaulle paid tribute to the role played by the French army, talking glowingly of its 'magnificent work of understanding and pacification' while also underlining the need for discipline and obedience. This recognition provoked a wave of emotion amongst the crowd who also listened as de Gaulle outlined new elections under a single college system within three months.[34] On the basis of these newly elected representatives, de Gaulle explained in a piece of calculated vagueness, 'we will see how to do the rest'.[35] No less significantly, the general extended a hand to those who, through 'desperation', were leading a fight which he himself recognized as 'courageous'.[36] To them, too, de Gaulle promised to open the way to 'reconciliation' before concluding, to

rapturous acclaim, with: 'Never more than here, nor more than this evening, have I felt how beautiful, how great, how generous is France! Long live
the Republic. Long live France.'[37]

The speech had lasted just over ten minutes. The true meaning of its
content, especially those first four words, have been interpreted and rein-
terpreted ever since. For the overwhelming majority of Europeans they
would become a byword for betrayal. But at the time, by seemingly
promising an Algeria firmly anchored within the Republic, they restored
trust. Thereafter de Gaulle's tour continued in triumph. Everywhere there
was euphoria, although de Gaulle still avoided all talk of French Algeria. In
fact, he only used this phrase once on 6 June at Mostaganem, and even then
with a degree of hesitation.

Figure 8.1 De Gaulle in Algeria, 4 June 1958.

A new constitution

In essence, de Gaulle's vision of equal citizens was the same as Mollet's two years earlier. What was different was the context within which this solution was received. In February 1956 the Europeans had felt vulnerable, but in May 1958 they felt strong because it was they and the army who had brought de Gaulle back to power. Although de Gaulle did not say French Algeria, he *did* say that France was still sovereign and that Algeria, 'composed of ten million French people', was an integral part of the Republic.[38] The Europeans saw this as the main message of May 1958, namely that independence was unthinkable.

However, if the Europeans saw the end of the Fourth Republic solely in terms of Algeria, de Gaulle did not. As his careful positioning throughout 1958 had shown, he had no wish to be a tool of the settlers or the army. He always had a wider vision of the future and here his first priority was popular approval for a new constitution. This alone would restore the authority of the state and immediately de Gaulle announced a referendum for 28 September which would give men and women in France, Algeria and the other overseas territories the right to say yes or no to the Fifth Republic's institutions.

As the referendum campaign got under way de Gaulle did everything for a 'yes' vote. One poster, with a photograph of the general, simply proclaimed 'Yes' in French and Arabic, while others showed Muslim families voting in favour of the new constitution.[39] Specifically, the 'yes' campaign reached out to Algerian women. One poster featured a black-and-white drawing of two European women and an Algerian woman casting their ballot with the titles 'I am a French citizen' in blue and 'I vote' in red.[40] A further one, simply entitled 'Why you must vote', listed why Algerian women had to use their franchise:

This vote enshrines your equality with men.
Women in the metropole all vote. You must do like them.
You should be proud of the new role that is opening up for you, since now you will have your say in the running of the country, since the new ALGERIA cannot be made without you.
The new Algeria will be what you make of it.
It is yourselves who will make your future and that of your children by making your voice heard. During the demonstrations, thousands of Muslim women

came to mix with men and prove that they want to play a role in the life of the country.

It is the sign of renewal.[41]

Equally de Gaulle sought to de-escalate the cycle of violence and counter-violence and win over the Algerian population by freeing 7,000 detainees and momentarily halting the guillotining of FLN prisoners on death row. On a different level, he tried to connect any future evolution to the Franco-African Community established by the constitution. By this measure he called on Africans to reject independence and vote in favour of autonomy within the Franco-African Community because it would offer a possible blueprint for Algeria. Indeed, at one point he even went as far as to say: 'It is for Algeria that I made the Community.' Yet, at the same time, the 'yes' campaign played on the anti-communist and anti-FLN feelings within the European community. One Gaullist sticker simply said 'Oui—Nyet',[42] while another, produced by Jacques Soustelle's Ministry of Information, was even cruder: 'FLN + Communists = Assassins'.[43]

In France the constitution was rejected by the Communist Party and some elements of the non-communist left who were worried that too much power was being handed over to the president. In Algeria the FLN warned that any Algerian who voted would be killed. However, despite this opposition, despite these threats, the referendum was a huge triumph for de Gaulle. In the metropole 84.94 per cent voted and 66.41 per cent said yes. In Algeria it was 80 per cent and 96 per cent. In French Africa only Guinea opted for independence.

Were the elections in Algeria clean, though? Certainly de Gaulle would immediately claim so. The sight of Algerian men and women queuing up to vote under a single college was, he argued, a victory for democracy against FLN terrorism. In contrast the journalist Edward Behr was less convinced. He saw 'no' votes thrown away. He saw Algerians being herded into the voting booths. He also recounted how the elections became the basis of a stand-up routine for Jean Rigaux, then France's funniest cabaret satirist. Within it Rigaux told the story of a Muslim making his way to a polling station in the Sahara, 160 km from his village. On the bus the army officer tells them that they are off to vote for de Gaulle, explaining that on arrival each person must put the white 'yes' ballot paper into the urn. When one Muslim asks what the purple 'no' ballot paper is for, the officer replies that it is the return bus ticket.[44]

The Constantine Plan

Armed with his electoral legitimacy, de Gaulle travelled to Constantine on 3 October to announce a major five-year development plan for Algeria. Making no mention of either French Algeria or integration, he situated the Constantine Plan within the 'yes' vote which had shown a France united in renewal and an African Community determined to build a common entity on the values of liberty, equality, and fraternity. Capitalizing on this success, he now promised that by 1963 the Constantine Plan would create 400,000 new jobs, house 1 million people, and redistribute 250,000 hectares of land to Muslims. Furthermore, this Plan would increase wages to the same level as in the metropole; provide an education for two-thirds of Muslim children; expand numbers of Muslims in the civil service, the law, and the army; and ensure the development of the Sahara's energy potential for the common good.

By acting in this way, de Gaulle explained, France would bring social and economic emancipation to the Algerian population:

> It is the profound transformation of this country, so courageous, so living, but also so difficult and suffering, that must be realized. That means it is necessary that the living conditions of each man and each woman improve from day to day; that means that, for the inhabitants, the resources of the soil, the value of the elites must be brought up to date and developed; that means children must be taught; that means that Algeria as a whole must have its share of what modern civilization can and must bring to men in terms of well-being and dignity.[45]

Although he was absolutely clear that the forthcoming elections to the National Assembly would be based on a single college and that two-thirds of those elected would be Muslim, de Gaulle was careful not to box himself into precise political solutions. Indeed he said that it was useless to say exactly where the process would end. The Constantine Plan had to concentrate on the here and now. The social and economic reforms had to have time to foster a spirit of political cooperation. Only in this way, over the next five years, de Gaulle argued, could the country move towards a new arrangement based on the dual notion of Algeria's distinctiveness (*sa personnalité*) and its direct link with France.

In conclusion de Gaulle contrasted his policies with those who only look 'to kill', 'to destroy', and 'to hate', telling his audience: 'For the race of men today, there are only two routes: war or fraternity. In Algeria as everywhere, France, for her part, has chosen fraternity. Long live the Republic! Long live Algeria and France!'[46]

Following on from the speech, bold posters trumpeted the Constantine Plan as a new era. In reality de Gaulle's initiative was the legacy of Mollet's third-way reformism, reflecting the role of specialist civil servants like Michel Piquard and Jean Vibert who had been working on welfare legislation in Algeria ever since 1954. Signalling the importance of the long-term development plans outlined under Mendès France in 1955 and Lacoste in 1956, Vibert stressed this fact in December 1959:

> The Constantine Plan was in effect the outcome of the work of several years, undertaken on their own initiative by a group of young civil servants in Algeria, economists, statisticians, financiers. Little by little the figures and ideas penetrated minds, formed the canvas for the economic future of Algeria, drew up an exit to the impasse to which a galloping demography had driven Algeria.[47]

Certainly, Mollet himself stressed this continuity in the legislative elections, telling journalists in Arras on 10 November 1958:

> we are proud to see that the essentials of our position are upheld by the government and by its leader. Patience and perseverance in the twin effort of economic progress (the Constantine Plan with which we are fully in accord) and political liberation are for us the keys to the solution.[48]

Like the Republican Front, Mollet further emphasized, de Gaulle understood that France had to help Algeria and the overseas territories become authentic democratic entities. He knew that it was in France's national interest to deliver economic and political modernization in Africa, otherwise these countries could fall prey to despair and ultimately communism.

Ten days later, in preparation for legislative elections on 30 November, de Gaulle ordered all army officers to stand down from the Committees of Public Safety. In part this was about reining in the military and placing it under civil authority. But in part, too, it was about keeping the military out of the elections. De Gaulle did not wish to be encumbered by French Algerian hardliners in the National Assembly. He wanted a fair ballot that would ensure a wider range of political tendencies, particularly from pro-French voices in the Algerian community. Then, on 23 October, de Gaulle made a direct appeal to the FLN: the 'peace of the brave' ('*paix des braves*'). It was an arresting phrase—projecting the image of an honourable enemy—and with it de Gaulle offered an amnesty. Inviting his adversaries to lay down their arms, he called on them to accept the democratic process and help build a solution recognizing Algeria's distinctiveness ('*la personnalité de l'Algérie*') and the country's special relationship with France.[49] Significantly, de Gaulle also gave the first French statistics on the loss of life since November 1954 which he put at 1,500 Europeans, 10,000 Muslims in Algeria, and 77,000 'rebels'.

Predictably, de Gaulle's offer was rejected. Nevertheless the elections went ahead on 30 November and, although Algerian participation fell to 64 per cent, they resulted in sixty-seven deputies, of whom forty-six were Muslim and twenty-one European. Collectively these deputies joined forces with the new Gaullist party, Union pour la Nouvelle République (UNR), which registered an overwhelming victory in mainland France. Then, on 21 December de Gaulle was elected by a college system to become President of the Republic and the Community.

In the meantime, in early December, de Gaulle brought about a final separation of military and civilian functions, transferring many leading army officers from May 1958 away from Algeria in early December. This included Salan himself, made military governor of Paris, who was replaced by two people: General Maurice Challe, one of the architects of the Suez campaign, and Paul Delouvrier, a smartly dressed technocrat who had taken a leading role in the establishment of the European Coal and Steel Community in the early 1950s. Within this division of power Challe's brief was the military side, while Delouvrier was to concentrate on making the Constantine Plan succeed.

FLN reaction

For the FLN, May 1958 was a shock. Although in public the FLN denounced the Franco–Muslim fraternization as a lie, in private the FLN leaders were fearful. Colonel Ouamrane spoke of these grave 'events'. In the same vein Ferhat Abbas was afraid that the Algerian people no longer had faith in the FLN's ability to deliver independence. If so, he confided on 28 July, then everything was lost and Algeria would suffer the same fate as Palestine.

In this mood of crisis the leadership recognized the need for dramatic action. The FLN had to regain the initiative. This led to a fresh offensive on the frontiers. It led, too, to a new front in France itself on 25 August when the FLN launched a series of coordinated attacks across the mainland, including an attempt to blow up the Mourepiane oil refinery in Marseille.[50]

Most dramatically of all, however, it led to the proclamation of a Provisional Government of the new Algerian Republic.

This momentous step took place at a press conference on 19 September in Cairo when Abbas, named president, unveiled his government to the world. Dressed in sober suits under the Algerian flag, Abbas and his ministers, including Benyoucef Ben Khedda at Social Affairs and Mohammed Yazid at Information, understood the symbolism of the moment. If they wished to challenge French sovereignty, they had to show that the FLN leaders were not 'murderers' or 'criminals'. They had to exude gravitas. They had to project the image of respectable statesmen ready for national office. This in turn explains why Abbas and Yazid were so important. As people of recognized political stature, they were reassuring figures in diplomatic circles, particularly in Britain and the US where Abbas's face appeared on the front cover of *Time* magazine. They were seen as men the French could sit down and talk to, even though the real power in the Provisional Government resided in the hands of the three B's: Belkacem Krim, vice-president and Armed Forces Minister, Lakhdar Ben Tobbal, Interior Minister, and Abdelhafid Boussouf, the head of the secret services.[51]

The hope was that the Provisional Government would seize back the political momentum. Did this succeed? On the negative side, de Gaulle ignored the Provisional Government's proposals to open negotiations. Likewise its existence did not prevent huge numbers of Algerians from voting in the September referendum. Nor was the news good on the military front. In the countryside and on the frontiers the ALN was more pinned back than ever. But, in the long run, these developments were more than outweighed by a major diplomatic victory when the Provisional Government was given immediate recognition by the Arab states and the Asian communist states. This legitimacy gave the FLN a decisive political strength because, in the absence of any alternative, who else were the French going to negotiate with?

The Challe offensive

On 9 January 1959 de Gaulle announced his first government of the Fifth Republic. Michel Debré was the prime minister, Jacques Soustelle Minister of the Sahara—two pro-French Algeria figures who reassured Europeans—while Pierre Guillaumat was the Army Minister and André Malraux the Culture Minister. Crucially this meant that there was no place for either

Mollet or Lejeune; a reflection of the way in which, with de Gaulle now firmly in the saddle, he could dispense with the Socialist Party, itself badly defeated in the November 1958 elections.

For this new government Algeria remained the number-one problem. There was no prospect of an end in sight because neither the '*paix des braves*' nor the Constantine Plan had coaxed the FLN into laying down arms. In this context de Gaulle turned to General Challe, asking him to deliver victory in six months. As such de Gaulle was following exactly the same logic as Mollet in 1956. Like Mollet, he knew that at some point the fighting would stop, and when it did de Gaulle wanted to be in the strongest position possible so that he could impose a solution of his own choosing.

In preparing his offensive Challe knew that the internal ALN maquis was in a perilous position. Effectively cut off from outside support by the two fortified frontiers and numbering 21,150 in October 1958, it had been on the back foot for over a year now.[52] Challe's aim, therefore, was to deliver a final hammer blow through a vast sweeping manoeuvre. This would begin in the west in February, where 'pacification' was the most advanced, followed by the centre in April and then climaxing with the east in July: the cradle of ALN resistance.

In seeking to finish off the ALN, Challe underlined the importance of the huge recruitment of pro-French Algerian units which were expanded from 26,000 to 60,000. Drawing on their local knowledge of the terrain, these units would be the eyes and ears of the hunt whose purpose was to pinpoint ALN guerrillas. Once this was accomplished the paratroopers would be immediately helicoptered in to finish off the ALN, hitting the guerrillas again and again until they were broken. Challe's strategy was based upon the principle of no safe havens. Neither the mountains nor the night, he stressed, would be left to the maquis. At the same time Challe aimed to starve the FLN of food and shelter. He wanted to cut them off from the people, and extended the regrouping policy so that by July 1959 1 million villagers had been relocated into makeshift camps.

This strategy, combined with the sheer weight of French numbers, meant that the Challe offensive was a one-sided battle. Harried on all sides the ALN tried to break down into smaller, more mobile units but there was no escape. Within months the ALN had lost half of its soldiers killed, captured, or converted to the French cause. It was now a skeleton of its former self. Relentless French pressure meant, Challe told *Le Monde* on 23 April 1959

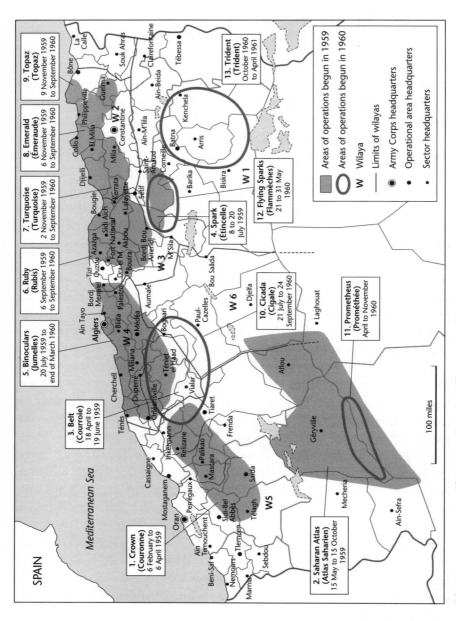

Map 8.1 1959–1960: The major French Offensives in Algeria.

SPAIN

Mediterranean Sea

1. Crown (Couronne) 6 February to 6 April 1959

2. Saharan Atlas (Atlas Saharien) 15 May to 15 October 1959

3. Belt (Courroie) 18 April to 19 June 1959

5. Binoculars (Jumelles) 20 July 1959 to end of March 1960

6. Ruby (Rubis) 6 September 1959 to September 1960

7. Turquoise (Turquoise) 2 November 1959 to September 1960

8. Emerald (Émeraude) 6 November 1959 to September 1960

9. Topaz (Topaz) 9 November 1959 to September 1960

13. Trident (Trident) October 1960 to April 1961

4. Spark (Étincelle) 8 to 20 July 1959

12. Flying Sparks (Flammèches) 21 to 31 May 1960

10. Cicada (Cigale) 21 July to 24 September 1960

11. Prometheus (Prométhée) April to November 1960

Areas of operations begun in 1959
Areas of operations begun in 1960

W   Wilaya
—   Limits of wilayas
◉   Army Corps headquarters
●   Operational area headquarters
•   Sector headquarters

100 miles

Oran
Mostaganem
Perrégaux
Cassaigne
Relizane
Inkermann
Palikao
Mascara
Frenda
Tiaret
Saïda
Télagh
Sidi-Bel Abbès
Ain-Temouchent
Tlemcen
Nemours
Beni-Saf
Sebdou
Marnia

W5

Mecheria
Géryville
Aflou
Laghouat
Ain-Sefra

W 6
Djelfa
Paul-Cazelles
Bou Saâda

W 4
Algiers
Blida
Médéa
Boghari
Aumale
Téniet el Haad
Vialar
Orléansville
Duperré
Miliana
Cherchell
Ténès

Ain Tayo

W 3
Tizi Ouzou
Bordj Menaïel
Azazga
Dra-el-M.
Fort National
Sidi Aïch
Bougie
Bordj Bou Arreridj
M'Sila
Boutra Akbou
Palestro

W 1
Biskra
Barika
Sétif
Lafayette
Kerrata
Mila
El Milia
Collo
Djidjelli

W 2
Constantine
Saint-Arnaud
Cornelia
Ain-Mlila
Batna
Arris
Kenchela
Ain-Beïda
Guelma
Philippeville
Bône
La Calle
Souk Ahras
Clairefontaine
Tébessa

that the ALN was no longer a viable force. It had imploded because the interior was no longer willing to fight for the exterior:

> It is clear that its members (of the government) do not have the same preoccupations as the rebels of the interior. The extremists of the exterior have certainly the desire to continue because they are risking nothing. In sum, we are taking prisoners who are putting up their hands more quickly than before, because they find themselves in a different situation. In other words, it is possible that those who we call the 'palace rebels' are fighting to the last man ... (Challe marked here a pause and smiled imperceptibly) ... of the interior.[53]

Impact on the FLN

Challe's claim of ALN disintegration and hence French victory was no false one. For the ALN, 1959 was the hardest year. Brought to its knees by the offensive, the interior did indeed feel abandoned, producing feelings of anger, paranoia, and disaffection. Amongst ordinary ALN soldiers morale plummeted. There was huge resentment towards the exterior military commanders and the Provisional Government who, it was believed, were doing nothing while living in luxury.[54]

Without doubt this mutinous atmosphere was fuelled by dirty tricks carried out by the French army. Already a certain Captain Léger had planted false information which trapped Colonel Amirouche, the Wilaya 3 commander, into thinking that his unit had been infiltrated by spies. This led to a purge during which 2,000 were killed, many of them students who had joined the maquis in spring 1956. Similarly, numerous French army tracts tried to drive a wedge between the interior and the exterior, describing the corrupt lifestyle of the leadership in Morocco and Tunisia and calling on ordinary maquisards to respond positively to de Gaulle's 'paix des braves'.[55] But it was also driven by rivalry and jealousy where, it must be stressed, the motivation was power not ideology. From top to bottom the FLN was riven by in-fighting as each faction was defined in terms of a combination of affinities whether it be family, tribe, region, wilaya, interior, exterior, or previous political involvement. For example, Ali Kafi, head of Wilaya 2, did not recognize the authority of the external military command structures put in place by Boussouf, Ben Tobbal, and Belkacem Krim. Ben Khedda the ex-MTLD member resented the head-of-state role accorded to Ferhat Abbas whom he saw as an old-style reformist. Belkacem Krim, as the only historic 1 November 1954 leader still not dead or imprisoned, saw himself as the one person who had the right to lead. Equally, when in March 1959 Amirouche, on his way to demand action from the Provisional Government in Tunis, was killed in an ambush, Wilaya 3 became immediately divided over who had the right to take his crown.[56]

Faced with implosion, Abbas sent an urgent message on 10 July 1959 to the Wilaya commanders. In it he called for a meeting that would designate another CNRA to resolve differences and fashion a new military, political, and diplomatic strategy. This took place in Tunis between 11 August and 16 December 1959 where the colonels, like a round table of medieval knights, became embroiled in a complex barter over who should enjoy the spoils of independence. The resultant CNRA, now clearly dominated by men loyal to Boumediène, then moved to Tripoli in Libya where, after four weeks of further talking, it appointed a fresh Provisional Government and a new military entity to replace the COM: the ALN general staff. For both these reasons, Tunis and Tripoli represented a significant shift in power. Belkacem Krim, Boussouf, and Ben Tobbal were on the wane while Boumediène was in the ascendant. He was the man in charge of the ALN general staff which, although in theory under political control, was in fact a rival power base to the Provisional Government.

Under the umbrella of the ALN general staff, Boumediène continued to build up the army of the frontiers, refining the system that he had inherited from Boussouf. Drawing upon the expertise of officers trained in Egypt, Iraq, and Syria and deserters from the French Army, he constructed a militarized society based on the values of obedience and discipline. On this basis Boumediène repressed the largest expression of interior dissent: the revolt led by Captain Zoubir, a maquis officer, who, starved of arms and food, had crossed over into Morocco in December 1959 and stirred up a protest movement against the ALN general staff.[57] In the meantime Boumediène ordered his own soldiers not to engage in costly attacks on the frontiers. Instead they were to sit tight and wait.

Impact on Algerian society

While the FLN reeled under the Challe offensive, the war continued to transform Algerian society at every level. More than ever this was a struggle for the allegiance of ordinary people. In this sense the Challe offensive was the climax of the 'pacification' process begun under the Fourth Republic. It was not just about defeating the FLN, but winning the population over to the Constantine Plan.

The authorities, therefore, continued to produce posters and films that extolled France's mission as one of long-term modernization where each Algerian would have their share. One poster, entitled 'The Constantine Plan: the Road to the Future', showed two children hand in hand at the beginning of a road leading to factories, tractors and electricity pylons.[58] Within the documentary films, such as *The Constantine Plan: Money, men, machines* which was in English and aimed at US audiences, little mention was made of the FLN.[59] Instead the images constructed the real battle in Algeria as one against illiteracy, underdevelopment, and female oppression under Islam. In *The Falling Veil*, a further film for US audiences, the narrator presents the arrival of de Gaulle in Algeria in June 1958 as a moment of liberation for Algerian women: an event which led them to reconsider their place in society: 'His confidence in women acted as almost an electric current to many of them, a kind of psychological shock which jolted them out of their old attitude of apathy and into a new awareness of themselves.'[60]

The Falling Veil, along with other documentaries such as *How to Vote*, *The Arab Women of the Bled*, and *Women, Blessing of God*, underlined how, for the French, Algerian women were a key battleground who had to be won over through a reform process which, begun under the Republican Front, was accelerated during the first year of the Fifth Republic.[61] Thus, the September 1958 Referendum saw Algerian women vote for the first time; the Constantine Plan contained specific clauses to improve women's education and employment in the public sector; and in December 1959 the government expanded opportunities for women to train as social workers and nurses in the civil service. Allied to this, three Algerian women were elected to the National Assembly in November 1958, including Nafissa Sid Cara who in 1959 became the first Muslim woman in a French government. In 1959 laws were introduced over marriage and divorce, designed to end discrimination and enhance women's rights as equal citizens with their husbands. Building upon proposals developed under Lacoste in 1956, these laws were intended to demonstrate how French rule was liberating them from conservative Islamic traditions.[62]

Particular attention was paid to rural women in this campaign. Already, in November 1957 the army had created thirty-five special mobile medical units whose brief was to reach out to Algerian women through an education programme.[63] Composed of a medical doctor plus three female assistants, one European and two Algerian, these teams went round the countryside and promoted healthcare and women's rights. Doubled in number by August 1958, their aim was to get 'Muslim women to participate in public life' in the run-up to the 1958 Referendum, a role that continued in 1959 with the promotion of the Constantine Plan and the reformed marriage laws. In fact by August 1960 there were 171 such units, peaking at 223 in February 1961.[64]

If these units were about treating Algerian women as equal citizens, they were also about eradicating the ALN's invisible infrastructures within the community. They were about weaning away female support that had been so vital to the ALN's survival. For this reason the targeting of women was part of a wider pattern of surveillance and control that was evident in the intensification of the regrouping of the Algerian population into camps. By October 1959 there were 1,242 camps holding more than 2 million people.[65] But if the military logic was to isolate the ALN, this aspect was down-played in official posters and pamphlets. Instead, official images underlined the theme of protection. Freed from FLN intimidation, it was claimed, these camps—many of which were purpose-built villages enjoying running water, electricity, a nurse, and a school—were part of the Constantine Plan's brave new future.

In tandem with the relocation policy, the army sought to recruit the Algerian population against the FLN. This involved the creation of self-defence villages, the recruitment of militiamen (*mokhaznis*) who were at-tached to an SAS officer, and the establishment of special Muslim units to hunt down the ALN: the *harkis*.[66] By 1958 the total of militiamen and *harkis* numbered 19,000 and 60,000 respectively, more than in the ALN maquis. What, however, motivated them? For some it was a genuine identification with France. Bachaga Boualam, was a prominent landowner and the head of the Beni Boudouane tribe from the Ouarsenis mountains in the north-west, an area relatively untouched by nationalism and from which he helped recruit a large number of *harkis*.[67] He always saw himself as French—a

Figure 8.2 The SAS providing lessons in hygiene for Algerian women in rural Kabylia, August 1959.

Boualam, he proudly asserted, had fought in every major campaign since the Crimean War, a patriotism that blended with a strong sense of anti-communism because, in his view, FLN victory would mean the expropriation of traditional landowners like himself.

For some it was revenge. Recruitment was a reaction against ALN excesses which many came to see as unfair, especially when local leaders were accused of exploiting their power to settle tribe and family disputes.[68] As one *harki* remembered:

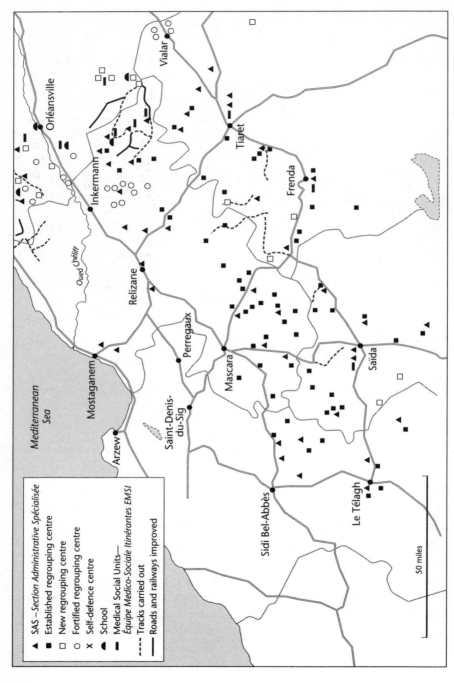

Map 8.2 1959: Western Algeria—French 'hearts and minds' operations amongst the Algerian population.

Legend:

▲ SAS – *Section Administrative Spécialisée*
■ Established regrouping centre
□ New regrouping centre
○ Fortified regrouping centre
✕ Self-defence centre
◗ School
▮ Medical Social Units—
 Équipe Medico-Sociale Itinérantes EMSI
- - - Tracks carried out
—— Roads and railways improved

50 miles

Labels on map:
Mediterranean Sea
Orléansville
Vialar
Inkermann
Tiaret
Frenda
Oued *Chéliff*
Relizane
Mostaganem
Arzew
Perregaux
Saint-Denis-du-Sig
Mascara
Saïda
Sidi Bel-Abbès
Le Télagh

Figure 8.3 Pamphlet aimed at recruiting Muslims into the French army, 1960.

You get up one morning and you discover that your neighbour has had his throat cut during the night. You, you know him, your neighbour, for a long time. You do not understand why he has been killed. You understand only that you must not ask questions ... So, in the beginning, you say to yourself to reassure you: 'It is astonishing but the moudjahidin know undoubtedly what they are doing. The men killed were perhaps playing a double game.' And then after a while, with all these deaths, the old people, the youngsters fifteen or sixteen years old, you say to yourself there is something not right here, that tomorrow it could be your turn, like that, for nothing.[69]

For some it was disillusionment with the ALN. Given the balance of forces they did not see how France could be defeated. For some it was survival. Money from the French army was a way of feeding hungry mouths. For others it was rejection by the maquis. By 1959 the ALN was a gateway to a political and social elite in waiting, and on these grounds local leaders turned away volunteers because, already looking ahead to independence, they did not want to share the fruits of victory.[70] And then, on the other side of the coin, were the French army tactics. On a regular basis, the army used psychological manipulation and entrapment to turn Algerians against the

ALN. Equally the makeshift camps created a culture of dependency which the military ruthlessly exploited to enlist Algerian volunteers.

Throughout 1959 de Gaulle's government played up images of loyal Algerians who, supposedly reaping the benefits of the Constantine Plan, were the basis of a pro-French and anti-FLN majority. In reality, although some Algerians did indeed enjoy greater social equality and some Algerians did identify with the French cause, many more did not. In fact the violent dimension of pacification continued to alienate huge numbers, deepening nationalist and pro-FLN feeling. These feelings were the product of the continued and systematic use of torture by the army.[71] These feelings were the product of the rape of Algerian women: acts of gender-specific violence by French soldiers which, although prohibited by the army, were intended to humiliate the local populations, an aspect of the war which is now being tentatively researched.[72] And these feelings were the product of the relocation policy. People resented being forced to leave their homes and they resented the poor living conditions of the camps which, as a report leaked to Le Monde in April 1959 showed, were characterized by disease and malnutrition on a huge scale.[73] And finally, they were the product of the brutalizing effect of war.[74] Algerians hated the way in which they were regularly stopped and searched by ordinary French soldiers. They hated, too, the way in which these soldiers, seeing all Muslims as a potential enemy, all too readily used derogatory words like melon, bougnoule, and raton.

At the same time the Algerians were subjected to pressure from the ALN. At regular intervals pro-French Muslims were warned that once the French left they would be subjected to terrible revenge. Women, too, were told to ignore French overtures. Through social reforms, as one FLN directive claimed in 1958, the French were not trying to liberate Algerian women but destroy the armed struggle from inside the FLN:

> After 100 years of occupation, and above all 4 years of revolution, the enemy proposes to free our Algerian sisters from archaic traditions...It shows a strong interest in her evolution and does not hesitate to employ every method to hasten her 'emancipation' based on that of French women.
>
> The enemy in undertaking the emancipation of women has two aims:
>
> IMMEDIATE AIM: Gain the confidence of Algerian women in order to get at the husband, the brother, the son, the supporters of the Algerian revolution, and, through that, make our struggle fail...

PROPAGANDA AIM: Allowing the papers, reviews, speeches, films to inform the world on the so-called 'humanitarian task' that France is accomplishing in respect to the Algerian people.[75]

Such a directive demonstrates how Algerians were being subjected to a whole host of competing pressures. For this reason it is vital to break away from seeing the war in terms of rigid absolutes. In 1959 Algeria many political choices were still not clear cut. Caught between the army and the ALN, commitment and opposition coexisted with hesitation, compromise, and ambiguous behaviour. In the case of the 13-year-old Saïd Ferdi, he was arrested by the army on 3 March 1958 at 6.00 a.m. in a remote village in the Aurès mountains.[76] As an ALN messenger boy he was then tortured horrifically before being offered a choice: either change sides or his father will be tortured too. Trapped, Ferdi fought for the French army, witnessing at first hand the savagery of the conflict. At one point, after an ALN unit had been wiped out, he saw:

> Infantrymen jump onto the corpses in order to grab what they had, rings, watches, wallets, helmets . . . Even more revolting was how they disembowelled the bodies with their bayonets. And into the burnt corpses, softened by napalm, they pushed pieces of wood picked up from the ground. The few wounded that they picked up were quickly finished off by a machine gun burst.[77]

It was a grotesque situation. But the army knew that it could count on Ferdi because it had locked him into a brutal logic. He had the most to fear from ALN reprisals even though he was a nationalist.

Europeans

Amongst Europeans the war produced a constant, nagging fear. On a daily level they were afraid of random acts of terrorism. They were watchful on buses, in cafés and at the cinema, creating a level of anxiety that tested the limits of Albert Camus's liberalism. When cornered over Algeria during his award ceremony for the Nobel Prize for Literature in Stockholm in December 1957, Camus chose his words carefully, explaining that he had always campaigned for a just Algeria where the two populations could live in peace and equality. Nevertheless, he underlined, in the final analysis FLN terrorism was a highly emotive issue: 'I have always condemned terror.

I must condemn also a terrorism that operates blindly, in the streets of Algiers for example, and which one day can strike my mother or my family. I believe in justice, but I will defend my mother before justice.'[78]

Furthermore, there was anger at how victims were left to cope with the consequences of this violence. In the case of the then 10–year-old Nicole Guiraud, she was with her father in the Milk Bar in Algiers on 30 September 1956 when the FLN bomb went off: 'I was nearly cut in two, I lost an arm, I am crippled. I had just turned ten years old. My father . . . had a leg torn off and became deaf as a result of the explosion.'[79] On coming out of hospital in December 1956 her father founded an association for the civilian victims of terrorism because he was incensed at their treatment by the government. He wished to overturn the law whereby their injuries were seen to be the result of a 'work accident' and not war.[80]

The FLN did make efforts to win over Europeans, producing tracts which claimed that they would have a place within the new Algerian nation.[81] But only a tiny micro-minority made this step. The overwhelming majority identified with French Algeria and this was why May 1958 was a moment of hope. They believed that de Gaulle's return was a definitive moment. With the integration of Algeria into France their future had been saved. This in turn explains the shift of emotion during 1959. Many Europeans disliked the open-ended tone of the Constantine Plan. By the same token they disliked the amnesty of FLN prisoners, including Saadi Yacef the man behind the 'Battle of Algiers', and they disliked de Gaulle's disdainful comment on 29 April 1959 that 'the Algeria of Papa [Dad] is dead'.[82] For Europeans these developments were a betrayal of their hopes raised by May 1958, hostility that was clear in graffiti that stated 'De Gaulle = Mendès' and the European student Mardi Gras parade on 5 March 1959 where a donkey, dressed up with big ears to resemble de Gaulle, was draped with the placard 'I have understood you'.[83]

Metropolitan France

If the sense of separation was palpable between the Europeans and de Gaulle, it was no less so between the metropole and French Algeria. By 1959 there was a war-weariness on the mainland. Fearful about the fate of the conscripts, metropolitan opinion wanted to bring an end to the Algerian crisis. This did not mean that people wanted an FLN victory.

Nor did it mean that they were indifferent to the plight of the Europeans. But it did mean that they did not want to be continually held to ransom by French Algeria. They wanted an honourable exit, a fact that was reflected in the opinion polls where a growing majority favoured ceasefire negotiations with the FLN, rising from 58% in January 1958, to 63% in January 1959 and 71% two months later.[84] This poll data points to how the 1958 elections meant something different on the French mainland. In Algeria they were about integration but in France they were about giving de Gaulle the mandate to find a palatable solution.

PART III

Dénouement 1959–62

9

Endgame

Wednesday, 16 September 1959

At 8.00 p.m. millions gathered round their televisions and radios to hear de Gaulle address the nation from the Élysée Palace in Paris. Sitting behind an elegant looking table, the besuited president spoke in a forceful manner for just over twenty minutes. As the longest and most detailed public pronouncement he ever made on the Algerian problem, de Gaulle was fully aware of the historical implications of the moment. This was the point when he intended to break the deadlock. Through a carefully prepared speech, backed up by a strong body language, de Gaulle wished to present the choices which, he considered, would lead to a lasting solution.

From the outset de Gaulle's tone was one of optimism tempered by realism. He claimed that renewal was a fact and that over the past fifteen months progress had been achieved in the form of national unity, enduring political institutions, and financial stability.[1] France was moving forward in terms of science and technology and had forged a new relationship with its African colonies under the banner of the African Community. However, the country was still confronted with the 'difficult, blood-soaked problem' of Algeria.[2] An answer, therefore, had to be found which eschewed 'sterile and simplistic slogans' and opened up the way for Algerians to exercise 'a free choice' over their future.[3]

To this end, de Gaulle continued, two preconditions had already been met. The country was largely 'pacified' and here de Gaulle spoke in glowing terms about the army's courage and loyalty, including the participation of 120,000 Muslim soldiers. By both dramatically improving the security situation and forging a real bond with the ordinary population, 'pacification', de Gaulle claimed, had brought about an atmosphere of peace: the prerequisite for any resolution. No less importantly, as the 1958 referendum and National Assembly elections had proved, Algerians now had the means to express themselves through universal suffrage based upon a single electoral college: 'a revolution' according to de Gaulle.

By the same token, de Gaulle explained, any solution was more than restoring law and order or according the right to self-determination. This was because Algeria was above all a human problem which was why, through the Constantine Plan, France had undertaken a vast programme of economic and social investment for the Muslim population that had led to the redistribution of 8,000 hectares of farming land; 5,000 more public service jobs; 860,000 children in school; and the development of the gas and oil industries. If, de Gaulle pondered, France continued with this cooperation then in fifteen years Algeria would be a 'prosperous and productive country'.[4] In the interim, the progress of 'pacification', 'democracy', and 'social evolution' meant that a stage had been reached where:

> We can look forward to the day when the men and women who live in Algeria will be in a position to decide their own destiny, once and for all, freely, in the full knowledge of what is at stake. Taking into account all these factors, those of the Algerian situation, those inherent in the national and international situation, I deem it necessary that recourse to self-determination be here and now proclaimed.
>
> In the name of France and of the Republic, by virtue of the power granted to me by our constitution to consult its citizens, granted that God let me live and that the people lend me their ear, I commit myself to ask, on the one hand, of the Algerians in their twelve departments, what it is they finally wish to be and, on the other hand, of all Frenchmen to endorse their choice.[5]

Having accepted the principle of self-determination de Gaulle then outlined the terms on which this free choice would be made. It would be put to Algerians as individuals because, de Gaulle emphasized, 'since the beginning of the world there has never been any true Algerian unity, far less any Algerian sovereignty'.[6] It would be for de Gaulle to decide the exact moment of the election which would be 'at the latest four years after the actual restoration of peace, that is to say, once a situation has been established whereby loss of life ... will not exceed 200 a year'.[7] Such a timescale, de Gaulle continued, would allow the country to resume a 'normal existence' by 'emptying the prisons and the camps' and 'allowing for exiles to return', thus 'restoring the free play of individual and public freedom' and 'enabling the population to be fully aware of what is at stake'.[8]

When consulted, de Gaulle explained, the Algerians would be offered three alternatives, the first of which would be secession. This scenario, de Gaulle was in no doubt, would be a disaster because: 'Algeria being what it is at the present time, and the world what we know it to be, secession would carry in its wake the most appalling poverty, frightful political chaos, widespread slaughter, and soon after the warlike dictatorship of the Communists.'[9]

Moreover, de Gaulle made it clear that this option would bring about France's immediate departure. The Constantine Plan would stop; those who wished to remain French would be grouped together; the flow of Saharan petrol, 'the work of France', would be protected within a French-ruled Saharan enclave: measures which implied that secession meant the partition of Algeria.

The second choice was what de Gaulle called 'complete francization' by which Algerians would enjoy the same political and social rights, making them an integral part of the French people that would henceforth stretch from 'Dunkirk to Tamanrasset';[10] while the third choice was:

> The government of Algerians by Algerians, backed up by French help and in close relationship with her, as regards the economy, education, defence, and foreign relations. In that case, the internal regime of Algeria should be of a federal type, so that the various communities—French, Arab, Kabyle, Mozabite—who live together in the country would find guarantees for their own way of life and a framework for cooperation.[11]

De Gaulle concluded in an emphatic manner, implicitly addressing himself to the FLN by reiterating his year-old *'paix des braves'* and calling on the rebels to lay down their weapons and enter into the electoral process. After all, de Gaulle was offering the Algerian people a democratic choice. Why should anyone oppose this unless they were 'a group of ambitious agitators, determined to establish by brute force and terror their totalitarian dictatorship and believing that they will one day obtain from the Republic the privilege of discussing with it the fate of Algeria, thus building up these agitators into an Algerian government'?[12]

In this way de Gaulle was trying to exert pressure in the battle for world opinion. If the Provisional Government failed to take up his offer, this was only because of FLN intransigence. It feared the democratic choice of the Algerian people.

By his weight of words and the order in which he outlined the three choices there is no doubt that the last scenario was de Gaulle's preferred option. It was a classic example of thesis (secession) followed by anti-thesis (integration) before de Gaulle presented his own synthesis: a third-way solution between the two extremes. In effect, de Gaulle was giving Algeria the choice that he had given Black Africa in September 1958. Clearly his hope was that the Algerian question would be resolved within the context of the African Community where, apart from Guinea, all the countries had chosen the path of partnership rather than outright independence.

In this manner, for all the talk of a brave new initiative, de Gaulle's address still bore the imprint of Mollet's Republican Front, even if he made no acknowledgement of his political predecessor. Like Mollet, de Gaulle was trying to find a solution from a position of military strength. Like Mollet, de Gaulle was trying to maintain French control of the Sahara.[13] And, like Mollet, de Gaulle was trying to win over the Algerian population through economic investment. Similarly, Mollet had always sought an outcome that anchored Algeria within a wider Franco-African entity, while the Republican Front 'triptych' of ceasefire, elections, and negotiations had always been justified in terms of choice and self-determination. The aim of this process, Mollet argued, was to open the way to talks with the democratic representatives chosen by Algerians. However, where de Gaulle's speech *did* represent a decisive break with Mollet was in the acceptance of outright independence if Algerians voted for it. This had never been countenanced before. All of the Fourth Republic blueprints, from the 1947 Statute through to the 1958 *loi-cadre*, had been about finding mechanisms that, while empowering Algerians, still shut the door on this possibility.

The fact that de Gaulle was prepared to concede the possibility of secession, even if he dismissed it as the route to disaster, was a measure of the importance he bestowed on this speech. Clearly, in the way in which he delivered the address and the words he used, de Gaulle wanted 16 September 1959 to be a milestone. He wanted to make world opinion stand up and listen. He wished to be seen as the man of democracy who was giving Algerians a free and unambiguous choice to decide their own destiny.

For this reason the speech has to be understood as the fruit of a long and measured deliberation throughout the first nine months of 1959. In different contexts and with different people he tested out ideas and opinions. Feeling around for an initiative he tried to get a sense of what would or would not be acceptable to the United Nations, the USA, domestic public opinion, and the army. Thus, in early July de Gaulle's perspective was transformed by an official visit to Madagascar. Witnessing for himself the strength of popular feeling for decolonization, he concluded that although the island had voted 'yes' to the Franco-African Community in 1958, independence (as elsewhere in Africa) was irreversible.[14] Later in the month he spoke at length with Modibo Keita and Léopold Senghor, two of the key leaders in the African Community, who both underlined that Algerians had to be given a choice through the ballot box. At the same time de Gaulle had asked one of his closest advisors, Bernard Tricot, to bring together a group of experts to reflect on how to get the FLN to agree to a ceasefire. Every eventuality was to be explored and here in the final confidential report Tricot was emphatic. Military success was not enough. Even if the FLN was defeated there would always be a stream of young men willing to become terrorists.[15] The FLN had to be enticed away from violence by a political solution: 'A request for a ceasefire by those on the other side only seems to us foreseeable if, convinced that the armed struggle had become hopeless, they had good reasons for thinking that a return to peace would permit them to attain their objectives by political means.'[16] A ceasefire was not a solution in itself. This was only a stage on the way to a referendum on autonomy within a Franco-African federation.

Reflecting on this ongoing advice, de Gaulle received Dag Hammarsk-jöld, the UN Secretary General, at the Élysée on 31 July where, although he did not go into detail, he talked about an imminent change in policy over Algeria that would surprise the world. Then on 12 August he asked all his government ministers to put down their proposals on Algeria in preparation for a cabinet meeting on 26 August. There he went round the table one by one listening to their thoughts which ranged from Edmond Michelet, the Justice Minister, who talked of an Algerian state linked to France, through to Bernard Cornut-Gentille, who warned against any abandonment, and Michel Debré, the prime minister, who, while underlining France's political and economic interests and rejecting any idea of an Algerian state, also admitted that it was impossible to conceive of an 'absolute identification' of Algeria with the metropole. Only Jean-Marcel Jeanneney, the Industry Minister, talked of independence.[17] Overall the cabinet was equally divided over the notion of a major diplomatic initiative. A minority supported Algerian autonomy while another opposed it. A third faction stood behind Debré who argued for a new political framework which Algerians would be invited to vote upon at a later date. At the end there was no discussion. De Gaulle merely thanked them for their ideas before concluding in a Delphic manner: 'In this order of affairs, it is necessary to march or die. I have chosen to march, but that does not prevent the fact that one can also die.'[18]

On the following day de Gaulle flew to Algeria to gauge the views of the army. Always dressed in uniform, de Gaulle went on a lightning tour of key military bases that began with Colonel Bigeard in the west before going on to General Buis in the Hodna region and the Morice Line in the east. The visit climaxed with a meeting at Challe's battle headquarters in Kabylia on 30 August. Throughout the tension was obvious. On 28 August de Gaulle clashed with Massu when the latter made plain his opposition to the three choices, arguing that this ran the risk of Algeria opting for independence like Guinea in 1958.[19] In the same vein de Gaulle lost his patience when General Faure called on him to declare publicly for French Algeria, quickly breaking off the conversation. Finally, at Challe's head-quarters de Gaulle spoke to a hundred senior officers where he underlined the importance of loyalty and obedience. These, he reminded his audience, were the cardinal military values: a warning that was intended to head off any rebellion.

In speaking candidly, de Gaulle was preparing the ground for his speech seventeen days later. He was trying to defuse anger within the army. In this sense his evolution during 1959 was marked by three interconnected trains of thought, the first of which was the movement away from integration. Although in June 1958 he had publicly stated that in Algeria there were equal citizens with equal rights, in private he had expressed doubts about whether this was feasible or desirable. In March 1959 de Gaulle confided to Alain Peyrefitte that he did not see how France could absorb 10 million Muslims who would become 20 million and then 40 million.[20] For him this cultural and religious difference was insurmountable. France would no longer be France, that is 'a European people of a white race, Greek and Latin culture and Christian religion'. There was a danger, he warned, that one hundred years hence his home village, Colombey-les-deux-églises (Colombey the two churches) could have become Colombey-les-deux-mosquées (Colombey the two mosques).[21] This did not mean that de Gaulle wanted an FLN victory, his second train of thought. On the contrary, his preferred outcome was a third-way solution that would prevent FLN domination, anchor Algeria into the Franco–African Community and pre-serve French geo-strategic interests. This in turn led into his third train of thought: his hope that NATO in general and the USA in particular would recognize a Eurafrican zone of anti-Soviet defence, led by France and centred on the Western Mediterranean, the Maghreb, and Black Africa.[22] Like Mollet, de Gaulle saw North Africa as a cold war front. He wanted the USA to accept the need to maintain French pre-eminence in Algeria, firmly tying any future solution into the NATO sphere of influence as well as the federal structure in French Africa.

As de Gaulle grappled with these three interconnected trains of thought, the evolution in his thinking was framed by international pressure to find a peaceful outcome. With another UN vote on Algeria looming large in December de Gaulle knew that he had to seize the moral high ground. He had to show world opinion that France was willing to offer Algerians a free vote because on 3 August 1959 nine newly independent African states had called on France to recognize Algeria's right to self-determination. Similarly, in Morocco and Tunisia both Mohammed V and Bourguiba, fearful of the way in which the FLN struggle was radicalizing opposition movements in their respective countries, were urging de Gaulle to find a solution. Meanwhile on 2 September de Gaulle received President Eisenhower at the Élysée Palace for an official state visit. Sounding out his US counterpart, de Gaulle was told that France should present its case to the UN. Moreover, having abstained from the United Nations vote on Algeria the previous December, Eisenhower also refused to endorse the French 'grand design' for a Eurafrican wing of NATO. He preferred to emphasize the US's 'anti-colonial tradition' as well as its opposition to force to solve problems. Only on this basis, Eisenhower explained to his host, could the United States support France, which is why it welcomed the imminent offer of self-determination. It was an exchange of views that further clarified the need for dramatic action in de Gaulle's mind. Rebuffed over his Eurafrican NATO strategy, de Gaulle understood the implications of Eisenhower's perspective, namely that if the war continued, then the American government would have to actively intervene to end it.[23] De Gaulle knew that he had to act or risk losing control of the whole process in Algeria, so threatening his ultimate goal: French renewal.

Reaction

Writing in 1961 Edward Behr, the veteran Algerian correspondent for US *Time* magazine, was in no doubt about the significance of de Gaulle's address: 'Whatever had gone before was forgotten; ever since this speech and in one form or another, the offer—and the deliberate or unconscious ambiguities it contained—have been at the heart of all discussions and speculations on Algeria.'[24] Behr argued that by foregrounding the Algerian right to self-determination, the speech simultaneously put paid to 'French Algeria', accepted a 'government of Algerians by Algerians', and conceded that the FLN would not be excluded from any future settlement. If such an offer had been made in the first three years after November 1954, Behr was convinced that the FLN leaders would have accepted it.

Initially, however, the speech did not provoke an immediate reaction from the FLN. This was because, as we saw in the last chapter, it was in complete disarray. Fixated with the in-fighting at the crisis meeting in Tunis, the FLN was in no position to make a united response. Only on 28 September did Ferhat Abbas, on behalf of the Provisional Government, welcome de Gaulle's recognition of the right to self-determination. This was a major victory which, Abbas emphasized, Algerians had won through the liberation struggle:

> The right to freely decide its destiny is at last accorded to the Algerian people. This evolution is only possible because for five years the Algerian people has resisted victoriously one of the bloodiest wars of colonial re-conquest. It has only been possible because the National Liberation Front and the National Liberation Army has continued and will continue if it is necessary the liberation struggle. It is only possible thanks to the support of our brother peoples and the support of international public opinion.[25]

Abbas posed a series of point-by-point objections to de Gaulle's arguments and framework. He challenged de Gaulle's assertion that independence would lead to political chaos. On the contrary for the FLN it was the prerequisite to progress and cooperation. He warned against de Gaulle's thinly veiled threat that independence would lead to partition. Algeria, Abbas argued, must not be divided along racial lines or separated off from the Sahara. All this would do, he continued, was aggravate the situation, making Algeria into a lasting danger to international peace. Abbas rejected the notion that Algerian self-determination had to be ratified by a vote on the French mainland. Equally Abbas questioned the order of de Gaulle's proposed self-determination. He wanted negotiations with the Provisional Government to begin before any vote, while for de Gaulle, still adhering to Mollet's formula, it was a question of 'pacification', ceasefire, and then a referendum. But leaving these differences aside the importance of Abbas's reply must be underlined. For the first time, a point of convergence had been found: both sides accepted a self-determination vote and by implication a ceasefire. In short, a political solution was on the horizon, even if the path to this solution was to be long and tortuous.

In metropolitan France a clear majority supported de Gaulle's initiative. Those who opposed it were limited to the extreme right and a minority current within the Gaullist UNR led by Soustelle and the Algiers deputy Lagaillarde, a fact underlined by the National Assembly vote on 14 October when de Gaulle's policy was approved by a crushing majority: 441 against 21. The government won support not just amongst the UNR but from the Socialist Party, where Mollet argued that de Gaulle's blueprint was a continuation of their own key tenets, and the Communist Party, which saw a convergence with its own policy for 'peace in Algeria'. Looked at through this lens, therefore, de Gaulle's September 1959 speech was a political success. He had carried most of the UNR with him and built a cross-party consensus behind self-determination; a conclusion reinforced by public opinion polls which showed that, by the end of 1959, 57 per cent of French people were in favour of negotiations.[26]

In Algeria the Europeans were devastated. Settler tracts and graffiti denounced de Gaulle's speech as a betrayal. Political meetings, fired up by Lagaillarde and Ortiz, the bar owner, reflected a mood of fear, anger, and recrimination. Why, settler activists asked, was de Gaulle turning his back on the 1958 referendum when Algeria was integrated into the Republic? Why was he about to let their world fall apart, abandoning the settlers to the wrath of the Algerian majority? In one meeting at the end of September in Algiers activists even openly shouted for a new Charlotte Corday.[27] Evoking the memory of the woman who famously assassinated the French revolutionary Jean-Paul Marat in 1793, it was a measure of the civil-war atmosphere. Reflecting the traditional hostility to a Paris-based solution, de Gaulle became the hate figure. He was seen as great a threat to French Algeria as the FLN, who would have to be removed, even murdered—a conclusion that was reinforced when the president reiterated his proposals on 10 November.

European anger was mirrored by disquiet within the army's ranks. Despite the fact that Delouvrier and Challe initially called on the troops to mobilize Algerians behind de Gaulle's preferred solution, many officers were unresponsive. They were angry that victory was being snatched away from them and none more so than Massu who, as the victor of the Battle of 'Algiers' and the last major figure from May 1958 still in place, was idolized by the Europeans. In an interview with a German journalist, Hans Ulrich Kempski for the Munich *Süddeutsche Zeitung*, published on 18 January, he publicly expressed his unhappiness at de Gaulle's policy:

> We no longer understand the policy of President de Gaulle. The army could not have anticipated that he would adopt such a policy ... Our greatest disillusion has been to see General de Gaulle become a man of the Left.[28]

Then when pushed even more, Massu did not hold back stating:

> De Gaulle was the only man available. Perhaps the army made a mistake.[29]

And:

> Myself, and the majority of officers in a position of command, will not execute unconditionally the orders of the Head of State.[30]

The interview was immediately picked up by the world's newspapers. In Britain *The Times*, like its counterparts in the American and European press, sought to verify Massu's words in a report by its German correspondent which included large extracts as well as a declaration from the *Süddeutsche Zeitung* defending the article's truthfulness.[31] This in turn was backed up by the paper's French correspondent who stated that 'whether or not General Massu was correctly reported, the sentiments attributed to him do mirror the mood of many officers in Algeria, and above all in Algiers'.[32]

De Gaulle was furious. This was a challenge to the Fifth Republic's political authority. It was a veiled threat that the army would not obey him. Four days later Massu was stripped of his command. Transferred back to a minor posting in Metz, he was banned from returning to Algeria.

The Week of the Barricades

As with the recall of Soustelle in February 1956 and Lacoste in May 1958, Massu's dismissal provoked rebellion in Algeria, although rumours about action had been circulating for weeks. Already on 19 January the Federation of Mayors had warned that people in Algeria wished to remain French, that they would defend this right 'even by taking up arms if necessary', and that they would not tolerate discussions with 'throat-cutters', adding that the only acceptable ceasefire would be 'the unconditional surrender of the rebels'.[33] This appetite for confrontation had been fuelled by fresh FLN attacks on civilians, vividly described in the European press, and on hearing of Massu's transfer, settler organizations immediately called for a demonstration in the Forum on 24 January, a Sunday, demanding his return and the rejection of self-determination. Grouped together as the 'French National Front' (FNF), the aim was insurrection—the hope that the army would side with them against de Gaulle. In short, a new May 1958.

The FNF leaders were the besuited Ortiz and the bearded Lagaillarde, dressed in military uniform, as well as a new face: the 25-year-old medical student, Jean Jacques Susini who, thin in physique, was a powerful orator and brilliant organizer. Choosing the emblem of the Celtic cross, the symbol of the explicitly fascist Jeune Nation movement, their activists had been preparing for confrontation for months by infiltrating the Territorial Units, the European militia trained for self-defence duties by the army, and on the evening of Saturday 23 January, Lagaillarde, sporting his military uniform and without telling Ortiz, occupied Algiers University at the head of 600 black-bereted paramilitaries.[34] Transforming the university into a fortress, Lagaillarde told the onlookers that he would not leave until de Gaulle had caved in to Algiers.

On the following morning by 11.00 a.m. some 20,000 demonstrators gathered on the Forum, many sporting small photographs of Massu in their button holes. By the afternoon these people began shifting to the streets below—Rue d'Isly, Rue Michelet, Rue Charras, and Rue Monge—where they dug up paving stones and built five barricades—the symbol par excellence of revolutionary insurrection against injustice—while the paratroopers, the deciding factor for Ortiz and Lagaillarde, refrained from intervening to quell the disturbances. Then at 6.00 p.m. the authorities sent in the gendarmerie to clear away the main bulk of the remaining crowd, some 6,000, and dismantle the barricades, leaving the more reluctant paratroopers to mop up the flanks. Moving down the steep slope from the Forum into the streets, the advancing gendarmes, helmeted and armed with batons, were fired upon by persons unknown before being caught in a volley of automatic fire from the surrounding windows and roof tops. What then ensued were scenes of incredible brutality, described in these terms by Edward Behr, still covering North Africa for *Time*:

> at least one gendarmerie trooper was killed in cold blood by maddened European youths; others were paraded up and down lifts in neighbouring buildings. European women were seen pouring shot after shot down on to the

trapped security squad from the windows of the buildings surrounding the War Memorial.[35]

In total the firefight led to 14 killed and 123 wounded on the side of the gendarmes and 8 killed and 24 wounded on the side of the demonstrators.

Metropolitan opinion was revolted by the pictures of ordinary policemen being gunned down by Europeans. But as the French mainland absorbed this new turn of events, the insurgents remained encamped in the centre of Algiers. Emblazoning the barricades with tricolores, one awash with the blood of fallen demonstrators, and banners proclaiming 'Vive Massu', they were fed by the European population, let through by parachutist officers, such as Pierre Sergent, whose sympathy for the revolt was self-evident. However, as the days went on it became clear that what became known as the 'Week of the Barricades' was no May 1958. The Algerians remained impassive. There were no scenes of reconciliation and fraternity. On mainland France there was overwhelming opposition. De Gaulle received thousands of letters and telegrams of support; Mollet accepted the leadership of a united front alliance stretching from Socialists to Gaullists in defence of the Republic; while large numbers of ordinary citizens, many with sons and husbands fighting as conscripts, wrote to soldiers in Algeria pleading with them not to side with the European rebels.[36] Finally, and most crucially, no senior army officer broke ranks, despite large-scale hostility to de Gaulle's self-determination policy. For all their bluster, the plain fact was that Ortiz and Lagaillarde and their few thousand supporters were isolated.

Oblivious to this reality, Lagaillarde maintained a strict discipline within his military redoubt. Convinced that the longer the stand-off went on the more likely it was that de Gaulle would be forced to change policy or go, he boasted to two paratroop officers: 'De Gaulle is determined to stick to his policy. But I, I am no less determined to go right to the end.'[37]

De Gaulle, however, remained firm as the crisis unfolded throughout the week beginning 25 January. Enraged by the conciliatory noises made in Algiers by Paul Delouvrier who, in a bid to get the insurgents to see the folly of their action, had even promised to shake Ortiz and Lagaillarde by the hand, the president intervened with a television address at 8.00 p.m. on Friday 29 January, dressed in his military uniform in order to underline his legitimacy, not just as the Head of State but as the leader of the French Resistance. His face determined, his fists clenched, his voice stern, de Gaulle made it clear that there was no going back. Self-determination was the only possible policy. Once peace had been achieved Algerians had to be given a free choice over their destiny:

> This will not be dictated to them. For if their response was not really their response, then, while for a time there might be military victory, basically nothing would be settled. On the contrary, everything can be settled and, I believe, settled in France's favour, when the Algerians have had an opportunity to make known their will in all freedom, dignity and security. In short, self-determination is the only policy that is worthy of France. It is the only possible outcome.[38]

Now, continued de Gaulle passionately, two different groups rejected this free choice. On one extreme there was the FLN, still wishing to build themselves up into a government in waiting, something de Gaulle claimed he would never agree to; while on the other there were the European insurgents in Algiers who, aided tacitly by parts of the army and exploiting the fears of the settlers, hoped to impose their will 'on the nation, on the state, on myself' through violent insurrection.[39] De Gaulle argued that, by killing the gendarmes and challenging the Fifth Republic's authority, this insurrection was madness. It was raising the spectre of a definitive rupture between the Europeans and the French nation, just at the moment when the FLN rebellion was in decline.

At this point de Gaulle spoke specifically to the Europeans. Emphasizing the special bond between him and them, the result of his time there at the head of the Provisional Government during World War Two, and their military contribution to the Liberation and May 1958, de Gaulle implored Europeans to ignore 'the liars and conspirators who tell you that in granting a free choice to the Algerians, France and de Gaulle want to abandon you, to pull out of Algeria and hand it over to the rebellion'.[40] How could this be so, given the ongoing presence of 500,000 troops, the economic investment in the Sahara and the social transformation of the Muslim population? In stressing these facts de Gaulle sought to win over the Europeans to his middle-way solution, underlining that nothing would give him greater joy than if the Algerians were to choose 'the one that would be the most French', in other words association.[41]

Next, de Gaulle addressed the other element in the insurrection: the army. Congratulating it on military victory, he warned against certain elements who believed 'that this war is their war, not that of France', before reiterating the terms of the military mission in Algeria:

You have to liquidate the rebel force that wants to chase France out of Algeria and rain down on this country its dictatorship of misery and sterility . . . you have to contribute to the moral and material transformation of the Muslim population, in order to bring them onto the side of France through hearts and minds. When the moment comes to proceed to the consultation, you will have to guarantee its complete and sincere freedom.[42]

Then, he stated, clearly and unambiguously;

no soldier, under the penalty of being guilty of a serious offence, may associate himself, may associate himself at any time, even passively, with the insurrection. In the last analysis, law and order must be re-established . . . your duty is to bring this about. I have given, and am giving, this order.[43]

Pausing briefly, to let the full significance of these words sink in, de Gaulle then climaxed by returning again to his unique June 1940 legitimacy. Straining every sinew in his body, he implored French people to follow him:

Well! My dear and old country, here we are together, once again, facing a harsh test. By virtue of the mandate that the people have given me and the national legitimacy that I have embodied over the last twenty years, I demand that everybody supports me whatever happens.[44]

It was a masterly performance. De Gaulle had judged the situation perfectly. Reflecting the exasperation of French metropolitan opinion with the European hardliners, he had conceded nothing: the first time Paris had not given way to the 'Algiers street'.

Listening in the rain which now lashed down on the city, the insurgents knew that they were defeated and by Monday morning, 1 February, the revolt had disintegrated. Ortiz went into hiding; Lagaillarde surrendered; and Alain de Sérigny, editor of *L'Écho d'Alger*, was arrested. Capitalizing on this victory, de Gaulle dissolved the army's Fifth Bureau, the specialist counter-FLN unit, which had been a locus of military discontent; disbanded the Territorial Units; and sent home disloyal officers, notably Colonels Argoud and Godard. At the same time he put in place new institutions to carry through a self-determination policy, underlining once again the separation of civil and military power as well as an explicit ban on torture and summary executions. Disgusted, Soustelle resigned from the government on 5 February but he was the only major minister to do so. The rest stood full-square behind de Gaulle—another measure of how the 'Week of the Barricades' had strengthened his hand.

The contrast with the events of 6 February 1956, when the Europeans rioted against Mollet, could not have been greater. The fact that de Gaulle did not capitulate was a measure of how perceptions had moved on in the intervening four years. In 1956 it was the FLN which was the 'other' within the Republican Front's political imagination: savage, totalitarian and fanatical. Against this FLN threat the Republican Front posited the ideal of a Franco-Muslim community based on the shared values of liberty, equality, and fraternity. By 1960, however, a new 'other' had entered the political equation: the settlers and army who, in the eyes of the mainland majority, were perceived as undemocratic, extremist, and fascist. This language did reflect patterns of prejudice going right back to the beginnings of French Algeria, namely that the *colons* were headstrong and emotional, classic Mediterranean types who thought with their hearts and not their minds. It did, too, dovetail with images, particularly strong on the left, of a minority of settlers who were regarded as rich and privileged: the so-called *ultras*. Now, though, this traditional alterity was given a fresh inflexion. In the face of de Gaulle's attempt at an honourable solution, the Europeans were seen to be an intransigent and unpatriotic threat to true republican values. Even worse, they seemed prepared to plunge the country into civil war in defence of their narrow interests, aided and abetted by a coterie of officers who, psychologically damaged by defeat in Indochina, were unable to countenance another one in Algeria.

This division between mainstream mainland opinion on one side and the settlers and elements of the army on the other was reflected in opinion polls. Seventy-five per cent, for example, endorsed de Gaulle's stance during the 'Week of the Barricades', while between February and March 1960 opinion-poll support for his preferred option of association surged from 48 to 64 per cent.[45] In another way, too, this division went back to the political choices of 1956. Then the Republican Front had justified the recall of reservists to French people on the grounds that increasing troop levels to over 400,000 would produce a quick victory, opening the way to a cease-fire, elections, and negotiations. When instead the army became entangled in a long and complicated conflict, one question began to impose itself above all others: how long could France maintain this level of economic and military commitment? In this sense, the comments of *Le Cri du Peuple*, the Socialist Party paper in the Somme region, on 7 February 1960 were symptomatic of a generalized mood of realism. In 1956 the paper had backed the measures introduced by Max Lejeune, the local Socialist Party deputy, but by 1960 there was recognition that there had to be renewed efforts at peace and reconciliation between the communities:

> We understand very well that our compatriots in North Africa cried out to us for help. We sent to protect them half of our army and we are spending on them a tenth of our budget. We never thought to abandon them, but we cannot do more, nor force the FLN to lay its arms down more quickly, nor above all stop the demographic disequilibrium growing each day between Europeans and Muslims. It would be absurd to fool our compatriots in Algeria with good words and false promises. We cannot eternally guarantee them the same effort: we must therefore help them, after this crisis, to find a durable harmony with the Muslims.[46]

In other words, after over five years of war it was clear to many French people that this effort could not go on forever. The 1 million Europeans had to face these facts. They could not dictate policy on a permanent basis. They had to accept de Gaulle's attempt to bring an end to the war. They had to embrace a free vote that, de Gaulle hoped, would see Algerians choose his third-way solution which would maintain the link with France and allow the Europeans to have a clearly allotted place within the new Algeria. If not, the separation could only deepen, bringing the Europeans and the metropole into a civil-war conflict that would make any compromise solution untenable.

Such comments underline how the 'Week of the Barricades' was a major turning point. By foregrounding the unbridgeable divisions between the metropole and French Algeria, these events did untold damage to the bonds between both sides of the Mediterranean. They weakened the French cause from the inside, handing a huge victory to the FLN, just at the moment when it was imploding militarily and politically.

Opposition to the war

As the mainland breathed a collective sigh of relief at de Gaulle's handling of the 'Week of the Barricades', it was shocked to learn of a new aspect of the war: networks of French people who had been hiding FLN members and smuggling FLN funds out of the country to finance the FLN war effort.[47] Announced by the French Secret Services in an official communiqué on 24 February, these arrests produced uproar in the right-wing press. Three days later *Paris-Presse* carried the headline 'Here are the Parisian women of the

FLN', drawing attention to the fact that of the eighty apprehended, sixty were women who (the article claimed) had been lured into betrayal by promises of money and sex.[48] This anger was intensified by news of a clandestine press conference in Paris on 15 April 1960 by Francis Jeanson, the ringleader of the Paris network of FLN supporters and hitherto one of the country's leading philosophers, who denounced the war, justified his network's action, and called on French soldiers to dodge the draft, talking of an organization *Jeune Résistance* (Young Resistance) that was organizing desertion networks.

The discovery of this underground pro-FLN movement put the spotlight on the Algerian community in France.[49] In 1954 this had stood at 211,000, mostly poor unskilled workers in construction and steel industries living in hostels or shanty towns, such as in Nanterre in the north-west suburbs of Paris. By 1960 this figure had risen to 350,000 as Algerians, many desperate to escape forced resettlement by the army, were enticed over by the prospect of employment and higher wages—the result of the ongoing economic miracle as well as the need, ironically, to replace workers called up for military service. Always highly politicized, the Algerian community in France had greeted 1 November 1954 with joy, although most believed that Messali Hadj was behind the attacks. The majority of the 7,000 MTLD activists, therefore, supported Messali's MNA which meant that the FLN found it difficult to implant itself, a fact exacerbated by wave after wave of arrests by the French police. With the arrival of Omar Boudaoud as leader in June 1957, a measure of order and continuity was established within the FLN's Fédération de France, whose clandestine headquarters was based in West Germany from spring 1958 onwards. In France, as in Algeria, the FLN became embroiled in a brutal, fratricidal conflict which resulted in 4,000 deaths on the mainland.[50] These tactics, as we have seen, caused uproar amongst Messali supporters on the left, like Maurice Pivert and Jean Rous, who saw them as Stalinist. But ultimately ruthlessness produced results. By the end of 1957, the FLN was dominant on the mainland, apart from Lille which remained an MNA bastion right until 1962.

Fédération de France was never a political party. It was not trying to transform opinion through petitions and meetings. It was a counter-society whose primary concern was the war effort. This meant opening a second front on the mainland in August 1958 through a series of coordinated attacks. It meant support for FLN prisoners who went on hunger strike in 1959 for political status. But most significantly it meant money for the FLN as the Fédération de France demanded money from Algerians on a sliding scale—500 old francs a month for students, 3,000 for workers, and 50,000 or more for shopkeepers—through a well-organized system of collectors.

In carrying out this war effort the Fédération was confronted with one enormous problem: France was *not* Algeria. FLN activists could not melt away into the crowd. Their visibility as Algerians meant that they were always liable to be stopped and searched by the police. As Ali Haroun, from 1958 onwards the Fédération leader responsible for press, communication, and support for FLN prisoners, later explained: 'FLN members were not like "fish in water" . . . they could not disappear because the 'water' that surrounded them (the mass of French people) was hostile.'[51]

Given this reality the FLN needed French people to transport money across the country, transfer these funds to bank accounts in Switzerland, hide FLN members, pass them across frontiers, and ferry arms.[52] In the case of Jeanson in 1956 this clandestine activity grew out of well-established links with FLN activists who, when they arrived in Paris, immediately contacted him because they knew he could be trusted. Jeanson in turn recruited amongst like-minded friends and activists, establishing the network in October 1957.[53]

The Jeanson group—subsequently known as the suit-case carriers (*porteurs de valises*)—was the nub of this clandestine activity, but it would be wrong to think of the underground anti-war movement as a purely Paris-based phenomenon. Georges Vanderkelen in Lille, Jean-Marie Boeglin in Lyon, Robert Bonnaud in Marseille: the Fédération de France divided France into six wilayas and within each wilaya FLN members sought out networks of support. Overall the numbers amounted to between five hundred and a thousand.[54] What motivated them to identify with the FLN cause? For some it was their direct experience of colonialism. Seeing for themselves, either as priests, journalists, teachers, or soldiers, the racial inequalities of French Algeria led them to the conclusion that the FLN struggle was just. For some it was bridges that they had already forged with the Algerian community since the late 1940s, a factor that was particularly important for Roman Catholic priests like Abbé Carteron in Lyon and Pierre Descheemaeker in Lille.[55] For others it was the impact of ideas, in particular the anti-colonial arguments of the psychiatrist Frantz Fanon who, after resigning from his post in Blida in 1956 to rejoin the FLN, became the most radical proponent of what he unashamedly called the Algerian Revolution.[56] For everybody, however, the common reference point was spring

1956. Mollet's capitulation to the 'tomatoes of Algiers', the voting of the special powers, the recall of the reservists: the Republican Front's intensification of the conflict was seen to be a betrayal of the electoral promise of 'peace in Algeria', a mockery of socialism and internationalism. Revulsion at the Republican Front was mirrored by disaffection with the Communist Party. The latter's support for the special powers was seen to be betrayal, a fact compounded by the way in which the party's anti-war campaign was deemed to be too timid, in particular the manner in which the central committee opposed desertion or any direct support for the FLN.[57]

These factors explain why a micro-minority, ranging from anarchists and Roman Catholic priests, to dissident communists and Trotskyists, sided with the FLN struggle. The path to this illegal action, though, was not a straightforward one. Georges Mattéi went through several stages.[58] Returning from service in December 1956, he felt hatred and aggression towards mainstream society because it showed so little understanding of what he and his fellow reservists had been forced to endure in Algeria. Fortunately for him, writing an eye-witness account for Jean-Paul Sartre and Simone de Beauvoir's journal Les Temps Modernes in July 1957 allowed him to get some of this anger out of his system. From that point on he sought to galvanize anti-war opinion through public meetings where he and other ex-servicemen described what they had witnessed in terms of torture and human rights. By 1959, however, he had come to the conclusion that this type of opposition was pointless because it did not go to the root of the problem: stopping the war itself. This feeling explains why, when contacted in that year by the Jeanson network, he was willing to pass over to illegal action because he wanted to bring about an FLN victory that would terminate the conflict. Nor did illegal work lead just to the FLN. Part of the French Trotskyist movement, led by Pierre Lambert, chose to support the MNA which it saw as more proletarian and revolutionary.

The pro-FLN underground movement drew in women no less than men. Madeleine Baudoin, France Binard, Hélène Cuénat, Claudie Duhamel, Anne Preiss, Micheline Pouteau, Cécile Verdurand: all played leading roles. In the case of Janine Cahen, support for the FLN stemmed from her Jewish identity, which meant for her that Jews, because of their history, should automatically identify with the oppressed, and from her sense of exclusion on gender grounds. As a woman she was intensely aware that she was not being directly confronted with the call-up in the way which young men were and her consciousness of this difference was a determining factor in her decision to cross over into pro–FLN clandestine activity: 'I came to see that, being a woman, and not being called upon to take up arms, there was a large matter on which I had no opinion to give, whereas a man has to reply 'yes' or 'no', and so my response was arrived at like that.'[59]

Janine Cahen's actions, like those of Mattéi, grew out of frustration with the wider legal opposition movement which mushroomed during 1957 in the wake of the 'Battle of Algiers'. The vast majority of those involved, however, preferred to hang back from directly aiding the FLN even if their activity did test the limits of the law. Above all, the focus of this wider movement was torture. In the face of ceaseless censorship, *Témoignage Chrétien*, *Esprit*, *L'Express*, *France-Observateur*, *Le Monde*, *L'Humanité*, and *Les Temps Modernes* defied the government with a stream of articles that documented French atrocities in Algeria. Equally, the publishers Maspero, Éditions de Minuit, and Seuil produced key eye-witness accounts that exposed systematic human rights abuses, while *Témoignages et Documents*, founded by Jacques Pagat in 1957, reproduced banned articles and books.[60]

Collectively these publications wanted to show that what was happening was not a 'law and order' problem, but a full-scale war with all its terrible consequences. This too was the purpose of the Audin Committee, established in September 1957 to investigate Maurice Audin's disappearance during the 'Battle of Algiers'.[61] The guiding light behind the Audin Committee was the historian Pierre Vidal-Naquet.[62] Drawing upon his historical training, he adopted a forensic approach which sought to establish the truth and set out the facts. On this basis the Audin Committee, in conjunction with the League of the Rights of Man, produced a comprehensive dossier in September 1958 that detailed the types of torture, named the military perpetrators, and listed the victims.[63] Prefacing the dossier with an unambiguous condemnation of FLN violence, the authors then underlined that nevertheless they had concentrated on the crimes of the French army because it was 'acting in the name of the French nation'.[64]

The advent of the Fifth Republic saw no let-up on the part of the Audin Committee. Confronted with the statement, made by André Malraux on 24 June 1958, that torture had stopped under de Gaulle, it set out to expose this claim as a lie, cataloguing abuses in Algeria and even more worryingly in France itself.[65] The increased incidents of torture in the metropole reinforced one of the Audin Committee's key arguments: that the war was an invasive entity, crossing the Mediterranean to fatally undermine human rights at home. This image of colonialism as a threat to democracy was ever present in the journal *Vérité-Liberté*, established in 1960 by many of the leading voices in the Audin Committee in collaboration with the left-wing Catholic journalist Robert Barrat. Giving information about meetings and demonstrations *Vérité-Liberté*, whose supporters numbered 10,000, hoped to produce a large-scale anti-war movement.

Without doubt the Audin Committee played a crucial role in politicizing the National Union of French Students (UNEF) which in 1960 became a vanguard force of anti-war protest. At its annual conference in Lyon the new president, Pierre Gaudez, a left-wing Catholic studying sociology at the Sorbonne, won a motion calling for negotiations with the Provisional Government. UNEF also re-established relations with the Union of Algerian Students that had been banned by the Gaillard government in January 1958. In response, a minority broke off to form a pro-French Algeria Union while the Ministry of Education cut the UNEF grant, but this did not deter it from signing a Communist Party and Catholic Trade Union declaration demanding negotiations with the FLN in Tunis in June 1960.

The fact that *Vérité-Liberté* and UNEF were operating outside the traditional parties was a measure of the dissatisfaction with the largest force on the left: the Communist Party. Many Communist Party intellectuals like the Sorbonne history student Madeleine Rebérioux did play a prominent role in the Audin Committee.[66] The party organized anti-war petitions and meetings. It also supported twenty-six party members, like Alban Liechti, who went to prison because they refused to fight in Algeria.[67] Yet, the general secretary, Maurice Thorez, was always carefully attuned to the thoughts and prejudices of the working class. Thorez argued that ordinary workers would recoil from any policy directly aiding the FLN, principally because many workers were conscripts. The Communist Party, therefore, had to be cautious or risk losing its electorate which is why the party line talked of 'Peace in Algeria' and negotiation rather than support for the FLN.

Opposition to clandestine support for the FLN was no less pronounced amongst the Parti Socialiste Unifié (PSU) founded in April 1960. Bringing together dissident anti-Mollet socialists like Alain Savary, Daniel Mayer, and Édouard Depreux with dissident communists such as Jean Poperen and François Furet, and Radical Party politicians like Pierre Mendès France, the PSU was promoted by the non-aligned weekly *France-Observateur*, edited by Claude Bourdet and Gilles Martinet: its programme was one of left renewal based on anti-Stalinism, anti-Gaullism, anti-Molletism, socialist humanism, and forthright opposition to the Algerian War.[68] But for all this radicalism the PSU still saw Jeanson's stance as dangerously misguided. Jeanson's logic, the PSU leadership argued, would not be understood by the vast majority of French people and, as such, could only damage the anti-war case.

Real though this anti-war anger was, it remained a minority current. Neither legal nor illegal opposition became mass movements. Jeune Résistance sought to make desertion into the great cause of their generation but in truth there were few deserters, perhaps no more than 3,000 in total.[69] This weakness of the Jeune Résistance movement takes us back to the mainstream majority, in particular their concern for the well-being of the 2.7 million soldiers who were conscripted from France to fight in Algeria during the course of the conflict. The patriotic bond between the home front and these raw 20-year-olds meant that most French people steered clear of extremism. They did not become involved in overt anti-war opposition, let alone pro-FLN support. They rejected the hard-line position of the pro-French Algeria movement. Instead, by 1960 this mainstream majority put their trust in de Gaulle to find an acceptable solution which would stop the war and bring the conscripts back home.

'Algerian Algeria'

In the spring of 1960 de Gaulle was still hanging on to the idea of a third-way solution. He hoped that local elections in May would produce a moderate Muslim elite to act as a counterweight to the FLN. With these thoughts in his mind de Gaulle visited the army leadership in Algeria on 3 March. These meetings were tense, especially as there were attempts within the army to manipulate reports of the president's pronouncements in a pro-French Algerian direction, but de Gaulle would not be deterred. He was frank that his preferred choice was an 'Algerian Algeria' associated with France and in this respect the army's mission continued to be clear and unambiguous: it had to complete the 'pacification' process as quickly as possible so that de Gaulle could negotiate from a position of strength.

But as de Gaulle grappled with the evolving situation his room for manoeuvre was constrained by new realities. First, there was the break-up of the Franco-African Community, as all the members pressed for full-blown independence which they won between January and December 1960. This rapid demise ended the possibility of a wider 'Eurafrican' entity within which both Mollet and de Gaulle had hoped to anchor an Algerian solution. Moreover, it strengthened the case for Algerian independence. After all, if the Black African territories had become independent nation states, why not Algeria? And then, allied to this, there was the wider process of decolonization. On 3 February 1960 Harold Macmillan delivered his landmark 'Wind of Change' speech in Cape Town to the South African parliament. Signalling that for the other major European power in Africa colonialism was now at an end, Macmillan declared:

> The wind of change is blowing through the continent. Whether we like it or not, this growth of political consciousness is a political fact. We must all accept this fact, and our national policies must take account of it.[70]

In this new context, Macmillan continued, the question was whether the uncommitted peoples of Asia and Africa would 'swing to the East or to the West':

> Will they be drawn into the Communist camp? Or will the great experiments in self-government that are now being made in Asia and Africa, especially within the Commonwealth, prove so successful, that the balance will come down in favour of freedom and order and justice? The struggle is joined, and it is a struggle for the minds of men.[71]

The issue in 1960, therefore, was about managing an orderly retreat from empire. It was about engineering a tactical withdrawal that would ensure the best strategic advantage. Equally, de Gaulle had to face the fact that neither Eisenhower nor the incoming Democrat President John F. Kennedy, elected in November 1960, was willing to support the concept of a French-led pillar of NATO covering Algeria, Africa, and the Mediterranean.[72] Quite the opposite; they wanted de Gaulle to bring about an end to the Algerian problem as quickly as possible.

Each of these factors formed the backdrop to the choreography between France and the FLN as both sides, knowing that direct contacts were about to resume, carefully positioned themselves to gain maximum advantage. The Provisional Government, fearful of the army hardliners who were ready to shout betrayal, did not want to be seen to concede anything, while de Gaulle tried to play off the interior against the exterior to his advantage. Thus, when the French authorities were secretly contacted by emissaries from Colonel Si Salah, head of Wilaya 4, in March, this produced a train of events that led Si Salah, with his adjoints Si Lakhdar and Si Mohammed, to go to the Élysée Palace to see de Gaulle in person on 10 June 1960 at 10.00 p.m. Stating that he represented 10,000 men, Si Salah accused the Provisional Government of abandoning the interior resistance before asking to negotiate directly with the French government on the basis of the 'paix des braves'.[73] In return, de Gaulle was courteous, but ultimately Si Salah left empty handed. De Gaulle did not take up his offer of negotiations, nor did he let Si Salah see the imprisoned Ben Bella, instead reiterating his decision to make another appeal to the Provisional Government. In this way, he exploited the meeting to put fresh pressure on the Provisional Government in advance of the 14 June speech: de Gaulle's first pronouncement on Algeria since the 'Week of the Barricades'.

In the speech de Gaulle called on his compatriots to embrace realism. Whether one liked the fact or not, colonialism was over:

> The spirit of the century ... also changes the conditions of our action overseas ... leads us to bring an end to colonization ... It is quite natural that one feels nostalgia for what was the Empire, just as one can regret the gentleness of oil lamps, the splendour of sailing ships ... But for what? No policy is worth anything outside of reality.[74]

Then de Gaulle restated his call for a ceasefire that would open the way to self-determination which, he hoped, would lead to 'union with France', cooperation between the communities, and 'the transformation of Algerian Algeria into a prosperous and fraternal country'.[75] Six days later, the Provisional Government responded with the view that de Gaulle's speech represented significant 'progress'. The path was clear for discussions, even if the Provisional Government was adamant that there was still a huge distance between the two sides.

Melun

This meeting, the first face-to-face contact since 1956, took place at the Prefecture of Melun south of Paris on 25 June. The FLN delegation was led by Ahmed Boumendjel and Mohammed Ben Yahia, but after three days the talks ended in failure. Largely this was because of the unbridgeable gap between the two sides. The French wanted to negotiate a ceasefire and then reach agreement on how the self-determination vote was going to be organized, while the FLN delegates wanted to do the opposite. But it was also because of the suspicion produced by the 'Si Salah affair'. President Abbas was petrified about being outmanoeuvred by de Gaulle and on this basis Si Salah was arrested and Si Lakhdar executed. Meanwhile Si Mohammed pledged his loyalty to the Provisional Government, purging Si Salah supporters and calling for a fresh offensive against the French army.[76]

Within France amongst the pro-Gaullist majority, Melun produced hope because it traced out how the war would be ended, namely through negotiations between France and the Provisional Government. Amongst pro-French Algerian supporters, however, Melun accelerated polarization. In Algeria the Front de l'Algérie Française (FAF) was formally established on 16 June and led by Bachaga Boualam, who had risen to become vice-president of the French National Assembly. Garnering 500,000 supporters, especially amongst young settlers, its slogans were: 'There will be no place in the French Algeria of tomorrow for defeatists'; 'Do not flee French Algeria needs you'; 'The FAF is not a party, it is France—not to join is to desert'; and 'The FAF strikes where it wants, when it wants'.[77] In France the Vincennes Committee, also launched in June, brought together Georges Bidault, André Morice, Jacques Soustelle, and Maurice Bourgès-Maunoury—all former Fourth Republic ministers, including two former prime ministers, whose sense of republican values led them to defend French sovereignty in Algeria and uphold 'the fraternity of all French people north and south of the Mediterranean' within one country.[78]

The presence of extreme right-wingers like Jean-Marie Le Pen in the Vincennes Committee led the Socialist Party leadership to block the participation of Max Lejeune. But, angry at the manner in which the Socialist Party had abdicated responsibility to de Gaulle over Algeria, Lejeune created a left-wing Committee for the 'Maintenance of Algeria in the French Republic', supported by Albert Bayet (who argued that the para-troopers were defending secular values), Robert Lacoste, Henri Laforest, Paul Rivet, and Jules Romains. Blaming the continuation of the war on the 'totalitarian' FLN but also upholding the progressive role played by repub-licanism, particularly over Algerian women's rights, this Committee explained that:

> A certain number of personalities belonging to left-wing parties, to trade union movements and Resistance organizations have met to put together the text of a declaration on the Algerian problem which, according to them, will only be resolved by the maintenance within the French Republic of a new and socially transformed Algeria.[79]

However, at the four-day Socialist Party Annual Conference which opened on 30 June at Issy, Lejeune was completely marginalized. His position, upholding Algeria's position within the Republic, mustered only 174 votes as against 1,299 for Gaston Defferre's motion in favour of 'Algerian Algeria' and 1,876 for Georges Brutelle's motion endorsing negotiations for a ceasefire and self-determination.[80]

In this atmosphere of argument and counter-argument, the opening of the trial of the Jeanson Network on 5 September made the public debate about Algeria more strident than ever, especially when 121 of the country's most prominent personalities, including the actress Simone Signoret, the philosopher Jean-Paul Sartre, and the writer Françoise Sagan signed a manifesto defending the accused and supporting the right of French soldiers to desert.[81] Furthermore, on 27 October, despite Communist Party opposition, the National Students' Union (UNEF) organized an anti-war demonstration in the Latin *quartier* where some 20,000 spilled out onto the streets, blocking the traffic and shouting 'Peace in Algeria', 'Paratroopers to the factories', and 'Yes, to negotiations'.[82]

In response, French Algeria supporters organized an alternative manifesto of the 185 on 7 October whose signatories included Marshal Juin and Henri Massis of the French Academy. Denouncing desertion as an act of betrayal, the counter-manifesto attacked the FLN as 'a minority of fanatical rebels, terrorists and racists, led by leaders whose personal ambitions are obvious— armed and financially supported by foreigners'.[83] Then one month later, Lagaillarde and the others from the 'Week of the Barricades' came up before the judges. Providing a platform for the hard-line supporters of French Algeria, the accused talked in stark terms. Public opinion, they argued, had to understand what was at stake. Their struggle was not just about Algeria. It was nothing less than the defence of Western values in the face of decadence and disintegration.

December 1960

By autumn 1960 the strain on de Gaulle was very clear. No end to the conflict was in sight, especially after a fresh wave of FLN violence in August seemed to bury the possibility of further talks. On 4 November, in a bid to break the deadlock, de Gaulle went further than any previous French leader, acknowledging that the future lay with an Algerian Republic that would 'exist one day' with its own government, institutions and laws.[84] It was a momentous phrase, slipped out at the end of his televised speech, which represented a further turning point in the war.[85]

Inevitably the speech produced deep divisions within the government. Even Debré offered to resign as prime minister, which de Gaulle refused. Elsewhere there was also condemnation from Soustelle and Lejeune's Committee for the 'Maintenance of Algeria in the French Republic' which argued that de Gaulle, by imposing an Algerian Republic as a solution, was not only dismembering the French Republic, but also betraying the principle of a free democratic choice envisaged in his original 16 September 1959 speech.[86] In contrast, amongst mainland public opinion there was a broad spectrum of support with 69 per cent favouring his pronouncement.[87] Heartened by this consensus de Gaulle quickly pushed through new institutions and people to carry out his policy. Delouvrier, who resigned as Delegate-General in protest, was replaced by two new faces: Louis Joxe, who occupied a new post, Minister of State for Algeria, reporting directly to de Gaulle and residing in Paris, and Jean Morin who, named Government-Delegate, remained in Algiers but under Joxe's orders.

Following these dramatic developments, de Gaulle made an official visit to Algeria on Friday 9 December 1960. In anticipation, settler hard-liners in the FAF organized a general strike, but, faced with this violent atmosphere, fuelled by ceaseless rumours about a putsch and assassination attempts on his life, de Gaulle's itinerary carefully avoided Algiers and Oran. Touching down in the west of the country, his cavalcade made its way to Tlemcen near the Moroccan border where, although he was booed by Europeans, another, even more decisive factor, entered the equation: Algerian counter-demonstrations in favour of de Gaulle's concept of 'Algerian Algeria'.[88] Encouraged by rumours that the authorities would not stand in their way, on Sunday 11 December these demonstrations, representing the expression of long-pent-up forces, took on an unprecedented size in Algiers and Oran. Thousands of Algerians, many armed with bike chains and clubs, poured onto the streets, brandishing green-and-white FLN flags and shouting 'Long live Ferhat Abbas! Long live the FLN! Long live the Provisional Government! Long live de Gaulle! Free Ben Bella!'; while others chanted 'Algerian Algeria!' and 'Muslim Algeria!', backed up by the 'you-you-you' ululations of countless women. Cars and buildings were set on fire, including a five-storey apartment in Belcourt, and in Bab-El-Oued there were clashes between Algerians and Europeans. On 12 December Algerians sacked the Great Synagogue in the Casbah, one of the most important places of Jewish worship in the country, tearing up the Torah scrolls and daubing the walls with slogans of 'Death to the Jews'—acts of violence that filled Jews with an ominous foreboding about their place within an 'Algerian Algeria'.

Writing in his diary, Mouloud Feraoun was in no doubt about the spontaneous nature of the demonstrations. They were not controlled and organized by the FLN. They were a 'direct' and 'truthful' reflection of Algerian feelings.[89] As one demonstrator told a reporter from Radio Luxembourg: 'No, the FLN have nothing to do with this. We are fed up, that is all. We want our independence. We want to shout that we have had enough. There was never any fraternization. They silenced us. We would rather die than accept this situation any longer.'[90]

These demonstrations were a shock to the Provisional Government since the FLN, pushed back to the mountains and the countryside by the end of 1957, had, at best, a rudimentary presence in the major cities.[91] For the most part this presence was limited to disaffected young Algerians who, given their patriotism, rejected the French authorities' attempt to win them over both through the creation of sporting clubs and the economic benefits of the Constantine Plain.[92] This was, therefore, a willing audience which FLN militants, still constantly tracked by the army and police, sought to discreetly organize by re-establishing scouting groups and football teams based on local *quartier*, in effect creating a politicization process whose end result—December 1960—far exceeded anything the FLN could have predicted.[93]

The demonstrations were also a shock to the French authorities who, ever since the 'Battle of Algiers', had claimed to have control of the capital. But, as ensuing rioting in both cities led to 120 Algerian dead and nearly 500 injured, the international impact of these demonstrations was clear and unambiguous. By occupying urban public space and expressing Algerian nationalism in such an audacious manner, the slogans and symbols were the climax of a politicization process that had begun in the 1920s, connecting December 1960 back to Sétif in 1945 and the Popular Front in 1936. 'Algerian Algeria', long denied by France but now recognized by de Gaulle, was a reality, even if the Provisional Government, fearful that it had lost control of the masses to the French army, was surprised by the depth of pro-FLN support. As one French officer, looking back to Indochina, admitted to *Le Monde*, the demonstrations were a defeat: 'We have suffered a veritable psychological Dien Bien Phu... On 16 May 1958, we did not have the military situation under control and... everybody shouted "long live France!". Today, we have won on the military front and... everybody was shouting "long live the FLN!" '[94]

For de Gaulle, forced to cut short what was to be his last visit to Algeria, the sheer scale of the Algerian demonstrations led him to one conclusion: the FLN enjoyed overwhelming support. From a French perspective this made December 1960 into *the* decisive moment of the Algerian War because it finally buried the concept of a third-way solution that had defined government policy from Mendès France onwards. Now there really was no alternative to the FLN, as December 1960 handed an unstoppable momentum to the Provisional Government causing the final remnants of an alternative anti-FLN Algerian force to melt away.

UN vote

At the same, this momentum was the result of an intense international diplomatic effort by the Provisional Government which, in the wake of the failed talks at Melun, reached out to other anti-colonial movements as well as the Communist-bloc countries.[95] Already in August, Belkacem Krim, the Foreign Minister, had called on the Algerian Provisional government to supply military aid to radical anti-French opposition parties in Cameroon and Senegal as a way of weakening France's military and political power.[96] In the following month the Provisional Government pledged solidarity with Fidel Castro's Cuban revolution and attacked NATO as a 'colonialist coalition'.[97] Then, in September and October Ferhat Abbas led a major delegation to Peking and Moscow, a visit that led to military support from China and the promise of de facto recognition for the Provisional Government from the Soviet Union: two major diplomatic victories.

In courting the communist world the Provisional Government intensified the international pressure on de Gaulle. Now, more than ever, Britain and the USA wanted an end to the conflict because they were petrified that French policy was pushing the FLN into the arms of the Soviet Union. Within the UN itself the FLN's New York delegation, still led by the ever resourceful Abdelkader Chanderli, continued to mount a formidable operation, seeking out allies amongst the newly independent African nations.

During 1960 it produced forty-six brochures on different aspects of the Algerian struggle; Chanderli appeared regularly in the media and addressed groups ranging from the Quakers to university students; while Abbas himself was on the front page of the *New York Times* and interviewed by CBS in an hour-long programme.

On 20 December this international strategy paid off handsomely, according the Provisional Government its greatest diplomatic victory so far: a United Nations General Assembly vote which endorsed Algeria's right to independence by sixty-three votes to eight with twenty-seven abstentions. Debated against the backdrop of the December demonstrations, the condemnation of French policies was unanimous, even amongst once-moderate delegations like India and pro-French African countries like Mali and Togo. In fact such was the level of anti-French feeling that the paragraph demanding an internationally supervised referendum only failed by one vote, while the final motion rejected de Gaulle's threat of partition, upheld Algeria's territorial integrity, and underlined the UN's role in ensuring self-determination. The UN vote exposed the limits to de Gaulle's power. It made plain that he alone could not impose peace. His only option was to negotiate with the FLN.

Referendum

After December 1960, events moved quickly. On his return de Gaulle organized a snap referendum timed for 8 January 1961 where he asked voters to respond to the following question: 'Do you approve the Bill submitted to the French people by the President of the Republic concerning the self-determination of the Algerian people and the organization of the public powers in Algeria prior to self-determination?' In campaigning for a massive 'yes' vote, de Gaulle made it clear that rejection would lead him to immediately resign and on this basis he was supported by his own UNR party, Christian Democrats in the MRP, and the Socialist Party. Against them the Communist Party and PSU urged voters to say 'no', claiming that de Gaulle could exploit the referendum to continue the war against the FLN. In Algeria the FLN called for a boycott and pro-French Algeria settlers argued for a 'no' vote.

In the event, on the mainland 75.5% voted with 76.25% of these endorsing de Gaulle, while in Algeria there was a massive abstention with 39%

voting 'yes' and 18% voting 'no'. Even so, on the basis of his support in the metropole, the referendum gave de Gaulle an undeniable mandate. He had the electoral authority to face the army, the Europeans and the Provisional Government, although in the following weeks de Gaulle went beyond the referendum's remit. Interpreting the result as a blank cheque, he despatched Georges Pompidou, close friend and director of Rothschild's Bank, to secretly re-establish contact with the FLN despite the fact that, strictly speaking, the referendum had only given him the right to organize a self-determination vote. Significantly, too, this move represented an abandonment of the triptych 'ceasefire, elections, negotiations', inherited from the Fourth Republic and which de Gaulle had persisted with at Melun. Now, without formally acknowledging the fact, de Gaulle had given in to the FLN demand that negotiations precede a ceasefire and elections.

Confronted with their worst nightmare—an Algerian Republic— European activists concluded that since France could no longer protect them then Europeans had to protect themselves, formally establishing the Organisation de l'Armée Secrète (OAS) at the end of January 1961 in Madrid. There the people leading the OAS were Salan, in theory retired from the army but still, as everybody knew, a fervent champion of French Algeria; and Susini and Lagaillarde, both of whom had jumped bail before they could be sentenced at the Barricades Trial. In choosing the name, the OAS wished to invoke the heroism of the Armée Secrète of the Resistance and turn it against de Gaulle, but in essence it belonged to the tradition of anti-Paris settler separatism going back to the 1890s and the Algiers Commune of 1870. In terms of strategy, the OAS based itself on the FLN, seeing its own use of terrorism as the way to victory. Theoretically there was a command structure to organize this violence; in practice there were many cells operating on their own initiative without a single well-defined aim. What united these disparate OAS activists was anti-Gaullism, anti-communism and anti-Algerian nationalism, tinged in some cases with the ideological trappings of racial superiority, in others with adherence to a united France from Dunkirk to Tamanrasset. What was less clear was what the OAS was proposing as a political solution. Was it fighting for the preservation of Algeria within the Fifth Republic, federation, or some form of settler independence?

Specifically the OAS wanted to destroy negotiations between its two mortal enemies: the Gaullist government and the FLN, thus ensuring that the preparations for official talks were conducted within a frantic atmosphere. Having accepted Switzerland's offer of protection for the FLN delegation, these negotiations were timed to begin on 7 April at Évian, the spa town on the French side of Lake Geneva, opposite Lausanne. However, when on 30 March Joxe suggested that the MNA should also be involved, even though Messali had recognized the right of his political rivals to talk with France, the FLN negotiators were furious.[98] The Provisional Government was adamant that the FLN alone represented the Algerian people and on the following day the FLN delegation pulled out. To make matters worse, that night the mayor of Évian was killed in a bomb attack by a pro-French Algeria commando group.

This collapse showed just how great the potential for misunderstanding was, especially at the start of what both sides knew was going to be a long and drawn-out process. In a bid to re-launch talks, de Gaulle gave a key press conference at the Élysée on 11 April 1961. He cut through the passion and emotion and made a hard-nosed economic assessment. What, he asked, was in Algeria for France: the question that had been there right from the beginning in 1830? And on this point he was in no doubt: 'Algeria is costing us, this is the least that one can say, much more than it brings into us.'[99]

Thus, whereas in 1956 Mollet's geo-strategic policy was predicated on the belief that, in the context of the cold war, rival Anglo-Saxon imperialisms, and pan-Arab nationalism, the economic and political future of France as a major power was inseparable from Algeria, five years on, de Gaulle rejected this premise. Disentangling France from Algeria was now seen to be in the national interest because, as Aron and Cartier argued in 1956, colonialism was a drain on finite financial resources that would be better invested in the metropole and in constructing a new relationship with independent African states.[100] In this manner, the Aron and Cartier reasoning, marginalized by Mollet, became the bedrock of de Gaulle's new economic calculations. In the final analysis Algeria was costing too much and on this basis France had no economic rationale for remaining there. In the same vein, de Gaulle continued, France had no objection to Algerians constructing an independent state that would be sovereign in terms of internal and external relations; a notable break with previous solutions that had talked about France still controlling foreign affairs. Nor, de Gaulle argued, was France worried about the USA and the Soviet Union encroaching on France's traditional sphere of influence. Indeed, in a flash of humour, causing consternation amongst the pro-French Algerian journalists present, de Gaulle wished both superpowers 'good luck'.[101]

In speaking so, de Gaulle was sending a clear peace signal to the Provisional Government. He was demonstrating that France no longer had any political, economic, or geo-strategic interests in Algeria, a message that was immediately picked up by Mohammed Yazid, the Provisional Government Minister of Information. Carefully tracing his finger under de Gaulle's text on the following day in Tunis, he nodded his head in agreement, stating: 'If he is sincere, three months from now we will have peace.'[102]

10

Bloody Conclusion

Friday, 21 April 1961

A t midnight paratroopers from the First Airborne Foreign Legion seized control of central Algiers, arresting de Gaulle's key representatives, including General Fernand Gambiez, the commander-in-chief, and Jean Morin, the Delegate-General. The following morning at 7.00 a.m. Radio-Algiers, renamed Radio-France, announced that under the leadership of Generals Challe, Jouhaud, and Zeller, and in liaison with Salan in Spain, the army had 'taken control of the Algero-Saharan territory'.[1] Like Challe and Salan, Jouhaud, a five-star air-force commander from Oran, and Zeller, a former chief of staff well known as an expert in logistics, had either retired or been retired out of the army because of their pro-French Algeria views. And like Challe and Salan, they were motivated by military honour. They wished to uphold what, in their opinion, the army had been fighting for ever since 1954: the maintaining of Algeria within the French Republic.

With Salan still in Madrid, Challe was the leader and it was he who took the key role in drafting the rebellion's first radio communiqué.[2] In it the generals underlined that their aim was not political power. This was a military operation which, after a lightning three-month campaign, intended to finally crush the ALN, in effect presenting the government with a fait accompli that would ensure that Algeria remained a 'French province'.[3] Through such action, the four generals would stay faithful to 'the pledge of the army to keep Algeria so that our dead have not died for nothing'; stop de Gaulle from selling out to 'the external organization of the rebellion'; and prevent the country from falling into the hands of the Soviet Union.[4] The communiqué, therefore, had a strictly limited intent. It was addressed only to the army units in Algeria. At no point did Challe consider the mass mobilization of Europeans. Settler leaders like Lagaillarde were viewed with disgust. They were to be kept at arm's length while the army completed the pacification process. In the meantime, Challe, the staunch republican, envisaged the country in terms of an integrated Franco-Muslim community of equal citizens that would have its own distinctive identity within a larger decentralized Republic, looking back to the language of the 1956 Republican Front government.[5]

The trail of powder for the putsch had been lit at the time of de Gaulle's speech on self-determination on 16 September 1959. As Massu's comments in January 1960 showed, large parts of the senior military were hostile to de Gaulle's policy. This feeling intensified when, instead of waiting for a free vote on integration, association, or independence, he began to impose a solution, talking of an 'Algerian Algeria' in June 1960, followed by an 'Algerian Republic' in November 1960, and then a 'sovereign Algeria' in April 1961. For them, each phrase was a betrayal of the army's blood sacrifice. Who, though, was prepared to cross the Rubicon and disobey de Gaulle? Jouhaud, Zeller, and Salan had already done so by January 1961, the latter in Madrid with the OAS, the first two in France testing out the depth of officer support for a military conspiracy. For Challe, the final turning point was de Gaulle's press conference on 11 April 1961.[6] This, he believed, was political cynicism of the very worst kind. By reducing Algeria to a negative economic equation, by opening the door to the Soviet Union and the USA, by recognizing the FLN as the sole negotiator, de Gaulle, in Challe's opinion, was acting in a shameful manner. He was selling out France's geo-strategic interests, and handing over the Europeans and pro-French Muslims to a future FLN state: the very people the army had pledged to protect.

Within army circles rumours of revolt had been circulating for months and here the pressure came upwards from middle-ranking officers: the lieutenants, the captains, the colonels. It was men such as Colonel Antoine Argoud, Colonel Yves Godard, and Captain Pierre Sergent who made the running. They believed that because their elite formations had borne the brunt of the fighting, they alone should have the last say on policy, testament to the way in which Algeria, along with the lost wars in Indochina, Tunisia, and Morocco, had politicized the army, making them bitter against government leaders who—they thought—had squandered their sacrifices. Argoud especially played a central role in the search for a senior leader who had the stature to stand up to de Gaulle. Several times he sounded out General Massu now stationed in eastern France. But each time he received a 'no' since by early 1961 Massu was convinced that independence was an inescapable fact, nor did he want to threaten army unity. At this point Argoud turned his attention to Challe, encouraging Jouhaud to propose that Challe should actually lead the putsch. Challe wavered but in the light of de Gaulle's pronouncements on 11 April he finally committed himself.

In the trawl for support Argoud and his fellow conspirators recruited significant figures right up to the eleventh hour. One was Colonel Jean Gardes, acquitted of complicity with European rebels at the Barricades Trial in March 1961; another was Major Denoix de Saint Marc who joined the night before the putsch when Challe himself made it clear that this was 'neither a Fascist *coup d'état* nor an action tending to racialism'.[7] Born into a right-wing Catholic and conservative milieu, inspired by de Gaulle's stance in June 1940, de Saint Marc's trajectory had led to the Resistance, deportation to Buchenwald Concentration Camp, and then Indochina as a volunteer with the Foreign Legion.[8] Shocked by the sudden tangent of de Gaulle's policy, de Saint Marc was very clear that for him self-determination was not about capitulation to the FLN, but the creation of a plural society where Europeans and *harkis* would both have their place. At his subsequent trial Saint Marc would justify his actions in the following manner: 'I never thought that I was fighting for any kind of colonialism, which I condemn, but for a just and humane cause.'[9]

Amongst the Europeans in Algiers there was total surprise at the putsch. But as news spread during early Saturday morning they spilled out onto the streets, waving tricolore flags, cheering the passing paratroopers and beating out on their car horns the notes of *Al-gé-rie française!* Momentarily the mood was euphoric: the army had saved them. Yet, almost immediately the putsch began to unravel. In Paris the ringleaders in the capital were all arrested that day. In Algeria it was quickly clear that only Algiers and its surrounding regions had been totally secured. In Kabylia, General Simon opposed the coup from the start; in the west, General Pouilly refused to commit himself, while in the east in Constantine General Gouraud wavered back and forth before finally throwing in his lot on the Sunday. To make matters even worse, the personal animosity between Challe and Salan created a basic disunity which plagued the putsch right from the start.

As Saturday gave way to Sunday, Paris was awash with rumours of an impending paratrooper invasion that evening. People looked anxiously to the skies as the government, using the state of emergency decreed by de Gaulle, cancelled flights, blocked the airport runways with lorries, stopped public transport, and closed cinemas.[10] Old World War Two Sherman tanks were trundled out of retirement and stationed in front of the National Assembly; while both André Malraux, the Minister of Culture, and the Communist Party called for volunteers to oppose any landing. Then at 8.00 p.m. on Sunday 23 April, de Gaulle finally intervened with a televised speech. Dressed in his two-star general's uniform, de Gaulle was eloquent and to the point. Deploying all his rhetorical skills to devastating effect, he was withering about the rebel leaders. They were nothing more than four retired generals. Detached from the reality of the modern world, they did not understand how they were doing untold damage to the national interest, threatening renewal and the recovery of great power status, and compromising France's role in Africa. And this, he complained sternly:

By men whose duty, honour and *raison d'être* it was to serve and obey.[11]

Then, banging his fist on the table to emphasize his words, he stated clearly:

In the name of France, I order that all methods, I say all methods, are used to block the path of these men . . . I forbid all French people and, first of all, all soldiers to carry out any of their orders.[12]

It was a stunning performance and the impact was immediate. Unlike Challe, de Gaulle had reached out to the people. Even more crucially, he had made a direct appeal to the conscripts who, crowded around their transistor radios in Algeria, followed his orders and refused to march with the putsch.[13] Despite promises from the rebel leaders to reduce military service from twenty-seven months to eighteen, only 25,000 soldiers out of 400,000 sided with the four generals. The rebellion was too small and too isolated to succeed.

In mainland France support for the president was unanimous. From Gaullists to Communists, all the parties opposed the putsch. Telegrams of support flooded into the Élysée from mayors underlining the loyalty of the population. Demonstrations took place across the country. Grass-roots anti-fascist committees were formed, proclaiming: 'Military Fascism will not pass'.[14] On Monday 24 April, there was a one-hour general strike against the putsch, while in the press at both a national and local level there was blanket condemnation. In Normandy *Le Courrier de la Mayenne* denounced the putsch as 'an act of desperation'; *Ouest-France* as 'an aberration'; and *Le Courrier Picard* as an 'insane undertaking'.[15] Significantly, though, what mobilized activists was anti-fascism and defence of the Republic, under-lining the way in which the Communist Party and Socialist Party were much more at ease with this language, evoking the Popular Front and the Resistance, rather than anti-colonialism or Algerian independence.

Figure 10.1 Putsch leaders: Generals Challe, Jouhaud, Salan, and Zeller in Algiers, 24 April 1961.

In Algiers, Salan remained defiant. Arriving from Spain on the Sunday he addressed 100,000 people crowded into the Forum in the city centre on Monday 24 April at 7.00 p.m., promising to maintain Algeria within France. In response Europeans shouted 'French Algeria' and 'De Gaulle to the execution stake [*au poteau*]' but in effect the putsch was finished. On Wednesday 26 April, Challe and Zeller handed themselves in. Salan and Jouhaud went underground to continue the struggle with the OAS. The operation had been a fiasco from start to finish, principally because the four generals had failed to win over the conscripts, underestimated the strength of metropolitan opinion, and provided no answer to de Gaulle's razor-sharp political instincts. Even the most basic logistics had been overlooked. By Monday the government had spirited away the transport planes from Algeria back to France, rendering it impossible to carry out a paratrooper drop on the mainland. Furthermore, the generals had no plan on how to supply Algeria—a fatal omission given the fact the country only had enough food and petrol to last two weeks. How, therefore, they hoped to sustain the rebellion beyond this period is difficult to envisage, especially if France had imposed a blockade.

De Gaulle himself muttered in cabinet that the gravest aspect of the putsch was that: 'It is not serious.'[16] Their failure, however, had strengthened his hand and on this basis three rebel regiments were disbanded; 200 officers arrested; Challe and Zeller imprisoned for fifteen years; and Salan and Jouhaud condemned to death. In this manner April 1961 has to be understood, from the French perspective, as the final and definitive tipping point. Confronted with the spectre of military rebellion, metropolitan opinion wished to finish with Algeria before the country was plunged into civil war. But, like the 'Week of the Barricades', April 1961 also strengthened the FLN because, if peace was to be achieved quickly, there was no alternative to FLN-dominated independence: the very opposite of what the putschists had wanted.

Negotiations: The first-round failure

During early 1961 de Gaulle made gestures which, he hoped, would entice the Provisional Government to the negotiating table. Already in the previous December, de Gaulle had stopped the execution of condemned FLN prisoners. Then in January 1961 the army reversed its regrouping policy. Finally, on the eve of the opening of negotiations on 20 May 1961 in Évian on Lake Geneva, the French government released 6,000 prisoners; transferred Ben Bella and his fellow inmates to the more luxurious surroundings of Château de Turquant; and declared a unilateral truce.[17]

In truth, though, the signals were contradictory, largely because of the discontents in the army which exploded so spectacularly with the putsch. The actual military directive, issued by General Gambiez on 23 March, continued to talk in terms of an ongoing conflict, albeit one now grounded in a humanitarian mission to win the Algerian people away from the FLN:

If a truce or a ceasefire comes into operation, it will represent most certainly the realization of the success of the Army. But the real, definitive victory will be to those to whom the Algerian people, the day when it will be called upon to vote, chooses to link its destiny: France or her adversaries of today. The struggle continues therefore, but under a new form. A new battle can now open up, which will perhaps no longer be a military one, but will be engaged on the human, material, psychological and economic levels. In place of operations 'Binoculars' or 'Ariège' will be substituted operation 'Youth', operation 'Degrouping', operation 'Rural renovation'. The French army must also win this battle.[18]

Such language explains why the Provisional Government broke off the first talks so abruptly on 31 March. They were suspicious of French intentions. They were worried that de Gaulle could exploit the negotiations to achieve victory by other means. They were petrified about appearing weak before the ever vigilant Boumediène. For this reason the Provisional Government issued no equivalent truce because this would be tantamount to an unconditional ceasefire, something the FLN had rejected right from the start. Furthermore, a truce would potentially weaken the FLN's power which is why, on the contrary, May and June witnessed a demonstration of force on the ground, leading to a fifty per cent increase in 'incidents' and 133 deaths.

It was in this tense climate that talks at last opened. The French side was led by Louis Joxe seconded by Bernard Tricot, Roland Cadet, and Bruno de Leusse. The Algerian team was headed by Belkacem Krim, backed up by Minister of Finance and Economic Affairs Ahmed Francis, Ahmed Boumendjel, and Mohammed Ben Yahia, the last two veterans of the Melun encounter. Also in the delegation were Saad Dahlab, Krim's second-in-command in foreign affairs, and, significantly, two senior officers from Boumediène's general staff: Major Mendjli and Major Slimane.

From the outset, the problem, typical of these situations, was how to edge towards a common ground, especially when both sides were so far apart both in their proposals and their manner of conducting face-to-face business.[19] Joxe wanted to get down to the specific details, whereas Krim, in a bid to wear down the French, preferred to drag the talks out by sticking to declarations of general principles. Comprising a mammoth thirteen sessions, the talks eventually broke down on 13 June. Resumed at nearby Lugrin on 20 July, they failed again eight days later. Specifically, the two major sticking points were the legal rights of the Europeans and the status of the Sahara. On the first issue Joxe wanted double nationality for Europeans; on the second he claimed that the Sahara was a French creation with no connection to Algeria: assertions that were rejected as an unacceptable infringement of their national sovereignty by the Algerian delegation.

Faced with failure, de Gaulle scrambled around for alternatives. He was not going to be dictated to by the Provisional Government. He was not going to make peace at any price and in response he threatened to expel Algerians from France, establish an executive without the FLN, and seek out the MNA as an alternative negotiating partner. He brandished, too, the idea of partition whereby settlers and pro-French Muslims would be concentrated into a French enclave.[20]

Dramatically, the Évian impasse was intensified even further by the incident at Bizerte, the French military base in Tunisia that had been a running sore between Bourguiba and Paris ever since independence in 1956. Frustrated at de Gaulle's refusal to negotiate or withdraw and desperate to counter his image in the Arab world as a Western puppet, Bourguiba ordered an attack on 19 July.[21] Enraged, de Gaulle immediately reinforced the base. He sent three warships to break the blockade, dropped 7,000 paratroopers, and ordered planes to bomb the Tunisian positions: firepower that crushed Bourguiba's troops in three days, inflicting 700 dead and 1,200 wounded.

By adopting such a muscular riposte, de Gaulle was thinking about the Provisional Government. He was trying to intimidate them back to the negotiating table by a display of military might. But here de Gaulle badly misjudged international opinion. In Washington the Kennedy administration was furious at his heavy-handed methods. They were angry at how de Gaulle's action had split NATO, leading countries like Denmark, Norway, and Turkey to join forces with Africa, Asia, and the Communist World to condemn France at the United Nations on 26 August. They were angry, too, at how France had provided another easy propaganda victory to the Soviet Union, allowing Moscow to present itself as the defender of African freedom against NATO imperialism.[22] Just at the moment when the Communist bloc was confronted with the mass exodus from East Germany via West Berlin, a crisis that threatened the very existence of the German Democratic Republic and led to the construction of the Berlin Wall on 13 August, the Bizerte crisis had pulled the Afro-Asian bloc in a communist direction.[23]

By August 1961 de Gaulle cut an isolated figure. He himself was deeply depressed because for all his bluff and thunder, the blunt truth was that the negotiations had failed. Moreover, the Bizerte affair had damaged French–US relations; alienated Tunisia, a potentially moderating force on the Provisional Government; and provoked hostility the world over. Meanwhile the war itself just went on and on as the army grappled with a conflict on two fronts: against the FLN *and* the OAS.

FLN internal politics

Although it ended on 12 August, the French truce provided the FLN with a vital breathing space. It allowed the maquis groups across the six wilayas to rebuild. It also handed the FLN an unstoppable political momentum. As in

December 1960, Algerians, sensing that with negotiations an end to their suffering was near, swung massively behind the FLN. This adherence was illustrated by the huge support for the FLN general strike upholding the unity of Algeria and the Sahara which lasted from 1 to 5 July. Tracts called on Algerians to show their loyalty to the Provisional Government and their rejection of 'any idea of partition, even provisional' as well as the notion of 'a so-called third force' and throughout the country there were demonstrations brandishing flags and chanting slogans.[24] In Algiers, Blida, and Constantine these turned into riots as Algerians surged forth into the European *quartiers*, necessitating the intervention of 35,000 troops to restore some semblance of law and order.

These confrontations led to eighty deaths, but most of the participants had little idea of the power struggles within the FLN. Here the Provisional Government and Boumediène were engaged in a bitter war of words. On the one hand, the Provisional Government denounced Boumediène's military inactivity as a betrayal of the interior resistance, even calling for the launch of an offensive before 31 March 1961. On the other hand, Boumediène and his general staff accused the Provisional Government of corruption, incompetence, and, worst of all, preparing the way for a sell-out to French neo-colonial interests. This confrontation came to a head at a crisis meeting of the National Council of the Algerian Revolution in Tripoli in Libya from 9 to 27 August 1961. The subject of debate was the failed negotiations, and in the bitter exchanges which followed each side tried to score points off the other. While Boumediène remained taciturn, his two officers, Kaïd and Mendjli, sharply criticized Krim's diplomacy.[25] They also argued that the war could still be won militarily. However, as the debate moved on to the election of the supreme leadership of the Provisional Government, it soon became clear that one immediate casualty of this internecine struggle was the incumbent president, Ferhat Abbas, widely seen as too moderate, too reformist, and too compromised by his engagement with French politics prior to 1954. Krim was the obvious candidate to succeed, but this would have provoked open conflict with Boumediène. The compromise candidate, therefore, was Benyoucef Ben Khedda, former general secretary of the MTLD, ex-centralist and veteran of the 'Battle of Algiers'. Elsewhere Saad Dahlab replaced Krim at Foreign Affairs who moved to Interior Minister; Abdelhafid Boussouf retained control of the omnipresent Secret Police; Mohammed Yazid remained Information Minister; while amongst the imprisoned leaders, Mohammed Boudiaf was promoted to vice-president along with Ben Bella and Krim. Lakhdar Ben

Tobbal was relegated from Interior Minister to a Minister of State, a measure of how Ben Khedda wished to reassert civilian control over the military.

In France the government and commentators interpreted Abbas's ousting as the rise of a more hard-line Marxist-orientated leadership, principally because Ben Khedda was an admirer of Mao's China. In reality it was less about ideology and more about power and in this new balance several factors were obvious: Krim's star was on the wane, along with his two allies Ben Tobbal and Boussouf; Abbas was completely marginalized; while the interior maquis continued to feel ignored by both the Provisional Government and the general staff. However, over and above these antagonisms, the major battle line was between Ben Khedda and Boumediène who, as a mark of revolt, left before the conclusion of the meeting.

Retreat over the Sahara

On 5 September, de Gaulle offered a significant olive branch to the Provisional Government. During a wide-ranging press conference at the Élysée, where he took questions on the Berlin crisis, Britain and the Common Market, and agricultural policy, he accepted that the Sahara was Algeria, stating: 'I know that there is not a single Algerian who does not think that the Sahara ought to be part of Algeria and any Algerian government, no matter what its relations with France, would unceasingly assert Algerian sovereignty over the Sahara.'[26] France still wanted to safeguard strategic interests—oil, military air bases, and the line of communication with Francophone Africa—but, in terms of the negotiating process, the sovereignty of the Sahara was no longer an issue.

The relatively relaxed manner in which de Gaulle announced this concession could not disguise the fact that this was a major retreat. Ever since the Republican Front, the Sahara had been a key geo-strategic justification in favour of the military effort. For Mollet the creation of the Organisation Commune des Régions Sahariennes (OCRS) in January 1957 had been one of his big ideas: the symbol of his 'Eurafrican' future whereby France, in cooperation with other African countries, would exploit the oil and gas riches for the common good. This vision had been taken up by de Gaulle who always underlined that the Sahara was a French creation, neither historically nor ethnically Algerian. Now, at a stroke, de Gaulle gave way, removing one of the last arguments inherited from the Republican Front.

Immediately, all the journalists present looked at each other. They knew the significance of de Gaulle's words. This was his attempt to unblock the negotiations. But it was also a measure of French weakness. By September de Gaulle was severely constrained. After Bizerte, his hopes of using Bourguiba as a lever in favour of a multilateral development of the Sahara were nil. Moreover, he was a man in a hurry, faced with growing domestic unease. French opinion, desperate for an end to the situation, was fearful that events had drifted out of control, a malaise that was reflected in Pierre Mendès France's call for a new interim government and Mollet's criticism that de Gaulle's leadership was becoming more 'weak' and 'vulnerable' by the day.[27] De Gaulle knew that he had to act quickly or risk prolonging the war.

This strategy produced tensions in the government with Debré even offering to resign. But de Gaulle was adamant. France had to sacrifice the Sahara for the greater cause of peace, angrily telling a meeting of sceptical civil servants: 'We must finish with this box of sorrows.'[28] In this way 5 September was a decisive step that, as de Gaulle hoped, transformed the Provisional Government's perceptions. By conceding over the Sahara the new Foreign Minister, Saad Dahlab, later explained, de Gaulle was sending a clear message. He was signalling that, after two false starts, France was ready to 'negotiate seriously'.[29]

OAS

Three days after the Sahara retreat, de Gaulle narrowly escaped being blown up by the OAS at Pont-sur-Seine. The fact that this was carried out by an autonomous cell, operating on the mainland under a dissident officer, Lieutenant-Colonel Bastien Thierry, emphasized the lack of overall control.[30] The acronym OAS was the facade for many different groups which, although paying lip-service to the leadership of Salan and Jouhaud, carried out bombings and assassinations on their own initiative. Beginning on 31 May 1961, when one cell stabbed to death a senior police officer, Commissaire Roger Gavoury, in central Algiers, these groups unleashed a spiral of bloodshed during the summer and autumn.[31] Some of this violence was aimed at specific targets—FLN opposite numbers, policemen, communists, 'third force' moderates—but some were indiscriminate killing as OAS operatives, circulating anonymously in cars and on scooters, machine-gunned Algerian cafés or seized upon Algerian passers-by on the grounds that 'any dead Arab will do'. In September alone one OAS commando unit, led by Roger Degueldre, a 36-year-old Foreign Legion lieutenant who had deserted in December 1960, killed 15 and wounded 155.

As the OAS imposed a climate of fear during 1961, it adapted tactics from the French Resistance, the Vietminh, and the Zionist Haganah.[32] Susini in particular was an admirer of the Haganah methods—notably the policy of aggressive defence and hard-hitting reprisals used during the war for the establishment of Israel in 1948—and he wanted the OAS to be the settler equivalent: 'A civil army powerful and with conviction, which would regain Muslim confidence from the FLN, and carry along the Europeans . . . to seize power in Algeria, in order to assume it one day in France.'[33]

The OAS also borrowed from the FLN and the French army. Drawing on the experience of Colonel Godard, 'Battle of Algiers' counter-insurgency veteran and now Susini's second-in-command, the OAS matched the violence with an all-out propaganda battle. Posters, tracts, and graffiti would magically appear in the European *quartiers*: their intention to instil an aura of OAS invincibility. The first tract in early May talked of a 'great army of the maquis' and called on Europeans to: 'Kill those who try to arrest you. Burn the government offices. Kill all the traitors, little and big.'[34] Another poster had an OAS dagger, superimposed onto a map of Algeria and France, shattering both the FLN's crescent and moon and the Gaullist Cross (see Figure 10.2); while one graffiti slogan, accompanied by a pair of glaring eyes, proclaimed menacingly: 'the OAS sees everything'.[35] In the post offices sympathizers stamped letters with OAS slogans; then, even more spectacularly, on 5 August the OAS momentarily seized control of the official television channel, interrupting the 1.00 p.m. news bulletin with an OAS speech inciting citizens to rise up against the 'Gaullist dictatorship'.

This was made clear on Friday 23 September when the Europeans of Algiers responded to Salan's call for a demonstration of popular unity behind the OAS. For three hours, from 8.00 p.m. to 11.00 p.m., thousands hammered out the rhythm of *Algérie française* on their pots, pans, and dustbin lids, backed up by car horns and whistles.[36] It was a deafening sound, accompanied by a provocative display of OAS banners, which seemed to support Salan's boast on 9 October that the OAS would have an army of 100,000 by the end of the year.

Who, therefore, did the OAS groups recruit? Although one poster showed French and Muslim together under the slogan 'Brothers . . . OAS', in reality its ranks were made up of young European men, mostly from modest backgrounds such as garage mechanics, barbers, car workers, gro-

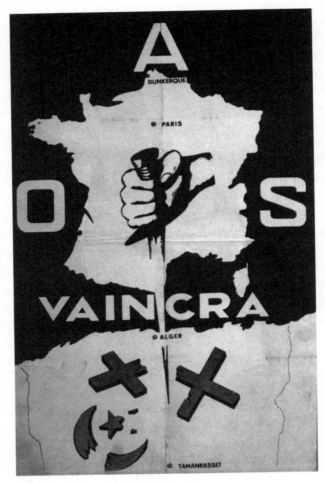

Figure 10.2 OAS Poster: 'The OAS will win'.

cers, and ice-cream sellers.[37] Pumped up and ready for action, the OAS was
a reflex action, an expression of their elemental anger. Through it they were
standing up and defending their community against de Gaulle and the FLN.
In terms of political persuasion many, reflecting long-standing settler traditions, were authoritarian and anti-communist, looking either backwards to
Pétain's Vichy France, upwards to Franco's Spain or downwards to the
apartheid regime in South Africa. Yet, it is important not to reduce the OAS

to a fascist caricature. The OAS included Spanish Civil War International Brigade veterans and ex-communists.[38] Similarly, Raoul Girardet, a young recruit in the metropole, saw the struggle as one of defending the fraternal bond between the two communities against the FLN; Adrien Badaracchi, a European, made the analogy with the French Resistance—'I considered the OAS as being like the resisters who defended France'; while for a small number of young Jewish men in Oran misgivings about racism were outweighed by the desire to avenge FLN attacks on their own *quartier* in September 1961.[39] Led by Jean Guenassia, described in the French press as a former member of the Zionist Stern Gang in Palestine, this group was at the forefront of the violence, although as one later admitted:

> It was necessary to hold your nose and close your eyes a little... The OAS included a lot of anti-Semites who in the name of the 'fraternity of arms', made the Celtic cross on the barricades. I avoided looking at them. Deep down, they were the children of those who had elected the anti-Semites Régis and Drumont, those who had applauded Vichy.[40]

In terms of numbers, by November 1961 *Le Monde* journalist Alain Jacob estimated the total of OAS underground operatives to be just over 1,500.[41] These shock troops were then backed up by a further 15,000 supporters in the Algiers region and 200 in Oran whose role was logistics and propaganda. As regards political support Jacob was emphatic: this amounted to 95 per cent amongst the European population in Algiers, Bône, and Oran which saw the OAS as a last hope against Gaullist treachery.[42]

In contrast, in France OAS recruitment was limited to overtly fascist groups such as Jeune Nation, idealistic students, and a small number of moles in the police, civil service, and army. Political support did come from the Vincennes Committee, led by the former Prime Minister Georges Bidault and the former Governor-General Jacques Soustelle, which argued the OAS case within and without parliament, even claiming that it should be represented at negotiations, but this found no echo amongst the wider public.[43] The overwhelming majority of French people recoiled in horror at the OAS which was now subjected to intense repression. Special anti-OAS units were sent to Algiers, while OAS prisoners were tortured for information and interned in camps, just like their FLN adversaries—a fact that was denounced by the anti-torture campaigner Pierre Vidal-Naquet in May 1962.[44]

The Battle of Paris

By the beginning of 1962 Algeria made grisly reading even by the standards of the previous seven years. Each day brought new horror. On 3 January alone two Algerian dock workers were blown up in the coastal town of Bône; the naked bodies of a young legionnaire and his fiancée were found with their throats slit in an abandoned car outside of Blida; while ten attacks, either by the FLN or the OAS, left seven dead in Algiers.[45] However, as Algeria became bloody beyond belief, the French capital also witnessed an upsurge in violence in what became known as the 'Battle of Paris'.

The first aspect of this violence was the confrontation between the FLN and the police. This had been ongoing with forty-seven gendarmes killed in the previous three years, but in September this tit-for-tat killing reached new levels. In response the Paris police chief, Maurice Papon, who had learnt his counter-insurgency trade as the prefect of Constantine between 1956 and 1958, intensified the repression.[46] Deploying specialized *harki* units, Papon also introduced a curfew for Algerian workers from 8.30 p.m. to 5.30 a.m. on 5 October.

Anger at Papon's measures led the FLN to organize a non-violent demonstration on 17 October.[47] At 5.30 a.m. 30,000 unarmed Algerians converged on the centre of Paris in the light rain, flooding in from the surrounding shanty towns and poor suburbs—Nanterre, Colombe, Gennevilliers. Mostly made up of young men and women, but also a scattering of older people and some mothers with young children, the demonstration was another example of politically engaged Algerians moving from the margins to the centre to occupy public space. This time, however, the challenge was in the capital of the colonial enemy and the crackdown was unforgiving. Some were chased through the streets and into the metro stations; others were beaten to death and thrown into the Seine; many more, 11,538, were herded into lorries and deported back to Algeria. Subsequently the FLN would claim that the police violence left 200 dead.[48]

It was a moment of extreme violence, but one that the authorities immediately denied. On 27 October in the Paris Municipal Council, Claude Bourdet, the veteran left-wing journalist, accused Papon in person of looking on as dozens of Algerians were killed in the actual courtyard of the Préfecture de Police. Papon remained silent, while the Minister of the Interior, Roger Frey, eager to protect the police, quickly pulled a veil over the whole affair.

The second aspect of the Paris violence was OAS terrorism. As in Algeria the OAS was riven by division with two groups challenging for authority over OAS/Métropole, the first led by the officer-deserter Pierre Sergent and the second by André Canal, a European in his mid-forties who operated under the pseudonym 'le Monocle'. Each tried to outdo the other in a bid to intensify the tempo of the war in France and the result was complete anarchy. By the beginning of 1962 Paris was under daily attack. Between 15 January and 28 January there were forty-eight bombings with one, detonated right inside the Foreign Office on the Quai d'Orsay at 4.34 p.m. on the 23rd, killing a porter and injuring twelve others.[49] Specifically, too, the OAS targeted the apartments of those deemed to be the enemies of Algérie Française such as the pro-FLN intellectual Jean-Paul Sartre, the communist journalist Vladimir Pozner and the *Figaro* Algerian correspondent, Serge Bromberger. This was why the OAS blew up the Boulogne-sur-Seine home of the Culture Minister André Malraux on Wednesday 7 February at 1.15 p.m. Malraux was absent but the blast, detonated on the ground floor, badly disfigured a neighbour's child, the 4-year-old Delphine Renard who was playing with her dolls. Rushed to the hospital, the image of the young girl, her face covered in blood, dominated the following day's newspapers.

Throughout the autumn there had been more and more demonstrations in Paris against the war and the OAS; on 18 November 10,000 students marched for 'Peace in Algeria' followed by a day of action on 29 November and a further march on 19 December. However, Delphine Renard was a real trigger for mass protest. Large numbers were angry, pointing the finger not just at the OAS but also the government which seemed utterly incapable of stopping the attacks. The call for a demonstration had gone out from the Paris trade unions, supported by the Communist Party and the Parti Socialiste Unifié, and on early Thursday evening 10,000 amassed in and around the Bastille, despite the ban on political gatherings put in place by the Minister of the Interior. Chanting 'OAS—As-sas-sins', the demonstrators, for the most part young, were soon engaged in skirmishes with the police. With the battle spilling out into the surrounding streets and boulevards, some sought refuge on the stairs of the Charonne Metro station. But, with the station locked, eight people, three of them women and a 16-year-old adolescent, were crushed to death trying to escape the police beatings.[50] According to *Le Monde*, these were the worst scenes of fighting since the right-wing riots on 6 February 1934.[51]

On the Tuesday morning, 13 February, an estimated 1 million mourners followed the eight coffins in silent procession to Père Lachaise cemetery: the largest crowd since the Liberation, which was backed up by a general strike in the Paris region and numerous demonstrations elsewhere, including 20,000 in Lyon, 150,000 in Rennes, and 10,000 in Marseille. Given these numbers, nobody was in any doubt about the mood they expressed. The majority was sick of the OAS violence and on this basis wanted de Gaulle, no matter what, to bring about a negotiated settlement. The depth of anti-OAS feeling drowned out those voices, like Lacoste and Lejeune, who continued to oppose de Gaulle's policy, fast-forwarding the path to independence.

Évian Agreement

The Paris violence framed the final push to a ceasefire agreement. The French government did not want the negotiations to break down again for fear that this would be exploited by the OAS. But neither did the Provisional Government. Ben Khedda was only too aware of how judgements about success or failure would play out in the unfolding power struggle with Boumediène. The question, therefore, was how to break out of the deadlock and bring a resolution that was acceptable to both sides. For the Provisional Government de Gaulle's concession over the Sahara had been the green light, and at the end of October secret meetings were held in Switzerland between Redha Malek and Mohammed Ben Yahia on the one side and Louis Joxe, Claude Chaylet, and Bruno de Leusse on the other. Their aim was to prepare the ground for the resumption of formal face-to-face talks which everybody knew were still going to be difficult. These opened on 11 February 1962 at Les Rousses, a remote hamlet high up in the Jura mountains on the Franco-Swiss border, where the two teams were made up of Joxe; Robert Buron, Minister of Public Works; and Jean de Broglie, Secretary of State for the Sahara, for the French and Saad Dahlab, Mohammane Yazid, Lakhdar Ben Tobbal, and Belkacem Krim for the Provisional Government. For another whole week, in freezing temperatures, the two delegations went back and forth over the well-furrowed ground—the status of the Europeans, the military bases, the nature of the transitional government—before coming to a preliminary agreement. This then formed the basis of the final round which began at Évian on 7 March 1962 and ended in the evening eleven days later with the signing of the Évian Agreement.

It had been an exhausting process for all concerned and the result was a long and complex document, stretching to ninety-three pages. From the beginning, though, there were two different interpretations. It was a basis not so much for understanding as for misunderstanding. For de Gaulle, Évian was an agreement that had to be ratified by the French and Algerian peoples through a referendum process. For the Provisional Government it was a treaty between two sovereign governments. Évian was about strengthening the hand of the Provisional Government in the unfolding battle with Boumediène.

In concrete terms the Évian Agreement broke down into two main aspects, the first of which was application of the self-determination process. Here the transition period would be run by a Franco-Algerian Provisional Executive empowered to organize the referendum, uphold the freedom and security of Europeans and Algerians, maintain the ceasefire, and oversee the release of political prisoners.

The second aspect was a declaration of principles which would lay the foundation of future relations between the two countries. Framed by the rights and freedoms enshrined in the United Nations Charter, these principles dealt with the status of French people in independent Algeria, the Sahara, future economic cooperation, and the military bases. French people would have three years to choose between Algerian and French nationality. In the meantime their rights would be upheld as regards protection of their property, participation in public affairs, and religious and cultural freedom. The Sahara would be exploited for a common good, although in comparison with international competitors the French would have privileged drilling and exploration rights. A blueprint for economic and financial cooperation was also enshrined in the Agreement, including a commitment to maintain the same level of developmental spending for the next three years. On the military front, French troops were to be reduced to 80,000 within one year, leading to total departure two years later; the naval and air bases in Mers-el-Kébir and Bou Sfer were leased to France for fifteen years; and the Sahara site for nuclear testing was kept for five years. With these clauses, therefore, the Agreement not only upheld, in the short run, France's military interests, but also contained an important element of the 1958 Constantine Plan and third-way reformism.

On Sunday 18 March a television news-flash announced that the Évian Agreement had been signed and at 8.00 p.m. de Gaulle gave a short address. In it de Gaulle, head held high, did not mention defeat. Instead, the Agreement reflected three clear truths, namely that self-determination was in the French national interest, reflected the wishes of Algerians, and laid the basis for a new future: association between the two countries. In this sense Évian was 'a common-sense solution' which he claimed to have pursued relentlessly over the last four years.[52] The challenge now was how to build positively on this history and ensure that both countries 'march together fraternally on the path to civilization'.[53]

It was a clever and selective rereading of history. There was no straight line from May 1958 to March 1962. Initially he had followed the Republican Front's precepts, but one by one, each precept had been peeled away, until de Gaulle had no option but to sit down with the FLN, before a ceasefire, before elections, and in full recognition of the Provisional Government as the sole negotiator. Judged by Mollet's war aims of January 1957, France had lost.

Amongst French people there was overwhelming relief.[54] They had no illusions about the Évian Agreement. Most recognized that they were 'disadvantageous' for the Europeans; most recognized too that, given the OAS, the violence would not end.[55] But only a minority really cared about these issues.[56] Most were grateful for some sort of end. For them Évian represented the basis of a credible exit strategy, even if de Gaulle had backed down over the Sahara and dual nationality for the Europeans.

Relief was also the dominant reaction amongst France's NATO allies, but particularly in Washington which had long seen Algeria as a running sore, damaging the construction of an anti-communist alliance in the Arab and African worlds. On the opposite side of the Iron Curtain Khrushchev sent a telegram congratulating the Provisional Government and establishing formal diplomatic relations—a measure of the way in which the Soviet Union, too, saw Algeria in terms of the cold war—while in Cairo Nasser hoped that the ceasefire would open a new era of rapprochement between France and the Arab world.

For Ben Khedda and the Provisional Government, however, Évian was a great victory. Spontaneously in Tunis the Algerian exiles descended into the streets, singing, dancing, and chanting 'Long live Ben Bella!' In front of Ben Khedda's modest villa, two impromptu orchestras, composed of drums and flutes, feted the president who emphasized that Évian was not a sell-out. By signing it the Provisional Government had adhered to all the principles of the revolution. It had upheld the territorial integrity of Algeria and it had steered Algeria to peace and national independence.

The war between France and the FLN was now at an end, although there had never in fact been a formal declaration of hostilities. From beginning to end, this conflict was always an undeclared war.

II

Independence

Monday, 19 March 1962

O n this day at midday the ceasefire between the French army and the FLN came into effect. In theory the official cessation of hostilities brought an end to 2,696 days of war, but there was no let-up in the violence. In fact the closer the final Évian Agreement, the worse the bloodshed became, as the different OAS groups, enraged by the prospect of 'betrayal', took their terror campaign to a new level. OAS documents seized by the French police in Algiers on 15 March included a six-page directive from Salan, dated 23 February, ordering a 'generalized offensive', as well as other tracts calling for the creation of maquis units, the targeting of the gendarmerie, and the killing of suspected pro-FLN 'Muslim intellectuals'.[1]

On this basis the OAS violence struck out in several directions. It struck out at the riot police, vilified as the 'Gaullist Gestapo'. It struck out at Europeans looking to leave, regularly bombing vacated apartments, travel agents, and the control tower at Algiers airport. It struck out at the Algerian professional classes—doctors, dentists, teachers, and chemists—with the explicit aim of eliminating the Algerian elite and making the Muslim population dependent on the continued 'French presence'.[2] At the same time the OAS violence aimed to create incessant chaos. Epitomized by 'Operation Rock and Roll' on the night of 5 March, which produced 120 explosions across Algiers in two hours, such uncertainty, the OAS hoped, would render the imminent Évian Agreement unworkable. It would force the Provisional Government to renounce the Accords and elements of the army, still ambivalent about Gaullist policy, to come over to the OAS cause.[3]

On 19 March itself the major cities were deserted as the Europeans, following OAS orders, registered a silent protest against Évian with a general strike. Nowhere was this insurrectionary mood more apparent than in the Bab-El-Oued *quartier*, the 60,000-strong European fiefdom in Algiers. Adjacent to the Casbah, Bab-El-Oued was to the OAS what the Aurès mountains were for the FLN: a bastion that had provided the initial foot soldiers for May 1958 and now became a no-go area for the authorities. Armed groups openly prepared to take on the FLN and the French army, while official posters, put up during the night of 18th and proclaiming 'For our children, peace in Algeria', were torn down and replaced by OAS ones telling Europeans 'To arms, citizens'. This was followed by a further tract which warned the police and army:

> you have until Thursday 22 March at midnight, to evacuate those *quartier* bordering on the Pélissier barracks, the Orléans barracks, Saint-Eugène, Climat-de-France (that is to say Bab-El-Oued). Cross over this deadline and you will be viewed as troops serving a foreign power.[4]

It was a tense atmosphere which really turned nasty when, on 21 March at midday, OAS groups in Bab-El-Oued launched six indiscriminate mortar bombs at passing Algerians on the nearby Place du Gouvernement, killing twenty-four and wounding fifty-nine. Then, on 23 March, two army trucks were cornered by an OAS commando in the centre of Bab-El-Oued and in the resulting firefight a lieutenant and five young conscripts lost their lives. On hearing this last news, the French commander-in-chief, General Ailleret, was furious. He wanted revenge for his fallen comrades and immediately replied with a full-scale attack on Bab-El-Oued, sealing off the area and sending in 20,000 troops to flush out the OAS. Backed up by fighter planes and helicopters, the soldiers used tanks, armoured cars, and rockets to claw back control street by street—a bitter battle that went on for three days and led to fifteen dead and seventy wounded on the army's side, and twenty killed and sixty wounded amongst the insurgents.

By 26 March it was clear that the insurrection had failed. The OAS groups had been dismantled with 3,309 arrests and 1,100 weapons seized. The FLN had not been provoked into revenge attacks that would have destroyed the Évian Agreement. Equally, the attitude of the army was transformed. Confronted with their own dead at the hands of the OAS, French soldiers from the high command downwards lost any lingering sympathy for the Europeans.[5] Nevertheless, in a bid to draw the general European population into the frame, the OAS organized an unarmed mass protest for the afternoon of the 26th. Ignoring the banning order issued by the new prefect of police, Vitalis Cros, hundreds of demonstrators, young

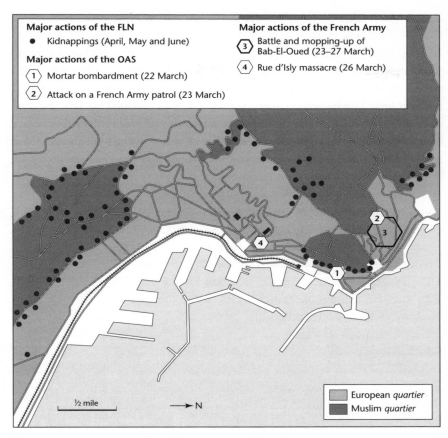

Major actions of the FLN
- ● Kidnappings (April, May and June)

Major actions of the OAS
- ① Mortar bombardment (22 March)
- ② Attack on a French Army patrol (23 March)

Major actions of the French Army
- ③ Battle and mopping-up of Bab-El-Oued (23–27 March)
- ④ Rue d'Isly massacre (26 March)

½ mile → N

☐ European *quartier*
■ Muslim *quartier*

Map 11.1 March–June 1962: The bloody end in Algiers.

men for the most part, converged on the centre of Algiers with the intention of marching up to the war monument on the Forum and then on to Bab-El-Oued to break the siege. By 2.50 p.m. this tightly packed crowd found the route forward blocked at the Rue d'Isly, when suddenly shots, fired by an unknown hand from a nearby rooftop, produced a general panic. The demonstrators scattered in all directions as the soldiers, ironically one of the last regular units composed of loyal Algerian troops, shot spontaneously back into the crowd. Despite shouts of 'Stop firing' this fusillade lasted six or seven minutes by which time 54 had been killed and 140 wounded.

The OAS immediately ordered a general strike as a sign of mourning for the martyrs of the Rue d'Isly massacre, but in truth the army now had the upper hand. Urged on by de Gaulle, who wanted the insurgency to be broken whatever the cost, French troops captured Jouhaud in Oran on 25 March followed by Salan himself on the outskirts of Algiers on 20 April. Yet, despite the decapitation of the leadership, the OAS violence reached new heights as the remaining diehards, bowing to the inevitability of independence, adopted a 'scorched earth' policy. Burning down town halls, schools, and public buildings, including the Algiers University Library on 7 June, their intention was to destroy the physical symbols of the 'civilizing mission'. Nothing of use was to be left for the new Algeria. The senselessness of this destruction led the imprisoned Salan and Jouhaud to plea for an end to the OAS campaign. They knew that the battle was lost, as did Jean-Jacques Susini who assumed leadership of the OAS after Salan's capture. Susini had already made contact with the president of the Provisional Executive, Abderrahmane Farès, in mid-May and these contacts eventually led to a truce signed on Sunday, 17 June, between Susini and Dr Chawki Mostefaï, one of the Algerian Provisional Government's nominees on the Executive. In return for an end to the violence, Susini obtained an amnesty for OAS members and on this basis he called for reconciliation, telling Europeans in a radio address from an OAS pirate station that these talks had won political, economic, and military guarantees that would allow: 'Algerians of European origin to remain in the country in complete security, in complete dignity, and then to realize the revolutionary integration with the Muslim community.'[6]

In Oran this agreement was rejected by the OAS. Instead, the OAS there talked of partition.[7] They momentarily envisaged an OAS-governed enclave, independent from both France and Algeria. This scenario, however, was never a long-term possibility and once this was clear, the OAS in Oran too succumbed to the 'scorched earth' policy, producing a final and dramatic spasm of violence on 24 and 25 June which witnessed the destruction of schools, clinics, and libraries right across the city.

In these difficult circumstances the Provisional Executive, based at Rocher Noir, 29 km to the east of Algiers, steered the country towards independence. The first stage was the hastily arranged referendum on mainland France and the overseas departments on 8 April. The 26,983,275 voters were asked to ratify the Évian Agreement and the response was an overwhelming 65.87 per cent 'yes' as against 6.65 per cent 'no', and 24.39 per cent abstentions.[8] De Gaulle's policy had been approved by the French people, opening the way to a referendum in Algeria itself on 1 July. There, however, the people were not given a choice, as de Gaulle had originally promised in his 16 September 1959 speech, between integration, association, or independence. Instead voters were asked to answer 'yes' or 'no' to one question: 'Do you want Algeria to become an independent state, cooperating with France, according to the conditions defined by the declaration of 19 March?'

In this campaign the FLN, the Algerian Communist Party, the Socialist Party Federations, and the PSU all called for a 'yes' vote. Significantly, though, there was no European party, while Messali Hadj's MNA, wishing to rename itself the Parti du Peuple Algérien, was excluded from the process, a move which Messali's party condemned as a violation of 'the principles of self-determination', aiming at the imposition of a one-party system.[9] On Sunday 1 July Algeria went to the polls with 91.2 per cent of the 6 million voters replying 'yes'. On Tuesday 3 July at 10.30 a.m. de Gaulle officially recognized Algerian independence in a short declaration, and during the hours that followed other countries followed suit, including Tunisia, Sweden, the USA, and Great Britian, while Egypt and Iran sent telegrams of congratulation to President Ben Khedda. The Algerian nation state was a diplomatic reality and the Provisional Government proclaimed Thursday 5 July to be Algeria's national independence day, nearly eight years after the events of 1 November 1954 and exactly 132 years after the original French invasion.

The human consequences

Without doubt the end of the Algerian War was a major moment in global affairs. This significance was signalled by countless editorials across the globe marking the event, including *The Times* and the *Daily Telegraph* in Britain, the *New York Times* in the USA, *Il Popolo* in Italy, and *Die Welt* in West Germany.[10] Algerian independence was history with a capital H at the time, but it has remained so because Algeria was one of the longest and most difficult episodes in the whole decolonization process. It was emblematic of the formal ending of European empires, a pivotal event in the shaping of the twentieth century which was intimately connected to other key processes, namely the impact of the two world wars, the cold war, pan-Arabism, the wider anti-colonial movement, and the movement towards Western European unity. How, though, did this macro-history impact on micro-history? How did Algerian independence in 1962 impact on the populations there?

The Europeans

Already in the period 1954 to 1960 a minority of Europeans, some 25,000, had left, while others had taken the precaution of buying bars and farms in France. Most, however, did not countenance departure until 1961 and 1962. This was the moment when the trickle became a flood. By the end of 1961 160,000 were in France, followed by another 70,000 during the first three months of 1962, so that by April a fifth of the European population had already gone. On one level this exodus was provoked by the general level of chaos and violence. Europeans left because by 1962 the country had broken down on a day-to-day level. Ordinary life was no longer possible as Jean-Paul Gavino, a pupil in a secondary school in Oran, remembered: 'During the last year, the country did not function any more. And we, the young, we no longer had a taste for studying . . . At the lycée, we used to go, we did not used to go, it was a shambles, people were beginning to leave, the teachers did not teach all their courses.'[11]

But for the most part it was motivated by a fear of the 'Algerian Algeria' to come. Already on 18 July 1961 Jean Morin had underlined this anxiety in a telegram to Michel Debré. In it he talked about how large numbers of Europeans had been shocked by what they saw as the 'xenophobic character' of the Algerian nationalist demonstrations on 5 July 1961.[12] Such unease, itself feeding the age-old fear of the 'Arab other', explains why the majority of Europeans had no faith in the guarantees contained in the Evian Accords. They trusted neither de Gaulle nor the FLN. They were convinced that once independence became a reality they would be exposed to terrible reprisals—a conclusion that deepened once it was clear that the OAS had lost.

Such fears were backed up by facts on the ground because, despite FLN assurances, violence against ordinary Europeans reached a new level after the Évian Agreement. Inevitably this violent conduct was fuelled by the actions of the OAS, but nevertheless the blunt truth was that after the ceasefire Europeans were more vulnerable than ever. Each day the European press carried photographs from families looking for lost relatives as, in the space of the next few months, 1,773 Europeans 'disappeared' and 1,165 certainly died: a number equalling the civilian casualty rate for the *whole* period from November 1954 until the Évian Agreement.[13] Such physical danger, when added to the fact that Algerians were seizing empty apartments and shops, produced a psychological pressure which pushed thousands of

INDEPENDENCE   319

Europeans to breaking point. Adrien Badaracchi, for example, remembered
that during the last two years he was afraid to go out. The anxiety that he
could be killed at random in the street was ever present. This is why his
family left in mid-June 1962:

> Two of my uncles were killed. From a knife attack. One was killed on the
> road, on his bike. The other was killed in his work yard. He was alone with his
> labourer, it was he who killed him. When he was arrested, he said: 'I had a lot
> of respect for him, but they told me: "If you do not kill him, it is you who will
> be killed." He was killed anyway afterwards. The police used to tell them:
> 'You must leave' and then kill them in the back.[14]

This meant that after Évian those Europeans still remaining were living
from one day to the next. Whether to go or to stay was a continual topic of
conversation, as thousands tried to make sense of the unfolding events
before committing themselves to a final, irreversible decision. That said,
many did not see this decision as permanent. They held out hope of a return
once the situation had calmed down and the contours of the new Algeria
were more apparent. As one European doctor from Constantine explained
to French journalists on 27 June: 'I am going to France for two months.
I have known for a long time that the soul of Algeria had changed, but
before returning I want to know what its new face will be.'[15]

Throughout April, May, and June Europeans readied themselves to leave
at any moment. In the case of the young Nicole Giraud, she and her sister
were told to pack immediately:

> I left Algeria all alone with my sister, the 18 June 1962, in the night, right at the
> end. One day, my mother told us: 'Pack your cases, you are leaving tonight.'
> We had learned not to pose questions, so we got ready without asking
> anything. Somebody came for us and took us in the middle of the night to
> the Maison-Blanche Airport. On the road, there were wrecks of cars that were
> burning. It was those of *pieds-noirs* who were arriving from the interior to take
> the boat or plane. As they could not take their cars and did not want above all
> to leave them there, they set fire to them.[16]

The symbol of the European predicament was the suitcase. Permitted only
two per person, each family had to make painful choices about which
possessions to take and which to leave. This is why photographs and footage
from the summer of 1962 show Europeans wearing thick overcoats and
pullovers, despite the scorching heat. Unable to cram them into their
luggage, these were deemed essential items for a France whose weather

was always perceived as dark and cold. It also explains why Europeans torched chairs, tables, sofas, and cars rather than let 'the Arabs' take them.

Within this uncertain context, the final factor which accelerated the European flight was Oran in the days following the referendum vote. There the Europeans had always been a majority. Not until November 1961 were the Algerians more numerous. But as the demographic scale tipped in favour of the Algerian population, the Europeans felt besieged. They were afraid that, with independence approaching, this Algerian majority was poised to overrun 'their territory'. This fear had led Europeans to retreat to the centre of the city where many felt protected by the OAS. By the end of June 1962 this OAS activism had been finally broken, although the situation remained tense. The referendum itself passed off without incident, but on 5 July the worst fears of the Europeans were realized. During independence celebrations in the centre of Oran, shots were fired into the Algerian crowd shortly after 11.00 a.m., creating a general panic.[17] To the cry of 'It's the OAS' Algerians surged into the European *quartier*, intent on revenge. The hunt had begun and by the end of the day twenty-five Europeans and a hundred Algerians had been killed. Then, in the days that followed, a further 356 Europeans were kidnapped, of whom 289 would never be accounted for.[18]

What petrified Europeans was not just the violence itself—crude face-to-face retribution—but the fact that the French army failed to intervene immediately. Not until 3.30 p.m. did the first French units arrive to protect civilians. Equally, Europeans noted the inability of the FLN to provide law and order, even if the local commander, Captain Bakhti, did execute a number of Algerians accused of carrying out the killings.[19]

In the wake of Oran most Europeans came to the conclusion that for their own safety they had to leave. The French government, however, had never envisaged total departure. It had always hoped that the majority of Europeans would stay. This is why official planning was so disorganized. Even in April 1962, the government had only one liner, *Gouverneur Chanzy*, operating to bring the Europeans 'back' to France. One month later this had been increased to twenty boats a day plus emergency flights, as the government finally accepted the reality of the European exodus which witnessed 46,030 leave in April, 101,250 in May, 354,914 in June, 121,020 in July, and 95,578 in August. By the autumn 99 per cent of the Europeans had left: one of the biggest population transfers of the twentieth century.

Figure 11.1 Settlers leaving with suitcases in 1962.

A few thousand did stay on after independence, like the doctor Pierre Chaulet, the poet Jean Senac, and the priest Abbé Scotto.[20] In contrast to the vast majority of Europeans, these three made a different choice about their national identity. They embraced independence which in turn underlines the inevitability, given the weight of the previous 132 years, of mass European departure. French Algeria was a segregated society based upon the denial of a separate Algerian nation state. It was a society, too, saturated with fears of Algerian violence—a state of mind intensified by eight years of FLN terrorism. For these reasons, Susini's appeal for reconciliation after the FLN–OAS Accords on 17 June was just too little too late.[21] By this point most had made up their minds. They could not envisage a future in an FLN Algeria. Day-to-day life would be turbulent and uncertain. They would feel anxious at every point. In contrast, France at least offered security and protection, even if they were angry at what they perceived as de Gaulle's great betrayal.

The Jews

The situation of the Algerian Jews was not same as the Europeans.[22] A minority, like the communist Henri Alleg, had embraced the idea of Algerian independence. A small number, too, sided with the OAS. Most rejected both European extremism and the FLN. They identified with French republicanism. They supported political and social equality. This is why so many Jews were prominent in 'The League of the Rights of Man' and the Socialist Party. It is also why in November 1956 Jewish community leaders publicly supported a middle way between extremists on both sides, echoing the line taken by the then Mollet government.[23]

By 1960 this measured neutrality was impossible to sustain. Jews had to make difficult personal and political choices about their future. Benjamin Stora, for example, was born in 1950 in Constantine in eastern Algeria, widely known as the 'Jerusalem of North Africa' due to the large Jewish population there.[24] His father could trace his lineage back to those Jews who arrived from Spain after their expulsion in 1492; his mother was descended from Jewish Berbers. By the late 1950s their life was over-shadowed by the unfolding violence, until his family decided to leave the 'Arab' *quartier* for the European one in 1959 because, like other Jews living there, they felt threatened. At primary school Stora remembers young Europeans shouting 'Vive Salan' in 1961.[25] Then, by the beginning of 1962, it was just too dangerous to go out:

> From January to June 1962, I no longer went to school. I stayed at home, like everybody. We did not have a television, only a radio . . . a terrible gulf had formed, everybody distrusted everybody. When people passed each other, it was fear which prevailed.[26]

Such separation was not just the product of the generalized tension. It was also the result of a series of specific events which shook Algerian Jews from 1959 onwards. One shock was a grenade attack by the FLN, on the eve of Yom Kippur in 1959, on the synagogue in Bou-Saada in the north-east of the Saharan Atlas region, which killed the 6-year-old daughter of the local rabbi. Another shock was the 11–12 December 1960 nationalist demonstrations when a group of Algerians sacked the main synagogue in the Algiers Casbah, daubing the walls with swastikas and slogans of 'Death to the Jews'.[27] But perhaps the biggest shock of all was the cold-blooded murder of the 48-year-old Raymond Leyris on 22 June 1961, killed with a bullet to the neck by an FLN commando while shopping with his daughter in the main market, Souk El Esser, in Constantine. Popularly known as Cheikh Raymond, he was one of the great figures in the Andalusian musical tradition, a truly gifted oud player who also possessed an astonishing voice.[28] And what gave his death an even greater poignancy was the fact that, in May 1961, a group of pro-independence Jews had underlined the significance of Cheikh Raymond as a bridge between Jews and Muslims. His music, they argued, encapsulated a common culture. It showed beyond doubt that Jews *did* have a place in a future Algeria:

> The singer and musician Raymond, is he not dear to the hearts of Muslims? They love him because he has contributed to the conservation and enrichment of Algerian folklore that the colonialists wanted to snuff out.[29]

Against these shocks the FLN did appeal to Jews as Algerians through specific tracts and posters.[30] Underlining a shared history stretching back over one millennia, these called on Jews to support the liberation struggle. One, in May 1961 in the Algiers region, took the form of a general letter sent out to individual Jews.[31] In it the authors recalled the way in which the colonial authorities had always tried to play Jew off against Arab by giving Jews greater political rights, a classic 'divide and rule strategy' which led directly to the 'absurd and distressing' violence in Constantine in 1934, in effect an apology for the anti-Jewish violence of the time.[32] Furthermore, they underlined how, between July 1940 and November 1942, Arabs had defended Jews against the Vichy regime's anti-Semitism. Calling on Jews to reflect hard about their position, the letter argued:

> Propaganda and colonial policy have they not constantly tried to make us forget the fact that Jews have been in Algeria for more than a thousand years and that they are an integral part of the Algerian People. Yet, history teaches us that Algeria has always been for us a place of welcome, above all when they were fleeing the Spanish inquisition and racial and religious persecution in Europe.[33]

At the beginning of 1962 the FLN made more pleas to the Jewish community, calling on them to join with their 'Muslim brothers', reminding them
of the anti-Semitism of the Europeans;[34] while at the end of April one FLN
tract in Algiers explicitly equated the OAS with fascism and the Holocaust,
calling on Algerian Jews not to forget:

Jews of Algeria

OAS: fascism

OAS: anti-Semitism

OAS: Auschwitz, Buchenwald, the Warsaw Ghetto

Do not forget.[35]

But most Jews were unconvinced. As a community they remembered their
inferior status during the Muslim pre-colonial period and feared that independence would return them to this second-class status. They remembered,
too, the anti-Jewish violence perpetrated by Algerians in Constantine in
1934. This was seen as a symptom of ingrained Muslim prejudice rather than
just the effect of a colonial 'divide and rule' policy, prejudice which was
reflected in private by some FLN leaders. In March 1960, during a series of
internal meetings with FLN activists in Morocco, Ben Tobbal admitted that
the Algerian people would not accept a Jew or a European at the heart of
government.[36]

And finally there was the question of Israel. Ever since the latter's
foundation on 14 May 1948 this had been a source of friction between
the two communities. It had sown distrust. It had fostered hostility, particularly because, going back to the Arab Revolt against the British Mandate in
the late 1930s, Algerian nationalism had always identified with the Palestinian cause. As a result most Jews were fearful of independence. They did
not believe FLN promises of a multicultural society. They were afraid that
the new Algerian state would be a monolithic entity, based on Arab and
Muslim values, which ultimately would be intolerant of a Jewish minority.

Then, added to all these factors, Jews were also targeted by OAS violence. On 20 November 1961 an OAS commando assassinated 61-year-old
William Levy, the Secretary-General of the Algiers Socialist Party Federation.[37] Inevitably this evoked memories of the endemic anti-Semitism
amongst Europeans, underlining how one strand of the OAS violence
went back to Vichy and the anti-Dreyfus activism of the 1890s, and in
this climate, caught between the FLN and the OAS, most of the 130,000

Jews chose to leave in the course of 1962. Identifying with French republican values, the overwhelming majority went to France rather than Israel, caught up in the mad rush to the airports and the coast which meant that the historical specificity of the Jewish population was lost. The 12-year-old Benjamin Stora, for example, remembers how his family queued for tickets in front of the Constantine Town Hall:

> The queue went on for several hundred metres. It was practically necessary to sleep there or to take turns in order not to lose one's turn. My mother, my sister and my father queued (one said 'the chain') for three days to get the tickets.[38]

Yet, if Jews were subjected to the same anxieties as Europeans, the historical significance of their departure was different from that of the Europeans. On the one hand, Jews like William Levy upheld the belief in a socialist solution, where all would live in equality under the banner of republican values. They, more than anyone else, encapsulated a third-way reformism crushed between European intransigence and Algerian nationalism. Then, on the other hand, these Jews carried with them much deeper roots in Algerian history than their European counterparts. For the likes of the Stora family it was not a question of 132 years of French rule. It was over 1,000 years of lived culture, encapsulated in food, dress, language, and the music of Cheikh Raymond. In this way, too, the case of the Jews in Algeria was part of a wider phenomenon in North Africa and the Middle East. It has to be understood in terms of the generalized hostility at the time which explains the wholesale departure of Jews from independent Arab countries during the 1950s and 1960s.

Harkis

On 20 March 1962, twenty-four hours after the ceasefire, *Le Monde* calculated the number of Algerians still in the army as being 60,000 conscripts, 45,000 *harkis*, 15,000 with the Section Administrative Spécialisée (SAS), and 10,000 in mobile police units to which must be added 20,000 professional soldiers, 60,000 in self-defence villages, and 50,000 civil servants.[39] The same day, the Armed Forces Minister, Pierre Messmer, issued a communiqué outlining how these 'French Muslims' in the army would be treated.[40] Under these provisions professional soldiers could either continue to serve or leave with a pension. Similarly, conscripts could either stay with their units or be integrated into the transitional local police force under the control of the Provisional Executive. The other Muslim auxiliaries, meanwhile, could be demobilized, join the transitional local police force or be absorbed into the Aid Centres that had replaced the SAS. In the Évian Agreement itself, although there was no specific clause referring to the 'French Muslims', Article 2 had explicitly forbidden any recourse to 'collective and individual violence'—a principle of 'non-reprisals' which had been accepted by the Provisional Government during the secret talks in November 1961.[41]

Many of those in the *harki* units, however, were under no illusions about these guarantees. After such a bitter and protracted conflict, where some *harki* units had developed a reputation for brutality, they knew that their position was exposed.[42] They were particularly vulnerable to *les marsiens*, a word adapted from the French for March (*mars*) to describe those Algerians who had joined the FLN after the ceasefire on 19 March 1962. Some of these *marsiens* were opportunists who had waited on events, but others were *harki* deserters. In both cases organizing *harki* purges became a way of effacing their past and proving their Algerian nationalism to the incoming FLN regime.

On the ground the FLN declarations were contradictory. Conciliatory declarations were matched by other tracts that threatened 'traitors' with death, a flagrant breach of the Évian Agreement. In this uncertain climate the first killings and kidnappings took place even before the ceasefire. In Constantine at the end of February a *harki* sergeant, Kalloul Rabah Ali, was knifed in the back by an FLN operative in broad daylight.[43] Then, after Évian, 487 'French Muslims' disappeared between 19 March and 1 June, before this anti-*harki* violence really intensified with independence in July. Now the *harkis* and their families—'enemies of the people' in the eyes of so many FLN activists—were hunted out and subjected to every conceivable form of torment. Throughout the summer and autumn of 1962 Bachaga Boualam, the most high-profile 'French Muslim', collected information cataloguing these reprisals. He was told how three *harkis* in Kabylia were killed and dismembered, before having their body parts displayed in the local market. He was told how Mebarki was castrated and cut up alive. He was told, too, how one sergeant Boucherit was paraded by rope through the Soummam valley before being beaten to death.[44] In the Akbou *arrondissement*, near Sétif in the east of the country, this bloodletting had petered out by mid-September.[45] It returned with the arrival of the 'Army of the

Frontiers' from Tunisia which, impatient to impose its authority, carried out a fresh wave of violence until December. By this point approximately 2,000 *harkis* had been killed out of a total Algerian population of 100,000 in this area.

Throughout the spring and summer the need for French action to protect the *harkis* was underlined by Bachaga Boualam who, feeling that his own life was in danger from FLN retribution, left Algeria for France.[46] At the end of June the newspaper *Combat* carried a specific appeal. Signed by public figures such as Jacques Bassot, Marcele Colombe, and Hyacinthe Dubreuil, it called on French people to mount a letter-writing campaign to trade unions and political parties which would force the government to give refuge to the *harkis*:

> You who have opened your doors to all the refugees in the world, Armenians, Spanish, Polish, Hungarian, do you accept that they will be shut to your own brothers?[47]

De Gaulle, however, was adamant. In government meetings he emphasized that the *harkis* were not the same as the Europeans, disparaging them on 3 April 1962 as 'a magma which had served no purpose, and which it was necessary to get rid of without delay'.[48] Given their different culture and religion, de Gaulle argued, they could not be integrated into French society and on 16 May and 15 July 1962 the government issued orders barring the *harkis* from France. When subsequently challenged by Pierre Messmer, the Armed Forces Minister, during a cabinet meeting on 25 July 1962, de Gaulle was categorical:

> We cannot agree to take all the Muslims who come here declaring that they do not agree with the Algerian government. The term repatriate obviously does not apply to Muslims; they are not returning to the land of their fathers. In their case, they would be refugees.[49]

Those ministers who disagreed, Messmer later wrote, did not continue the argument.[50] Silenced by de Gaulle's outburst, they bowed their heads in shame. In contrast, many SAS officers, like Nicolas d'Andoque, disgusted by official policy, contravened government orders and organized clandestine networks to bring them to France.[51] In eastern Algeria French officers procured false identity papers in order to pass seven *harki* families from the town of M'sila on to Paris. One of those involved was Taouès Titraoui-Coll, a young girl at the time, who remembers her father's anxiety once his *harki* unit had been disarmed at the end of March. Already in April her father had warned that they might be obliged to leave for France. Then, at the beginning of June, the army officers came in secret in the early morning in lorries, jeeps, and two tanks:

> My parents woke us at 3 a.m. We left at 4 a.m. . . . They told us not to make any noise. This departure had to be secret, because it was forbidden to repatriate the *harkis*, they were risking a lot, the officers who did that. They were breaking their orders in order to save us, if not we were destined to a certain death . . . As soon as they left the town, they accelerated. We took the plane from Sétif to Algiers, a military plane put at our disposal . . . Once at Algiers airport, we were mixed in with the *pieds-noirs* . . . we had to wait forty-eight hours before being able to get on a plane.

Given the clandestine nature of these operations, just how many *harkis* escaped is difficult to calculate. One subsequent study would put the total at 270,000, many of whom were transferred to disused internment camps in the south of France.[52] To this figure, however, must be added the 10,000 prisoners who were freed and 'returned' to France through the actions of the International Red Cross.

The Algerians

In its campaign of violence, successive OAS tracts claimed that it was anti-FLN and not anti-Muslim. In reality, little attempt was made to discriminate between the FLN and the 'ordinary Muslim'. The various OAS groups dealt out a summary justice. Just to be suspected of pro-FLN sympathies merited execution, and at regular intervals the bodies of murdered Algerians were left on the street as a warning. Particular venom was reserved for the middle classes—hated symbols of Algerian advancement. The bespectacled Mouloud Feraoun, for example, was a prize-winning author and school inspector of the Ministry of Education. Throughout the conflict he had kept a diary which, by describing his inner feelings in the face of French and FLN bloodshed, gave a remarkable inside view of the war. By early 1962 he had already sent the diary as a manuscript to his publisher Seuil in Paris. Continuing with his entries, he wrote on 28 February of the anti-Algerian violence in Algiers:

> For two days I have been holed up at home to avoid the Arab hunt [*ratonnades*]. There was a large attack on Muslims at Bab-El-Oued with scores of

casualties and wounded, on Michelet Street and on d'Isly. The day before yesterday on d'Isly street, I watched the gunfire. Across from the Monoprix at 11:05 a.m.—crowds, flying bullets, and the reckless flight of bystanders. On the street not far from me, state police in a jeep slowly cruise by. Indifferent, they turn their back on the murderers.[53]

Moments later Feraoun witnessed an OAS member—a 'young, stocky, and chubby man' wearing a light blue sweater—gun down two fleeing Algerians. Too afraid to go over to the two outstretched corpses, he ran away 'fear in my belly and sweat on my brow'.[54] In his 14 March entry, six days after his forty-ninth birthday and five days before the ceasefire, terror still 'reigns in Algeria'.[55] He tried to cope in the same way as many other people at the time:

> Of course, I do not want to die, and I certainly do not want my children to die. But I am not taking any special precautions, aside from those that have become habits for the past couple of weeks: limiting reasons to go out, stocking up for several days, cutting out visits to friends. Just the same, every time that anyone goes out, he comes back to describe a murder or report a victim.[56]

On the following morning Feraoun was involved in a day conference on training opportunities for Algerian children at a social centre in the El-Biar district of Algiers. At 11.00 a.m., a three-man OAS commando drove up to the centre and led away the six participants—two school principals and four inspectors.[57] They were all lined up against a wall and shot, Feraoun was the last to be killed with twelve bullets in the chest.

Given the writer's high profile, Feraoun's murder was a shocking event widely covered in the press.[58] His fate, like his diary entries, was a measure of how much grief was a daily occurrence for the Algerian population. In the major cities of Algiers and Oran just to go out was to risk death, either at the hands of OAS death squads or OAS mortar attacks on the Algerian *quartier*. Yet, in the months from January to July 1962 this fear coexisted with relief and hope because, after nearly eight years of war, Algerians knew that the end was near. This was especially true for prisoners and their waiting families who, in the wake of the Évian Agreement, greeted their release with elation. In the case of Ali Zamoum, captured in early 1955, the journey from his prison in France to his mountain village in Kabylia was an emotive one. In this moment of victory he felt a surge of joy at seeing the greenery of the Kabyle countryside, at being reunited with his wife and having 'defeated colonialism'; but this joy was tempered by the wish to remember those who had died in the struggle.[59] Walking around the main square of Taddert, Zamoum embraced everybody, declaring 'Glory to our martyrs' whenever the name of a fallen comrade was evoked.[60] Such human gestures were a mark of a grieving process, which was also apparent in the need to find out about the dead. Families wanted to know about the fate of their close ones which is why, between 19 March and 25 May, the local ceasefire commissions received a staggering 187,304 demands for information on missing Algerians.[61]

This desire to look backwards and acknowledge the fallen was paradoxically a measure of how much people were looking forwards. Expectation gripped huge numbers of Algerians. Everywhere there was a sense of approaching victory and, during the referendum campaign, public FLN meetings (now permitted for the first time) became independence celebrations. On 25 June, 20,000 Algerians converged on the village of Arba, situated at the foot of the Atlas Mountains to the south of Algiers, for one of these FLN meetings.[62] Following lorries covered in green-and-white flags into the village, the crowd watched a march-past by maquisards, including a detachment of women nurses in olive-green battle fatigues, before Si Mokhtar, one of the leaders of Wilaya 4, called on people to vote 'yes' in the referendum, respect the Évian Agreement and reach out in a fraternal manner to Europeans. In conclusion a female nurse exalted the important role of women in the revolution who, like Djamila Bouhired during the 'Battle of Algiers', had fought alongside their brothers, husbands, and sons.

In this euphoric atmosphere hundreds of thousands of rural Algerians gravitated towards the coastal towns and cities during May and June. After years of penury and deprivation this mass sensed that their time had come. This was the moment when their pent-up anger could be finally released, and the result was chaos (fawda) on a grand scale which peaked in the weeks after independence on 3 July. This disorder, particularly acute in Algiers and Oran, meant that there was no orderly hand-over of power. The Provisional Executive was simply swept away by a great movement from below and within this vacuum uncontrolled joy mingled with uncontrolled anger. The colonial world had been overturned. The 'other' Algeria had stood up. Everywhere there was an explosion of Muslim national identity through music, dancing, and flag-waving. French statues were draped in a sea of white, red, and green or, as in the case of the 1930 centenary monument at Sidi-Ferruch, blown up, while in Guelma, near the Tunisian border, the local imam oversaw the destruction of the Roman temple, a hated example of pagan idolatry in the eyes of Muslims.[63]

Symbolic retribution was mirrored by physical retribution. In the heightened emotions of July 1962, a moment of rigid absolutes where Algerians could only be for or against national liberation, any past relationship with French power was potentially suspect. There was no room for error, compromise, or ambiguous behaviour. The choice was simple and those who had chosen the French side, whether in the administration, as a *harki*, or one of the women who had burnt their veils on 13 May 1958, were subjected to summary justice. Their behaviour was a public act which demanded public vengeance: a psychological aspect at the root of the *harki* massacres, as well as the humiliation of women who had slept with French soldiers, and Muslim elites deemed to have benefited from the colonial system. Inflamed by eight years of war, the ferocity of this revenge was marked by a reassertion of male dominance that was class and gender specific. In many places local dignitaries were forced to run a gauntlet of popular hatred, before being made to sweep the streets or made to marry off their daughters to men from the lower orders: a settling of personal and political scores which expressed a fusion of social and sexual resentments.[64]

But if part of July 1962 was about retribution, another part was about personal enrichment. With all the Europeans leaving, thousands of impoverished Algerians saw their opportunity for rich pickings in the towns and cities. This was a lawless moment when everything was possible and during July empty European shops, businesses, and property were taken over with no legal process. Equally, hundreds of cars were stolen while farms, schools, factories, and workshops were stripped bare of anything worthwhile. Within this chaos some FLN officers did try to impose order. In Oran Captain Bakhti introduced martial law and executed looters. But elsewhere, as Ali Zamoum observed, some officers exploited the situation, using their authority to requisition the best villas for themselves.[65]

Overall these mass seizures of property make it difficult to see how Europeans could have stayed because, for all the appeals for reconciliation during the referendum process, the explosion of July 1962 was powered by an all-encompassing rage against the last vestiges of French rule. The need to end colonial humiliation was deeply felt and in this manner July 1962 takes us back to the millenarian roots of Algerian nationalism. The belief that at some point French rule would disappear in a climactic moment had been part of the Muslim imaginary ever since 1830, particularly in eastern Algeria.

Figure 11.2 Independence July 1962: Algerians demonstrating in front of the colonial monument celebrating the centenary of French rule at Sidi-Ferruch, the site of the 1830 invasion. The political significance of this monument as a symbol of the French 'civilizing mission' is dicussed on page 49.

This sentiment had underpinned the May 1945 uprising, the elections of April 1948 and 1 November 1954, and was finally realized in July 1962. Independence was the millenarian event so many Algerians had been waiting for.

The Algerian Civil War

Within this generalized chaos most Algerians were unaware of the FLN's internal divisions which exploded into public view for the first time. In essence, across all the rivalries and divisions, this civil war was not about ideology. It was a clash for power between the Provisional Government and Boumediène. In terms of allies Boumediène could count upon the support of the wilayas of the Aurès, North Constantine, Oran, and the Sahara, along with Ferhat Abbas, still angry at the way in which he had been ousted from the presidency by Ben Khedda. Crucially, the Boumediène alliance was fronted by Ben Bella himself.[66] As the face of the Algerian Revolution, Ben Bella endowed the alliance with a historical legitimacy which meant that Boumediène was also able to win over famous figures such as the two founder FLN leaders, Mohammed Khider and Rabah Bitat, as well as Yacef Saadi, Djamila Bouhired, and Zohra Drif from the 'Battle of Algiers'. Even so, Ben Bella was no dupe. He was perfectly aware of Boumediène's ambitions for power, but for him this was a tactical alliance. It would allow him to become the first post-independence president.

On the Provisional Government's side stood President Ben Khedda, Ben Tobbal, Belkacem Krim, the wilayas of Kabylia and Algiers, the Fédération de France, and the other two historic prisoners, Aït Ahmed and Boudiaf. At the Tripoli Conference in Libya, lasting from 28 May to 7 June, this conflict erupted into a war of words. Any lingering facade of unity ended as Ben Bella consistently accused the Provisional Government of selling out the FLN's principles at Évian and with the OAS ceasefire. Moreover, Ben Bella called for a new leadership made up uniquely of the historic leaders of 1 November 1954 which would marginalize politicians like Ben Khedda. Judging time to be of the essence in this rush for power Ben Khedda left with seven ministers for Tunis before the end of the conference. There he issued a communiqué dismissing Boumediène and dissolving his general staff, before arriving in Algiers on 3 July. It was a triumphant welcome, although many Algerians were mystified by the absence of Ben Bella, nor did they understand Ben Khedda's warnings of an army coup.

In response, Boumediène denounced Ben Khedda's action as illegal and, on 11 July, Ben Bella, backed up by the Army of the Frontiers, entered Algeria via the Moroccan border and established a power base at Tlemcen. A tense stand-off ensued, which deepened further when Ben Bella established a Political Bureau with five members on 22 July. Reiterating the accusation that the Provisional Government had betrayed the FLN's original ideals, the Political Bureau denounced Ben Khedda and his ministers as 'usurpers' whose departure from the Tripoli Conference had undermined the institutions of the 'Algerian revolution'.[67] In the meantime the Provisional Government de-camped to Tizi-Ouzo in Kabylia, the fiefdom of Wilaya 3, where it prepared for armed conflict under the leadership of Belkacem Krim, Mohammed Boudiaf, and Mohand Oul Hadj, leader of Wilaya 3.

With bloodshed seemingly imminent, one last attempt was made to reach a compromise and on 2 August an agreement was brokered setting elections for a Constituent Assembly on 27 August. The next day Ben Khedda welcomed this recourse to the 'will of the people', while continuing to attack the Army of the Frontiers which 'had never known the revolutionary war like their brothers in the maquis' and, he claimed, represented a 'military caste' such as those found in Latin American countries.[68] But in truth, the Provisional Government had been effectively marginalized. The Provisional Executive was working solely with the Political Bureau towards the final transfer of political power and on 4 August the latter, under Ben Bella's leadership, established itself in Algiers. Unwilling to accept Ben Bella's authority, Wilayas 4 and 5 dug in and on 20 and 29 August there were exchanges of gunfire in the Algiers Casbah. Even more provocatively, both refused to be absorbed into the new National Army under Boume-diène, with the result that on 30 August the Political Bureau ordered its troops to march on Algiers.

This 'March on Algiers' took the form of three columns, one coming from the west and two others from the south, and from the beginning it was an unequal battle. Boumediène's troops were better equipped and superior in number and after fifteen days the maquisards of Wilayas 3 and 4 had been defeated, although in places the intensity of the fighting matched anything during the war against the French—a rude shock to many Algerians who, weary of violence, demonstrated against this civil war to the shouts of 'Seven years, that is enough!' In the ensuing days Ben Bella would claim that he had won 'thanks to the people'.[69] This was a lie. Ben Bella had triumphed because he had sided with the most powerful military clique within the FLN. By the same token it was not true, either, that July 1962 was a *coup d'état* against the democracy. Within the Provisional Government the key figures—Boussouf, Ben Tobbal, and Belkacem Krim—were as authoritarian as Boumediène. They, too, had subordinated politicians to their will. In 1962 they lost because of one simple fact: their side could not match the firepower of the Boumediène machine, honed outside of Algeria in anticipation of this final reckoning.

In this manner the victory of the Army of the Frontiers takes us back to two intertwined historical factors: the origins of the FLN and the consequences of French 'pacification'. From the beginning, the FLN was defined by a cult of the gun which looked down upon politicians as weak and ineffectual. The sheer length of the conflict, totally unexpected according to the activist Mohammed Harbi, meant that this cult of the gun predominated.[70] The adherence to 'pacification', the *raison d'être* of the Republican Front government's intensification of the war in spring 1956 which de Gaulle continued until the end of 1960, ensured that politicians were marginalized and the maquis reduced to a skeleton, opening the way to Boumediène's victory. Given the political objectives of Guy Mollet in 1956, such a consequence was the most unexpected outcome of his policy.

The pity of an undeclared war

Amidst the explosion of joy and anger that greeted independence amongst Algerians, one unifying narrative was asserted over all others: national suffering. Again and again demonstrators in July proclaimed that this was the war of 'one million martyrs' or even 'two million martyrs': evoking a claim made by *El-Moudjahid* on 9 March 1962 that the blood sacrifice for independence was one and a half million victims—500,000 killed and disappeared and 1 million wounded and injured—which would be officially inscribed in the 1963 Constitution.[71] Immediately, these figures became embedded in popular and official mythology, fashioning an image of an Algerian resistance which, it was declared, had begun in 1830 and where all the Algerian casualties were victims of French colonialism: an epic resistance narrative that, by linking the dead and the living into one seamless continuum, formed the basis of a post-independence identity.

But, short-lived though it was, the Algerian Civil War showed how the violence of the Algerian War was a diverse violence. This was never a struggle between two monolithic blocs. It was never *just* colonizer versus colonized. It was a violence which drew in a range of political and social actors and, at different stages, set French against French and Algerian against Algerian. In 1962 the Civil War bloodshed within the FLN was motivated by the lust for power. FLN activists were killing other FLN activists for political and social advancement—a pattern of violence with deep roots in Algerian society that pre-dates the colonial period.[72] However, the potency of the 'one and a half million martyrs' narrative eclipsed this more complicated reality. Nuance and complexity were obscured, above all in determining one of the most basic consequences of the fighting: who was killed, how many, and by whom.

This is why historical research calculating how many died has led to some of the fiercest polemics over the Algerian War. The attempt by professional historians such as Charles-Robert Ageron, Guy Pervillé, Kamel Kateb, and Xavier Yacono to sift through the figures has provoked an ongoing controversy because their numbers immediately raise questions about the meaning and legitimacy of the conflict. In trying to get nearer to an empirical 'objectivity', they have challenged received truths, whether it be the 'one and a half million martyrs' Algerian narrative, the amnesia of subsequent French governments, or the various European and *harki* lobbies who want their 'own' suffering to be quantified and recognized.

The most exhaustive work on these statistics, the one that has produced the widest consensus amongst historians, has been that carried out by Charles-Robert Ageron.[73] Drawing upon official documents, as well as calculations based upon a comparison of the census of 1954 and that of 1966, he made a series of estimates which have become reference points even if they, too, have been challenged.[74] In particular, however, this statistical research underlines how this was a war of *different* peaks and troughs. The confrontation on the ground between the FLN and the French Army took time to take off. From 1 November 1954 onwards there was an upward graph of violence which climaxed in April 1958, when 3,500 Algerian maquisards were killed in that month as against 2,500 in January 1957 and 500 in January 1956, before falling away in the wake of the Challe Offensive in 1959.[75] By the same token the OAS violence reached its high point after the Évian ceasefire in 1962, while the worst of the anti-*harki* massacres occurred in July 1962.

In terms of the precise records the easiest to determine, and the least contested, are the French military losses. According to official records these are said to stand at 24,614, with 15,583 killed in fighting and terrorist attacks, while one-third died in accidents and from illness. Added to this, 450 prisoners were never accounted for and a further 64,985 were wounded. More controversial are the figures for the civilian casualties of Algerian terrorism. In 1962 the French government, drawing up a balance sheet stretching from 1 November 1954 until the signing of the Évian Agreement, put this at 2,788 French and 16,378 Algerians killed, 7,541 French and 13,619 Algerians injured, and 375 French and 18,296 Algerians disappeared. What is striking, therefore, is that Algerians represented a much greater preponderance of these victims. Paradoxically, they suffered the most from FLN attacks. Equally, these figures do not take into account those killed or kidnapped after the ceasefire which, on 24 November 1964, the French government put at 3,018 Europeans between 19 March and 31 December 1962.[76] As regards OAS terrorism, the French government never produced equivalent information, although the French military calculated that, between 19 March and 19 May 1962, OAS violence accounted for 1,658 people, of whom 58 were soldiers, 104 European, and the rest Algerian.[77] Against this, the FLN activist Redha Malek would subsequently claim that the OAS killed 12,000 Algerians.

Without doubt the greatest violence was perpetrated by the French army which, according to its own documents, inflicted 141,000 losses on the ALN—a figure largely substantiated by the Algerian Government in 1974 when it put the figure killed in battle at 132,290. One of the great unknowns, however, is the number of Algerian civilians who were killed or disappeared during French military operations. In his authoritative history of the FLN, Gilbert Meynier, citing French army documents from November 1959, puts this figure at between 55,000 and 65,000.

On the issue of FLN violence against Algerians and the rival nationalist organizations, Meynier, drawing on French documents, gives a round figure of 30,000. He also concludes that between 6,000 and 7,000 were killed by FLN internal purges, while the September 1962 Algerian Civil War led to around 1,000 deaths. As regards the *harki* massacres this, too, remains a great unknown. In November 1962, *Le Monde* journalist Jean Lacouture wrote of 10,000 slaughtered in the reprisals, but others have since claimed the figure to be as high as 150,000. Meynier puts the number at 30,000.[78]

When added together these figures come to between 250,000 and 300,000 Algerian dead, although this remains open to debate because of the unreliability of the documentary evidence. The Algerian demographer, Kamel Kateb, has raised questions about the validity of both the 1954 and 1966 censuses, while the French historian, Sylvie Thénault, has pointed to the fact that the French military had a vested interest in massaging these figures. It wished to cover up summary executions and torture.[79] Nevertheless, even if we accept the 300,000 figure, it in no way minimizes the violence. Out of the total of a 9 million Algerian population, this is equivalent to the percentage of French losses during World War One: a point of comparison which underlines the devastating impact of the eight-year undeclared war.

Postscript

Tuesday, 25 September 1962

Algeria

Shortly after 4.00 p.m. the new Algerian Assembly was inaugurated and during this first session Ferhat Abbas, elected leader of the Assembly, formally declared the establishment of the Algerian Republic: 'democratic', 'popular', 'socialist', and one that would belong to Europeans 'as much as us'.[1] This Assembly was the outcome of elections five days earlier when Algerians were asked to vote for a single list of 196 candidates drawn up by Ben Bella's Political Bureau. As an exercise in popular consultation this process had nothing to do with democratic choice, even if large numbers, over 90 per cent, did vote, largely because they were desperate for a government that would restore order. The result was a foregone conclusion, enshrining Ben Bella's victory in the FLN civil war. Those who had opposed the 'March on Algiers' were excluded from political power and at 5.00 a.m. on Saturday 29 September, after a long debate, Ben Bella was elected president by 159 to 1 with 19 abstentions.[2] In his acceptance speech the new president characterized the values that would define the new Algeria. This was to be a country founded upon 'socialism', 'agrarian reform', 'Arabism', and 'non-alignment', which would allow the Algerian peasantry, 'four-fifths of our population', to break the chains of colonialism and underdevelopment.[3]

On 8 October Algeria formally entered the UN as a separate nation state. Membership was supported by ten other countries: Chile, France, Ghana, Ireland, Romania, the Soviet Union, the United Arab Republic, the United Kingdom, the USA, and Venezuela, and in their addresses the delegates welcomed the resolution of a principal source of tension in international relations. Speaking on behalf of Ghana, the first sub-Saharan country to achieve independence in 1957, the Ghanaian representative to the UN, Alex Quaison-Sackey, went much the furthest in emphasizing the depth of Algerian suffering and the extent of the French crime. Describing the '800,000 Algerians' who had laid down their lives, he declared:

> Looking around and knowing the historic struggles for freedom from colonial domination that were waged by some of the Member States here in this Council chamber, my delegation is struck by the fact that Algeria's price for freedom has been too high: it has been so much higher than our own. Not the United States with its Boston Tea Party, not Chile not Venezuela with their Bolivar's struggles, not Ireland with its Sinn Fein, not the United Arab Republic with its Suez experience, not Romania with its Nazi oppressors, not even Ghana with our positive action—not one of us suffered so much when the hour of triumph was upon us.[4]

Quaison-Sackey's words underlined the power of the 'one and a half million martyrs' narrative; one that endowed Algeria with a moral legitimacy on the international scene throughout the 1960s and 1970s. At home, however, the unifying force of this resistance narrative could not disguise the huge challenges of independence. In autumn 1962 the country was still highly unstable. In part this instability was because of the environmental consequences of eight years of conflict. The French military strategy, involving the laying of mines, the burning down of whole forests, and the regrouping of vast parts of the rural Algerian population, had done untold damage to what had been previously productive farmland. Moreover, once the regrouping was reversed in 1961, this policy created a rootless mass which needed food, employment, and housing. But this instability was also the result of the departure of the Europeans. Their flight left Algeria bereft of key technical expertise. The lack of trained managers, accountants, lawyers, teachers, and civil servants meant that businesses collapsed, unemployment— already endemic—shot up even further, and the new school year was chaotic, making day-to-day life very difficult. For all these reasons Algeria in 1962 was in a far more difficult position than, say, France in 1944, because at least with the end of the Vichy regime elements of the state remained in place, smoothing the transition to a post-Liberation government. In Algeria there was no such continuity. The break was more sudden and more profound.

This reality made it impossible for the Ben Bella government to deliver one of its most basic promises: a better economic life for ordinary Algerians.

Already, within a year, many of the population were talking of a 'bitter peace'.[5] The country was bankrupt and, to survive, Ben Bella resorted to emergency measures, notably the establishment of a National Solidarity Fund where compatriots were called upon to contribute jewellery, bank notes and deeds of land. Even more embarrassingly, Ben Bella was obliged to ask de Gaulle for greater economic aid, while quietly ignoring the continuing emigration to France. By 1964 this stood at 450,000 Algerians on the other side of the Mediterranean—a staggering figure that was, in effect, a safety valve for his own government.

As Ben Bella grappled with these huge social problems, his legitimacy was further undermined by defeat in a brief war with Morocco in October 1963 over the disputed Saharan frontier.[6] He also slid from political crisis to political crisis as his dictatorial manner alienated allies, leading to the resignation of Mohammed Khider on 16 April 1963 as Secretary-General of the FLN's Political Bureau, followed by Ferhat Abbas three months later. Standing down as president of the National Assembly, Abbas was above all angry over the new constitution which rejected pluralism in favour of a one-party state. More dramatically still, in September 1963 Ben Bella was confronted with an armed uprising in Kabylia led by Aït Ahmed who had founded the Front des Forces Socialistes (FFS). Supported by Abbas and Ben Khedda, Aït Ahmed aimed to ignite a country-wide revolt, but in reality it was restricted to Kabylia and by the summer of 1964 it had been crushed and the leaders arrested. Boudiaf cherished the same hopes of overthrowing Ben Bella but he, too, failed to spark mass revolt before going into exile in Morocco in 1964.[7]

Within this world of plot and counter-plot Ben Bella's greatest enemy was Boumediène whom, given his reliance upon the army of the frontiers, Ben Bella had no choice but to appoint as Minister of Defence. Once in power, Ben Bella tried to marginalize Boumediène by purging pro-Boumediène ministers, building up a popular militia to rival the army and preparing the way for an Afro-Asia Conference in Algiers that would enshrine himself as the leader of the Third World. Conversely, Boumediène fine-tuned his system by promoting professional officers, many of whom, like Khaled Nezzar and Larbi Belkheir, had been trained in the French army and only came over to the liberation struggle after 1958, at the expense of former maquis commanders, while patiently extending the power of the shadowy Military Security (Sécurité Militaire—SM) which installed networks of spies everywhere.[8] The authoritarian military model developed in

Morocco from 1957 was now being applied to Algeria itself so that, although, in theory, the country was a one-party state, in reality the FLN was under the thumb of Boumediène's machine. Power depended on force, not the constitution or elections, and in the early hours of 19 June 1965 Ben Bella was deposed by this machine and imprisoned.[9] Just after midday Boumediène announced the creation of a Revolutionary Council that would assume all powers and which he would lead as the new head of state.

Ben Bella's fall was greeted with indifference both at home and abroad. There was no mass opposition to the coup, although Boumediène's accession made plain the cardinal rule of Algerian politics: the army is the determining force. Ever since, the country's future has been decided in secret by an inner circle of high-ranking officers, despite the regime's dictum, proclaimed on every government building, that Algeria was 'ruled by the people and for the people'. First and foremost, Boumediène wanted to replace the anarchy of the Ben Bella years with the military values of discipline, reverence, and authority. He wished to make the army synonymous with the people and the revolution. He wanted to enshrine the army as the custodian of the national liberation struggle, thereby portraying his coup as a return to the true roots of Algerian nationalism which stressed egalitarianism, social justice, and the recovery of Muslim and Arab values.

Until his death in December 1978, Boumediène ruled the country with an iron fist. Ben Bella was imprisoned throughout these years, while opponents were either forced into exile or, as in the case of Mohammed Khider in 1967 and Belkacem Krim in 1970, hunted down and killed by the military security.[10] At the same time, Boumediène did not govern by fear alone. He displayed considerable political skills, overcoming the initial indifference to inspire genuine popular enthusiasm. Boumediène had an instinctive understanding of the feelings of ordinary Algerians and knew that the populace admired his modest life style, an incorruptibility which became a pillar of his personal legitimacy. He knew, too, that, given the nationalism that characterized the country after such a long war of independence, much more intense than in either Morocco or Tunisia, Algerians would acclaim the way in which he stood up to the former colonial master and won, notably through the nationalization of French oil and gas assets in the Sahara on 24 February 1971—a move which Boumediène justified as the continuation of the decolonization process into the economic sphere. Equally, Boumediène knew that Algerians would take pride in the country's stature as a beacon for Third World revolution. Whether it was through his military and diplomatic support for the Palestinian cause, his close alliance with Fidel Castro's Cuba, or his address to the United Nations General Assembly in May 1974 calling for the transfer of resources from the North to the South, Boumediène knew that Algerians would enjoy these displays of international strength. They made Algerians stand tall because their country stood for something. Revolutionary, socialist, and a leading voice in the 'Non-Aligned Movement' which rejected the two cold war blocs, Algeria was seen to be a model of how to overcome poverty and under-development.

If Boumediène was one part of Algeria's international standing during the late 1960s and 1970s, the other was the enormous impact of the ideas of Frantz Fanon. Born in 1925 in the French-ruled Caribbean island of Martinique, a veteran of the Free French campaign in Italy during World War Two, Fanon studied psychology at Lyon University in the late 1940s, before arriving in Algeria in October 1953 as a psychiatrist in a hospital in the town of Blida just south of Algiers. Coming to the conclusion that Algerian patients were suffering from mental-health problems because of the psychological effect of colonialism, Fanon resigned in 1956 and made his way to Tunis to join the FLN where he became one of the editors of *El-Moudjahid* who, in articles and books, analysed the unfolding liberation struggle.[11] The role of women; relations with parental authority; attitudes towards technology: in each case, Fanon argued, the FLN struggle was transforming traditional mentalities and laying the foundation of new post-independence identities.

Fanon died of leukaemia on 6 December 1961, shortly after the publication of his most influential work, *Les Damnés de la terre* (*The Wretched of the Earth*).[12] Writing in angry and confrontational style, Fanon extolled the virtues of mirror violence, justifying this as a liberational act against the inherent violence of colonial rule—a necessary stage which would purge Africans and Asians of any inferiority complex in regard to white settler society. Containing a preface by Jean-Paul Sartre, who embraced Fanon's vision of a third revolution led by a dispossessed peasantry, *The Wretched of the Earth* had a global resonance. It became an iconic text of the new 1960s radical movements: *the* classic vindication of the Algerian cause and a permanent indictment of colonialism.

Fanon's influence was explicit in the other international icon to emerge from independent Algeria, the 1966 film *The Battle of Algiers*. Directed by the Italian Gillo Pontecorvo and produced by Saadi Yacef, the 'Battle of Algiers' leader who played himself under the name Jaffar, the film's depiction of the role of women in carrying out the bomb attacks on the European community drew heavily from Fanon. In particular, this sequence was framed by his 1959 book *L'An cinq de la révolution algérienne* (*Year Five of the Algerian Revolution*), which had stressed how their action, either using the veil for hiding weapons, or discarding it to pass themselves off in a decoy function as sexually available French females, was challenging traditional values.[13] Winner of the Venice Film Prize in 1966, initially banned in France, the film, shot in black and white, had a newsreel documentary quality. This authentic feel was part of the film's raw power, which distilled into celluloid form Fanon's theory of revolutionary violence, namely that terrorism is justified and wins.[14]

This message had an enduring impact throughout the 1960s and 1970s. From Cape Verde through to Angola and Mozambique, it inspired other Africans fighting colonialism, not least Nelson Mandela in South Africa who visited FLN training camps in Morocco in 1962 and saw in Algeria the 'closest model to our own in that the rebels faced a large white settler community that ruled the indigenous majority'.[15] In France it inspired Georges Mattéi, the former reservist in Algeria in 1956 who had gone over to work clandestinely with the FLN in Paris. He, along with two other militant anti-colonialists, Gérard Chaliand and François Maspero, founded the journal *Partisans* in November 1961. Convinced that the locus of revolution was no longer to be found in the European working class, but amongst the dispossessed peasantry of Africa, Asia, and Latin America, the February 1962 issue was dedicated to the recently deceased Fanon who had given 'a new direction to their thinking, their decisions, their political acts and their very lives'.[16]

The wider significance of the Algerian War for revolutionaries was self-evident in the first ever Pan-African Cultural Festival which began in Algiers on 21 July 1969. Lasting until 1 August, the Festival saw 4,000 painters, poets, photographers, musicians, and intellectuals converge on the capital. Representing thirty-one nations from across the continent, these activists transformed the streets into a meeting place of creative culture. They embodied the belief that, free from imperialism, Africans had the capacity to shape their own history.

The idea for a Pan-African Cultural Festival had originated from within the Organization of African Unity two years earlier. Since Boumediène was

Figure 12.1 Poster for Gillo Pontecorvo's 1966 film, *The Battle of Algiers*, which inspired anti-imperialist struggles across Africa, Asia, and Latin America.

Figure 12.2 Black Panthers paying homage to the Algerian anti-colonial struggle during the Pan-African Cultural Festival in Algiers in 1969.

the president of the Organization of African Unity, Algeria was the obvious choice to be the host and within the Festival the connection between political, cultural, and psychological liberation was everywhere. Belittled or misunderstood by European colonizers, the Festival was a celebration of African cultures past, present, and future: a cathartic moment whose aim was to decolonize the mind by breaking away from European modes of thought.

One of the Festival's major themes was the unfinished anti-colonial revolution. It foregrounded the continuing struggles against Portuguese colonialism in Angola, Cape Verde, Guinea-Bissau, and Mozambique, the apartheid system in South Africa, and white minority rule in Rhodesia. No less importantly, the Festival stressed the link with the Afro-American diaspora—the lost sons and daughters of the continent. Pride in African roots had been one of the cornerstones of the rising tide of black radicalism in the USA, whether in politics, literature, or music, and this aspect was represented in the Festival by the singer Nina Simone, the drummer Max Roach, and the saxophonist Archie Shepp whose improvised, free-form style was explicitly political. By dispensing with a European-derived harmonic system, Shepp argued, he was reconnecting with what he saw as the African roots of jazz.

This Afro-American connection was further represented by the Black Panther Party. Formed in 1966 in San Francisco by Huey Newton and Bobby Seale, the Black Panthers, inspired by Mao and dressed in trademark black berets and sunglasses, espoused a revolutionary, far-left politics that underlined black self-determination and pride. By 1968 the FBI Chief J. Edgar Hoover had identified the Panthers as 'the gravest threat to internal security'. Decreeing 1969 to be the year that the Panthers would be destroyed, he unleashed a wave of FBI repression and under this pressure the Panthers, racked too by ideological and personal differences, began to implode.

On the run from the US police, Panther leaders like Eldridge and Kathleen Cleaver headed for Algeria. Inspired by Fanon, they saw Algiers as the beacon of the Third World and the Black Panthers were a huge presence at the Festival. An exhibition tracing the Panthers' history and including paintings and prints by Emory Douglas, the Panthers' Minister of Culture, was inundated by adoring crowds. Eldridge Cleaver was followed for three days by the radical film-maker William Klein and in the resultant documentary Cleaver poured forth on the crimes of American imperialism while visiting the North Vietnamese delegation. In addition, the Black Panthers' own paper had a front cover entitled 'the Panthers in Kasbah', as Cleaver toured the Casbah in homage to the Algerian liberation struggle—a measure of Algeria's revolutionary standing across the globe.

France

In France the consequences of independence in 1962 were just as enormous, not least because the country was truly at peace for the first time since September 1939. Algeria might have been an undeclared war, but by spring 1956 French people were under no illusion about the scale of the violence. Given the deployment of over 400,000 troops, France was at war. This fact meant that, when added to World War Two, as well as Indochina, Morocco, and Tunisia, military conflict was a constant presence for nearly twenty-three years, even if its impact varied according to place, time, and the particularities of each conflict.

Independence produced far-reaching geographical and legal changes. No longer did the French nation state stretch from Dunkirk to the Sahara Desert. Shorn of Algeria, France had been returned to something approaching its original 1830 entity.[17] The Deputies and Senators from the former Algerian departments, which had made up 9.5 per cent of the National Assembly between October 1958 and July 1962, were formally excluded from the legislature. Stripped of their electoral constituencies, these politicians had no place in the new, resolutely hexagonal landscape, while Algerians residing in France were divested of French citizenship and became foreigners. It was a constitutional revolution, redefining what and where France was—one that went even further when de Gaulle, using the continuing threat of the OAS, won a referendum on 28 October 1962 for his proposal to elect the president by universal suffrage.[18]

This revolution meant that there was never any question of France looking to recover Algeria. Although an integral part of France, Algeria never assumed the status of the lost provinces of Alsace-Lorraine after the Franco–Prussian War of 1870–1. In July 1962 Gaullist France turned away from Algeria in an emphatic manner. For de Gaulle the army rebels and the settlers belonged to the past. They had lost touch with the realities of the mid-twentieth century. France's future, he argued, was elsewhere. It was to be found in a modern, technological society which, unencumbered with

Algeria, could now, in de Gaulle's famous June 1960 expression, 'marry its epoch'.[19] For this reason the power of de Gaulle's decolonization narrative was in the way in which, during the following years, it reinvented historical perspectives and made the end of the Algerian War into a victory. In this narrative the loss of Algeria had not sent France into terminal decline. On the contrary, it had galvanized the country's outward-looking energies. It had allowed French policy to move boldly forward into the unfolding 1960s. These were the assumptions of post-1962 France. They underpinned prestige projects, such as the building of Concorde, the first supersonic passenger plane; dramatic foreign policy initiatives, notably the reconciliation with West Germany in January 1963; and de Gaulle's strident opposition to Anglo-Saxon influence, whether it be his vetoing of British entry into the European Economic Community (EEC) in 1963 or his withdrawal from NATO's command structure in 1966, both justified as a rejection of US dominance. In each case de Gaulle wanted to demonstrate that France had emerged from Algeria as a strengthened power, still able to operate as a global actor in international relations.

The impact of this modernization narrative was particularly apparent in respect to de Gaulle's reconfiguration of the army. When France exploded its first atomic bomb in the Sahara on 13 February 1960 de Gaulle greeted this as a great day because the Fifth Republic had joined the international nuclear club. For de Gaulle this fact, not the possession of empire, was the new yardstick of great power status. It was symbolic of a forward-thinking army whose superiority was based upon cutting-edge technology rather than a colonial mission. On another level this modernization policy ensured that the army was finally and definitively republicanized. The purge of the putschists and pro-OAS supporters brought to an end the military's role in politics stretching from Algeria and Vichy right back to Napoleon Bonaparte at the end of the eighteenth century. Henceforth the army would be subordinate to the civilian powers. It was the servant of elected politicians—an opposite outcome to the one in Algeria.

The amnesty for humans rights abuses contained within the Évian Agreement meant that the careers of Bigeard, Massu, and Aussaresses continued throughout the 1960s and 1970s. In 1975 Bigeard, by now a four-star general, was appointed State Secretary in the Ministry of Defence by President Valéry Giscard d'Estaing. Massu was appointed commander of the French forces in Germany and it was there in May 1968 that he extracted a final concession from de Gaulle: an amnesty for the remaining imprisoned putschist officers as the price for the army's support in the face of the student revolt.[20] In 1961 Aussaresses delivered a series of lectures to US officers on the lessons of the Algerian War, moulding the military minds of those who would use similar strategies in the Vietnam War.[21] In the same vein, in 1959 de Gaulle signed a series of accords with Argentina whereby France supplied a raft of military advisors to Buenos Aires. With this training the Algerian War became the blueprint for a counter-insurgency war fought in the name of anti-communism, one connection with France's undeclared war that remained secret and was not exposed until Marie-Monique Robin's acclaimed 2003 television documentary—*The Death Squads: The French School*.[22]

If looking to new futures was one way in which de Gaulle turned the page, the other was indifference. De Gaulle offered no contrition over Algeria, let alone an apology. He never extended any sympathy to the Europeans or the *harkis*. In his opinion he had made the right choice and he never retracted this view, either publicly or privately. The higher interests of the French nation state outweighed their trauma—which meant that, at an official level, the social consequences of the Algerian War became a taboo subject. There was no public acknowledgement of their suffering. Europeans and *harkis* were expected to piece together their lives themselves, reflecting a level of unconcern within wider French society. Thankful that the Algerian nightmare had been put behind them, by September 1962 only 13 per cent thought that Algeria was the number-one preoccupation for the government. Embracing the new consumerist society of refrigerators, washing machines, and televisions, the majority wanted to enjoy the increased living standards and turn away from the passions raised by 'French Algeria'.[23] By 1962 France was in the middle of an unprecedented period of economic growth which was not held back by the loss of Algeria. Indeed, in providing a much-needed expansion of workforce in the form of Europeans, *harkis*, and Algerian immigrants, the end of the Algerian War contributed to the continuation of this miracle.

Social and political consequences

Within France many 'returning' Europeans endured hostility. Large numbers of French people, forgetting the strategic decisions made by Mollet in 1956 to defend national sovereignty in Algeria, blamed 'European intransigence' for the Algerian War. They identified all Europeans with the OAS which meant that repatriation was regarded with suspicion. They feared that it would give fresh impetus to fascism and extremism. With anti-European prejudice rife, some town hall authorities, such as Marseille, were reluctant to take too many which, in turn, led European families to occupy empty houses and apartments in protest at their plight.[24] This hostility was a defining event for the 'return-ing' Europeans. It was the moment when the term *pied-noir* entered common currency as a marker of their separate history from other French people. In the face of official forgetting and public indifference, *pied-noir* organizations sprang up as the returning Europeans turned in on themselves to establish their own community identity through music, language, food, and commemorative activities.[25]

For the *harkis* too their arrival in France was a humiliating experience. Most were housed in squalid camps and made to reapply for French nationality; an experience made worse by the icy winter of 1962–3, one of the coldest on record. From that point on the government policy was segregation. The majority were relocated to makeshift villages, far from the public eye, and employed in forest clearance. Little attempt was made to integrate them, for the most part illiterate peasants, into French society or help them cope with the psychological cost of loss and exile. Consequently, despised by their country of origin and disowned in large part by the French authorities, many male veterans retreated into silence. They were unable to communicate their personal experience to their daughters and sons, princi-pally because they found it difficult to comprehend the consequences of their choices for them and their families.[26]

The specificity of the Algerian Jews (most of whom chose France rather than Israel) was lost in the repatriation process, although on 5 October 1962 French television featured a documentary about a 24-year-old singer, Gaston Ghrenassia, who went by the Spanish-sounding stage name Enrico Macias.[27] Born into a Jewish family in Constantine, Macias was trained in the Maalouf musical tradition by Cheikh Raymond Leyris whose daughter, Suzy, he married. Leaving shortly after Cheikh Raymond's assassination in June 1961, Macias's first single, 'Goodbye my Country' ('*Adieu mon pays*'), was seen to encapsulate the pain of the *pied-noir* community for their lost country. It was indicative of the manner in which much of the Jewish experience was subsumed into a generalized *pied-noir* identity of regret and nostalgia. Against the cold individualism of Gaullist France, Macias pined for the sun, sea, and warm sociability of Algeria—an attitude that was also prevalent amongst Benjamin Stora's Algerian Jewish family who ended up in Paris in 1962.[28] Again and again, Stora's mother complained to her son about the impersonal nature of the mainland. She found it difficult to adapt to the wet weather, and was alarmed by the fact that one could walk down the streets for days without seeing a friend or acquaintance.

If the 'return' of Europeans, *harkis*, and Jews was one social consequence, the other was Algerian immigration. Between 1954 and 1962 this rose from 210,000 to 350,000, followed by another 100,000 by the end of 1964 who wished to escape poverty in Algeria. No longer French citizens, these Algerians had the status of foreign nationals. They were symptoms of an unregulated labour market which needed immigrant labourers to fuel the economic miracle. They did the jobs in building and construction that no one else wanted, and the result was a rapidly growing underclass of families. Living in hostels or in shanty towns (*bidonvilles*) on the outskirts of Paris, Lyon, and Marseille, these immigrants continued to be defined by the legacy of the Algerian War. Thus, whereas Rachid Mekhloufi, who had defected to the FLN in Tunis in 1958, was welcomed back with open arms by the football supporters of Saint-Étienne after 1962, this was the exception rather than the rule.[29] Within France there was no reconciliation or for-giveness. Instead, Algerians were identified with an undesirable immigrant underclass, and anti-Algerian racism, a product of colonialism and war, became endemic to all levels of French society.

The political consequences were no less far-reaching than the social consequences. Algeria catapulted de Gaulle back to power in 1958. It was the event which launched the Gaullist transformation of France, making him and his movement the dominant force in politics until his resignation in April 1969. On the left, the Communist Party lost its hegemony. The National Union of Students in particular challenged the Communist Party's monopoly of action over opposition to the Algerian War, organizing a major demonstration on 27 October 1960 despite Communist hostility. This experience left an enduring legacy and thereafter a younger generation of student activists saw the PCF as too conformist—a part of the electoral system and therefore one of the barriers to revolutionary change. There is, therefore, a direct connection between 27 October 1960 and the student revolt of May 1968. Both situated themselves to the *left* of the Communist Party. This connection is also clear in the way in which during May 1968 the students showed banned films from the opposition movement to the Algerian War. By showing Jacques Panijel's exposé of the 17 October 1961 anti–FLN repression in Paris and René Vautier's hand-held camera documentary of life in the FLN maquis in 1957, the student movement wished to break taboos. They wanted to end Gaullist censorship over Algeria.[30]

The consequences for the Socialist Party were equally enduring as the SFIO's electoral appeal was forever tarnished by the Fourth Republic's inability to solve the Algerian crisis. The SFIO was perceived as a party of the past which is why it remained on the sidelines during the 1960s, unable to break the political dominance of the Gaullists and the Communists. In trying to carve out a new political role, few in the SFIO wished to revisit the Algerian War, although in March 1962 Marcel-Edmond Naegelen, the former Governor-General in Algeria between 1948 and 1951, published a counter-factual scenario arguing that a third way could have won.[31] If France had done what it did in 1956 eight years earlier, investing resources and giving the Governor-General cabinet status, as Naegelen had demanded, then the outcome could have been different. Mollet himself returned to 1956 during a television interview on 26 January 1966 with four journalists on the tenth anniversary of the Republican Front coming to power, but only under duress.[32] The exchanges were bad tempered because Mollet wanted to talk about the party's political future, while the journalists—Jean Cau, Michel Droit, Jean Farran, and Françoise Giraud—wished to revisit his time in power, laying the blame at Mollet's feet for the SFIO's lost support over the past ten years. In the cross-examination, Mollet defended the political choices he made in 1956. He took responsibility for all of them although, a decade on, he admitted that for him the one unambiguously positive outcome of 1956 was his government's role in the survival of Israel. In the following days the press applauded Mollet as the victor in this trial by television. There was even speculation about a crucial role in the realignment of left politics: a measure of the way in which, by 1966, the key question was not the whys of the Algerian War, but the construction of a non-communist left capable of challenging de Gaulle.[33] For the French minority who had opposed the war, however, Mollet could never be rehabilitated. For Pierre Vidal-Naquet, Mollet remained as a hate figure who was symbolic of a 'certain attitude of mind'.[34] This is why, on the latter's death on 3 October 1975, Vidal-Naquet gladly celebrated: 'The man that I hate the most—besides of course the archetypes that were Hitler and his gang—it is certainly Guy Mollet. I have the impression of being politically formed by the hatred of Guy Mollet, and I can tell you that I drank champagne on the evening of his death.'[35]

By this point the SFIO had ceased to exist. At two bitter party conferences in 1969, the SFIO changed its name to the Parti Socialiste (PS), with Mollet standing down as party leader to be replaced by Alain Savary who, given his resignation from the Republican Front government in October 1956 over the hijacking of Ben Bella, was identified with decolonization. Two years later, on 16 June 1971 at the party conference at Épinay in the northern suburbs of Paris, François Mitterrand, coming from outside the party, stepped in to win the leadership in a tightly fought contest. Like Mollet, Mitterrand was very much bound up with the Algerian War. As a member of the Republican Front government he had defended the recall of the reservists and the Suez expedition. But, unlike Mollet, he had opposed the return of de Gaulle in 1958, a stance further reinforced by his strong showing against de Gaulle in the 1965 presidential elections. Moreover, unlike Mollet, he had a new party which, in using much of the language of May 1968 and identifying itself with radical change, allowed for a reinvention. It gave Mitterrand the chance to escape from the shadow of Algeria and present himself as the future, a strategy which culminated in his narrow presidential victory in May 1981.[36]

Algeria: October 1988

On Wednesday 5 October 1988, central Algiers was ransacked by thousands of disaffected youths. With demonstrators chanting 'Rise up, youth', the violence lasted several days and quickly spread to the rest of the country. In response the army declared a state of siege and used tear gas and tanks to restore law and order. By 10 October some 500 people, mostly young men, had been killed.

'Black October', the most significant single event in post-independence Algeria, was the result of a decade of social hardship where the country had been hit very badly by the worldwide economic crisis. The collapse of oil and gas prices, and hence the revenue from Algeria's key exports, forced the government to introduce austerity measures that had a terrible impact on the ordinary population. Unemployment mushroomed to over 25 per cent. Life became very hard, principally because between 1966 and 1987 the population had nearly doubled to 23 million: a new post-independence generation which, in bearing the brunt of the 1980s crisis, felt nothing but anger towards the elite, known popularly as 'the power' (*le pouvoir*).

Figure 12.3 Two cartoons by Gyps from his comic book *Algé-rien*. Both are a satirical comment on the falsification of history in post-independence Algeria. In the first, a history lecturer recites in an unenthusiastic fashion from a textbook glorifying the martyrs of the war of liberation. In the second, Gyps casts doubts on le Pére Lakhdar Benqueuqueli's status as a war veteran, describing him as 'former shepherd, former *moudjahid* (that is what he says, his companions having been all killed in the maquis), former commander, former minister, today a black market dealer'.

This resentment manifested itself in cynicism towards the official memory of the War of Liberation. The younger generation was instinctively suspicious of the 'one million martyrs' narrative. This narrative was seen to be spurious and indiscriminate, the measure of a secretive system which justified the status quo by blaming all of Algeria's ill on the colonial past. This distrust became a rich vein of humour in post-1962 Algeria, in particular the exposing of those who had inflated or invented their roles during the War of Liberation for political and social advancement, a theme brilliantly explored in the films of Merzac Allouache, the stand-up comic

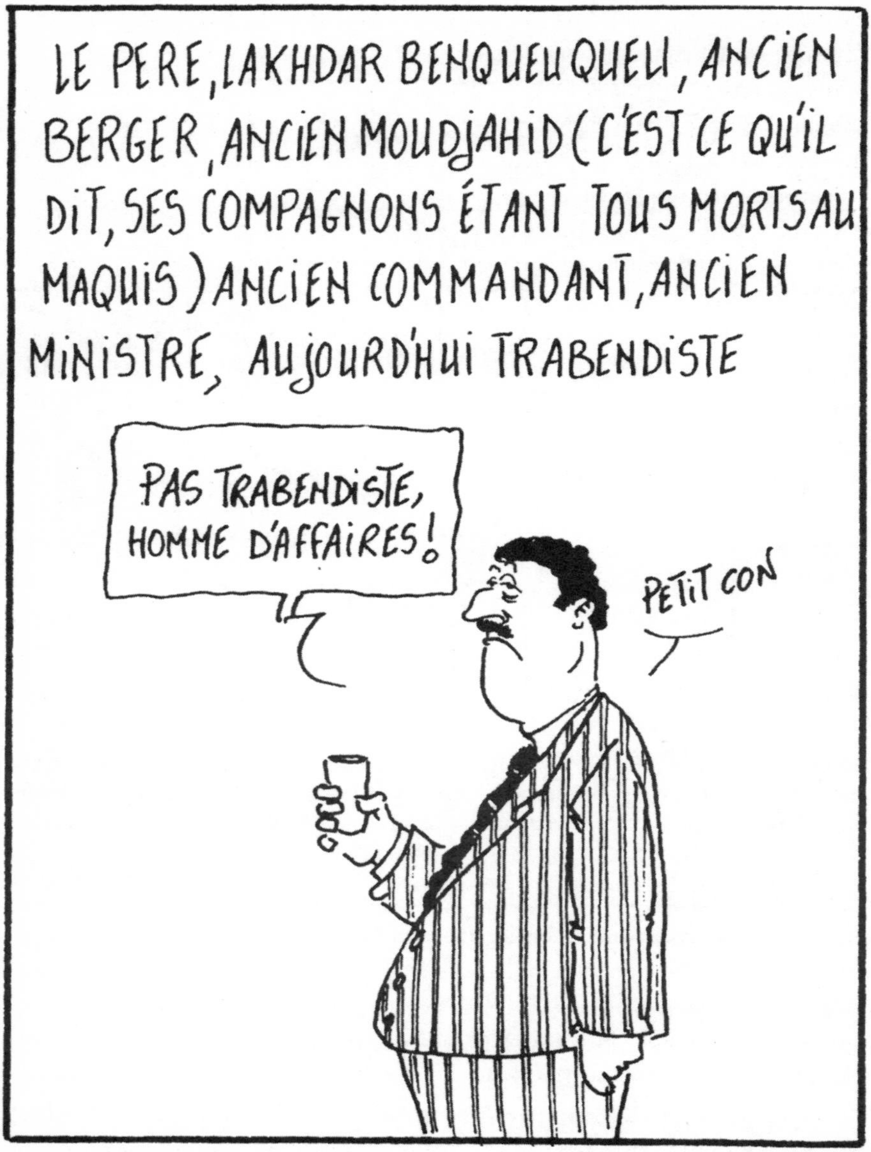

Figure 12.3 (continued)

routines of Fellag, and the satirical cartoons of Ali Dilem and Karim Mahfouf (aka Gyps).

This cynicism explains why rioters attacked the symbols of FLN power in October 1988, a process of unravelling which had begun eight years earlier with the 'Berber Spring' when, in March, April, and May 1980, the government banning of a lecture by the writer Mouloud Mammeri on the Berber language provoked a general strike across the Kabylia region which was severely repressed and led to thirty deaths amongst the protestors. Specifically, the 'Berber Spring' was about the articulation of a Berber identity which, the Berber activists claimed, was under threat from the imposition of a narrow identity based on the Arab language. In this way the 'Berber Spring' gave rise to a movement which challenged one of the cornerstones of Algerian nationalism. It contested the official doctrine that Berberism was a legacy of the colonial divide-and-rule policy, setting Arab against Berber. It reopened the long-suppressed argument about Algeria's Berber roots.[37] It questioned the doctrine of a unitary nationalism based upon Arab and Muslim values.

In the wake of 'Black October' President Chadli Bendjedid, War of Liberation veteran, protégé of Boumediène, picked out by the military to replace the latter in 1979, ushered in a multi-party system which, in theory, limited the army to a purely military role. Chadli's hope was that this experiment would give fresh impetus to the FLN, but in practice the main beneficiaries were the new Islamist party: the Islamic Salvation Front (*Front Islamique du Salut*—FIS). Led by Abassi Madani, a veteran of 1 November 1954, and the firebrand cleric, Ali Belhadj, the FIS offered an alternative interpretation of the War of Liberation. They argued that the original Islamic principles of November 1954 had been betrayed by independence, when pro-French Algerians, such as French-trained officers like Khaled Nezzar, had infiltrated the FLN and imposed an alien system on the Arab-speaking masses. This, Madani and Belhadj railed, was clear from the erection of monuments to the War of Liberation. By building memorials, such as the huge Riadh el-Feth monument in 1982 that dominates the Algiers skyline, the system, Madani and Belhadj continued, was anti-Islamic, encouraging Algerians to worship idols rather than God. Faced with these practices, the FIS leaders maintained, Algeria needed a new *jihad* that would return the country to the purity of November 1954 and finally cleanse the country of the colonial legacy, whether it be secular ideologies, the French language or Western-style fashions and music.

In January 1992 the FIS was poised to win national elections, at which point the army intervened to stop the electoral process. The military leadership, largely unknown to Algerians and operating behind the scenes, managed to convince Mohammed Boudiaf, one of the historic FLN leaders and the architect of 1 November 1954, to return from a twenty-nine-year exile in Morocco.[38] However, on 29 June 1992 Boudiaf was assassinated in dramatic circumstances, almost certainly on the orders of someone from within the military who felt threatened by Boudiaf's promise to root out the high-level corruption that had blossomed under Chadli. The country was on the edge of a precipice and finally tipped over into it in spring 1993, when armed Islamist groups unleashed a maelstrom of violence which met with full-scale repression by the army. Over the next decade some 200,000 people would perish in this horrific undeclared civil war.

At the centre of this new war was the memory and meaning of the first undeclared war. In pursuing a ruthless anti-terrorism campaign, the government purported to be defending the country's most cherished values against sons and daughters of *harkis* who were seeking revenge on independent Algeria. On the opposite side, the armed groups denounced the army leadership as 'the new settlers' or as 'Lacoste's corporals', a reference to the promotion that some Algerians enjoyed in 1956 under the Republican Front before subsequently joining the FLN.[39] Meanwhile, in France, François Gèze, the editor at the left-wing publisher La Découverte, published a series of eye-witness accounts which claimed to show that, in resorting to torture and summary executions, the Algerian army was modelling its counter-insurgency tactics on those of its erstwhile enemy.[40] In short, Gèze argued, 'Lacoste's corporals' had learnt the lessons from their former colonial masters.

France: The return of the repressed

In France the official memory had been defined by Gaullist amnesia, but this too was impossible to sustain by the 1980s. Censorship and silence was challenged from all sides, but most obviously with the ongoing polemic on torture. This had been the *raison d'être* behind so much of the anti-war testimony at the time and it continued to be after 1962. From the beginning, anti-torture campaigners like Pierre Vidal-Naquet condemned the amnesty contained within the Évian Agreement as a mechanism through which perpetrators could escape justice.[41] French people, Vidal-Naquet warned, must not forget what had been done in their name and in 1971 and 1972 he became involved in a fierce public debate with Jacques Massu in the columns of *Le Monde*, when the latter published his memoir justifying French tactics during the 'Battle of Algiers'.[42]

This public debate never went away and reached a new intensity in June 2000 when the FLN activist Louisette Ighil-Ahriz described in *Le Monde* the torture inflicted upon her by Massu's paratroopers in August 1957.[43] Her subsequent book reiterated these claims, underlining one of the paradoxes of 'pacification', namely the extent to which the male violence practised upon Algerian women contradicted the image of female liberation preached by the Republican Front government.[44] In reply Massu, now ninety-two, apologized for the use of torture, although he still drew attention to the horrors inflicted by the FLN on French and Algerian civilians. FLN terrorism, he argued, was the context for torture, even if he accepted that this practice should be formally condemned. In contrast, Paul Aussaresses, now eighty-two, displayed no such regrets. He told *Le Monde* on 23 November 2000: 'Torture gave me no pleasure . . . but if forced to relive it . . . I would do the same thing again because I believe one could not have done otherwise.'[45] Both, however, underlined the ultimate responsibility of the Republican Front government. Mollet, Mitterrand, Lacoste, Lejeune, Pineau: all, Massu and Aussaresses argued, knew exactly what was happening on the ground. This fact was emphasized still further by Aussaresses in his memoirs, published in 2001, where the detailed revelations about torture led human rights organizations to take him to court.[46] Unable to prosecute over the events themselves because of the Évian amnesty, they made a case on the basis of 'complicity in apologies for war crimes'; one that they won in January 2002, which led to Aussaresses being fined.

Immigration was the other ongoing debate which regularly returned France to the Algerian War. By 1982 there were 800,000 Algerian immigrants, still clearly at the bottom of the social ladder. Much of this immigration had been predicated on the belief that families would go back to Algeria, once the father and mother had come to the end of their working lives. However, this unfolding scenario was complicated by the question of the second generation: the sons and daughters who were born in France and therefore had the automatic right to French citizenship under French nationality law. As these sons and daughters tried to find a place in French society, they were confronted with racism and discrimination, which inevitably raised questions about their relationship both with France's colonial past and with Algeria.[47] Between October and December 1983 these sons and daughters gave vent to their grievances with 'The March for Equality' which went from town to town before ending up in Paris, where they were greeted by President Mitterrand. In asserting their right to equality, the marchers described themselves as 'Beurs', a corruption of the word 'Arabe' which had emerged during the 1970s and seemed to encapsulate their struggle: the search for a citizenship that involved an acceptance of their North African identity. This struggle during the 1980s saw an explosion, not just of political activism in anti-racist organizations such as SOS–Racisme and France–Plus, but also a Beur culture which manifested itself through a specific radio station, Radio Beur, novels, music, cinema, strip cartoons, theatre, and stand–up comics.[48] Within this culture the exploration of unresolved tensions was central, whether it be the place of Islam in a secular society, historical knowledge about colonialism, or the link with Algeria.

The ongoing immigration debate was fuelled by the dramatic rise of the National Front during the 1980s led by Jean–Marie Le Pen, the former die-hard supporter of French Algeria and veteran of the 'Battle of Algiers', who himself was accused of torturing prisoners in articles carried by the left-wing daily newspaper *Libération* in February and March 1985.[49] The National Front talked about an 'immigration invasion'. It argued that the presence of Muslim Algerians was a long-term threat to France's Roman Catholic identity, a platform which regularly garnered 10 per cent of the vote. In particular, the National Front attracted support amongst the *pied-noir* community along the Mediterranean coastline, who warmed to Le Pen's anti-Gaullist and pro-French Algeria credentials as a way of expressing their own community difference. Even more significantly, this electoral success pulled all the other parties to the right and made immigration into the number-one political issue.

As questions over the Algerian past proliferated within the media, a concerted attempt was made by professional historians to reclaim the Algerian War from nostalgia, triumphalism, lobby groups, and political manipulation. Until the 1980s literature on Algeria had been dominated by the memoirs of former actors. Now historians, using archive sources and oral interviews, made the Algerian War into an object of legitimate study. A landmark publication in this regard was Mohammed Harbi's study of the FLN published in 1980.[50] Harbi was a former FLN combatant who was incarcerated after the 1965 Boumediène coup as a Ben Bella supporter.

Transferred to house arrest in 1971, Harbi escaped to Paris in 1973 where he became a history lecturer at the University of Paris. Drawing upon his personal archives, his unique position as an insider with the wartime FLN, and notes written during his imprisonment, Harbi argued that the image of the FLN as a revolutionary liberation movement was a mirage. In reality the eight-year struggle had allowed 'the army of the frontiers' to seize power. Banned in Algeria, Harbi's study sent shock waves across France's third-worldist left who were accustomed to the heroic image promoted by Fanon and in Pontecorvo's *Battle of Algiers*. A further landmark publication was Benjamin Stora's biography of the veteran nationalist Messali Hadj in 1982.[51] Politicized by May 1968, an adherent of the Trotskyist movement, Stora's research was based on police archive reports tracking Messali in the late 1920s and early 1930s. Through them he was able to recover the central significance of Messali to modern Algerian nationalism (he had been written out of the official record in Algeria and died in exile in 1974).

Harbi and Stora exemplified the quest for a pluralist historical perspective. This need was also the driving force behind the attempt by Jean-Pierre Rioux, the renowned historian of the Fourth Republic then based at the Institute of Contemporary History (*Institut d'Histoire du Temps Présent*—IHTP), to open up the Algerian War through three conferences in Paris in 1987 and 1988 on the 'War and Christian Opinion', the 'War and Intellectuals', and the 'War and the French'. These conferences were followed by a raft of others throughout the 1990s, as well as a body of research carried out by a new generation of doctoral researchers, less directly implicated in the events themselves than a Harbi or a Stora. This new spirit was epitomized by the theses on the justice system and on torture by Sylvie Thénault and Raphaëlle Branche, born after the Algerian War, in 1969 and in 1972 respectively. Through detailed archival work, they eschewed triumphalism or amnesia in favour of a rigorous method which, in this case, proved beyond doubt that successive French governments had covered up about torture. Subsequently published as books, Thénault's and Branche's research pointed to another crucial dimension of this new academic context: the opening up of official archives.[52] Under the thirty-year rule, declassified documents were being released, but, given the sensitive nature of the subject, the flow of material was restricted. Consequently, much of the professional historical battle during the 1990s was about the fight for unfettered access to documents in the name of openness, a pressure which led the then prime minister of the left coalition government, Lionel Jospin,

to send out an official circular on 13 April 2001 to all government departments, aiming to facilitate greater speed and transparency over the release of
archives.

Without doubt, anniversaries played a key role in fuelling media and
historical speculation about the Algerian War. In the run-up to the thirtieth
anniversary of the end of the Algerian War, French television featured a
major four-part series by Benjamin Stora, *The Algerian Years* (*Les Années
Algériennes*) which brought together actors from all sides of the conflict. In
each case they spoke simply and directly to the camera, bringing their own
perspectives on the conflict as FLN combatants, French conscripts, *harkis*, or
Europeans.[53] For Stora, this series was about setting these very different
experiences and memories side by side. Through the medium of television,
he wanted to bring these painful stories into the open: a therapeutic act
which at last acknowledged the enormity of France's Algerian past. The
hidden emotional wounds of the conflict were at the centre of Bertrand
Tavernier's four-hour documentary film *The Undeclared War* (*La Guerre sans
nom*), also released to coincide with the thirtieth anniversary.[54] Structured
around twenty-nine retrospective interviews with conscripts from the Grenoble region, which took place in the home, the workplace, or the local
bar, the film used personal photographs as *aides-memoires* to help the veterans
reconstruct their memories.[55] Tavernier wanted a grass-roots perspective
and throughout the interviews no subject was taboo. Some talked about the
day-to-day stress of the war against the FLN, often for the first time. Some
talked about the loss of comrades. Some talked about torture. Some, too,
talked about the use en masse of Algerian prostitutes for paid sex, who were
commandeered by the army and sent to follow units in special vans into field
operations. Serge Puygrenier recounts how he lost a leg in action which, he
tells in a scene of mounting anger, has left him feeling like a freak. He
cannot do normal activities like swimming in the sea. Recently made
redundant, and with little prospect of finding work, he is forced to relive
the Algerian War every day. By exploring the aftermath of Algeria, one of
the film's subtexts is the long-term consequences of political decisions made
by the Mollet government in spring 1956. There is an undercurrent of
resentment to this generation of political leaders whose careers continued
throughout the 1960s, 1970s, and 1980s, while thousands of veterans were
forced to cope with the psychological cost of war in the form of depression,
insomnia, and violent mood swings.

Another factor fuelling media and historical interest in the war and its legacy was the unfolding violence in Algeria. This troubled present, at times in 1997 bloody beyond belief, led to a re-examination of political choices during the original Algerian War. This was true of Albert Camus who died on 4 January 1960 in a car crash. The publication of *The First Man* (*Le Premier Homme*) in 1994, the unfinished text of which was discovered in his wrecked vehicle, was a major event because at the centre of the novel was the lost world of French Algeria, told through the eyes of Jacques Cormery whose life, as a dirt-poor European in Algiers who wins a scholarship to secondary school, was clearly based on Camus's own life. Selling over 200,000 copies and immediately translated into English, the novel was a statement of Camus's third way. It was a plea for a multicultural Algeria which, from the perspective of 1994, was hailed by many commentators as visionary; a more hopeful future which could have avoided this second undeclared war. As Catherine Camus, his daughter, explained in the introduction:

> for Algeria, he advocated a federation in which the Arab and European peoples would be equally represented. Those who read this book may better understand his position. So, in denouncing totalitarianism, and in advocating a multicultural Algeria where both communities would enjoy the same rights, Camus antagonized both the right and the left. At the time of his death he was very much isolated and subject to attacks from all sides designed to destroy the man and the artist so that his ideas would have no impact.[56]

The apparent failure of Algerian independence led to a reimagining of *harki* memories that was strengthened by the historical research of Mohand Hammoumou, who recovered the full complexity of the *harki* experience in a more sympathetic light.[57] By casting themselves as the victims of FLN violence, *harki* organizations asserted that they had made the right choice. They were no longer simply the losers in history who had betrayed Algeria—a claim that became the basis of a campaign for *harki* rights which united fifty groups in 1997 under the title 'Justice for the *harkis* and their Families'. Demanding truth, dignity, and justice from the French government, the campaign called for a specific public monument, greater efforts to combat anti-Muslim racism and a better public understanding of the positive role played by Islam within France.[58] The same process of reimagining was to be observed amongst Jewish Algerians, albeit in a different direction that led to an affirmation of their specifically Algerian roots. This was clearly one of the key themes of Benjamin Stora's historical research which underlined their precarious position between European anti-Semitism and Algerian nationalism during the colonial period. Similarly, the philosopher Jacques Derrida campaigned in defence of Algerian intellectuals threatened by the bloodshed there: his solidarity was inspired by a 'Jewish–North African' identity which united Jewish Algerians like himself with their long origins in the Maghreb.[59]

Across these conflicts over memory and identity during the 1990s, one common theme was the demand for a public recognition on the part of groups most affected by the Algerian War. At the national level this pressure led to a partial retreat from the rigidities of the de Gaulle era which resulted, in June 1999, in a National Assembly vote in favour of a change of terminology. Henceforth, thirty-seven years after independence, France officially recognized the Algerian conflict to have been a full-scale war and not a 'police operation'. In the same vein, on 25 September 2001, President Chirac unveiled a plaque in the Invalides in central Paris to the *harkis* and established a national day for them: an act of recognition that, Chirac emphasized, demonstrated that they and their children were part of the national community. On the local level, responsiveness varied from place to place, depending on the nature of regional politics and its particular relationship to the Algerian issue. In Aix-en-Provence in the south, a *pied-noir* fiefdom, a square was named after the most prominent pro-French Muslim, Bachaga Boualam, and a monument erected to commemorate the French soldiers who fell in Morocco, Tunisia, and Algeria between 1952 and 1962. In Paris, the left-wing mayor, Bertrand Delanoë, inaugurated a plaque on the Saint Michel bridge to the memory of the Algerian victims of the events of 17 October 1961, forty years after the event, that was complemented by a square named in honour of Maurice Audin, one of the disappeared from the 'Battle of Algiers'.

The inscription of these Algerian memories into France's commemorative landscape raised a further question about apologies. In this respect Algeria was intertwined with the public debates over the Vichy regime and the Holocaust (which, in July 1995, led Chirac to officially acknowledge the French nation state's responsibility in the deportation of the Jews) and slavery (where a specific law, passed on 21 May 2001, recognized slavery as a 'crime against humanity'). Yet, given the polemics that still exist, it is impossible to imagine any equivalent pronouncement or law over the Algerian War. This would demand an unequivocal consensus on the rights and wrongs of the Algerian War that is still absent in official discourse. Algeria is too controversial. It continues to divide French society, although there have been some elements of public remorse from the left. In 2004 the Communist Party apologized for its support for the special powers in March 1956 which, it admitted, intensified the conflict and was a serious mistake. Then, in 2006, in an interview with the journalist Edwy Plenel, François Hollande, the Socialist Party general secretary, recognized, 'in the name of the Socialist Party', that: 'The SFIO lost its soul in the Algerian War. It had its justifications but we still owe an apology to the Algerian people. And we must make sure that it never happens again.'[60]

An unfinished war

On 14 April 1999, Abdelaziz Bouteflika was voted president of Algeria in dubious circumstances after the other six contenders withdrew in protest at electoral fraud. At sixty-two, Bouteflika was a Boumediène protégé who, in the summer of 1962, had acted as the liaison between the latter and Ben Bella, before going on to a long career as the Algerian representative at the United Nations. Given this background, as well as the fact that he was the official candidate, backed by the highest echelons of the army, Bouteflika's accession was another example of the enduring consequences of the Algerian War: the power of the military.

As president, Bouteflika immediately sought to end the cycle of violence and counter-violence. This involved a reconciliation process which aimed to transform a ceasefire with key Islamist armed groups into a permanent peace. In parallel with this strategy, Bouteflika tried to unite the country through a reappropriation of the past which legitimized his presidency and isolated Islamists. This centred upon a new public memory of the liberation struggle where the role of controversial figures, like Ferhat Abbas, Messali Hadj, Abane Ramdane, Belkacem Krim, and Mohammed Khider, was fully recognized. It included, too, a more inclusive national identity where Bouteflika spoke openly about the contribution of Jews and Christians to Algerian national culture. But, in equal measure, Bouteflika did not hang back from a continued condemnation of French colonialism. Appealing to nationalism, he talked in forthright terms about the need for an official French apology which, in effect, became one of the stumbling blocks to a long-mooted treaty of reconciliation and friendship between the two countries.

These political perspectives embroiled Bouteflika in a series of controversies that underlined the unfinished nature of the Algerian War on both sides of the Mediterranean. The first of these was his official invitation in June 1999 to Enrico Macias to come and perform in Algeria, thirty-eight years after the Jewish singer left his native Constantine—an invitation that had to be cancelled because of hostility from Islamists and FLN veterans. Then there was the polemic over the 23 February 2005 bill: the product of *pied-noir* pressure, proposed by the right-wing deputy Christian Vanneste and passed by the French National Assembly, which decreed that France's overseas civilizing mission had to be taught in schools, colleges, and universities in a positive fashion. In a speech to mark the sixtieth anniversary of the Sétif repression in May 1945, Bouteflika expressed his revulsion at the law. France, he maintained, was a country in denial about colonialism, even making an explicit link between the May 1945 anti-Algerian violence and the Holocaust.

In France the unfinished nature of the Algerian War was still clear in a myriad of ways, but in particular with a manifesto, issued in January 2005 and entitled the 'Natives of the Republic', which talked angrily about the connection between colonial racism and contemporary discrimination against French citizens of African and Caribbean descent, an argument that took on an even greater urgency with the urban riots in France in autumn 2005.[61] Concentrated in the run-down neighbourhoods where immigrants from the former colonies resided, these civil disturbances, the worst since May 1968, led commentators to reflect upon the after-effects of empire in general and Algeria in particular, not least because the government enacted 'state of emergency' laws for the first time since the Algerian War itself.

The riots of 2005 were just one example of how the legacy of the Algerian War is still being played out: an 'Algerian syndrome' that is permanently present. For instance, on 21 May 2010, 1,000 *pieds-noirs*, *harkis*, and army veteran demonstrators converged on Cannes to show their outrage at one of the contenders for the prestigious Palm d'Or award: *Outside the Law* (*Hors-la-loi*) by the French-born director Rachid Bouchareb, which traces the story of three Algerian brothers caught up in their country's struggle for independence. Organized by the National Front, the demonstrators sang the Marseillaise, waved French flags, and carried placards, including one with a graphic photograph of Europeans killed and mutilated by Algerians in May 1945. To feel the intensity of these arguments, any researcher has only to surf the World Wide Web. By typing in 'pied-noir', 'harki', 'FLN', 'natives of the Republic', 'veteran of the Algerian War', or 'Algerian government', they will enter an unfinished history, where different communities and organizations are each transmitting their own versions of the Algerian War.

This intensity of these arguments underlines how this undeclared war is permanently present in France and Algeria. In France, when one adds together the *pieds-noirs*, *harkis*, the sons and daughters of Algerian immigration, as well as the professional and conscript veterans, at least 17 million people are still directly affected by the war. In Algeria the conflict against French colonialism is the foundation stone of the nation state; yet France and French culture still moulds the country in a profound way. The length of French rule has left a deep and lasting impact whether in terms of food, most obviously the baguette, the French language, or the fact that France is still the number-one destination for Algerian emigrants. In 2010 Algeria is still the most Francophone country after France, the one whose 34 million population contains the most French speakers outside the hexagon. There is a French dimension to Algeria and an Algerian dimension to France: multiple, complex, and evolving aspects that have transformed, and will continue to transform, the histories of both countries.

At the same time, it is vital to underline the wider significance of 1954–62 beyond Algeria and France. To fully understand this significance, the Algerian War needs to be seen in a much broader historical context.[62] It has to be seen as a central episode in the global phenomenon of empire: one of the most ubiquitous forms of political organization across time and space. It has to be situated as part of the multifaceted stories of invasion, rule, accommodation, ambivalence, resistance, and breakdown that characterized not just European colonization of the non-European world during the nineteenth and twentieth centuries, but so many other forms of imperial control down the ages, from the Roman to the Ottoman Empires.

No less importantly, the Algerian War must be seen as part of the history of modern warfare. In this respect, the shape of the Algerian conflict was quite different from that of the two world wars in the first half of the twentieth century. Those wars were mammoth conflicts where the objective was military victory at all costs. The only acceptable outcome was unconditional surrender. In Algeria in 1956 the French aims were more nuanced because the military and political dimensions were inseparable. Learning the lesson of the 1954 defeat in Indochina, the intention was not to crush the enemy, but to reach out and change minds. Repression of 'FLN terrorism' was complemented by the introduction of social reform, major investment, and the promise of new political structures which, Guy Mollet hoped, would win over the Muslim majority from Algerian nationalism. 'Pacification', Mollet recognized, was a struggle fought for the people and among the people, where linguists and anthropologists were more important than tanks, where the support of the Muslim population was the strategic goal, and where the word 'war' was withheld. It was a battle for the political allegiance of Algerians in the face of pan-Arab nationalism and communism.

In contrast, anti-war campaigners such as Pierre Vidal-Naquet sought to expose Mollet's language as a lie. He wanted to show how the word 'pacification' concealed a horrific reality of torture and summary executions carried out by the French army. For Vidal-Naquet this was a full-scale war and it was this reality which isolated France on the international scene. No matter how much France claimed to be promoting democracy, reform, and Muslim empowerment, the scale of the French violence horrified international opinion, far outweighing any reservations about FLN terrorism. It revolted the Arab and Muslim worlds. It provoked the hostility of newly decolonized countries such as India. It produced dismay in the USA and Britain and, in the end, this international opinion was too strong to ignore. It made French military success meaningless, giving de Gaulle no option but to concede independence.

Ultimately, however, France lost because the Algerian nationalist sentiment was too rooted in the Algerian people. This nationalism, drawing upon deeply held grievances stemming from colonial dispossession, developed from the 1920s onwards and climaxed with the demonstrations of December 1960. Owing little to the FLN, these demonstrations articulated the desire for national independence. The FLN's strength was that its leaders instinctively understood the ideas, beliefs, and prejudices which underpinned this desire, a fact which explains why the FLN could lose militarily but triumph politically.

This outcome underlines why the Algerian War was such a paradigmatic conflict for the second half of the twentieth century. It involved a completely different mindset from that of the 'total war' mentality of the two world wars. And it was not simply about the securing of resources and strategic influence, as with classic imperialism. It was a battle for the 'people' where, in a post-1945 world, both sides appealed to the language of human rights. In this battle the FLN won because its basic aim—the right to an independent nation state—expressed Algerian aspirations in a way which the third-way solution, put forward by the French, never could.

Glossary

FRENCH WORDS

Metropole   Although Algeria was legally a sovereign part of the French nation state, a distinction was made, both in everyday conversation and at an official level, between Algeria and the French mainland which was commonly referred to as the metropole

ARABIC WORDS

Bachaga	regional leader in the Ottoman and French systems
Cha'b	people
Chahid	martyr
Harki	Muslim auxiliary who fought in the French Army
Hogra	humiliation
Jihad	effort, struggle, a legitimate war
Katiba	military company
Marabout	holy man
Nahia	region
Qadi	judge
Qaïd	local governor/tax collector
Qawmiyya	nationality
Roumi	Christian
Salafiyya	return to the practices of early Islam
Ulama (pl. ulema)	group of religious scholars
Umma	Islamic community
Watan	nation
Wilaya	administrative region; the FLN divided Algeria into six such regions

Endnotes

PRELIMS

1. Quoted in Raoul Girardet, *L'Idée colonial en France 1871–1962*, Paris: La Table Ronde, p. 183.
2. These special power laws are reproduced in Patrick Eveno and Jean Planchais (eds.), *La Guerre d'Algérie*, Paris: La Découverte, 1989, p. 96.
3. On this reform aspect of the special powers see Daniel Lefeuvre, *Chère Algérie 1930–1962*, Paris: Société Française d'Histoire d'Outre-Mer, 1997, pp. 269–79.
4. Guy Mollet, '13 April Press Conference' in *Cahier et revue de l'Office Universitaire de Recherche Socialiste*, July–August 1988, p. 13.
5. On this see Pierre Vidal-Naquet, *Torture: Cancer of Democracy*, London: Penguin, 1963; and Raphaëlle Branche, *La Torture et l'armée pendant la guerre d'Algérie 1954–1962*, Paris: Gallimard, 2001.

CHAPTER 1

1. The Barbary pirates operated out of Algeria from the sixteenth century onwards. On the place of the Barbary pirates in the European imaginary see Linda Colley, *Captives: Britain, empire and the world 1600–1850*, London: Jonathan Cape, 2002.
2. Napoleon had wished to protect French commercial shipping from Algerian pirates.
3. On population statistics for Algeria see Guy Pervillé, *Atlas de la guerre d'Algérie*, Paris: Autrement, 2003, p. 15.
4. On the complex ethnic origins of the Algerian population see Michael Brett and Elizabeth Fentress, *The Berbers*, Oxford: Blackwell, 1996; Martin Evans and John Phillips, *Algeria: Anger of the dispossessed*, London: Yale University Press, 2007; Samy Hadad, *Algérie: autopsie d'une crise*, Paris: L'Harmattan, 1989; Patricia Lorcin, *Imperial Identities: Stereotyping, prejudice and race in colonial Algeria*, London: I. B. Tauris, 1995; Gilbert Meynier, *L'Algérie des origines*, Paris: La Découverte, 2007.
5. Apart from these main areas there were also pockets speaking variants of Berber in the Atlas Mountains to the south of Blida and to the south of Tlemcen.

6. Jean Graniage, *Histoire contemporaine du Maghreb*, Paris: Fayard, p. 30.

7. On the role of Christianity in Algerian history see Gilbert Meynier, *L'Algérie des origines*.

8. On Abd el-Kader see Raphael Danzinger, *Abd el-Kader and the Algerians: Resistance to the French and internal colonisation*, New York: Africana Publishing Company, 1977; Ismail al-Arabi, *Al muqawama al jaza'iriyya that liwa' al amir Abd al Qadir*, Algiers: Société Nationale d'Édition, 1982; Bruno Étienne, *Abd el-Kader*, Paris: Hachette, 1994; and Julia Clancy-Smith, *Rebel and Saint*, California: University of California Press, 1994.

9. In fact it was through fighting Spanish irregular forces during this campaign that the Spanish word *guerrilla* entered the English and French languages.

10. In exile in Damascus Abd el-Kader was involved in protecting Christians in the 1860s.

11. They were known popularly as the 'yellow gloves' (*gants jaunes*) because of their aristocratic origins. In the case of Max de Tonnac, he learnt to speak fluent Arabic and dressed in Arab robes.

12. Bugeaud tried to recruit soldiers who had ended their military service as settlers with the promise of land concessions.

13. Friedrich Engels, 'Extraordinary revelations; Abd el-Kader; Guizot's foreign policy', *Northern Star*, XI: 535, 22 January 1848 in K. Marx and F. Engels, *Collected Works*, London: Lawrence &Wishart, VI, pp. 469–72.

14. On Tunisia see Graniage, *Histoire contemporaine du Maghreb*, p. 294. On Morocco see C. R. Pennell, *Morocco: From empire to independence*, Oneworld: Oxford, 2003, pp. 136–42.

15. Growing up in the 1930s in El-Arrouch in eastern Algeria, Mohammed Harbi remembers how his mother frightened him with stories about Bugeaud, who would come and eat him up if he did not sleep. On this see Mohammed Harbi, *Une vie debout: mémoires politiques*, Paris: La Découverte, 2001, p. 10.

16. Confronted with 4,000 Muslims, who had occupied the mosque in protest, French troops blew up the doors and forced them out, wounding several.

CHAPTER 2

1. Jules Ferry was prime minister between September 1880 and November 1881 and again between February 1883 and April 1885. In both cases he vigorously pursued colonial expansion into Africa and Asia.

2. Algeria was claimed as a territory of France in 1834 and began sending deputies in 1848 under the Second Republic. The significance of 1881, therefore, is that this is the first time Algeria is *administered* as an integral part of France.

3. On this see Kamel Kateb, *Européens, 'indigènes' et juifs en Algérie (1830–1962: Représentations et réalités des populations)*, Paris: INES, 2001, pp. 338–46.

4. European women did not have the right to vote until 1945. The overwhelming majority of Muslim men did not vote until 1945. Muslim women only voted for the first time in 1958.

5. On how the arguments for and against empire played out in French politics under the Third Republic between 1870 and 1940 see Raoul Girardet, *L'Idée coloniale en France*, Paris: La Table Ronde, 1972; Charles-Robert Ageron, *France Coloniale ou parti colonial?*, Paris: Presses Universitaires de la France, 1978; Robert Aldrich, *The Greater France: A history of French overseas expansion*, London: Macmillan, 1996.

6. On the highly specific history of Jews in Algeria see Robert Attal, *Regards sur les juifs d'Algérie*, Paris: L'Harmattan, 1996; Aïssa Chenouf, *Les Juifs d'Algérie, 2000 ans d'existence*, Algiers: El Maarifa, 1999; Benjamin Stora, *Les Trois Exils. Juifs d'Algérie*, Paris: Hachette, 2006; and Benjamin Stora, 'L'impossible neutralité des juifs d'Algérie' in Mohammed Harbi and Benjamin Stora (eds.), *La Guerre d'Algérie 1954–2004: la fin de l'amnésie*, Paris: Hachette, 2004.

7. In Arabic this was known as *dhimmi* status and also applied to Christians.

8. On the complex relationship between citizenship, race, and nationality in respect to Islam in French Algeria see Patrick Weil, *Qu'est-ce qu'un Français? Histoire de la nationalité française depuis la révolution*, Paris: Grasset, 2002.

9. 178 of these applications were turned down. On this see Charles-Robert Ageron, *Les Algériens musulmans et la France (1871–1919)*, 2 vols., Paris: Presses Universitaires de la France, 1968.

10. Within the 196 communes based upon the metropolitan model of a ruling mayor and elected municipal council only 5 per cent of the adult male Muslim population was allowed to vote until 1919 and even then the percentage of Muslim representatives could not exceed one-quarter. Within the seven mixed communes all Muslim representatives were appointed by the French administration.

11. The 1881 law codified practices in place since 1834.

12. Within the French Empire the newly conquered subjects were considered to be subjects and not citizens. Nevertheless there were anomalies. People of African descent in the French Caribbean and the original inhabitants of the 'old' colonies of Senegal (the Four Communes) were considered to be citizens and elected deputies to the National Assembly. In the last case, in contrast to Algeria, inhabitants had the rights of citizens without giving up their Islamic civil status.

13. On this see Aldrich, *The Greater France*, pp. 216–19.

14. In 1931 the European population accounted for 79 per cent of the total population of Oran, 69 per cent in Algiers, 48 per cent in Constantine, and 57 per cent in Bône.

15. On this as a Europe-wide phenomenon see Richard Vinen, *A History in Fragments: Europe in the twentieth century*, London: Little Brown, 2000.

16. On this diversity see Daniel Lefeuvre, 'Les Pieds-Noirs' in Harbi and Stora (eds.), *La Guerre d'Algérie*; and Andrea L. Smith, *Colonial and Postcolonial Europe: Maltese settlers in Algeria and France*, Bloomington: Indiana University Press, 2006.

17. Phylloxera was an insect which arrived in Europe from North America in the 1860s and ravaged vineyards throughout Southern Europe.

18. Recruitment centres were set in Belfort and Nancy through which 2,000 left in the summer of 1871. In Algeria they were given plots of land, and helped with bringing in their first harvest by the army. Their settlement was supported financially by the rich industrialist Jean Dollfus.

19. Andrea Chazot in Dominique Fargues, *Mémoire des pieds noirs*, Paris: Flammarion, 2008, p. 49.

20. *Ibid.*, p. 36.

21. *La Dépêche Algérienne*, *La Dépêche d'Algérie*, *La Dépêche Oranaise*, and *La Dépêche de Constantine et de l'Est Algérien* were all established by the eve of World War One.

22. The first season included Verdi's *Rigoletto* and *Les Huguenots*. The actress Sarah Bernhadt performed there in 1889.

23. August Robinet, *Cagayous, ses meilleurs histoires*, Paris: Gallimard, 1931.

24. Louis Bertrand, *Le Sang des races*, Paris: P. Ossendorff, 1899; and Robert Randau, *Les Algérianistes. Roman de la patrie algérienne*, Paris: Laffont, 1979 (orig. pub. 1911).

25. In 1894 Alfred Dreyfus, a young Jewish staff officer born in Alsace, was court-martialled for supposedly passing military secrets to Germany and sentenced to life imprisonment. Over the next three years the 'Dreyfus Affair' mushroomed into a huge scandal as doubts about his guilt began to surface. In January 1898 the celebrated novelist Emile Zola wrote an open letter, 'J'accuse', in which he accused the army of an anti-Semitic conspiracy that had fabricated a case against Dreyfus because he was Jewish. On this see Eric Cahm, *The Dreyfus Affair in French Society and Politics*, London: Longman, 1996; and Ruth Harris, *The Man on Devil's Island: Alfred Dreyfus and the affair that divided France*, London: Allen Lane, 2010.

26. Edouard Drumont's most infamous anti-Semitic polemic was *La France juive*, Paris: C. Marpon & E. Flammarion, 1886.

27. Félix Dessoliers, *L'Algérie libre*, Algiers: Gojosso, 1895.

28. Docteur X, *Simples réflexions d'un colon algérien*, Paris: J.-D. Maillard, 1891.

29. Jean-Pierre Peyroulou, *Guelma, 1945*, Paris: La Découverte, 2009, p. 211.

30. In Jacques Borgé and Nicolas Viasnoff (eds.), *Archives d'Algérie*, Paris: Éditions Michèle Trinckvel, p. 197.

31. Jules Roy, 'Étrange patrie' in *Le Nouvel Observateur: La guerre d'Algérie: trente ans aprés*, 1992.

32. Jean Daniel, *Le Temps qui reste*, Paris: Stock, 1973.

33. *Ibid.*, p. 84.

34. Interview with Roger Rey, Paris, 9 November 1989. Rey went on to work with the FLN in France as part of the far-left group *La Voie Communiste*. On this see Martin Evans, *Memory of Resistance: French opposition to the Algerian War 1954–1962*, Oxford: Berg, 1997, pp. 96–7.

35. Bernard Coll in Fargues, *Mémoires des Pieds Noirs*, p. 58.

36. On this crucial difference see Mohammed Harbi, 'L'Algérie en perspectives' in Harbi and Stora (eds.), *La Guerre d'Algérie*.

37. For detailed statistical information on this process see Guy Pervillé, *Atlas de la Guerre d'Algérie*, Paris: Autrement, 2003.

38. In Jacques Borgé and Nicolas Viasnoff (eds.), *Archives d'Algérie*, Paris: Éditions Michèle Trinckvel, 1995, p. 41.

39. Interview with Rabah Bitat, 12 July 1988, Algiers in Patrick Eveno and Jean Planchais (eds.), *La Guerre d'Algérie*, Paris: La Découverte, 1989, p. 38.

40. Camille Sabatier, *Les Difficultés algériennes. La question de la sécurité, insurrection, criminalité*, Algiers: Jourdain, 1882, p. 53.

41. This famine continued in Kabylia into 1939 and was covered by Albert Camus for the left-wing daily *Alger Républicain*. His articles are reproduced in Albert Camus, *Chroniques algériennes 1939–1958*, Paris: Gallimard, 1958.

42. Ali Zamoum, *Le Pays des hommes libres. Tamurt Imazighen: mémoires d'un combatant algérien*, Paris: La Pensée Sauvage, 1998, p. 53.

43. On this discrimination within the army see Abdelkader Rahmani, *L'Affaire des officiers algériens*, Paris: Seuil, 1959. Anti-North African racism within the French army during World War Two was the subject of Rachid Bouchareb's 2006 film *Indigènes* (released as *Days of Glory* in English).

44. Mohammed Harbi, *Une vie debout: mémoires politiques*, Paris: La Découverte, 2001.

45. Mohammed Harbi, *Aux origines du FLN, le populisme révolutionnaire en Algérie*, Paris: Christian Bourgois, 1975; and Mohammed Harbi, *La Guerre commence en Algérie*, Brussels: Éditions Complexe, 1984.

46. Discussion with Gilbert Meynier, London 17 June 2008.

47. On the image of the 'honourable outlaw' see Eric Hobsbawm, *Primitive Rebels*, Manchester: Manchester University Press, 1959.

48. On such stories of outlaws and other legends see Georges Robert, *Voyage à travers l'Algérie: notes et croquis: la province d'Alger, la province de Constantine, la province d'Oran, le Sahara algérien*, Paris: E. Dentu, 1891.

49. Sabatier, *Les Difficultés algériennes. La question de la sécurité, insurrection, criminalité*.

50. On this as a generalized phenomenon within peasant societies see James C. Scott, *Weapons of the Weak: Everyday forms of peasant resistance*, Yale: Yale University Press, 1985.

51. Zamoum , *Le Pays des hommes libres. Tamurt Imazighen: mémoires d'un combatant algérien*, p. 1.

52. *Ibid.*, p. 49.

53. After the expulsion of Jews and Muslims from Spain in 1492 this tradition was dispersed right across North Africa often in the form of orchestras.

54. Harbi, *Une vie debout*.

55. Centre des Archives d'Outre Mer (CAOM), Aix-en-Provence, Sous-Série Gouvernement Général de l'Algérie, 9H/7, 'Circulaire du 11 août 1880. Objet surveillance politique et administrative des indigènes. Etablissement d'un registre à feuillets mobiles'.

56. On the experience of Muslims in primary schools at the end of the nineteenth century see Benjamin Stora, *Messali Hadj*, Paris: Hachette, 2004, p. 27.

57. Mouloud Mammeri, *Entretien avec Tahar Djaout*, Algiers: Éditions Laphonic, p. 14.

58. Harbi, *Une vie debout*.

59. Other words included *lagara* (station), *biskleta* (bicycle), *lamba* (lamp).

60. On this see Gilbert Meynier, *L'Algérie révélée: la guerre de 1914–1918 et le premier quart du vingtième siècle*, Geneva: Librairie Droz, 1981; and Ahmed Koulakssis and Gilbert Meynier, *L'Émir Khaled*, Paris: L'Harmattan, 1987.

61. 'Le Manifeste jeune algérien' was discussed in the National Assembly on 2 July 1912. The full text is reproduced in Claude Collot and Jean-Robert Henry (eds.), *Le Mouvement national algérien: textes 1912–1954*, Paris: L'Harmattan, 1978, pp. 23–4.

62. Stora, *Messali Hadj*, p. 27.

63. Frederick Cooper, *Colonialism in Question: Theory, knowledge, history*, Berkeley: University of California Press, p. 176.

64. As a prisoner Louise Michel was sent to New Caledonia where she had met Muslims who had been deported there after the 1871 uprising. In befriending them she promised to visit Algeria and report on their plight.

65. Ernest Girault, *Une colonie d'enfer*, Paris: Éditions Libertaires, 2007. See also Clotilde Chauvin, *Louise Michel en Algérie*, Paris: Éditions Libertaires, 2007.

66. Léon Blum, quoted in François Lafon, *Guy Mollet*, Paris: Fayard, 2006, p. 533.

67. Lafon, *Guy Mollet*, p. 533.

68. Maurice Viollette in Jacques Marseille (ed.), *France et l'Algérie: journal d'une passion*, Paris: Larouse, 2002, p. 154. His proposals were outlined in Maurice Viollette, *L'Algérie vivra-t-elle?*, Paris: F. Alcan, 1931.

CHAPTER 3

1. Jacques Marseille (ed.), *France et l'Algérie: journal d'une passion*, Paris: Larouse, 2002, p. 163.

2. Jean Renoir's *Le Bled*, a silent comedy set in Algeria and partly financed by the French government, was released to coincide with the centenary.

3. Marseille (ed.), *France et Algérie: journal d'une passion*, p. 163.

4. On this movement within the history of Islam see Malise Ruthven, *Islam*, Oxford: Oxford University Press, 1997. On the impact of this movement in Algeria see Michael Willis, *The Islamist Challenge in Algeria*, London: Ithaca, 1996.

5. e.g. *Abou El Adjayeb, Ach Charia, Ach Chiheb, El Fourkane, En Nadjah.*

6. Gilbert Meynier describes it as a bestseller. See Gilbert Meynier, *L'Histoire intérieure du FLN, 1954–1962*, Paris: Fayard, 2002, p. 53.

7. On this see James McDougall, *History and Culture of Nationalism in Algeria*, Cambridge: Cambridge University Press, 2006.

8. Mohamed Derouiche, *Le Scoutisme, école du patriotisme*, Algiers: ENAL-OPU, 1985.

9. Charles-Robert Ageron, 'L'Algérie est ma patrie', *Les Collections de l'Histoire*, 2002.

10. 'From our Mountains (Min gibâlinâ)', Ageron, 'L'Algérie est ma patrie', p. 12.

11. Ageron, 'L'Algérie est ma patrie', p. 12.

12. Eugene Rogan, *The Arabs*, London: Allen Lane, 2009.

13. On the Muslim Brotherhood see Ruthven, *Islam*.

14. A special 'Native Affairs Unit' (Affaires Indigènes) closely monitored Algerian links with the wider Muslim world.

15. Benjamine Stora and Zaky Daoud, *Ferhat Abbas: une autre Algérie*, Paris: Denoël, 1995.

16. Ferhat Abbas, *Le Jeune Algérien*, Paris: Garnier, 1981 (orig. pub. 1931).

17. Benjamin Stora, *Messali Hadj*, Paris: Hachette, 2004, p. 31.

18. Messali Hadj, *Les Mémoires de Messali Hadj*, Paris: Jean-Claude Lattès, 1982.

19. During the same period 10,000 Moroccans and 10,000 Tunisians came to France in search of work. Conquered in 1912 and 1881 respectively, they were ruled as protectorates and did not experience the same destruction of traditional structures or expropriation of the land as in Algeria. On this see Benjamin Stora, *Ils venaient de l'Algérie: l'immigration algérienne en France, 1912–1992*, Paris: Fayard, 1992; and Neil Macmaster, *Colonial Migrants and Racism: Algerians in France, 1900–1962*, London: Macmillan, 1997.

20. This immigration wave did stir up fears amongst the Europeans. They feared that the prospect of better-paid work in France for Algerians would threaten their own supply of cheap labour back in Algeria. There were mutterings, too, that these immigrants could use the money to buy back land in Algeria.

21. On 12 September 1924 the Governor-General introduced measures to control this immigration.

22. Songs became a very important way of expressing this immigrant experience and gave rise to a rich musical tradition encapsulated in the work of Dahmane El Harrachi and Mohammed Mazouni. Many of these songs underlined the significance of Algerian solidarity in a foreign land and created a strong feeling of national identity—why Algerians were different from the French. Many of

the key songs in this repertoire were covered by Rachid Taha on Diwan 1 (2000) and Diwan 2 (2006).

23. Initially the Communist Party tried (and failed) to forge an alliance with Emir Khaled.

24. Stora, *Messali Hadj*. This political activism also included opposition to British repression in Egypt.

25. *Ibid.*, pp. 70–1.

26. The party's paper was *Ikdam*. The members were divided into fifteen sections, eight of which were in Paris.

27. The French Communist Party stopped paying Messali and did not allow him to use their meeting halls.

28. Archives de la Préfecture de Police de Paris, 'Rapport des renseignement généraux: Notes sur l'activité de l'Étoile Nord-Africaine depuis sa création jusqu'au 15 novembre 1934', 174 pages.

29. Stora, *Messali Hadj*, p. 99.

30. In Morocco Marshal Lyautey courted the Berber populations, arguing that they were different from the Arabs. The Berber Dahir (Decree) of 1930 inscribed customary law, and not the sharia, within the Berber-speaking areas.

31. This was the view of Jean Longuet, Karl Marx's grandson and SFIO member who was one of the party's specialists on the colonial question. Georges Oved, 'Jean Longuet et l'anticolonialism' in Gilles Candar (ed.), *Jean Longuet, la conscience et l'action*, Paris: Éditions de la Revue Politique et Parlementaire, 1988.

32. Marseille (ed.), *France et l'Algérie*, p. 147.

33. On this see also Charles-André Julien, *Une pensée anti-coloniale*, Paris: Sindbad, p. 58. Julien momentarily joined the French Communist Party in Algeria before rejoining the SFIO. At the time of the Sidi Bel-Abbès motion he also conducted a questionnaire amongst Communist Party members in Algeria which in 1921 demonstrated 'the predominance of a fundamentally colonial mindset, even amongst the most committed activists', *ibid.*, p. 58. See also Emmanuel Sivan, *Communisme et nationalisme en Algérie*, Paris: Presses de la Fondation Nationale des Sciences Politiques, 1976.

34. Stora, *Messali Hadj*, p. 49.

35. Marseille (ed.), *France et l'Algérie*, p. 163.

36. Picked up and translated by the French authorities. CAOM 9H/37/18, 'Le Chef de la Sûreté au Gouverneur-Général de l'Algérie', 15 March 1935.

37. Omar Carlier, *Entre nation et jihad*, Paris: Presses de la Fondation National des Sciences Politiques, pp. 53–5.

38. Two days earlier a scuffle had broken out between a Jewish soldier and a group of Muslims outside the Si Lakhdar Mosque. Despite a curfew and an appeal for calm by local Muslim political leaders, including Doctor Ben Djelloul, there was a very tense atmosphere on the borders between the Jewish and Arab *quartier* during the following days, fuelled by rumours that Ben Djelloul had been assassinated.

39. Stora, *Messali Hadj*, p. 113–14.

40. CAOM 9H/39/24, 'Le Maire de la Commune d Djidjelli à Monsieur le Sous-Préfet Bougie', 15 May 1936.

41. The intersection between sport and politics is not unique to Algeria. One only has to think of the role of cricket in Trinidad in the Caribbean during British rule. On this see C. L. R. James, *Beyond the Boundary*, London: Yellow Jersey, 2005, orig. pub. 1963.

42. CAOM 9H/39/24, 'Sociétés sportives musulmanes: Le Préfet du Département de Constantine à Monsieur le Gouverneur-Général', 24 July 1933.

43. Benjamin Stora, *Le Front populaire*, Paris: L'Harmattan. On the Popular Front in France see Julian Jackson, *The Popular Front in France*, Cambridge: Cambridge University Press, 1988.

44. On this see the work of Samuel Kalman, 'Le combat par tous les moyens: Colonial violence and the extreme right in the 1930s', *French Historical Studies* (2011), pp. 125–53.

45. *El-Ouma*, May–June 1936, p. 1.

46. The demands of 20 June 1936 were reprinted in *El-Ouma*, July–August 1936.

47. *L'Entente franco-musulmane*, 27 February 1936.

48. *Ibid.*

49. *Ach-Chihab*, April, 1936.

50. CAOM 9H/37/18, ' Le Commissaire Central de Constantine à Monsieur le Gouverneur-Général de l'Algérie', 2 June 1937.

51. Published in *El-Ouma*, July–August 1936.

52. The speech was published in *El-Ouma*, September–October 1936. It is also reproduced in Claude Collot and Jean-Robert Henry (eds.), *Le Mouvement national algérien: textes 1912–1954*, Paris: L'Harmattan, 1978, pp. 82–5.

53. *Ibid.*, p. 84.

54. *Ibid.*

55. Messali Hadj, *Les Mémoires*, pp. 223–4.

56. By autumn 1936 the party had 7,000 members.

57. *El-Ouma*, 29 January 1937. Stora, *Messali Hadj*, p. 158.

58. This atmosphere is superbly described by Mohammed Dib in his novel *L'Incendie*, Paris: Seuil, 1954.

59. The Paris Mosque was built in recognition of the sacrifice of Muslim troops in World War One.

60. Only on two occasions did the reports note the presence of Europeans—in Bône 10 out of an audience of 650 and in Perrégaux 50 out of 300.

61. CAOM 9H/37/18, 'Le Chef de la Sûreté Départementale de Constantine au Directeur de la Sécurité Générale de l'Algérie', 5 February 1938.

62. CAOM 9H/37/18, 'Le Commissaire de la Sûreté de Bône au Directeur de la Sécurité Générale de l'Algérie', 24 January 1938.

63. CAOM 9H/37/18, 'Le Commissaire de Police de Relizane à Monsieur le Préfet d'Oran', 26 February 1938.

64. CAOM 9H/37/18, 'Le Maire de la Commune d'Inkerman à Monsieur le Préfet d'Oran', 2 April 1937.

65. CAOM 9H/37/18, 'Bulletin de renseignements des questions musulmanes', 15 November 1937. This report underlined that the authorities must control what films Muslims are exposed to. It warned that scenes that ridicule authority, particularly military authority, will have a detrimental influence on Muslims.

66. CAOM 9H/37/18, 'Le Commissaire de Police à Monsieur Préfet du Département d'Alger', 28 February 1938.

67. Key extracts of the speech can be found in Benyoucef Ben Khedda, *Les Origines du premier novembre 1954*, Algiers: Éditions Dahlab, 1989, p. 292.

68. Jacques Cantier, *L'Algérie sous le régime de Vichy*, Paris: Odile Jacob, 2002.

69. Annie Rey-Goldzeiguer, *Aux origines de la guerre d'Algérie, 1940–1945, de Mers el-Kébir aux massacres du Nord-Constantinois*, Paris: La Découverte, 2002.

70. Hélène Cixous, 'Celle qui ne se ferme pas' in Sofiane Hadjadj (ed.), *Derrida à Alger*, Paris: Actes Sud, p. 48.

71. Benjamin Stora, *Les Trois Exils. Juifs d'Algérie*, Paris: Hachette, 2006, pp. 124–5.

72. Hocine Aït Ahmed, *Mémoires d'un combatant*, Algiers: Barzah, 2009, p. 24.

73. Marvine Howe, *Morocco: The Islamist awakening and other challenges*, New York: Oxford University Press, 2005, p. 70.

74. These words were noted down by the President's son, Elliot Roosevelt, who was present at the meeting. Elliot Roosevelt, *As He Saw It*, New York: Duell, Sloan and Pearce, 1946, pp. 109–12.

75. 'Le Manifeste du Peuple Algérien' in Collot and Henry (eds.), *Le Mouvement national algérien*, pp. 155–165.

76. 'Statuts de l'Association des Amis du Manifeste et de la Liberté' in Collot and Henry (eds.), *Le Mouvement national algérien*, pp. 186–7.

77. Ferhat Abbas, *J'Accuse l'Europe*, Algiers: Les Amis du Manifeste et de la Liberté, 1944.

78. Abbas, *J'Accuse l'Europe*, p. 10.

79. Hocine Aït Ahmed, *Mémoires d'un Combatant*, p. 29.

80. CAOM 9H/31/36, 'Commissaire de Police de Biskra à Monsieur le Préfet de Constantine', 16 May 1944.

81. This dimension was underlined to me by Henri Alleg who was an Algerian Communist Party member at the time. Interview with Henri Alleg, 24 November 2010, Paris.

82. CAOM 9H/31/36, 'Objet: Nationalism à Biskra. Source: Commissaire de Police de Biskra', 14 May 1944.

83. CAOM 9H/31/36, 'Le Commissaire Lalande Jean, chef de la Circonscription de Police de Biskra à Monsieur le Préfet de Constantine', 11 April 1944.

84. 'Le Rapport du Général Paul Tubert' in Marcel Reggui, *Les Massacres de Guelma*, Paris: La Découverte, pp. 142–3. This was an official government report into the causes of the violence of May 1945 in Algeria.

85. Foreign Office Archive, J. E. M. Carvell, 'Letter to the Foreign Office', 9 February 1945.
86. Foreign Office Archive, J. E. M. Carvell, 'Letter to the Foreign Office', 11 May 1945.
87. *Ibid.*
88. *Ibid.*
89. *Ibid.*

CHAPTER 4

1. Annie Rey-Goldzeiguer, *Aux origines de la guerre d'Algérie, 1940–1945, de Mers el-Kébir aux massacres du Nord-Constantinois*, Paris: La Découverte, 2002, p. 278. See also Jean-Louis Planche, *Sétif 1945*, Paris: Perrin, 2006.
2. Redouane Ainab Tabet, *8 Mai 45 en Algérie*, Algiers: Office des Publications Universitaires Entreprise Algérienne, 1985, p. 204.
3. Foreign Office Archives, J. E. M. Carvell, 1945.
4. *Ibid.*
5. Tabet, *8 Mai 45 en Algérie*, p. 204.
6. Gilbert Meynier, *L'Histoire intérieure du FLN, 1954–1962*, Paris: Fayard, 2002, p. 67.
7. Abelkader Rahmani, *L'Affaire des Officiers Algériens*, Paris: Seuil, 1959, p. 24.
8. Jean-Pierre Peyroulou, *Guelma, 1945*, Paris: La Découverte, 2009.
9. Meynier, *L'Histoire intérieure du FLN*, p. 66.
10. Overall there were 5,560 arrests, of which two-thirds were in the Constantinois department. Of those 1,307 would receive prison sentences and 20 would be condemned to capital punishment.
11. Foreign Office Archives, J. E. M. Cavell, 'Letter to the Foreign Office', 12 June 1945.
12. CAOM 9H44/27 and 9H51/42. These boxes, relating to the violence in Sétif and Guelma and the surveillance of Algerians nationalism, contain a number of opened letters from Europeans and Algerians which describe this tension.
13. Mohammed Harbi, *Une vie debout: mémoires politiques*, Paris: La Découverte, 2001, p. 47.
14. Born in Guelma in 1905 his family was Tunisian in origin. Reggui's person inquest would not be published until 2006: Marcel Reggui, *Les Massacres de Guelma*, Paris: La Découverte, 2006.
15. The full text of the Tubert Report is reproduced *ibid.*
16. The Tubert Report was in many ways very candid about the roots of the violence. Reggui did try to alert the SFIO to the contents of his manuscript but was ignored.
17. Jean-Pierre Peyroulou, *Guelma, 1945*, p. 198.
18. Rey, *Aux Origines de la Guerre d'Algérie*, p. 333.

19. Foreign Office Archives, J. E. M. Cavell, 'Letter to the Foreign Office', 12 June 1945.

20. Jean-Pierre Peyroulou, *Guelma, 1945*, p. 192.

21. On this see *L'Humanité*, 25 May 1945.

22. Friction between Britain and France was evident in Lebanon and Syria at this point since Britain was demanding that both countries, French possessions, be brought up under British military authority. De Gaulle initially thought that there was a link between Syria and Algeria. In an interview with *The Times* in September 1945, de Gaulle sought to repair the rift, emphasizing common imperial interests.

23. During 1946, the British Consulate in Algiers received 20,000 applications from Europeans who were looking to leave for the British Empire; in particular they were seeking passage to Australia. Tabet, *8 Mai 45 en Algérie*, p. 144.

24. Lefeuvre, 'Les Pieds-Noirs' in Mohammed Harbi and Benjamin Stora (eds.), *La Guerre d'Algérie 1954–2004: la fin de l'amnésie*, Paris: Hachette, 2004.

25. Albert Camus, *Chroniques algériennes 1939–1958*, Paris: Gallimard, 1958.

26. Camus's writings were part of a new intellectual current that emerged during the mid-1930s: the École d'Alger. This trend, also apparent in the writings of Gabriel Audisio, talked about a common Mediterranean culture which broke away from traditional European perspectives and called for harmony and not domination of the 'native' population.

27. Camus, *Chroniques algériennes 1939–1958*, pp. 93–122.

28. *Ibid.*

29. *Ibid.*

30. André Mandouze, *Mémoires d'outre siècle: d'une résistance à l'autre*, Paris: Vivianne Hamy, 1998. See also Martin Evans, *Memory of Resistance: French opposition to the Algerian War*, Oxford: Berg, 1997.

31. In 1946 he introduced measures aimed at those Algerian peasants in financial difficulty. He also sought to improve Algerian living and working conditions by widening their access to education and sanitation.

32. Interview with Zina Haraigue, Algiers, 14 October 1989. See also Danièle Djamila Amrane-Minne, *Des femmes dans la guerre d'Algérie*, Paris: Karthala, 1994, pp. 165–6.

33. Jean-Pierre Peyroulou, *Guelma, 1945*, p. 242.

34. CAOM 9H51/42, 'L'Autre Musulman', 23 February 1946.

35. For a comprehensive analysis of the origins and politics see Malika Rahal, *L'Union Démocratique du Manifeste Algérien (1946–1956)*, Paris: L'Institut National des Langues et Civilisations Orientales, Thesis, 2007.

36. 'Face au crime colonial et à la forfeiture de l'administration. Appel à la jeunesse algérienne française et musulmane', 1 May 1946 in Claude Collot and Jean-Robert Henry (eds.), *Le Mouvement national algérien: textes 1912–1954*, Paris: L'Harmattan, 1978, pp. 219–23.

37. *Ibid.*, p. 222.

38. *Ibid.*

39. e.g. Abbas put forward his arguments for the creation of an Algerian state in the left-wing newspaper *Combat* on 26 June 1946 in an article entitled: 'Les Nouveaux Élus musulmans nord-africains demandent la creation d'un état algérien'. The article is reproduced in Collot and Henry (eds.), *Le Mouvement national algérien*, pp. 224–7.

40. 'Appel du troisième congrès du parti communiste algérien. Union pour la démocratie, gage du bien-être de toutes les populations algériennes', 24 March 1946, in Collot and Henry (eds.), *Le Mouvement national algérien*, pp. 215–19.

41. Boualem Khalfa, Henri Alleg, and Abdelhamid Benzine, *La Grande Aventure d'Alger républicain*, Algiers, Libraire El-Ijtihad, p. 130.

42. Mohammed Harbi, *Le FLN. Mirage et réalité*, Paris: Jeune Afrique, 1980, pp. 35–7.

43. *Ibid.*, p. 36.

44. On this see Martin Shipway, *Decolonization and its Impact*, Oxford: Blackwell, 2008, pp. 88–90.

45. Martin Shipway, *The Road to War: France and Vietnam, 1944–1947*, Oxford & Providence, RI: Berghahn, 1996, pp. 60–1.

46. Commission de la Constitution: Comptes Rendus Analytiques de l'Assemblée Constituante Élue le 21 octobre 1945, Paris: Imprimerie de l'Assemblée Constituante, 1946, Marius Moutet, pp. 258–9.

47. Commission de la Constitution: Comptes Rendus Analytiques de l'Assemblée Constituante Élue le 2 juin 1946, Paris: Imprimerie de l'Assemblée Constituante, 1946.

48. *Ibid.*, Ferhat Abbas, p. 578.

49. *Ibid.*, pp. 784–93.

50. 'Projet de Statut de l'Algérie propose par le conseil federal d'Oran', 9 March 1947, Guy Mollet Archive, OURS A2, Correspondances avec les Fédérations, Correspondances avec la Fédération d'Oran 1944–7. See also Claire Marynower, *Joseph Begarra. Un socialiste oranais dans la guerre d'Algérie*, Paris: L'Harmattan, 2008.

51. This blueprint is reproduced in Collot and Henry (eds.), *Le Mouvement national algérien*, pp. 236–47.

52. The full text of the UDMA proposal can be found *ibid.*, pp. 247–60.

53. Léon Blum, 'L'Algérie' in *L'Oeuvre de Léon Blum 1947–1950*, Paris: Albin Michel, 1963, p. 408.

54. CAOM 9H/51/42. These files contain regular reports to the authorities on nationalist graffiti and the defacing of French posters.

55. CAOM 9CAB 64/65 Fonds du Gouverneur-Général de l'Algérie, Marcel-Edmond Naegelen Cabinet Civil 9CAB 64/65.

56. Harbi, *Une vie debout*. This evidence was backed up in an oral interview with Mohammed Harbi, Paris, 22 May 2008.

57. CAOM 9CAB 64/65 Fonds du Gouverneur-Général de l'Algérie, Marcel-Edmond Naegelen Cabinet Civil 9CAB 64/65.

58. Marcel-Edmond Naegelen, *Mission en Algérie*, Paris: Flammarion, 1962, p. 65.

59. Ferhat Abbas, 'Un huit mai electoral', *La République Algérienne*, 23 April 1948, p. 1. 'Tout le peuple algérien doit lutter contre la repression coloniale', *La République Algérienne*, 23 April 1948, p. 1.

60. Interview with Mohammed Harbi, Paris, 22 May 2008.

61. Harbi, *Le FLN. Mirage et réalité*, p. 44.

62. Meynier, *L'Histoire intérieure du FLN*, p. 83.

63. On developments in West Africa see Tony Chafer, *The End of Empire in French West Africa*, Oxford: Berg, 2002.

64. Naegelen, *Mission en Algérie*, pp. 122–41.

65. *Ibid.*, p. 89.

66. *Ibid.*, p. 157.

67. Meynier, *L'Histoire intérieure du FLN*, pp. 94–6. They were taking issue with a report that had been submitted by Messali to the United Nations in 1948 and claimed that the history of Algeria began with the arrival of Islam.

68. Harbi, *Le FLN. Mirage et réalité*, p. 66.

69. Abdelkader Ougouag, *Les Grands Procès*, Algiers: Dahlad, 1989.

70. Roger Léonard, *Quatre ans en Algérie*, Algiers: Imprimerie officielle du gouvernement générale, Paris, 1955, pp. 84–5.

71. Mohammed Dib, *La Grande Maison*, Paris: Seuil, 1952; *L'Incendie*, Paris: Seuil, 1954; *Le Métier à tisser*, Paris: Seuil, 1957; Mouloud Feraoun, *La Terre et le sang*, Paris: Seuil, 1953; Kateb Yacine, *Nedjma*, Paris: Seuil, 1956.

72. Meynier, *L'Histoire intérieure du FLN*, p. 72.

CHAPTER 5

1. Jean Servier, *Dans L'Aurès sur les pas des rebelles*, Paris: Éditions France-Empire, 1955. Guy Monnerot's wife survived.

2. For a full geographical survey of all the FLN attacks see Mohammed Harbi, *La Guerre commence en Algérie*, Brussels: Éditions Complexe, 1984, pp. 19–25.

3. About 1,000 copies were printed by roneo in the village of Ighil Imoula in Kabylia. On this see Ali Zamoum, *Le Pays des hommes libres. Tamurt Imazighen: mémoires d'un combatant algérien*, Paris: La Pensée Sauvage, 1998, pp. 36–7.

4. In Mohammed Harbi, *Les Archives de la révolution algérienne*, Paris: Jeune Afrique, 1981, pp. 101–3.

5. On this see Martin Evans and John Phillips, *Algeria: Anger of the dispossessed*, London: Yale University Press, 2007, pp. 5–6.

6. Servier, *Dans L'Aurès sur les pas des rebelles*, p. 18.

7. Gilbert Meynier, *L'Histoire intérieure du FLN, 1954–1962*, Paris: Fayard, 2002, pp. 275–8.

8. Mohammed Harbi, *Le FLN. Mirage et réalité*, Paris: Jeune Afrique, 1980, pp. 96–8.

9. *Ibid.*, p. 100.

10. The centralists created a new party which explicitly excluded Messali.

11. They were headed by the lawyer Abderrahmane Kiouane who voted in favour of Chevallier's budget—a first.

12. The Comité Révolutionnaire pour l'Unité et d'Action (CRUA) was founded at the end of March 1954. Retrospectively the French authorities would draw a straight line from CRUA to the FLN. This was wrong. The CRUA was an attempt by the centralists to ally themselves with disgruntled OS members to outmanoeuvre the Messalists. The centralists were not opposed to armed action but feared that such armed action would be suicidal. The CRUA met in Berne in Switzerland, under cover of the 1954 World Cup, and Cairo, but it led to no common platform. On this see Harbi, *FLN. Mirage et réalité*, pp. 119–20.

13. Ben Bella had escaped from prison in 1952; Aït Ahmed had been accused of Berberist sympathies by Messali in the fallout of the 1949 crisis; while Khider had been a MTLD deputy in the French National Assembly.

14. Ben Boulaïd was a miller; Krim the son of a hawker who had became a *qaïd*; and Didouche was the son of a café owner.

15. Meynier, *L'Histoire intérieure du FLN*, p. 131.

16. Rabah Bitat, 'Rabah Bitat: la creation du FLN et l'insurrection de 1954' in Patrick Eveno and Jean Planchais (eds.), *La Guerre d'Algérie*, Paris: La Découverte, 1989, pp. 86–9.

17. Zamoum, *Le Pays des hommes libres*, pp. 135–6.

18. This point was underlined by a Mohammed Harbi interview, Paris May 2008.

19. The phrase is James C. Scott's. On this see his classic *Weapons of the Weak: Everyday forms of peasant resistance*, New Haven: Yale University Press, 1985, pp. 28–47.

20. Roger Léonard, *Quatre ans en Algerie*, pp. 133–4.

21. Mohammed Harbi, *La Guerre commence en Algérie*, Brussels: Éditions Complexe, 1984, pp. 25–7.

22. Mohammed Harbi, *Une vie debout: mémoires politiques*, Paris: La Découverte, 2001.

23. 'Déclaration du Bureau Politique du PCF', *L'Humanité*, 9 November 1954. On this see Danièle Joly, *The French Communist Party and the Algerian War*, London: Macmillan, 1991.

24. Only the Trotskyist left supported the concept of Algerian independence. Harbi, *La Guerre commence en Algérie*, p. 29.

25. *Journal Officiel de la République Française*, 1954, p. 4961.

26. *Journal Officiel de la République Française*, 1954, p. 4968.

27. Harbi, *La Guerre commence en Algérie*, p. 46.

28. *Ibid.*, pp. 38–45.

29. Sylvie Thénault, *Histoire de la guerre d'indépendance algérienne*, Paris: Flammarion, 2005, p. 46.
30. Natalya Vince, 'To be a Moudjahida in independent Algeria: Itineraries and memories of women veterans of the Algerian War', University of London: PhD, pp. 33–4. I am grateful to Dr Natalya Vince in underlining this point to me.
31. *Ibid.*, p. 34.
32. 'Règlement intérieur de la wilaya 4', Les Archives du Services Historique de l'Armée de Terre (SHAT), Vincennes, 1H1095–1.
33. Evans and Phillips, *Algeria: Anger of the dispossessed*, pp. 11–25.
34. Adherence to this religious discipline varied according to each wilaya. Wilaya 3 was the most rigorous. There women wishing to join the maquis were tested for their virginity.
35. For a detailed sociological profile of the ALN see Meynier, *L'Histoire intérieure du FLN*, pp. 138–57.
36. These accounts were published on 21–3 January 1955. They were reproduced as André Leveuf , 'La révolte kabyle' in Eveno and Planchais (eds.), *La Guerre d'Algérie*, pp. 77–82. Leveuf was subsequently killed while reporting in Morocco on 20 August 1955.
37. *Ibid.*, pp. 78–9.
38. Ramdane Abbane, 'Tract diffuse par le FLN', June 1955 in Mohammed Harbi and Gilbert Meynier (eds.), *Le FLN: Documents et histoire 1954–1962*, Paris: Fayard, 2004, pp. 219–20.
39. Mabrouk Belhocine, *Le Courier Alger-Le Caire, 1954–1956*, Algiers: Casbah Éditions, p. 150.
40. *Ibid.*, pp. 108–9.
41. Marcel-Edmond Naegelen, *Le Populaire*, 13 December 1954, p. 1.
42. François Mayle and Benjamin Stora, *François Mitterrand et la guerre d'Algérie*, Paris: Calmann-Lévy, 2010, pp. 74–80.
43. For a summary of these debates see Alexander Werth, *The Strange History of Pierre Mendès France and the Great Conflict over French North Africa*, London: Barrie Books, pp. 168–77.
44. Jacques Soustelle, 'Jacques Soustelle: l'échec de la cohabitation' in Eveno and Planchais (eds.), *La Guerre d'Algérie*, pp. 103–6.
45. Jacques Soustelle, *Aimée et souffrante Algérie*, Paris: Plon, 1956.
46. CAOM, 11CAB 14 Soustelle, 'Télégramme aux préfets', 15 December 1955.
47. Soustelle, *Aimée et souffrante Algérie*.
48. Soustelle, 'Jacques Soustelle: l'échec de la cohabitation', p. 105.
49. Nancy Wood, *Germaine Tillion, une femme mémoire*, Paris: Autrement, 2003.
50. Sylvie Thénault, *Une drôle de justice: les magistrats dans la guerre d'Algérie*, Paris: La Découverte, 2001.
51. 'L'instruction ministérielle française du 1 juillet 1955', SHAT 1H1944.
52. These letters to Soustelle are contained in CAOM, 11CAB 14 Soustelle.
53. Dominique Fargues, *Mémoire des pieds noirs*, Paris: Flammarion, 2008, pp. 95–6.

54. Claude Bourdet, 'Votre Gestapo d'Algérie', *France-Observateur*, 13 January 1955; and François Mauriac, 'La question', *L'Express*, 15 January 1955.

55. This conference was covered by the American left-wing activist Richard Wright who published his insights on the conference in *The Colour Curtain: A report on the Bandung Conference*, London: Dobson, 1956.

56. Ali Kafi, *Du militant politique au dirigeant militaire. Mémoire 1946–1962*, Algiers: Casbah Éditions, 2002, pp. 58–69.

57. Meynier, *L'Histoire intérieure du FLN*, p. 280.

58. Paul Aussaresses, *Services spéciaux, Algérie, 1955–1957*, Paris: Perrin, 2001.

59. Meynier, *L'Histoire intérieure du FLN*, p. 281.

60. Union Française Nord-Africaine, *Le Martyr de l'Algérie française: le massacre d'El-Alia 20 août 1955*, Algiers: Prestiger Français, 1955.

61. *Ibid.*, p. 1.

62. Meynier, *L'Histoire intérieure du FLN*, p. 179.

63. 'La motion des 61' in Harbi and Meynier (eds.), *Le FLN: Documents et histoire 1954–1962*, pp. 220–1.

64. Robert Barrat, 'Un journaliste chez les hors-la-loi Algériens', *France-Observateur*, 15 September 1955 in Robert Barrat, *Les Maquis de la Liberté*, Paris: Témoignage Chrétien, 1987.

65. *Ibid.*, p. 76.

66. *Ibid.*, p. 3.

67. *Ibid.*, p. 72.

68. *Ibid.*, p. 183.

69. CAOM, 11CAB 14 Soustelle, 'Discours à l'Assemblé Algérienne', 21 November 1955.

70. Werth, *The Strange History of Pierre Mendès France and the Great Conflict over French North Africa*, p. 254.

71. Guy Mollet, 'Numéro un: l'Algérie', *L'Express*, 19 December 1955, p. 3. On this see also Denis Lefebvre, *Guy Mollet*, Paris: Plon, 1992, p. 172.

72. Mollet, l'Office Universitaire de Recherche Socialiste, AGM 118 Elections Législatives 1956. At the meeting of the SFIO's Comité Directeur on 15 June 1955 Mollet stated: 'We must find a political solution to the problem.' At the SFIO's 47th Annual Conference from 30 June to 5 July 1955 Mollet supported a strategy based upon a proper application of the 1947 Statute, the dissolution of the Algerian Assembly, and fresh elections to find proper democratic representatives to negotiate with. Within the final Conference resolution on the crisis in the French Union, the Socialist Party identified the key roots of this crisis to be racism, the use of force that contravened the Geneva Conventions of 1950 on the protection of the civilian population, the under-representation of 'natives' in the running of their own affairs, and misery and unemployment. 'Débats internes sur l'Outre-Mer', *Cahier et revue de l'Office Universitaire de Recherche Socialiste*, May/June 1988, pp. 36–8.

73. 'La constitution du gouvernement', *Cahier et revue de l'Office Universitaire de Recherche Socialiste*, July/August 1988, p. 1. These are a summary of the debates within the *Comité Directeur du Parti Socialiste*.

74. *Ibid.*, p. 1.

75. *Ibid.*, p. 2.

76. Mollet, *ibid.*, p. 2. The controversy over why Mollet became prime minister rather than Mendès continued throughout February. At a meeting of the ruling committee of the SFIO on 22 February Mollet claimed that Mendès told him in January: 'It is you who must become prime minister because if it was me, I would have the votes of the Communist Party, those of the Republican Front, and not one more. Now, to carry through the necessary policy, that is not possible with a support limited to the Popular Front.' 'La constitution du gouvernement', *Cahier et revue de l'Office Universitaire de Recherche Socialiste*, July/August 1988, p. 3.

77. Initially linked with the Communist Party, Rassemblement Démocratique Africain had split with the PCF in 1951 and aligned itself with the UDSR.

78. Guy Mollet, 'Declaration d'investiture', 31 January 1956 in 'La constitution du gouvernement', *Cahier et revue de l'Office Universitaire de Recherche Socialiste*, July/August 1988.

79. *Ibid.*, p. 4.

80. Importantly key members of the government, notably Pineau and Gazier, advised him against going, saying that the government needed to wait and to take stock of the situation. Christian Pineau, 'La question algérienne', *Cahiers de l'Office Universitaire de Recherche Socialiste*, May/June 1986.

CHAPTER 6

1. Mohammed Harbi and Gilbert Meynier (eds.), *Le FLN: Documents et histoire 1954–1962*, Paris: Fayard, 2004, p. 222–4.

2. Jo Ortiz, *Mon combat pour l'Algérie française*, Paris: Éditions Jean Curutchet, 1998, p. 17.

3. Jean-Baptiste Biaggi, 'Le six février d'Alger' in Philippe Héduy (ed.), *Algerie Française 1954–1962*, Paris: Société de Production Littéraire, 1980, p. 168.

4. Albert Camus, 'Appel pour une trêve civile en Algérie' in *Chroniques Algériennes*, Paris: Gallimard, 1958.

5. Biaggi, 'Le six février d'Alger', p. 169.

6. *La Documentation socialiste: bulletin hebdomadaire de la SFIO—la situation en Algérie*, 26 February 1956, p. 215.

7. Biaggi, 'Le six février d'Alger', p. 169. European tracts had been circulating for some weeks talking of using tomatoes as a weapon to teach Parisian politicians a lesson.

8. François Lafon, *Guy Mollet*, Paris: Fayard, 2006, pp. 512–13; and Denis Lefebvre, *Guy Mollet*, Paris: Plon, 1992, p. 185–6. Joseph Begarra, 'Guy Mollet et l'Algérie' in Augustin Laurent (ed.), *Témoignages: Guy Mollet 1905–1975*, Arras: Fondation Guy Mollet, 1977.

9. *La Documentation socialiste: bulletin hebdomadaire de la SFIO—la situation en Algérie*, 26 February 1956, p. 218.

10. *Ibid.*

11. *Ibid.*, p. 221.

12. Alain de Sérigny, 'Un passé à rappeler', *Écho d'Alger,* 8 February 1956, p. 1.

13. *Ibid.*

14. *Cahier et revue de l'Office Universitaire de Recherche Socialiste*, July/August 1988, p. 12.

15. *Ibid.*

16. *Ibid.*, pp. 12–13.

17. Interview with Mohammed Harbi, 22 May 2008, Paris.

18. Mouloud Feraoun, *Journal 1955–1962*, Nebraska: University of Nebraska Press, 2000, 69–74.

19. *Ibid.*, p. 73.

20. Gilbert Meynier, *L'Histoire intérieure du FLN, 1954–1962*, Paris: Fayard, 2002, p. 179.

21. Edward Behr, *The Algerian Problem*, London: Hodder & Stoughton, 1961, p. 93.

22. Martin Evans, *Memory of Resistance: French opposition to the Algerian War*, Oxford: Berg, 1997, p. 107.

23. Guy Mollet, 'Déclaration du 10 Février à l'Assemblée Nationale', *La documentation socialiste: bulletin hebdomadaire de la SFIO—la situation en Algérie*, 26 February 1956, p. 221.

24. *Ibid.*, p. 225.

25. Interview with Mohammed Harbi, 22 May 2008, Paris.

26. For example the information pamphlet *L'Algérie?* produced by the Service de l'Information du Gouvernement Générale de l'Algérie.

27. This immigration was seen to be a unique bond by the Mollet government. Without it Algeria, the government argued, would not be able to survive.

28. Albert Gazier, *Albert Gazier (1908–1997). Autour d'une vie de militant*, Paris: L'Harmattan, 2006.

29. 'Discours de Robert Lacoste à la séance de l'assemblée algérienne', 21 February 1956, Guy Mollet Archive, OURS, Guy Mollet AGM 81. See also Daniel Lefeuvre, *Chère Algérie*, Paris: Sociétée Française d'Histoire d'Outre-Mer, 1997, pp. 269–9.

30. *Algérie?*, Service de l'Information du Gouvernement Générale de l'Algérie, 1956, p. 8.

31. Marcel Champeix, 'Réorganisation territorial de l'Algérie', 21 June 1956; and 'Prise de position sur le problème Algérien', 10 September 1956, Guy Mollet Archive, OURS, Marcel Champeix 6APO4.

32. Marcel Champeix, 'Discours au conseil général d'Oran', 4 May 1956, Guy Mollet Archive, OURS, Marcel Champeix 6APO2.

33. Tony Chafer, *The End of Empire in French West Africa*, Oxford: Berg, 2002.

34. Foreign Office 80–0/734, 'Record of Meeting held at Chequers', Sunday, 11 March 1956.

35. Foreign Office 371/124431, 'From Jebb (Paris)', 27 March 1956. WF 1022/35. Nasser's *Philosophy of the Revolution* was translated into French and widely discussed in the French media.

36. 'Parodi à Pineau', 7 March 1956, T.50077, Archives diplomatiques françaises (ADF).

37. Meeting of the Council held at the Palais de Chaillot, 5 May 1956, NATO C-R (56)23, p. 6.

38. Avi Shlaim, *The Iron Wall: Israel and the Arab world*, London: Allen Lane, 2000.

39. *Ibid.*, pp. 164–5.

40. On 1940 as an event in French and world history see Julian Jackson, *The Fall of France*, Oxford: Oxford University Press, 2003.

41. Jean-Marc Binot, *Max Lejeune*, Amiens: Martelle Éditions, II, pp. 26–8.

42. Max Lejeune, *Le Populaire*, 15 March 1956, p. 1.

43. Claude Bourdet, *France-Observateur*, 29 March 1956.

44. Henri Marrou, 'France, ma patrie . . . ', *Le Monde*, 5 April 1956.

45. Patrick Rotman and Bertrand Tavernier, *La Guerre sans nom*, Paris: Seuil, 1992, p. 43.

46. Evans, *Memory of Resistance*, p. 106. Jean-Luc Einaudi, *Franc-Tireur: Georges Mattéi de la guerre d'Algérie à la guérilla*, Paris: Éditions du Sextant, 2004, p. 25.

47. Interview with Jean Masson, Lyon, 22 October 2008.

48. These telegrams are contained in the Guy Mollet Archive, OURS, Guy Mollet AGM88.

49. 'Y-a-t-il des maquis des disponibles insoumis?', 18 May 1956, Guy Mollet Archive, OURS, Guy Mollet AGM 88. Annie Martin, 'La rumeur en Limousin: Le maquis des rappels' in Sylvie Thénault and Raphaëlle Branche (eds.), *La France en guerre 1954–1962*, Paris: Autrement, 2008, p. 35. Martin identifies the authors of the tract as being anarchists within the Fédération Communiste Libertaire led within the Limousin area by Georges Fontenis. On this see Georges Fontenis, *Changer le monde, histoire du mouvement communiste-libertaire 1945–1997*, Paris: Le Coquelicot/Alternative libertaire, 2000. Martin also underlines the importance of the memory of the World War Two maquis which was particularly strong in this area.

50. 'Télégramme arrive. Préfecture Isère à Ministère Intérieur Cabinet', 18 May 1956 and 'Message téléphone. Renseignements généraux Grenoble. Manifestation contre le depart des disponibles', 19 May 1956, Guy Mollet Archive, OURS, Guy Mollet AGM88.

51. Rotman and Tavernier, *La Guerre sans nom*, pp. 39–40.

52. Jean-Charles Jauffret, 'Le movement des rappelés en 1955–1956' in Mohammed Harbi and Benjamin Stora (eds.), *La Guerre d'Algérie 1954–2004: la fin de l'amnésie*, Paris: Robert Laffont, 2004.

53. Hervé Hamon and Patrick Rotman, *Les porteurs de valises: la résistance française à la guerre d'Algérie*, Paris: Albin Michel, 1979, pp. 48–9.

54. 'Y-a-t-il des maquis des disponibles insoumis?', 18 May 1956, p. 2.

55. Hamon and Rotman, *Les porteurs de valises*, p. 67.

56. Evans, *Memory of Resistance*, pp. 128–9.

57. *La Lettre d'Algérie* was an anonymous pamphlet sent from Algiers to Mollet during 1956 which informed him of this insurrectionary mood amongst arriving reservists on 7 May 1956 in Algiers.

58. Jean-Yves Alquier, Robert Barberot, Raoul Girardet, Michel Massenet, and Thierry Maulnier, *Ceux d'Algérie: lettres de rappelés*, Paris: Plon, 1957, p. 5.

59. Rotman and Tavernier, *La Guerre sans nom*, pp. 44–5.

60. Raphaëlle Branche, *L'embuscade de Palestro*, Paris: Amand Colin, 2010, p. 70.

61. *Ibid.*, pp. 78–9.

62. *Ibid.*, p. 61.

63. In 1956 the newspaper *Écho d'Alger* organized trips for wives to meet their husbands doing military service in Algeria.

64. Although not the other Radical Party ministers who remained in the government.

65. Patrick Eveno and Jean Planchais (eds.), *La Guerre d'Algérie*, Paris: La Découverte, 1989, p. 102. Mendès France had wanted to go earlier but did not want to appear disloyal to reservists whose call-up he supported.

66. Binot, *Max Lejeune*, II, p. 20.

67. For example the cover of 16 June *Paris Match* had a full-colour photograph of French troops in action with the title 'De nos envoyés spéciaux en Algérie: OFFENSIVE "ESPÉRANCE"'.

68. On this see Serge Kastell, *Le Maquis Rouge: L'aspirant Maillot et la guerre d'Algérie 1956*, Paris: L'Harmattan, 1997.

69. Jean-Charles Jauffret, *Soldats en Algérie 1954–1962*, Paris: Autrement, 2000, p. 56.

70. Interview with Robert Bonnaud, 4 April 1989, Paris.

71. Comité de Résistance Spirituelle, *Des rappelés témoignent*, Paris, 1957.

72. The French army paper *Le Bled* asked soldiers to refrain from detailed descriptions of operations.

73. Comité de Résistance Spirituelle, *Des rappelés témoignent*, p. 23.

74. *Ibid.*, p. 55.

75. *Ibid.*, p. 61.

76. *Ibid.*, p. 13.

77. Interview with Georges Mattéi, 13 April 1989, Paris.

78. Jean Martin, *Algérie 1956: pacifier, tuer*, Paris: Éditions Syllepse, 2001, p. 63.

79. *Ibid.*, p. 78.

80. Alquier *et al.*, *Ceux d'Algérie: lettres de rappelés*, p. 25.

81. Jauffret, *Soldats en Algérie 1954–1962*, p. 115.
82. Benjamin Stora, *Appelés en guerre d'Algérie*, Paris: Gallimard, pp. 76–7.
83. Jean-Charles Jauffret, 'The war culture of French combatants in the Algerian conflict' in Martin S. Alexander, Martin Evans, and J. F. V. Keiger (eds.), *The Algerian War and the French Army, 1954–1962*, Basingstoke: Palgrave, 2002.
84. *Ibid.*, p. 107.
85. Harbi and Meynier (eds.), *Le FLN. Documents et histoire 1954–1962*, pp. 145–6.
86. *Ibid.*, p. 112.
87. Radio sets were quickly bought up by the Algerian population, many of whom had always been suspicious of French-controlled radio stations.
88. Khaoula Taleb Ibrahimi, 'Les Algériennes et la guerre de libération nationale—l'émergence des femmes dans l'espace public au cours de la guerre et l'après-guerre' in Harbi and Stora (eds.), *La Guerre d'Algérie*.
89. On the figures concerning female participation the key study is Djamila Amrane, *Les Femmes algériennes dans la guerre*, Paris: Plon, 1991.
90. Natalya Vince, 'To be a Moudjahida in independent Algeria: Itineraries and memories of women veterans of the Algerian War', University of London: PhD, p. 72.
91. *Ibid.*
92. *Ibid.*
93. *Ibid.*
94. *Ibid.*, p. 74.
95. Ali Kafi, *Du militant politique au dirigeant militaire, mémoires 1946–1962*, Algiers: Casbah Éditions, pp. 68–9.
96. *Ibid.*
97. *Ibid.*
98. Harbi and Meynier (eds.), *Le FLN. Documents et histoire 1954–1962*, p. 53.
99. *Ibid.*, p. 58.
100. Mabrouk Belhocine, *Le Courier Alger–Le Caire, 1954–1956*, Algiers: Casbah Éditions, pp. 168–9.
101. The Soummam Platform is reproduced in Harbi and Meynier (eds.), *Le FLN. Documents et histoire 1954–1962*, pp. 241–9.
102. Within the document it was calculated that the numbers fighting were approximately 7,500—made up of 3,100 in Kabylia, 1,669 in the North Constantinois, 1,500 in the West and 1,000 in the Algiers region. These were supported by 15,000 auxiliaries—half of which are in Kabylia, 5,000 in the North Constantinois, 2,000 in the Algerois, and 1,000 in the west of the country. Weapons too was a constant issue with the report calculating that the maquis had just 2,500 modern weapons.
103. These are contained at the Guy Mollet Archive OURS. The contents of the Marcel Champeix papers (APO 1–APO 10) are listed online at <http://www.lours.org>.

104. François Mayle and Benjamin Stora, *François Mitterrand et la guerre d'Algérie*, Paris: Calmann-Lévy, 2010, pp. 135–6.

105. On 18 July 1956 Egypt, India, and Yugoslavia issued a joint statement of 'Non-Alignment' rejecting dependence on the Western powers.

106. Marcel Champeix, 'Notes Champeix, conseil du 3 août 1956', Guy Mollet Archive, OURS. Marcel Champeix 6APO2.

107. Jean-Luc Einaudi, *Pour l'exemple: l'affaire Fernand Iveton*, Paris: L'Harmattan, 1986; and Mayle and Stora, *François Mitterrand et la guerre d'Algérie*.

108. Binot, *Max Lejeune*, II, p. 42.

CHAPTER 7

1. Jacques Massu, *La Vrai Bataille d'Alger*, Paris: Plon, p. 39.

2. Guy Pervillé, *Atlas de la guerre d'Algérie*, Paris: Autrement, 2003, p. 33.

3. Patrice Buffotot, *Le Socialisme français et la guerre*, Brussels: Bruylant, p. 289.

4. 'Guy Mollet rend publique la déclaration d'intentions du gouvernement à l'égard de l'Algérie', *Le Populaire*, 10 January 1957, pp. 3–4. The speech was translated into English by the French Embassy at the United Nations and became the first document in a 'Dossier on Algeria' which put the French case and was widely distributed at the United Nations. 'Dossier on Algeria', Guy Mollet Archive, OURS, APO 6.

5. 'Statement by Premier Mollet on January 9', Guy Mollet, Guy Mollet Archive, OURS, APO 6, p. 2.

6. *Ibid.*

7. *Ibid.*

8. *Ibid.*, p. 6.

9. *Ibid.*

10. *Ibid.*, p. 1.

11. *Ibid.*, p. 5.

12. *Ibid.*, p. 7.

13. *Ibid.*, p. 11.

14. Guy Mollet, 'Basic principles underlying France's European, Algerian and Black African Policy', 25 January 1957. This speech was given at a luncheon organized in his honour by the 'Cercle Républicain' and 'Société des Études Économiques' in Paris. It was translated into English by the French Embassy at the UN. Guy Mollet Archive, OURS, APO 6.

15. *Ibid.*, p. 2.

16. *Ibid.*

17. Darrius Le Corre, 'Pour ou contre une evolution démocratique des pays sous-développés', *Le Populaire,* 14 January 1957, p. 2.

18. 'Guy Mollet répond aux journalists américains', *Le Populaire,* 28 February 1957, p. 1.

19. Michel Debré's seven-page letter contained a comprehensive critique of the Fourth Republic's institutions and revulsion at any contact with FLN, while Mendès France underlined the need for quicker reforms and greater contact with the Muslim population. 'Lettre de Michel Debré à Guy Mollet', 31 January 1957 and 'Lettre de P. Mendès France à Guy Mollet', 17 February 1957, Guy Mollet Archive, OURS, APO 6.

20. 'Lettre de Joseph Perrin à Guy Mollet', 31 January 1957, p. 2, Guy Mollet Archive, OURS, APO 6. Perrin was the UDSR Senator for the Ivory Coast.

21. 'Lettre d'André Morice et de Henri Queuille à Guy Mollet', 29 January 1957, Guy Mollet Archive, OURS, APO 6. Attached to the letter was a three-page declaration from the Parti Radical-Socialiste which talked of this idea of a blood sacrifice.

22. 'Lettre de Michel Debré à Guy Mollet', 31 January 1957, Guy Mollet Archive, OURS, APO 6.

23. *Ibid.*, p. 6.

24. Maurice Vaïsse, 'La guerre perdue a l'ONU' in Jean-Pierre Rioux (ed.), *La Guerre d'Algérie et les français*, Paris: Fayard, 1990.

25. Whether it be over Algeria, Israel or leadership of the independent Euratom initiative into peaceful atomic research which, the Americans rightly suspected, was a means of securing enriched uranium for their nuclear weapons programme, Eisenhower disliked the Republican Front's independent course. In his opinion, this independence signalled France's inability to accept the needs of NATO's wider anti-Soviet strategy. On this see Matthew Connelly, *A Diplomatic Revolution: Algeria's fight for independence and the origins of the post-cold war era*, New York: Oxford University Press, 2002; and Irwin Wall, *France, the United States and the Algerian War*, Berkeley: University of California Press, 2001.

26. The Republican Front government handed over key nuclear technology secrets to Israel in exchange for the latter's support against Nasser's Egypt. On this see Avi Shlaim, *The Iron Wall: Israel and the Arab world*, London: Allen Lane, pp. 175–6; and Patrice Buffotot, *Le Socialisme français et la guerre*, pp. 280–3.

27. André Philip, *Le Socialisme Trahi*, Paris: Plon, 1957.

28. Julien was very clear on this in a debate published in *Le Figaro* on 17 December 1956. This is reproduced in Charles-André Julien, *Une pensée anti-coloniale*, Paris: Sindbad, pp. 174–5; Marceau Pivert, *Office Universitaire de Recherche Socialiste: Cahier et revue*, November–December 1988, p. 15.

29. Gilles Deroche, 'Les socialistes et l'Algérie. Les Ardennes, terre de minorité' in Raphaëlle Branche and Sylvie Thénault (eds.), *La France en guerre 1954–1962*, Paris: Autrement, 2008, p. 242.

30. Raymond Cartier, 'En France noire avec Raymond Cartier', *Paris Match*, 18 August 1956, pp. 34–7.

31. *Ibid.*, p. 37.

32. Raymond Aron, *La Tragédie algérienne*, Paris: Plon, 1957.

33. Alexander Werth, *La France depuis la guerre*, Paris: Gallimard, 1957.

34. On this opinion poll data see Jean-Pierre Rioux, *The Fourth Republic 1944–1958*, Cambridge: Cambridge University Press, 1987, pp. 299–300; and Ageron, 'L'opinion française à travers les sondages' in Rioux (ed.), *La Guerre d'Algérie et les français*.

35. Mabrouk Belhocine, *Le Courier Alger–Le Caire, 1954–1956*, Algiers: Casbah Éditions, 2000, p. 187.

36. Patrick Eveno and Jean Planchais (eds.), *La Guerre d'Algérie*, Paris: La Découverte, 1989, p. 113.

37. Gilbert Meynier, *L'Histoire intérieure du FLN, 1954–1962*, Paris: Fayard, 2002, p. 322.

38. Mohammed Harbi, *Le FLN. Mirage et réalité*, Paris: Jeune Afrique, 1980, p. 195.

39. *Ibid.*, p. 197. Already in 1956 FLN tracts in and around Oran warned that if the 'killing of innocents continues' then the FLN will attack European civilians.

40. Meynier, *Histoire intérieure du FLN*, p. 325.

41. Eveno and Planchais (eds.), *La Guerre d'Algérie*, p. 122.

42. Yacef Saadi, *Souvenirs de la bataille d'Alger*, Paris: Julliard, 1962; and *La Bataille d'Alger*, Algiers: Casbah Éditions, 1997, 3 vols.

43. Meynier, *Histoire intérieure du FLN*, pp. 325–6.

44. Danièle Djamila Amrane-Minne, *Des femmes dans la guerre d'Algérie*, Paris: Karthala, p. 138.

45. Antoine Argoud, *La Décadence, l'imposture et la tragédie*, Paris: Fayard, 1974.

46. Pierre Vidal-Naquet, *Torture: Cancer of democracy*, London: Penguin, 1963, p. 43.

47. Raphaëlle Branche, *La Torture et l'armée française pendant la guerre d'Algérie*, Paris: Gallimard, 2001.

48. Meynier, *Histoire intérieure du FLN*, p. 328.

49. Pierre Vidal-Naquet, *La Raison d'état*, Paris: Éditions de Minuit, 1962, p. 274.

50. Philippe Bourdrel, *La Dernière Chance de l'Algérie française*, Paris: Albin Michel, pp. 111–14.

51. On 4 February 1957 FLN the amateurs of the Algiers settler team Sporting Club Universitaire d'El Biar caused a major shock in the French Cup by beating Reims, European Cup finalists in 1956, 2–0.

52. Pierre Pellissier, *La Bataille d'Alger*, Paris: Perrin, p. 128.

53. *Ibid.*, p. 151.

54. Branche underlines the way in which the isolation of the countryside allowed the army to torture prisoners in different ways, e.g. in the open air. Branche, *La Torture et l'armée française pendant la guerre d'Algérie*, p. 128.

55. Paul Aussaresses, *Services Spéciaux*, Paris: Perrin, 2001, p. 169.

56. The Aussaresses version of events has also been contested; e.g. Saadi Yacef is certain that Ben M'Hidi was shot. On this see Meynier, *Histoire intérieure du FLN*, p. 328.

57. Malika Rahal, *Ali Boumendjel*, Paris: Les Belles Lettres, 2010, pp. 183–240.

58. Pellissier, *La Bataille d'Alger*, p. 189.

59. Meynier, *Histoire intérieure du FLN*, p. 329.

60. Harbi, *Le FLN. Mirage et réalité*, p. 199.

61. In military terms Massu calculated that by this point his troops had arrested 1,827, killed 200, while seizing 812 arms, 88 bombs, 166 grenades, and 200 kg of explosives. Massu, *La Vrai Bataille d'Alger*, p. 173.

62. Jean Daniel, 'Des faits terribles qu'il faut connaître', *L'Express,* 29 December 1955, pp. 8–9.

63. *Esprit* was a leading independent, left-of-centre Catholic journal. The key articles on the Algerian War are collected in Joël Roman, *Esprit: Écrire contre la guerre d'Algérie 1947–1962*, Paris: Hachette, 2002.

64. Vidal-Naquet would later call this one of the most important actions in his life. Pierre Vidal-Naquet, *Mémoires*, II: *Le Trouble et la lumière*, Paris: La Découverte, 1998, p. 38.

65. Robert Bonnaud, 'Paix des Nementchas', *Esprit*, April 1957.

66. Jean Müller, 'Le "Dossier Jean Muller"', *Témoignage Chrétien*, February 1957; Comité de Résistance Spirituelle, 'Des rappelés témoignent', March 1957; Georges Mattéi, 'Jours Kabyle', *Les Temps Modernes*, July 1957. Jean-Jacques Servan-Schreiber's account would subsequently be published as *Lieutenant en Algérie*, Paris: Julliard, 1957.

67. Beuve-Méry cornered Mollet on 16 October 1956 at an event launching a 'week of solidarity in support of Algerian children'. There he told Mollet of the numerous letters he had received about torture. Denis Lefebvre, *Guy Mollet*, Paris: Plon, 1992, p. 236.

68. Hubert Beuve-Méry, 'Sommes-nous les vaincus de Hitler', *Le Monde*, 13 March 1957, p. 1.

69. Léon-Étienne Duval, *Au nom de la vérité*, Paris: Éditions Cana/Jean Offredo, 1982.

70. *Ibid.*, p. 70.

71. Jacques Pâris de Bollardière, *Bataille d'Alger, bataille de l'homme*, Paris: Desclée De Brouwer, 1972.

72. In writing to Salan, Bollardière was bypassing his immediate superior officer Massu. On 8 March Massu wrote to Salan where he underlined that, by re-inscribing laborious legal procedures, Bollardière's tactics were going back on special powers that had been given to the army. In this letter Massu also drew attention to the fact that Lejeune was totally opposed to Bollardière's methods. On this see Massu, *La Vrai Bataille d'Alger*, pp. 223–5.

73. *L'Express*, 28 March 1957, p. 13.

74. Eveno and Planchais (eds.), *La Guerre d'Algérie*, p. 144. The resignation letter would not be made public until 1 October 1960 when it was published in *Le Monde*.

75. Guy Mollet, 'Discours devant la federation socialiste', 14 April 1957 in Vidal-Naquet, *La Raison d'état*, p. 111.

76. Claude Fuzier, 'Une odieuse diversion', *Le Populaire,* 27 March 1957, p. 1.
77. Albert Camus was asked but refused on the grounds that the remit was not clear.
78. With 221 votes for, 188 against, and 110 abstentions.
79. 'Le Voyage en France d'Elisabeth et Philip', *Paris Match,* 20 April 1957.
80. 'La declaration ministérielle Bourgès-Maunoury', *Le Populaire,* 13 June 1957, p. 1. This continuity was also underlined by Claude Fuzier—Claude Fuzier, 'Un programme identique', *Le Populaire,* 13 June 1957, p. 1.
81. Meynier, *Histoire intérieure du FLN,* p. 453.
82. *Ibid.*
83. *Ibid.*
84. Jean-Charles Jauffret, *Soldats en Algérie,* Paris: Autrement, 2000, p. 73.
85. 'Le Massacre: Seule Doctrine du FLN', *Le Populaire,* 1–2 June 1957, p. 1.
86. This assassination is recreated in Rachid Boudjedra's novel *Le Vainqueur de coupe,* Paris: Denoël, 1981.
87. Charles-Robert Ageron, 'Les Français devant la guerre civile algérienne' in Rioux (ed.), *La Guerre d'Algérie et les français.*
88. Bourdrel, *La Dernière Chance de l'Algérie française,* p. 168.
89. Claude Bourdet, 'Qui sont les Chefs du FLN?', *France-Observateur,* 7 November 1957 pp. 5–6.
90. Maisonneuve had been president of the Gas and Electricity Board in Algeria since 1948. His knowledge of Algeria, allied to his long-standing friendship with Lacoste, is why the latter asked him to coordinate relations between civil and military authorities.
91. Eveno and Planchais (eds.), *La Guerre d'Algérie,* p. 120–1.
92. François Mauriac, 'le Bloc-Notes de François Mauriac', *L'Express,* 14 June 1957, p. 32.
93. Germaine Tillion, *Les Ennemis complémentaires,* Paris: SARL Éditions Tirésias, 2005, pp. 58–81.
94. *Ibid.,* p. 72.
95. By June 1957 membership had increased to 113,033 from 110,102 in 1956 and 106,940 in 1955, *Office Universitaire de Recherche Socialiste: Cahier et revue,* November–December 1988, p. 15.
96. Conseil National, 12 May 1957, p. 196. For a summary of the debates see *Office Universitaire de Recherche Socialiste: Cahier et revue,* November–December 1988, pp. 21–2.
97. Bourdrel, *La Dernière Chance de l'Algérie française,* pp. 144–5.
98. Guy Mollet, *Bilan et perspectives socialistes,* Paris: Plon, 1958, p. 65.
99. Ageron, 'L'opinion française à travers les sondages' in Rioux (ed.), *La Guerre d'Algérie et les français.*
100. Jean-Paul Sartre, Preface to Henri Alleg, *La Question,* Paris: Éditions de Minuit, 1958.
101. Mouloud Feraoun, *Journal 1955–1962,* Nebraska: University of Nebraska Press, 2000, p. 114.
102. Tillion, *Les Ennemis complémentaires,* p. 175.
103. *Ibid.,* p. 183.

CHAPTER 8

1. 'Abbane Ramdane est mort au champ d'honneur', *El-Moudjahid*, 29 May 1958, p. 1.
2. *Ibid.*
3. *Ibid.*
4. For a description of these events see Mohammed Lebjaoui, *Vérités sur la révolution algérienne*, Paris: Gallimard, 1970, pp. 153–62.
5. Mohammed Harbi, 'Le Système Boussouf', *Le Drame algérien*, Paris, 1995, pp. 88–9.
6. Gilbert Meynier, *L'Histoire intérieure du FLN, 1954–1962*, Paris: Fayard, 2002, p. 336.
7. Mohammed Harbi, *Le FLN. Mirage et réalité*, Paris: Jeune Afrique, 1980, p. 305.
8. Meynier, *Histoire intérieure du FLN*, p. 337.
9. *Ibid.*, p. 345.
10. Harbi, *Le FLN. Mirage et réalité*, p. 201.
11. Meynier, *Histoire intérieure du FLN*, p. 344.
12. Saad Dahlad, *Pour l'independance de l'Algérie*, Algiers: Dahlab, p. 87.
13. Meynier, *Histoire intérieure du FLN*, p. 345.
14. Belkacem Krim in Mohammed Harbi and Gilbert Meynier (eds.), *Le FLN: Documents et histoire 1954–1962*, Paris: Fayard, 2004, pp. 270–1.
15. Meynier, *Histoire intérieure du FLN*, p. 349.
16. Harbi, *Le FLN. Mirage et réalité*, p. 205.
17. *Ibid.*, pp. 310–13.
18. Kader Abderrahim, *L'Indépendance comme seul but*, Paris: Paris-Méditérannée Éditions, 2008.
19. Maurice Vaïsse, 'La guerre perdue à l'ONU', Jean-Pierre Rioux, *La Guerre d'Algérie et les français*, Paris: Fayard, 1990, p. 455.
20. Irwin Wall, *France, the United States and the Algerian War*, Berkeley: University of California Press, 2001, pp. 104–7.
21. Martin Thomas, *The French North African Crisis: Colonial breakdown and Anglo-French relations, 1945–1962*, London: Macmillan, 2000.
22. Raoul Salan, *Mémoires: Fin d'un empire*, Paris: Éditions Presses de la Cité, 1972, p. 285.
23. These were carried out at dawn on 30 April 1958 in response to the guillotining of Abderrahmane Taleb, key bomb-maker during the 'Battle of Algiers', six days earlier.
24. Patrick Eveno and Jean Planchais (eds.), *La Guerre d'Algérie*, Paris: La Découverte, 1989, p. 207.
25. For detailed examination of the meaning of this unveiling see Neil Macmaster, *Burning the Veil: The Algerian War and the emancipation of Muslim women*, Manchester: Manchester University Press, 2009, pp. 121–44.
26. *Ibid.*, p. 137. On 29 May *El-Moudjahid* carried an article entitled 'Operation "Fraternization"' which argued that the parades had been completely orchestrated by the army.

27. Jacques Massu, *Le Torrent et la digue*, Paris: Plon, 1972, p. 107.

28. Wall, *France, the United States and the Algerian War*, pp. 127–33.

29. Charles de Gaulle, *Discours et messages*, Paris: Plon, 1970, II, pp. 666–7. On this see Matthew Connelly, *A Diplomatic Revolution: Algeria's fight for independence and the origins of the post-cold war era*, New York: Oxford, 2002, pp. 173–80.

30. Massu, *Le Torrent et la digue*, p. 165.

31. *Ibid.*

32. *Ibid.*

33. *Ibid.*, pp. 165–6.

34. *Ibid.*, p. 166.

35. *Ibid.*

36. *Ibid.*

37. *Ibid.*

38. *Ibid.*, pp. 166–7.

39. 'Général de Gaulle Affiche', 1958, CAOM 9 Fi 43.

40. Benjamin Stora and Tramor Quemeneur, *Algérie 1954–1962: Lettres, carnets et récits des français et algériens dans la guerre*, Paris: Les Arènes, 2010, p. 53.

41. *Ibid.*, p. 52.

42. Philip M. Williams, *French Politicians and Elections 1951–1969*, Cambridge: Cambridge University Press, 1970, p. 98.

43. *Ibid.*

44. Edwar Behr, *The Algerian Problem*, London: Hodder and Stoughton, 1961, pp. 153–4.

45. Eveno and Planchais (eds.), *La Guerre d'Algérie*, p. 237.

46. *Ibid.*, p. 240.

47. Daniel Lefeuvre, *Chère Algérie 1930–1962*, Paris: Société d'Outre Mer, 1997, p. 284. See also Daniel Lefeuvre, 'L'echec du plan de Constantine' in Rioux (ed.), *La Guerre d'Algérie et les français*.

48. Guy Mollet, 'Conférence de Presse', 10 November 1958, p. 2, Guy Mollet Archive, OURS, 118 AGM.

49. Charles de Gaulle, *Discours et messages*, III, p. 54.

50. Ali Haroun, *La Septième Wilaya. La guerre du FLN en France, 1954–1962*, Paris: Seuil, 1986.

51. Ahmed Francis was Minister of Economic Affairs, Abdelhamid Mehri Minister of North African Affairs, Tawfiq El Madani Minister of Cultural Affairs, and Lamine Debaghine Minister of Foreign Affairs. The imprisoned leaders were given honorary positions by which Ben Bella became vice-president and Aït Ahmed, Khider, and Boudiaf Ministers of State, along with Rabah Bitat, arrested in March 1955.

52. Jacques Vernet, 'Les barrages dans la guerre d'Algérie' in Jean-Charles Jauffret and Maurice Vaïsse (eds.), *Militaires et guerrilla dans la guerre d'Algérie*, Brussels: Éditions de Complexe, 2001.

53. Eveno and Planchais (eds.), *La Guerre d'Algérie*, p. 223.

54. Charles-Robert Ageron, 'Complots et purges dans l'armée de libération Algérienne (1958–1961)' in Raphaëlle Branche (ed.), *La Guerre d'indépendance des algériens*, Paris: Perrin, 2009.

55. For examples of this propaganda see SHAT 1H1101–5, 1775–3, and 3217.

56. Said Saadi, *Amirouche*, Blida: Imprimerie Mauguin, 2010.

57. Zoubir was eventually executed in August 1960 during purges organized by Boumediène. See Meynier, *Histoire intérieure du FLN*, pp. 412–16.

58. 'Le Plan de Constantine: La Route de l'Avenir Affiche', 1958, CAOM 9 FI 345.

59. Connelly, *A Diplomatic Revolution*, pp. 215–21. See also Macmaster, *Burning the Veil*, pp. 159–64.

60. Connelly, *A Diplomatic Revolution*, p. 216.

61. Macmaster, *Burning the Veil*, p. 161. See also Ryme Seferdjeli, '"Fight with us, women, and we will emancipate you": France, the FLN and the struggle over women during the Algerian War of National Liberation 1954–1962', PhD, London School of Economics, 2005.

62. Seferdjeli, '"Fight with us, women, and we will emancipate you"', pp. 224–55.

63. These were known as *Équipes medico-sociale itinérantes* (EMSI). On this see Macmaster, *Burning the Veil*, pp. 90–5, 245–66.

64. Ryme Seferdjeli, 'French "reforms" and Muslim women during the Algerian War (1954–1962)', *Hawwa*, 2005, pp. 50–1.

65. Guy Pervillé, *Atlas de la guerre d'Algérie*, Paris: Autrement, 2003, p. 40.

66. This term is derived from the Arab word (*harka*) for movement. Traditionally it referred to militias raised during the Ottoman period to extract the payment of taxes from the local populations. On their specific history see Mohand Hamoumou, *Et ils sont devenus harkis*, Paris: Fayard, 1993.

67. Bachaga Boualam, *Mon pays la France*, Paris: France Empire, 1962.

68. In his diaries Mouloud Feraoun conjures up an image of wanton FLN violence which, in a society with a strong code of honour, fuelled a cycle of revenge and counter-revenge. Mouloud Feraoun, *Journal 1955–1962*, Nebraska: University of Nebraska Press, 2000.

69. Jean-Jacques Jordi and Mohand Hamoumou, *Les Harkis, une mémoire enfouie*, Paris: Autrement, 1999, p. 29.

70. Martin Evans, 'The *harkis*: The experience and memory of France's Muslim auxiliaries' in Martin S. Alexander, Martin Evans, and J. F. V. Keiger (eds.), *The Algerian War and the French Army, 1954–1962*, Basingstoke: Palgrave, 2002.

71. Significantly André Malraux claimed that under the Fifth Republic torture had stopped. On this see Raphaëlle Branche, *La Torture et l'armée française pendant la guerre d'Algérie*, Paris: Gallimard, 2001.

72. Raphaëlle Branche, 'Des viols pendant la guerre d'Algérie', Branche (ed.), *La Guerre d'indépendance des algériens*.

73. This report was drawn up by a young civil servant, Michel Rocard, and submitted to Paul Delouvrier in December 1958. *Le Monde* obtained a leaked copy from an undisclosed source and published extracts on 18 April 1959 under

the title 'Un million de "regroupés"'. This article is reproduced in Eveno and Planchais (eds.), *La Guerre d'Algérie*, pp. 223–8.

74. On this brutalizing effect see the eye-witness accounts of three French officers in Algeria, J. M. Darboise, M. Heynard, and J. Martel, *Officiers en Algérie*, Paris: Maspero, 1960, pp. 54–5.

75. SHAT 1H1623–1.

76. Saïd Ferdi, *Un enfant dans la guerre*, Paris: Seuil, 1981.

77. *Ibid.*, pp. 72–3.

78. Eveno and Planchais (eds.), *La Guerre d'Algérie*, pp. 196–7.

79. Dominique Fargues, *Mémoire des pieds noirs*, Paris: Flammarion, 2008, p. 102.

80. *Ibid.*

81. See examples of these tracts in Harbi and Meynier (eds.), *Le FLN: Documents et histoire 1954–1962*, pp. 590–603.

82. Jean Lacouture, *De Gaulle*, III: *Le Souverain*, Paris: Seuil, 1986, p. 60.

83. 'Lettre de François Gilbert à Guy Mollet', 5 March 1959, Guy Mollet Archive, OURS, AGM 91 Algérie 1958–1959.

84. Charles-Robert Ageron, 'Opinion française à travers les sondages', Rioux (ed.), *La Guerre d'Algérie et les français*, p. 37.

CHAPTER 9

1. Charles de Gaulle, *Discours et messages*, Paris: Plon, 1970, III, p. 117.

2. *Ibid.*

3. *Ibid.*

4. *Ibid.*

5. *Ibid.*

6. *Ibid.*

7. *Ibid.*

8. *Ibid.*

9. *Ibid.*

10. *Ibid.*

11. *Ibid.*

12. *Ibid.*

13. In talking about Algeria, de Gaulle excluded the two departments of the Sahara which he saw as a French creation belonging to France.

14. Jean Lacouture, *De Gaulle*, III: *Le Souverain*, Paris: Seuil, 1986, p. 64.

15. Bernard Tricot, *Les Sentiers de la paix*, Paris: Plon, 1972, pp. 103–4.

16. *Ibid.*

17. Lacouture, *De Gaulle*, III, p. 67.

18. Jacques Soustelle, *L'Espérance trahi*, Paris: Éditions Alama, 1962, p. 112.

19. Jacques Massu, *Le Torrent et la digue*, Paris: Plon, 1972, pp. 285–6.

20. Alain Peyrefitte, *C'était de Gaulle*, Paris: Fayard, 1994, I., p. 68.

21. *Ibid.*

22. Irwin Wall, *France, the United States and the Algerian War*, Berkeley: University of California Press, 2001, p. 180.

23. *Ibid.*, pp. 188–91.

24. Edward Behr, *The Algerian Problem*, London: Hodder and Stoughton, 1961, pp. 162–3.

25. Patrick Eveno and Jean Planchais (eds.), *La Guerre d'Algérie*, Paris: La Découverte, 1989, p. 252.

26. Charles-Robert Ageron, 'L'opinion française à travers les sondages' in Jean-Pierre Rioux (ed.), *La Guerre d'Algérie et les français*, Paris: Fayard, 1990.

27. Lacouture, *De Gaulle*, p. 79.

28. *Ibid.*, p. 88.

29. *Ibid.*

30. *Ibid.*

31. Bonn Correspondent, 'The General's reported remarks', *The Times*, 20 January 1960, p. 12.

32. Paris Correspondent, 'General Massu summoned to Paris', *The Times*, 20 January 1960, p. 12.

33. *Ibid.*

34. These paramilitary units were under the military and could be called up for active duty for anything between twenty-four hours and one month.

35. Behr, *The Algerian Problem*, p. 168.

36. Merry and Serge Bromberger, Georgette Elgey, and J.-F. Chauvel, *Barricades et colonels. 24 Janvier 1960*, Paris: Fayard, 1960, p. 338.

37. *Ibid.*, p. 343.

38. De Gaulle, *Discours et messages*, III.

39. *Ibid.*

40. *Ibid.*

41. *Ibid.*

42. *Ibid.*

43. *Ibid.*

44. *Ibid.*

45. Charles-Robert Ageron, 'L'évolution de l'opinion publique française face à la guerre d'Algérie' in Rioux (ed.), *La Guerre d'Algérie et les français*, p. 165.

46. Jean-Marc Binot, *Max Lejeune*, Amiens: Martelle Éditions, 2003, II, p. 124.

47. Martin Evans, *The Memory of Resistance: French opposition to the Algerian War 1954–1962*. See also Hervé Hamon and Patrick Rotman, *Les Porteurs de valises: la résistance française à la guerre d'Algérie*, Paris: Albin Michel, 1979; and Jacques Charby, *Les Porteurs d'espoir*, Paris: La Découverte, 2003.

48. Evans, *The Memory of Resistance*, p. 220.

49. Ali Haroun, *La Septième Wilaya: la guerre du FLN en France, 1954–1962*, Paris: Seuil, 1986.

50. Charles-Robert Ageron 'Les Français devant la guerre civile algérienne' in Rioux (ed.), *La Guerre d'Algérie et les français*.

51. Interview with Ali Haroun, 9 October 1989, Algiers.

52. This amounted to 500 million old francs per month.

53. Eveno and Planchais (eds.), *La Guerre d'Algérie*, p. 270.

54. Evans, *The Memory of Resistance*.

55. On the role of French pro-FLN activists in Lyon see the excellent Béatreice Dubell documentary *El Biar; Le Puits*, 2008.

56. Frantz Fanon, *L'An cinq de la révolution algérienne*, Paris: Maspero, 1959. The book was banned.

57. Danièle Joly, *The French Communist Party and the Algerian War*, London: Macmillan, 1991; Jacques Jurquet, *La Révolution nationale algérienne et le Parti Communiste français*, Paris: Éditions du Centenaire, 1984; Jacob Moneta, *Le PCF et la question coloniale, 1920–1965*, Paris: Maspero, 1971.

58. Jean-Luc Einaudi, *Franc-Tireur: Georges Mattéi, de la guerre d'Algérie à la guérilla*, Paris: Éditions du Sextant.

59. Evans, *The Memory of Resistance*, p. 59.

60. Anne Simonin, 'Les Éditions de Minuit et les Éditions du Seuil. Deux stratégies editorials face à la guerre d'Algérie', Jean-Pierre Rioux and Jean-François Sirinelli (eds.), *La Guerre d'Algérie et les intellectuels français*, Paris: Les Cahiers de l'IHTP, 1988.

61. See above Ch. 7.

62. Pierre Vidal-Naquet, *Face à la raison d'état: un historien dans la guerre d'Algérie*, Paris: La Découverte, 1989; and *Mémoires*, II: *Le Trouble et la lumière*, Paris: La Découverte, 1998.

63. *Nous accusons . . . Dossier sur la torture et la repression en Algérie*. This was sent to René Coty, president of the Repubic, and Charles de Gaulle, prime minister, on 16 September 1958, and seized immediately by the police. Vidal-Naquet, *Mémoires*, II, pp. 91–3.

64. *Ibid*.

65. e.g. *La Gangrène*, Paris: Éditions de Minuit, 1959 contained five eye-witness accounts by Béchir Boumaza, Mustapha Francis, Benaïssa Souami, Abd el-Kader Belhadj, and Moussa Khebaili, which described how they had been tortured in the metropole.

66. On this see the interview with Madeleine Rebérioux in Eveno and Planchais (eds.), *La Guerre d'Algérie*, pp. 200–2.

67. e.g. in October 1957 the Communist Party monthly newspaper, *La Défense*, carried the front-page banner headline 'To liberate Alban Liechti' and had a front-page article calling for his release. J. E. Mazubert, 'Une grande bataille à gagner', *La Défense*, October 1957, p. 1. In January 1959 the Communist Party published a pamphlet drawing attention to their plight entitled *Des Jeunes qui servent l'intérêt de la France*.

68. PSU members were drawn from the Union de Gauche Socialiste (UGS), founded in 1957, and the Parti Socialiste Autonome (PSA), founded in 1958.

69. Tramor Quemeneur, 'Réfractaires français dans la guerre d'Algérie' in Jean-Charles Jauffret and Maurice Vaïsse (eds.), *Militaires et guerilla dans la guerre d'Algérie*, Brussels: Éditions de Complexe, 2001.

70. Harold Macmillan, 'The Wind of Change' in Simon Heffer (ed.), *Great British Speeches*, Chester: Quercus Publishing, 2007. In 1957 Macmillan had already asked his officials to give him 'something like a profit and loss account for each of our Colonial Possessions'. On this see Frederick Cooper, *Africa since 1940*, Cambridge: Cambridge University Press, 2002, pp. 76–84.

71. Macmillan, 'The Wind of Change', p. 215.

72. Wall, *France, the United States and the Algerian War*, p. 188.

73. Gilbert Meynier, *L'Histoire intérieure du FLN, 1954–1962*, Paris: Fayard, 2002, p. 426.

74. De Gaulle, *Discours et messages*, III.

75. *Ibid.*

76. Si Salah was killed in action on 19 July 1961.

77. CAOM 9Fi 408, CAOM 9Fi 409, CAOM 9Fi 410; and Anne-Marie Duranton-Crabol, *Le Temps de l'OAS*, Brussels: Complexe, 1995, p. 45–6.

78. Serge Bernstein, 'La peau de chagrin de "l'Algérie française"' in Rioux (ed.), *La Guerre d'Algérie et les français*, p. 215.

79. Binot, *Max Lejeune*, p. 126.

80. *Ibid.*, p. 130.

81. 'Le Manifeste de 121: Déclaration sur le droit à l'insoumission dans la Geurre d'Algérie', Eveno and Planchais (eds.), *La Guerre d'Algérie*, pp. 273–7.

82. Hamon and Rotman, *Les Porteurs de valises: la résistance française à la guerre d'Algérie*.

83. 'Le Manifeste des intellectuels français', Eveno and Planchais (eds.), *La Guerre d'Algérie*, pp. 273–7.

84. De Gaulle, *Discours et messages*, III.

85. Significantly this phrase had not figured in the original typescript.

86. Binot, *Max Lejeune*, p. 131.

87. Ageron, 'L'opinion française à travers les sondages', p. 37.

88. Meynier, *Histoire intérieure du FLN*, p. 465.

89. Mouloud Feraoun, *Journal 1955–1962*, Nebraska: University of Nebraska Press, 2000, p. 281.

90. *Ibid.*

91. Meynier, *Histoire intérieure du FLN*, p. 466. Both Ben Tobbal in Tunis and Boumediène in Morocco were worried that the FLN had lost control. For them demonstrations had to be strictly controlled.

92. Established by the Sections d'Administrations Urbaines, the urban equivalent of the SAS.

93. Mohamed Derouiche, *Le Scoutisme, école du patriotisme*, Algiers: ENAL-OPU, 1985.

94. Meynier, *Histoire intérieure du FLN*, p. 466.

95. Matthew Connelly, *A Diplomatic Revolution: Algeria's fight for independence and the origins of the post-cold war era*, New York: Oxford, 2002, p. 229.

96. *Ibid.*

97. *Ibid.* André Mandouze, *La Révolution algérienne par les textes*, Paris: Maspero, 1961, p. 68.

98. Jean Lacouture, 'Les étapes de la négotiation', *Le Monde*, 20 March 1962, p. 11.

99. De Gaulle, *Discours et messages*, III.

100. On this see Jean-Pierre Rioux, 'Les Français et la guerre deux républiques' in Mohammed Harbi and Benjamin Stora (eds.), *La Guerre d'Algérie 1954–2004: la fin de l'amnésie*, Paris: Robert Laffont, 2004.

101. De Gaulle, *Discours et messages*, III.

102. Lacouture, *De Gaulle*, p. 155.

CHAPTER 10

1. Maurice Vaïsse, *Alger, le Putsch*, Brussels: Éditions Complexe, 1983, p. 166.

2. *Ibid.*

3. *Ibid.*

4. *Ibid.*

5. Jean Lacouture, *De Gaulle*, III: *Le Souverain*, Paris: Seuil, 1986, p. 158.

6. He underlined this point at his subsequent trial and in his memoirs. Maurice Challe, *Notre Révolte*, Paris: Presses de la Cité, 1968.

7. Philip M. Williams, *Wars, Plots and Scandals in Post-War France*, Cambridge: Cambridge University Press, 1970, p. 199.

8. Laurent Beccaria, *Hélie de Saint Marc*, Paris: Perrin, 1988.

9. Williams, *Wars, Plots and Scandals in Post-War France*, p. 199.

10. De Gaulle had these powers under Article 16 of the Constitution. They were kept in place until 29 September 1961.

11. Charles de Gaulle, *Discours et messages*, Paris: Plon, 1970, III, pp. 306–8.

12. *Ibid.*

13. The late 1950s witnessed the introduction of cheap portable radios as the transistor replaced the vacuum tube. These transistor radios, a new portable way of listening to broadcasts, played a crucial role in defeating the putsch because conscripts could actually hear de Gaulle's words.

14. Marc Coppin and Alain Trogneux, 'Face au putsch' in Raphaëlle Branche and Sylvie Thénault (eds.), *La France en guerre 1954–1962*, Paris: Autrement, 2008.

15. *Ibid.*, pp. 215–16.

16. Alain-Gérard Slama, *La Guerre d'Algérie*, Paris: Gallimard, 1996, p. 110.

17. The truce was to be renewed on a month-to-month basis.

18. 'Directive du general Gambiez', 23 March 1961, Mohammed Harbi and Gilbert Meynier (eds.), *Le FLN: Documents et histoire 1954–1962*, Paris: Fayard, 2004, p. 825.

19. Redha Malek, *L'Algérie à Évian. Histoire des négociations secrètes, 1956–1962*, Paris: Seuil, 1995.

20. This idea was explored in a series of articles by Alain Peyrefitte in *Le Monde* in September and October 1961 which appeared as a book: Alain Peyrefitte, *Faut-il partager l'Algérie?*, Paris: Plon, 1962.

21. For an eye-witness account of the impact of the attack See Jean Daniel, *Le Temps qui reste*, Paris: Stock, 1973, pp. 143–64.

22. See Irwin Wall, *France, the United States and the Algerian War*, Berkeley: University of California Press, 2001, p. 247.

23. On the Berlin Crisis see Tony Judt, *Postwar: A history of Europe since 1945*, London: Pimlico, 2007, pp. 249–53.

24. 'Tract de Wilaya 4', June 1961, Harbi and Meynier (eds.), *Le FLN. Documents et histoire 1954–1962*.

25. Mohammed Harbi, *Le FLN. Mirage et réalité*, Paris: Jeune Afrique, 1980, p. 286.

26. Lacouture, *De Gaulle*, III, p. 202.

27. Raymond Barrillon, 'M. Mendès France préconise la formation d'un "gouvernement intérimaire"', *Le Monde*, 27 September 1961, p. 5; and Raymond Barillon, '"Réformistes" et "révolutionnaires" de la SFIO durcissent leur opposition au régime et au gouvernement', *Le Monde*, 29 September 1961, p. 5.

28. Lacouture, *De Gaulle*, III, p. 203.

29. *Ibid.*

30. T. Bastien Thierry would be condemned to death and executed for this assassination attempt.

31. The week beginning 13 July 1961 saw 138 OAS bombing attacks across the country. Jean-Jacques Susini, *Histoire de l'OAS*, Paris: La Table Ronde, 1963, p. 211.

32. This means defence in Hebrew and was established by the Zionist Movement in 1939 in order to combat Arab resistance.

33. Susini, *Histoire de l'OAS*.

34. Alistair Horne, *A Savage War of Peace*, London: Macmillan, 1977, p. 486.

35. *Ibid.*

36. André Pautard, 'Les Européens d'Alger ont organisé pendant trois heures un vacarme étourdissant', *Le Monde*, 24–5 September 1961, p. 3.

37. Rémi Kauffer, 'OAS: guerre franco-française d'Algérie', Mohammed Harbi and Benjamin Stora (eds.), *La Guerre d'Algérie 1954–2004: la fin de l'amnésie*, Paris: Robert Laffont, 2004, p. 666.

38. *Ibid.*

39. Dominique Fargues, *Mémoire des pieds noirs*, Paris: Flammarion, 2008, p. 147.

40. Benjamin Stora, 'L'impossible neutralité des juifs d'Algérie', Harbi and Stora (eds.), *La Guerre d'Algérie*, pp. 439–40.

41. Alain Jacob, 'L'OAS telle que voient les Européens d'Algérie', *Le Monde*, 15 November 1961, p. 1.

42. *Ibid.*

43. The Vincennes Committee was banned and Soustelle went into exile, although he subsequently made it clear that he was never an OAS member.

44. Pierre Vidal-Naquet, *Face à la raison d'état: un historien dans la guerre d'Algérie*, Paris: La Découverte, 1989, pp. 170–86. These documents were originally published in *Esprit*, May 1962.

45. 'Alger: dix attentats commis mardi ont fait sept morts dix-neuf blessés', *Le Monde*, 4 January 1962, p. 4.

46. On Maurice Papon see Stephanie Hare, 'Duty, death and the Republic: The career of Maurice Papon from Vichy France to the Algerian War', PhD, London School of Economic and Political Science, 2008.

47. Jean-Luc Einaudi, *Octobre à Paris: un massacre à Paris*, Paris: Fayard, 2001; and Jim House and Neil Macmaster, *Paris 1961: Algerians, state terror, and memory*, Oxford: Oxford University Press, 2006.

48. Ali Haroun, *La Septième Wilaya: la guerre du FLN en France, 1954–1962*, Paris: Seuil, 1986, p. 374.

49. 'L'engin qui a explosé au Quai d'Orsay', *Le Monde*, 24 January 1962, p. 2.

50. 'Trois femmes et un jeune homme de seize ans parmi les morts', *Le Monde*, 10 February 1962, p. 2. A further demonstrator would die from his injuries several months later, thereby making it nine deaths in total.

51. 'La plus sanglante affrontement entre policies et manifestants depuis le 6 février 1934', *Le Monde*, 10 February, 1962, p. 2.

52. De Gaulle, *Le Monde*, 20 March 1962, p. 2.

53. *Ibid.*

54. Charles-Robert Ageron, 'L'opinion française à travers les sondages' in Jean-Pierre Rioux (ed.), *La Guerre d'Algérie et les français*, Paris: Fayard, 1990, p. 39.

55. *Ibid.*

56. In January 1962, 53 per cent no longer felt solidarity with the Europeans, while 28 per cent thought that the war could go on for another two or three years. Ageron, 'L'opinion française à travers les sondages', p. 39.

CHAPTER 11

1. Alain Jacob, 'Le plan de l'OAS pour saboteur les accords', *Le Monde*, 20 March 1962, p. 7.

2. *Ibid.*

3. *Ibid.*

4. Alain Jacob, 'Militaires, gendarmes et CRS font prevue dans l'ensemble d'un remarquable sang-froid', *Le Monde*, 23 March 1962, p. 4.

5. Alain Jacob, 'Dans Bab-El-Oued en État d' "Insurrection Armée"', *Le Monde*, 25–6 March 1962, p. 2.

6. Radio address given by Jean-Jacques Susini, Tuesday 19 June, reproduced in *Le Monde*, 21 June 1962, p. 2.

7. Todd Shepherd, *The Invention of Decolonization: The Algerian War and the remaking of France*, Ithaca: Cornell University Press, 2006, p. 219.

8. The full results were tabulated in *Le Monde*, 10 April 1962, p. 1.

9. 'Le parti de M. Messali Hadj est exclu de la champagne électorale' and 'Le PPA: procédé dictatorial', *Le Monde*, 17–18 June 1962, p. 5.

10. For a round-up of this global reaction see *Le Monde*, 3 July 1962, p. 3.

11. Dominique Fargues, *Mémoires de pieds-noirs*, Paris: Flammarion, 2008, pp. 196–7.

12. Daniel Lefeuvre, 'Les pieds-noirs' in Mohammed Harbi and Benjamin Stora (eds.), *La Guerre d'Algérie 1954–2004: la fin de l'amnésie*, Paris: Robert Laffont, 2004, p. 400.

13. Gilbert Meynier, *L'Histoire intérieure du FLN, 1954–1962*, Paris: Fayard, 2002, p. 642.

14. Fargues, *Mémoires de pieds-noirs*, p. 200.

15. 'Les responsables FLN de Constantine s'inquiètent du depart des Européens', *Le Monde*, 28 June 1962, p. 3.

16. Fargues, *Mémoires de pieds-noirs*, p. 201.

17. On the different versions of what happened see 'Le fusillade d'Oran aurait fait plus de trente morts', *Le Monde*, 7 July 1962, p. 2.

18. Meynier, *Histoire intérieure du FLN, 1954–1962*, p. 641. See also Alain-Gérard Slama, 'Oran, 5 juillet 1962: le massacre oublié', *L'Histoire. La Guerre d'Algérie: sans mythes ni tabous*, 2002, pp. 102–3.

19. Meynier, *Histoire intérieure du FLN, 1954–1962*, pp. 641–2.

20. Jean Scotto, *Curé pied-noir évêque algérien*, Paris: Desclée de Brouwer, 1991.

21. e.g. Lagaillarde sent a declaration to Agence France-Presse calling on Europeans to return to Algeria, 'Pierre Lagaillarde demandent aux Français qui ont quitté l'Algérie de "rentrer le plus rapidement possible"', *Le Monde*, 6 July 1962, p. 2.

22. Benjamin Stora, 'L'impossible neutralité des juifs d'Algérie' in Harbi and Stora (eds.), *La Guerre d'Algérie*.

23. 'Déclaration du Comité juif algérien d'études sociales sur la situation en Algérie (novembre 1956)', Stora, 'L'impossible neutralité des juifs d'Algérie, pp. 433–4. This underlined the need to bring about racial equality.

24. Benjamin Stora, *La Dernière Generation d'octobre*, Paris: Hachette, 2003, pp. 24–8.

25. *Ibid.*, p. 27.

26. *Ibid.*, pp. 27–8.

27. During demonstrations in Oran a Jewish cemetery was also desecrated.

28. Other prominent Algerian Jewish singers included Reinette l'Oraniase and Lili Boniche who pioneered a Judeo-Arab form of tango.

29. Stora, 'L'impossible neutralité des juifs d'Algérie', p. 437.

30. Meynier, *Histoire intérieure du FLN 1954–1962*, p. 255.

31. Mohammed Harbi and Gilbert Meynier (eds.), *Le FLN: Documents et histoire 1954–1962*, Paris: Fayard, 2004, pp. 594–6.

32. *Ibid.*, p. 595.

33. *Ibid.*, pp. 594–5.

34. Stora, 'L'impossible neutralité des juifs d'Algérie', p. 441.

35. 'Tracts FLN à l'intention des juifs d'Algérie', *Le Monde*, 27 April 1962, p. 5.

36. Mohammed Harbi, *Les Archives de la révolution algérienne*, Paris: Jeune Afrique, 1981, p. 298. See also Meynier, *Histoire intérieure du FLN 1954–1962*, p. 254.

37. This shows the disorganized nature of the OAS. This group was unaware that the order to kill Levy had been rescinded the week before by Colonel Godard. On this see Georges Fleury, *Histoire secrète de l'OAS*, Paris: Grasset, 2002, p. 459. Tragically Levy's son was killed by the FLN in 1956, while his niece lost two arms in the FLN bombing attack on the Corniche dance hall in Algiers in 1957.

38. Stora, *La Dernière Generation d'octobre*, p. 29.

39. Alain Jacob, 'Les forces en présence', *Le Monde*, 20 March 1962, p. 12.

40. Guy Pervillé, 'La tragédie des harkis: qui est responsable', *L'Histoire. La Guerre d'Algérie: sans mythes ni tabous*, 2002, pp. 88–93.

41. 'L'analyse des accords conclus entre la France et le GPRA', *Le Monde*, 20 March 1962, pp. 4–5. This principle of no reprisals had been a sticking point for the French negotiators which the Algerian Provisional Government had conceded. On this see Benyoucef Ben Khedda, *Les Accords d'Évian*, Algiers: Publisud-OPU, 1986, pp. 27–30.

42. This was particularly true in Paris during winter 1961/62 where Maurice Papon had deployed *harki* units against the FLN. Paulette Péju, *Les Harkis à Paris*, Paris: Maspero, 1961.

43. *Paris Match* contained a photograph of his blood-soaked body looked over by his grieving family. 'Dans Alger avec l'armée qui veille', *Paris Match*, 24 February 1962, pp. 30–1.

44. Bachaga Boualam, *Les Harkis au service de la France*, Paris: France-Empire, 1963.

45. Evans, 'The *harkis*: The experience and memory of France's Muslim auxiliaries' in Martin S. Alexander, Martin Evans, and J. F. V. Keiger (eds.), *The Algerian War and the French Army, 1954–1962*, Basingstoke: Palgrave, 2002, p. 127.

46. Michel Goué, '"C'est le FLN qui commande chez nous . . . il ne me restait plus qu'à partir" declare le Bachaga Boualam', *Le Monde*, 22 May 1962, p. 6. On 28 June 1962 Bachaga Boualam, vice-president of the National Assembly, gave an impassioned speech where he denounced the way in which pro-French Muslims had been abandoned by France.

47. *Combat*, 'Appel aux Français', reprinted in *Le Monde*, 26 June 1962, p. 3.

48. Pervillé, 'La tragédie des harkis: qui est responsable', p. 91.

49. *Ibid.*

50. Alain Peyrefitte, *C'était de Gaulle*, Paris: Fayard, 1994.

51. Nicolas d'Andoque, *1955–1962, guerre et paix en Algérie*, Paris: SPL, 1977.

52. Abd-El-Aziz Méliani, *Le Drame des harkis*, Paris: Perrin, 1993.

53. Mouloud Feraoun, *Journal 1955–1962*, Nebraska: University of Nebraska Press, 2000, p. 313.

54. *Ibid.*, pp. 313–14.

55. *Ibid.*, p. 314.

56. *Ibid.*

57. Alain Jacob, '"Vous êtes condamnés à mort"', *Le Monde*, 16 March 1962, p. 1; Sylvie Thénault, 'Mouloud Feraoun, un écrivain dans la guerre d'Algérie', *Vingtième Siècle*, July–September 1999, pp. 65–74.

58. See *Le Monde* 17 March 1962 which included shocked reactions from the writers Jean Amrouche, Gabriel Audisio, and Jules Roy, all of whom condemned the OAS in forthright terms.

59. Ali Zamoum, *Le Pays des hommes libres. Tamurt Imazighen: mémoires d'un combatant algérien*, Paris: La Pensée Sauvage, 1998, p. 299.

60. *Ibid.*

61. Meynier, *Histoire intérieure du FLN 1954–1962*, p. 642.

62. André Pautard, 'Les meetings FLN sont des fêtes de la victoire plus que des reunions électorales', *Le Monde*, 26 June 1962, p. 3.

63. Meynier, *Histoire intérieure du FLN 1954–1962*, p. 643.

64. Mohammed Harbi, *Le FLN. Mirage et réalité*, Paris: Jeune Afrique, 1980, p. 364; and Meynier, *Histoire intérieure du FLN 1954–1962*, p. 643.

65. Zamoum, *Le Pays des hommes libres*, pp. 315–16.

66. All the detainees captured on 22 October 1956 were released after the signature of the Évian Agreement. Initially Boumediène approached Boudiaf but was rejected. At this point he turned to Ben Bella.

67. Harbi, *Les Archives de la révolution algérienne*, pp. 350–2.

68. Meynier, *Histoire intérieure du FLN 1954–1962*, p. 665.

69. *Ibid.*, p. 670.

70. Interview with Mohammed Harbi, 22 May 2008, Paris.

71. Charles-Robert Ageron, 'Les pertes humaines de la guerre d'Algérie', in Laurent Gervereau, Jean-Pierre Rioux, and Benjamin Stora (eds.), *La France en guerre d'Algérie*, Nanterre: BDIC, 1992, p. 171.

72. On this see Luis Martinez, *The Algerian Civil War 1990–1998*, London: Hurst & Company, 2000, pp. 12–13.

73. He was then based at Tours University. Ageron had been a teacher at Lycée Gautier in Algiers between 1947 and 1957. In 1956 and 1957 he was part of the liberal current which produced the journal *L'Espoir*. His calculations are cited by Meynier, *Histoire intérieure du FLN 1954–1962*; Guy Pervillé, 'Combien de morts', *L'Histoire. La Guerre d'Algérie: sans mythes ni tabous*, and Sylvie Thénault, *Histoire de la guerre d'indépendance algérienne*, Paris: Flammarion, 2005.

74. Ageron, 'Les pertes humaines de la guerre d'Algérie', in Laurent Gervereau, Jean-Pierre Rioux and Benjamin Stora (eds.), *La France en guerre d'Algérie* .

75. Guy Pervillé, *Atlas de la guerre d'Algérie*, Paris: Autrement, 2003, p. 54.

76. *Ibid.*, p. 55.
77. *Ibid.*
78. Meynier, *Histoire intérieure du FLN 1954–1962*, p. 289.
79. Thénault, *Histoire de la guerre d'indépendance algérienne*, p. 267.

POSTSCRIPT

1. 'Le discours de M. Ferhat Abbas', *Le Monde*, September 1962, p. 6.
2. Within the new government Rabah Bitat was vice-president; Amar Bentoumi, Minister of Justice; Ahmed Medeghri, Minister of the Interior; and Houari Boumediène, Minister of Defence. No European was appointed as a minister.
3. 'Le discours d'investiture du president du conseil algérien', *Le Monde*, 30 September 1962, p. 2.
4. United Nations, Security Council Official Record, 1020, Seventeenth Year, 4 October 1962, p. 6. Dag Hammarskjöld Library, United Nations, New York, <http://www.un.org/Depts/dhl>.
5. Edward Behr, 'Algeria's bitter peace', *Sunday Times*, 7 July 1963.
6. Morocco was unhappy at the frontiers imposed by France in 1856. In July 1961 the Algerian Provisional Government signed an agreement which Hassan II believed laid the basis for a revision of the Sahara frontiers.
7. In September 1962 Boudiaf founded the Parti de la Révolution Socialiste (PRS).
8. These French-trained officers became known as the Déserteurs de l'Armée Française, quickly abbreviated to the acronym DAF.
9. He would not be released until 1980.
10. Krim was strangled to death by Algerian Secret Services in Frankfurt on 18 October 1970.
11. Frantz Fanon, *L'An cinq de la révolution algérienne*, Paris: Maspero, 1959.
12. Frantz Fanon, *Les Damnés de la terre*, Paris: Maspero, 1961, trans. *The Wretched of the Earth*, London: Penguin, 1967.
13. Fanon, *L'An cinq de la révolution algérienne*.
14. Remnants of the OAS threatened to bomb any cinema showing the film. It was eventually shown in Paris in 1971 at a limited number of cinemas with leftist students mounting guard.
15. Nelson Mandela, *Long Walk to Freedom*, London: Little Brown, 1994, p. 286.
16. 'À Frantz Fanon', *Partisans*, February 1962, p. 1.
17. But with Savoie which was ceded to France in 1860.
18. On this see the excellent Todd Shepherd, *The Invention of Decolonization*, Cornell: Cornell University Press, 2006.
19. Jean Touchard, *Le Gaullisme, 1940–1969*, Paris: Seuil, 1978, p. 271.
20. Salan, the most politicized of the four putsh leaders, was released. Challe and Zeller were amnestied in 1966 and Jouhaud amnestied in 1967. On 24 July

1968 the National Assembly passed a general amnesty on infractions carried out by the army during the 'events'.

21. Roger Trinquier, *La Guerre moderne*, Paris: Éditions de la Table Ronde, 1961, trans. *Modern Warfare*, New York: Praeger, 1964.

22. Marie-Monique Robin, *Les Escadrons de la mort, l'École Française*, Paris: La Découverte, 2004.

23. By 1959 France had the highest per capita consumption in Europe. On this see Roderick Kedward, *La Vie en Bleu: France and the French since 1900*, London: Allen Lane, 2005, p. 375.

24. 'Des Réfugiés d'Algérie s'installent en "squatters" dans les immeubles vides', *Le Monde*, 11 August 1962, p. 5.

25. Joëlle Hureua, 'Associations et souvenir chez les Français rapatriés d'Algérie' in Jean-Pierre Rioux (ed.), *La Guerre d'Algérie et les français*, Paris: Fayard, 1990.

26. On this silence see Laurent Muller, *Le Silence des harkis*, Paris: L'Harmattan, 1998.

27. This programme was part of a regular documentary slot, *Cinq Colonnes à la une*, which had consistently covered the Algerian War issue.

28. Benjamin Stora, *La Dernière Generation d'octobre*, Paris: Hachette, 2003.

29. He went on to win the French Championship in 1964, 1967 and 1968. On 12 May he captained them to victory in the French Cup, scoring twice. He received the Cup from President de Gaulle. Martin Evans, 'Patriot games: Algeria's football revolutionaries', *History Today*, July 2010.

30. René Vautier, *Algérie en Flames* (1958) and Jacques Panijel *Octobre à Paris* (1962). On how the Algerian War became a reference point for the French extreme-left see Manus McGrogan, '*Tout!* In context 1968–1974: French radical press at the crossroads of the far-left, new movements and counterculture', PhD Thesis, University of Portsmouth, October 2010.

31. Marcel-Edmond Naegelen, *Mission en Algérie*, Paris: Flammarion, 1962.

32. Denis Lefebvre, *Guy Mollet*, Paris: Plon, 1992, pp. 431–4.

33. *Ibid.*

34. Marc Sadoun, 'Les socialistes entre principles, pouvoir et mémoire' in Rioux (ed.), *La Guerre d'Algérie et les français*, p. 232.

35. *Ibid.*

36. Mitterrand did express regret at his support for the 'special powers' in March 1956, describing it as the biggest mistake in his career. But there was no apology and during the rise of the Socialist Party during the 1970s, Mitterrand's Algerian past became a taboo. Significantly, Mitterrand did reach out to the *pied-noir* vote during the 1981 presidential election. Once in power he also oversaw the final amnesty of Salan in October 1982. On this see François Mayle and Benjamin Stora, *François Mitterrand et la guerre d'Algérie*, Paris: Calmann-Lévy, 2010.

37. This Berber component had been categorically rejected by Messali Hadj in the late 1940s.

38. Martin Evans and John Phillips, *Algeria: Anger of the dispossessed*, London: Yale University Press, 2007.
39. *Ibid.*, pp. 208–10.
40. Habib Souaïda, *La Sale Guerre*, Paris: La Découverte, 2001.
41. Un appel du Comité Maurice Audin, 'À propos du décret du 22 mars sur l'amnistie', *Le Monde*, 28 June, 1962, p. 4.
42. This exchange is reproduced in Patrick Eveno and Jean Planchais (eds.), *La Guerre d'Algérie*, Paris: La Découverte, 1989, pp. 126–43.
43. Kedward, *La Vie en Bleu: France and the French since 1900*, pp. 629–30.
44. Louisette Ighil-Ahriz, *L'Algérienne*, Paris: Fayard, 2001.
45. *Le Monde*, 23 November 2000, p. 11.
46. Paul Aussaresses, *Services spéciaux, Algérie, 1955–1957*, Paris: Perrin, 2001.
47. Benjamin Stora, *La Guerre des mémoires*, Paris: Éditions de l'Aube, 2007, p. 12.
48. Alec Hargreaves, *Immigration and Identity in Beur Fiction*, Oxford: Berg, 1997.
49. Peter Davies, *The National Front in France: Ideology, discourse and power*, London: Routledge, 1999.
50. Mohammed Harbi, *Le FLN. Mirage et réalité*, Paris: Jeune Afrique, 1980.
51. Benjamin Stora, *Messali Hadj*, Paris: Hachette, 2004.
52. Raphaëlle Branche, *La Torture et l'armée française pendant la guerre d'Algérie*, Paris: Gallimard, 2001; Sylvie Thénault, *Une drôle de justice: les magistrats dans la guerre d'Algérie*, Paris: La Découverte, 2001.
53. Benjamin Stora, *La Gangrène et l'oubli: la mémoire de la guerre d'Algérie*, Paris: La Découverte, 1991. The book also drew upon interviews from the television series.
54. Patrick Rotman and Bertrand Tavernier, *La Guerre sans nom*, Paris: Seuil, 1992. This book also drew upon interviews from the film.
55. Martin Evans, 'Rehabilitating the traumatized war veteran: The case of French conscripts from the Algerian War, 1954–1962' in Martin Evans and Ken Lunn (eds.), *War and Memory in the Twentieth Century*, Oxford: Berg, 1997.
56. Catherine Camus, 'Editor's Note', Albert Camus, *The First Man*, 1995, p. vi.
57. Mohand Hamoumou, *Et ils sont devenus harkis*, Paris: Fayard, 1993.
58. On this memory see Claire Eldridge, *Memories of the Algerian War of Independence*, University of St Andrews, 2009.
59. Nancy Wood, *Vectors of Memory: Legacies of trauma in post-war Europe*, Oxford: Berg, 1999.
60. François Hollande, *Devoirs de Vérité. Dialogue avec Edwy Plenel*, Paris: Stock, 2006.
61. See <http://www.indigenes-republique.org>.
62. Linda Colley, 'The difficulty of empire: Present, past and future', *Historical Review*, August 2006. Martin Evans and Raphaëlle Branche, 'Where does colonial history end' in Robert Gildea and Anne Simonin (eds.), *Writing Contemporary History*, London: Hodder, 2008.

Guide to Research Sources
and Select Bibliography

This is a guide to the archive sources used and a select bibliography of the primary and secondary sources. There is also a list of key Internet sources that have been used.

ARCHIVE SOURCES

Archives Nationales (AN), Paris
www.archivesnationales.culture.gouv.fr/chan/chan/caran.

André Boutemy
553AP29-30: Algérie: documentation. 1954–1958.

Marcel-Edmond Naegelen
518AP5: Gouverneur générale de l'Algérie. Février 1948–avril 1950.
518AP9: Algérie. Cabinet du minister-resident.
518AP10: Algérie. Documentations et divers. 1947–1964.
518AP11: Algérie. Documentations et divers. Documents non datés.

Parti Socialiste Unifié
581AP1: SFIO, Comité socialiste d'étude et d'action pour la paix en Algérie. 1957–1958.

Centre d'Archives d'Outre Mer (CAOM), Aix-en-Provence
<http://www.archivesnationales.culture.gouv.fr/anom/fr/>

Gouvernement Générale de l'Algérie (GGA)

Marcel-Edmond Naegelen (1948–1951)
9CAB: Plan quadriennal d'équipment; sécurité sociale; économie; associations; partis politiques algériens; surveillance politique; syndicalisme; assemblée algérienne; insurrection de 1945.

Roger Léonard (1951–1955)
10CAB: Partis politiques algériens; election de 1951; éducation nationale; assemblée algérienne; attentats; courrier parlementaire; économie; office administratif de l'Algérie; séisme d'Orléansville; chronos 1951–1955.

Jacques Soustelle (1955–1956)

11CAB: Composition du cabinet; séisme d'Orléansville; attentats; réorganisation administrative de l'Algérie; hydraulique; finances; état d'urgence; élections législatives de 1955; chronos; réformes.

Robert Lacoste (1956–1958)

12CAB: Finances; économie; éducation nationale; situation en Algérie; municipalités; chronos; état d'urgence; colonisation; pouvoirs spéciaux; exactions; centres d'hébergement; partis politiques; loi cadre; syndicalisme musulman; assemblée algérienne; dossiers d'internés.

Affaires Indigènes (Série H)

9H: Surveillance politique (1844–1958).
10H: Études et notices sur l'Algérie et l'Islam (1845–1957).
15H: Presse indigène et radiodiffusion (1867–1956).

National Archives, London

<http://www.nationalarchives.gov.uk>

Foreign Office: British Consul in Algiers 1944–1945

FO 371/49276: despatch n°116 from Algiers to FO—9th July: report on interview with members of PPA (Political situation in North Africa: French administration: Arab national movement in Algeria 1945).

FO 371/49275: despatch n°96 from Algiers to FO: Situation in Algeria—12th June (Political situation in North Africa: French administration: Arab national movement in Algeria 1945).

FO 371/49275: despatch n°111—7th July (Political situation in North Africa: French administration: Arab national movement in Algeria 1945).

FO 371/49275: telegram from Algiers to FO—11th May (Political situation in North Africa: French administration: Arab national movement in Algeria 1945).

FO 371/49275: telegram from Algiers to FO—12th May (Political situation in North Africa: French administration: Arab national movement in Algeria 1945).

Office Universitaire de Recherche Socialiste, Paris

<http://www.lours.org>

Ernest Cazelles

30APO2: Mission d'étude en Algérie, 1949.

Marcel Champeix

6APO1: Textes et discours, 1936–1981.
6APO2: Secrétaire d'État aux Affaires Algériennes, 1956–1957.
6APO3: Notes diverses, missions en Algérie, 1956–1957.
6APO4: Réorganisation administrative de l'Algérie et statut de l'Algérie, mai 1956–janvier 1957.

6APO5: Délégué à la IIe session générale des Nations Unis, 23 janvier–17 février 1957.

6APO6: Algérie, 1956–1957.

6APO7: Documentation et dossier de presse sur l'Algérie.

Maurice Deixonne

1APO44: Algérie, 1956-1960.

Guy Mollet

AGM65: Formation du gouvernement et dossiers de presse, 1956–juin 1956.

AGM66: Dossier de presse, juillet 1956–mai 1957.

AGM67: Discours, declarations à la presse, communiqués, interviews, correspondance avec les journalists, janvier–juin 1956.

AGM68: Idem suite, juin–septembre 1956.

AGM69: Idem suite, septembre–décembre 1956.

AGM70: Idem suite, janvier–juin 1957.

AGM72: Sondage IFOP sur l'état d'esprit des Français mai–novembre 1956.

AGM76: Outre mer.

AGM79: Politique extérieure, Affaire de Suez.

AGM80: Idem suite.

AGM81: Le Président du Conseil et l'Algérie, 1956.

AGM82: Idem suite, 1957.

AGM83: Statut de l'Algérie 1956–1957.

AGM84: Algérie, 1956–1957.

AGM85: Présidence du Conseil, Algérie, 1956–1957.

AGM86: Idem suite.

AGM87: Idem suite.

AGM88: Idem suite.

AGM89: Idem suite.

AGM90: Programme des emissions arabes, novembre 1956, janvier–mai 1957.

AGM91: Algérie, 1958–1959.

AGM92: Algérie, 1960–1968.

AGM93: Divers Algérie, 1956–1962.

AGM94: OAS, 1960–1963.

SFIO

A2: Correspondances avec les Fédérations, Correspondances avec la Fédération d'Oran 1944–1947.

C1: Vie interne, dont sténographie des congrès et conseils nationaux, 1950–1971.

C3: Comptes rendus des comités directeurs, 1944–1969.

SFIO publications

L'Œuvre du gouvernement Guy Mollet du 2 février 1956 au 21 mai 1957. La Loi-Cadre dans les territoires d'Outre Mer, Arras: Société d'Éditions du Pas-de-Calais, 1957.

French official publications

Assemblée Nationale Constituante élue le 21 octobre 1945, Séances de la Commission de la Constitution, Paris: Assemblée Nationale Constituante, 1946.

Assemblée Nationale Constituante élue le 2 juin 1946, Séances de la Commission de la Constitution, Paris: Assemblée Nationale Constituante, 1946.

DOCUMENT COLLECTIONS

Belhocine, Mabrouk, *Le Courrier Alger–Le Caire*, Algiers: Éditions Casbah, 2000.

Collot, Claude and Jean-Robert Henry, *Le Mouvement national algérien par les textes*, Paris: L'Harmattan, 1978.

Eveno, Patrick and Planchais, Jean (eds.), *La Guerre d'Algérie*, Paris: La Découverte, 1989.

Harbi, Mohammed (ed.), *Les Archives de la revolution algérienne*, Paris: Éditions Jeune Afrique, 1981.

Harbi, Mohammed and Gilbert Meynier (eds.), *Le FLN: Documents et histoire 1954–62*, Paris: Fayard, 2004.

Léonard, Roger, *Quatre ans en Algérie*, Algiers: Imprimerie Officielle du Gouvernement Générale de l'Algérie, 1955.

Mandouze, André, *La Révolution algérienne par les textes*, Paris: Maspero, 1961.

OAS Parle, Paris: Julliard, 1964.

Paillat, Claude, *Dossier Secret de l'Algérie, 13 mai 1958–28 avril 1961*, Paris: Le Livre Contemporain, 1961.

INTERVIEWS

Henri Alleg, 24 November 2010, Paris.
Robert Bonnaud, 4 April 1989, Paris.
Mohammed Harbi, 22 May 2008, Paris.
Jean Masson, 22 October 2008, Lyon.
Georges Mattéi, 13 April 1989, Paris.
Zina Harraigue, 14 October 1989, Algiers.

PRESS

Alger Républicain
Le Canard Enchainé
L'Écho d'Alger
Egalité
Espoir
Esprit
L'Express
L'Humanité

Le Monde
El Moudjahid
Paris Match
Le Populaire
La République Algérienne
The Sunday Times
Temoignages et Documents
Les Temps Modernes
The Times
Vérite-Liberté

EYE-WITNESS ACCOUNTS

Alleg, Henri, *La Question*, Paris: Éditions de Minuit, 1958.
—— *Prisonniers de Guerre*, Paris: Éditions de Minuit, 1961.
Behr, Edward, *The Algerian Problem*, London: Penguin, 1961.
Bonnaud, Robert, *Itinéraire*, Paris: Éditions de Minuit, 1962.
Boumaza, Bachir, Mustapha Francis, Benaissa Souami, and Moussa Khebaili, *La Gangrène*, Paris: Éditions de Minuit, 1959.
Bromberger, Serge, *Les Rebelles algériens*, Paris: Plon, 1958.
Bromberger, Merry, Serge Bromberger, Georgette Elgey, and J. F. Chauvel, *Barricades et colonels. 24 janvier 1960*, Paris: Fayard, 1960.
Charby, Jacques, *L'Algérie en prison*, Paris: Éditions de Minuit, 1961.
Darboise, J. M., M. Heynaud, and J. Martel, *Officiers en Algérie*, Paris: Maspero, 1960.
Davezies, Robert, *Le Front*, Paris: Éditions de Minuit, 1959.
Feraoun, Mouloud, *Journal 1955–1962*, Paris: Seuil, 1962.
Jeanson, Colette and Francis Jeanson, *L'Algérie Hors-La-Loi*, Paris: Seuil, 1955.
Ouzegane, Amar, *Le Meilleur Combat*, Paris: Julliard, 1962.
Rahmani, Abdelkader, *L'Affaire des officiers algériens*, Paris: Seuil, 1959.
Reggui, Marcel, *Les Massacres de Guelma*, Paris: La Découverte, 2006.
Servan-Schreiber, Jean-Jacques, *Lieutenant en Algérie*, Paris: Julliard, 1957.
Servier, Jean, *Dans l'Aurès sur les pas des rebelles*, Paris: Éditions France-Empire, 1955.

POLITICAL WRITING FROM THE PERIOD

Arnaud, Georges and Jacques Vergès, *Pour Djamila Bouhired*, Paris: Éditions de Minuit, 1957.
Aron, Raymond, *La Tragédie algérienne*, Paris: Plon, 1957.
Blum, Léon, *L'Oeuvre de Léon Blum 1947–1950*, Paris: Albin Michel, 1963.
Camus, Albert, *Chroniques algériennes 1939–1958*, Paris: Gallimard, 1958.
Fanon, Frantz, *L'An cinq de la révolution algérienne*, Paris: Maspero, 1959.
—— *Les Damnés de la terre*, Paris: Maspero, 1961.

—— *Pour la révolution africaine*, Paris: Maspero, 1964.

Jeanson, Francis, *Notre guerre*, Paris: Éditions de Minuit, 1960.

Péju, Marcel, *Le Procés du Réseau Jeanson*, Paris: Maspero, 1961.

Philip, André, *Le Socialisme trahi*, Paris: Plon, 1957.

Mollet, Guy, *Bilan et perspectives socialistes*, Paris: Plon, 1958.

Roman, Joël, *Esprit. Écrire contre la guerre d'Algérie 1947–1962*, Paris: Hachette, 2002.

Simon, Pierre-Henri, *Contre la torture*, Paris: Seuil, 1957.

Soustelle, Jacques, *Aimée et souffrante Algérie*, Paris: Plon, 1956.

Tillion, Germaine, *L'Algérie en 1957*, Paris: Éditions de Minuit, 1957.

Vidal-Naquet, Pierre, *L'Affaire Audin*, Paris: Éditions de Minuit, 1958.

—— *La raison d'état*, Paris: Éditions de Minuit, 1962.

Yacine, Kateb, *Abdelkader et l'indépendance algérienne*, Algiers: Enahda, 1947.

NOVELS

Camus, Albert, *L'Étranger*, Paris: Gallimard, 1942.

—— *La Peste*, Paris: Gallimard, 1947.

—— *L'Exil et le royaume*, Paris: Gallimard, 1957.

—— *Le Premier Homme*, Paris: Gallimard, 1994.

Dib, Mohammed, *La Grande Maison*, Paris: Seuil, 1952.

—— *L'Incendie*, Paris: Seuil, 1954.

—— *Le Métier à tisser*, Paris: Seuil, 1957.

Feraoun, Mouloud, *Le Fils du pauvre*, Paris: Seuil, 1954.

Yacine, Kateb, *Nedjma*, Paris: Seuil, 1956.

—— *Le Cercle des représailles*, Paris: Seuil, 1959.

MEMOIRS

Algerian

Abbas, Ferhat, *La Nuit coloniale*, Paris: Julliard, 1962.

—— *L'Indépendance confisquée, 1962–1968*, Paris: Flammarion, 1984.

Aït Ahmed, Hocine, *Mémoires d'un combattant*, Paris: Messinger, 1983.

Azzedine, Commandant, *On nous appelait Fellaghas*, Paris: Stock, 1976.

Ben Khedda, Benyoucef, *Les Origines du premier novembre 1954*, Algiers: Dahlab, 1989.

Dahlab, Saad, *Pour l'indépendance de l'Algérie. Mission accomplie*, Algiers: Dahlab, 1990.

Farès, Abderrahmane, *La Cruelle Vérité. L'Algérie de 1954 à l'indépendance*, Paris: Plon, 1982.

Harbi, Mohammed, *Une vie debout: mémoires politiques*, Paris: La Découverte, 2001.

Haroun, Ali, *La Septième Wilaya: la guerre du FLN en France 1954–1962*, Paris: Seuil, 1986.

Ighil-Ahriz, Louisette and Anne Nivat, *Algérienne*, Paris: Fayard, 2001.

Kafi, Ali, *Du militant politique au dirigeant militaire. Mémoires 1946–1962*, Algiers: Casbah Éditions, 2002.

Malek, Redha, *L'Algérie à Évian. Histoire des négociations secrètes, 1954–1962*, Paris: Seuil, 1995.

Ougouag, Abdelkader, *Les Grands Procès*, Algiers: Éditions Dahlab, 1992.

Saadi, Yacef, *La Bataille d'Alger*, III: *Le Démantèlement*, Algiers: Casbah Éditions, 2000.

Zamoum, Ali, *Le Pays des hommes libres. Tamurt Imazighen*, Paris: La Pensée Sauvage, 1998.

European
Ortiz, Jo, *Mon combat pour l'Algérie française*, Paris: Éditions Jean Curutchet, 1998.
Fargues, Dominique, *Mémoires des pieds-noirs*, Paris: Flammarion, 2008.
Susini, Jean-Jacques, *Histoire de l'OAS*, Paris: La Table Ronde, 1963.

Pro-French Algeria
Bidault, Georges, *D'une résistance à l'autre*, Paris: La Table Ronde, 1965.
Soustelle, Jacques, *Vingt-huit ans de Gaullisme*, Paris: La Table Ronde, 1968.

French political
Gazier, Albert, *Autour d'une vie de militant*, Paris: L'Harmattan, 2006.
Naegelen, Marcel-Edmond, *Mission en Algérie*, Paris: Flammarion, 1962.
Pineau, Christian, *1956 Suez*, Paris: Laffont, 1976.
Tricot, Bernard, *Les Sentiers de la paix en Algérie*, Paris: Plon, 1972.

French opposition
Barrat, Robert, *Les Maquis de la liberté*, Paris: Éditions Témoignage Chrétien, 1987.
Julien, Charles-André, *Une pensée anti-coloniale*, Paris: Sindbad, 1979.
Mandouze, André, *Mémoires d'autre siècle: d'une résistance à l'autre*, Paris: Vivianne Hamy, 1998.
Vidal-Naquet, Pierre, *Face à la raison d'état. Un historien dans la guerre d'Algérie*, Paris: La Découverte, 1989.
—— *Mémoires. La brisure et l'attente*, Paris: Seuil, 1995.
—— *Mémoires. Le trouble et la lumière (1955–1998)*, Paris: Seuil, 1998.
Winock, Michel, *La République se meurt*, Paris: Seuil, 1978.

French military
Argoud, Antoine, *La Décadence, l'imposture et la tragédie*, Paris: Fayard, 1974.
Aussaresses, Paul, *Services spéciaux, Algérie, 1955–1957*, Paris: Perrin, 2001.
Bigeard, Marcel, *Pour une parcelle de gloire*, Paris: Plon, 1975.

Bollardière, Jacques Paris de, *Bataille d'Alger, bataille de l'homme*, Paris: Desclée Brouwer, 1972.

Challe, Maurice, *Notre révolte*, Paris: Presses de la Cité, 1968.

Massu, Jacques, *La Vrai Bataille d'Alger*, Paris: Plon, 1971.

—— *Le Torrent et la digue*, Paris: Plon, 1972.

Salan, Raoul, *Mémoires. Fin d'un empire*, III: *Algérie française*, Paris: Éditions Presses de la Cité, 1972.

Trinquier, Roger, *La Guerre moderne*, Paris: La Table Ronde, 1961.

Harkis

Boualam, Bachaga, *Mon pays la France*, Paris: Éditions France-Empire, 1962.

—— *Les Harkis au service de la France*, Paris: France-Empire, 1964.

Ferdi, Saïd, *Un enfant dans la guerre*, Paris: Seuil, 1981.

SECONDARY SOURCES

General histories

Abécassis, Frédéric and Gilbert Meynier (eds.), *Pour une histoire franco-algérienne*, Paris: La Découverte, 2008.

Ageron, Charles-Robert, *Modern Algeria: A history from 1830 to the present*, London: Hurst, 1991.

Ageron, Charles-Robert (ed.), *L'Algérie des français*, Paris: Seuil, 1993.

Alleg, Henri (ed.), *La Guerre d'Algérie*, 3 volumes, Paris: Temps Actuel, 1981.

Bennoune, Mahfoud, *The Making of Contemporary Algeria: Colonial upheavals and post-independence development*, Cambridge: Cambridge University Press, 1988.

Branche, Raphaëlle, *La Guerre d'Algérie: une histoire apaisée*, Paris: Seuil, 2005.

Branche, Raphaëlle (ed.), *La Guerre d'indépendance des algériens 1954–1962*, Paris: Perrin, 2009.

Carlier, Omar, *Entre nation et jihad: histoire sociale des radicalismes algériens*, Paris: Presses de Science Po, 1995.

Droz, Bernard and Evelyne Lever, *Histoire de la guerre d'Algérie*, Paris: Seuil, 1982.

Elsenhans, Hartmut, *La Guerre d'Algérie, la transition d'une France à une autre*, Paris: Publisud, 2000.

Harbi, Mohammed and Benjamin Stora (eds.), *La Guerre d'Algérie 1954–2004: la fin de l'amnésie*, Paris: Robert Laffont, 2004.

Horne, Alistair, *A Savage War of Peace: Algeria 1954–1962*, London: Macmillan, 1977.

Lefeuvre, Daniel, *Chère Algérie 1930–1962*, Paris: Société Française d'Outre Mer, 1997.

Naylor, Phillip C., *France and Algeria: A history of decolonization and transformation*, Gainesville: University Press of Florida, 2000.

Pervillé, Guy, *Pour une histoire de la guerre d'Algérie*, Paris: Éditions Picard, 2002.

—— *La Guerre d'Algérie*, Paris; Presses Universitaires de France, 2007.

Rioux, Jean-Pierre (ed.), *La Guerre d'Algérie et les français*, Paris: Fayard, 1990.

Ross, Kristin, *Fast Cars, Clean Bodies: Decolonization and the reordering of French culture*, Cambridge: MIT Press, 1995.

Ruedy, John, *Modern Algeria: The origins and development of a nation*, Bloomington: Indiana University Press, 1992.

Stora, Benjamin, *Algeria 1830–2000*, Ithaca: Cornell University Press, 2001.

Thénault, Sylvie, *Histoire de la guerre d'indépendance algérienne*, Paris: Flammarion, 2005.

Pre-colonial Algeria

Brett, Michael and Elizabeth Fentress, *The Berbers*, Oxford: Blackwell, 1996.

Julien, Charles-André, *Histoire de l'Afrique du nord*, I: *Des origines à la conquête Arabe*, Paris: Payot, 1951.

Meynier, Gilbert, *L'Algérie des origines*, Paris: La Découverte, 2007.

The French conquest

Al-Arabi, Ismail, *Al Muqawama al Jaza'irriya that liwa' al Amir Abd al Qadir*, Algiers: Société National d'Édition, 1982.

Clancy-Smith, Julia A., *Rebel and Saint: Muslim notables, populist protests, colonial encounters (Algeria and Tunisia, 1800–1904)*, Berkeley: University of California Press, 1994.

Étienne, Bruno, *Abd-el-Kader*, Paris: Hachette, 1994.

Fleming, Fergus, *The Sword and the Cross*, London: Granta, 2003.

French Algeria

Ageron, Charles-Robert, *Les Algériens musulmans et la France (1871–1919)*, 2 vols., Paris: Presses Universitaires de France, 1968.

Guilhaume, Jean-François, *Les Mythes fondateurs de l'Algérie française*, Paris: L'Harmattan, 1992.

Haddour, Azzedine, *Colonial Myths, History, Narrative*, Manchester: Manchester University Press, 2000.

Lorcin, Patricia, *Imperial Identities: Stereotyping, prejudice and race in colonial Algeria*, London: I. B. Tauris, 1995.

Prochaska, David, *Making Algeria French*, New York: Cambridge University Press, 1990.

Vatin, Jean-Claude, *L'Algérie politique*, Paris: Armand Colin, 1974.

Algerian Jews

Abitbol, Michel, *Les Juifs d'Afrique du nord sous Vichy*, Paris: Maisonneuve et Larose, 1983.

Attal, Robert, *Regards sur les juifs d'Algérie*, Paris: L'Harmattan, 1996.

Bel-Ange, Norbert, *Les Juifs de Mostaganem*, Paris: L'Harmattan, 1990.

Stora, Benjamin, *La Dernière Génération d'octobre*, Paris: Stock, 2003.

—— *Les Trois Exils. Juifs d'Algérie*, Paris: Stock, 2006.

Algerian nationalism

Derouiche, Mohamed, *Le Scoutisme, école du patriotisme*, Algiers: ENAL-OPU, 1985.

Gadant, Monique, *Islam et nationalisme en Algérie*, Paris: L'Harmattan, 1988.

Kaddache, Mahfoud, *Histoire du nationalisme algérien*, Algiers: SNED, 1980.

Lacheraf, Mostefa, *L'Algérie, Nation et Société*, Paris: Maspero, 1965.

McDougall, James, *History and the Culture of Nationalism in Algeria*, Cambridge: Cambridge University Press, 2006.

McDougall, James (ed.), *Nation, Society and Culture in North Africa*, London: Frank Cass, 2003.

Meynier, Gilbert, *L'Algérie révélée: la guerre de 1914–1918 et le premier quart du vingtième siècle*, Geneva: Librairie Droz, 1981.

Rahal, Malika, *L'Union démocratique du manifeste Algérien (1946–1956)*, Paris: L'Institut National des Langues et Civilisations Orientales, Thesis, 2007.

Stora, Benjamin, *Messali Hadj (1898–1974), pionnier du nationalisme algérien*, Paris: L'Harmattan, 1986.

World War Two and May 1945

Ainad Tabet, Redouance, *8 Mai 45 en Algérie*, Algiers: Office des Publications Universitaires, 1985.

Cantier, Jacques, *L'Algérie sous le régime de Vichy*, Paris: Odile Jacob, 2002.

Peyroulou, Jean-Pierre, *Guelma, 1945*, Paris: La Découverte, 2009.

Rey-Goldzeiguer, Annie, *Aux origines de la guerre d'Algérie 1940–1945. De Mers-el-Kébir aux massacres de Nord-Constantinois*, Paris: La Découverte, 2001.

FLN

Ageron, Charles-Robert (ed.), *La Guerre d'Algérie et les algériens*, Paris: Armand Colin, 1997.

Benkhedda, Benyoucef, *La Crise de 1962*, Algiers: Dahlab, 1997.

Harbi, Mohammed, *Aux origins du FLN: le populisme révolutionnaire en Algérie*, Paris: Christian Bourgois, 1975.

—— *Le FLN: Mirage et réalité*, Paris: Éditions Jeune Afrique, 1980.

—— *La Guerre commence en Algérie*, Bruxelles: Complexe, 1984.

—— *L'Algérie et son destin: croyants et citoyens*, Paris: Arcantère, 1992.

Meynier, Gilbert, *Histoire intérieure du FLN, 1954–1962*, Paris: Fayard, 2002.

Rahal, Malika, *Ali Boumendjel, une affaire française, une histoire algérienne*, Paris: Les Belles Lettres, 2010.

Sadi, Said, *Amirouche, une vie, deux morts, un testament*, Blida: Mauguin, 2010.

The French left

Binot, Jean-Marc, *Max Lejeune. L'enfant chérie du socialisme Picard*, Amiens: Éditions Martelle, 2002.

—— *Max Lejeune. Du ministre de la quatrième au notable de la cinquième*, Amiens: Éditions Martelle, 2003.

Brana, Pierre and Joëlle Dussea, *Robert Lacoste (1898–1989)*, Paris: L'Harmattan, 2010.

Bourdel, Philippe, *La Dernière Chance de l'Algérie française. Du gouvernement socialiste au retour de De Gaulle, 1956–1958*, Paris: Albin Michel, 1996.

Buffotot, Patrice, *Le Socialisme français et la guerre*, Brussels: Emile Bruylant, 1998.

Lafon, François, *Guy Mollet*, Paris: Fayard, 2006.

Lefebvre, Denis, *Guy Mollet*, Paris: Plon, 1992.

—— *Guy Mollet face à la torture en Algérie 1956–1957*, Paris: Éditions Bruno Leprince, 2001.

Maquin, Étienne, *Le Parti socialiste et la guerre d'Algérie*, Paris: L'Harmattan, 1990.

Marynower, Claire, *Joseph Begarra. Un socialiste Oranais dans la guerre d'Algérie*, Paris: L'Harmattan, 2008.

Mayle, François and Benjamin Stora, *François Mitterrand et la guerre d'Algérie*, Paris: Calmann-Lévy, 2010.

Ménager, Bernard, Philippe Ratte, Jean Louis Thiébault, Robert Vandenbussche, and Christian-Marie Wallon-Leducq (eds.), *Guy Mollet. Un camarade en république*, Lille: Presses Universitaires de Lille, 1987.

Simmons, Harvey, *The French Socialists in Search of a Role, 1956–1967*, Ithaca: Cornell University Press, 1970.

Werth, Alexander, *The Strange History of Pierre Mendès-France and the Great Conflict over French North Africa*, London: Barrie Books, 1957.

The French Communist Party

Joly, Danièle, *The French Communist Party and the Algerian War*, London: Macmillan, 1991.

Sivan, Emmanuel, *Communisme et nationalisme en Algérie (1920–1962)*, Paris: Presses de la Fondation National des Sciences Politiques, 1976.

The French military

Alexander, Martin, Martin Evans and J. F. V. Keiger (eds.), *The Algerian War and the French Army: Experiences, images, testimonies*, Basingstoke: Macmillan, 2002.

Branche, Raphaëlle, *L'Embuscade de Palestro. Algérie 1956*, Paris: Armand Colin, 2010.

Jauffret, Jean-Charles, *Soldats en Algérie 1954–1962. Expériences contrastées des hommes du contingent*, Paris: Autrement, 2000.

Jauffret, Jean-Charles and Maurice Vaïsse (eds.), *Militaires et guérilla dans la guerre d'Algérie*, Brussels: Éditions Complexe, 2001.

Mauss-Copeaux, Claire, *Appelés en Algérie. La parole confisquée*, Paris: Hachette, 1998.

Pellissier, Pierre, *La Bataille d'Alger*, Paris: Perrin, 1995.

Stora, Benjamin, *Appelés en guerre d'Algérie*, Paris: Gallimard.

Torture

Branche, Raphaëlle, *La Torture et l'armée pendant la guerre d'Algérie 1954–1962*, Paris: Gallimard, 2001.

Einaudi, Jean-Luc, *Pour l'exemple. L'affaire Iveton*, Paris: L'Harmattan, 1986.
Thénault, Sylvie, *Une drôle de justice: les magistrats dans la guerre d'Algérie*, Paris: La Découverte, 2001.
Vidal-Naquet, Pierre, *Torture: Cancer of democracy*, London: Penguin, 1963.

Algerian women and the Algerian War
Amrane-Minne, Danièle Djamila, *Des Femmes dans la guerre d'Algérie*, Paris: Karthala, 1994.
Gadant, Monique, *Le Nationalisme algérien et les femmes*, Paris: L'Harmattan, 1995.
Macmaster, Neil, *Burning the Veil*, Manchester: Manchester University Press, 2009.
Natalya, Vince, 'To be a moudjahida in independent Algeria: Itineraries and memories of women veterans of the Algerian War', University of London: PhD, 2009.
Seferdjeli, Ryme, 'Fight with us, women, and we will emancipate you: France, the FLN and the struggle over women during the Algerian War of National Liberation', University of London: PhD, 2005.

De Gaulle and the Algerian War
Lacouture, Jean, *De Gaulle*, III: *Le Souverain*, Paris: Seuil, 1986.
Peyrefitte, Alain, *C'était de Gaulle*, Paris: Fayard, 1994.
Stora, Benjamin, *Le Mystère de Gaulle. Son choix pour l'Algérie*, Paris: Laffont, 2009.

French opposition to the Algerian War
Charby, Jacques, *Les Porteurs d'espoir. Les réseaux de soutien au FLN pendant la guerre d'Algérie: Les acteurs parlent*, Paris: La Découverte, 2004.
Einaudi, Jean-Luc, *Franc-Tireur. Georges Mattéi, de la guerre d'Algérie à la guérilla*, Paris: Éditions Sextant, 2004.
Evans, Martin, *The Memory of Resistance: French opposition to the Algerian War 1954–62*, Oxford: Berg, 1997.
Hamon, Hervé and Patrick Rotman, *Les Porteurs de valises. La Résistance française à la guerre d'Algérie*, Paris: Albin Michel, 1979.
Sueur, James D. Le, *Uncivil War, intellectuals and identity politics during the decolonization of Algeria*, Philadelphia: University of Pennsylvania Press, 2001.

The war in France
Amiri, Linda, *La Bataille de France. La guerre d'Algérie en métropole*, Paris: Laffont, 2004.
Branche, Raphaëlle and Sylvie Thénault (eds.), *La France en guerre 1954–1962. Expériences métropolitaines de la guerre d'indépendance algérienne*, Paris: Autrement, 2008.
Einaudi, Jean-Luc, *La Bataille de Paris, 17 octobre 1961*, Paris: Seuil, 1991.
House, Jim and Neil Macmaster, *Paris 1961, Algerians, State Terror, and Memory*, Oxford: Oxford University Press, 2006.
Williams, Philip M., *Wars, Plots and Scandals in Post-War France*, Cambridge: Cambridge University Press, 1970.

April 1961 putsch

Vaïsse, Maurice, *1961, Alger, le Putsch*, Brussels: Éditions Complexe, 1983.

OAS

Delarue, Jacques, *L'OAS contre de Gaulle*, Paris: Fayard, 1981.

Kauffer, Rémi, *OAS, histoire d'une organisation secrète*, Paris: Fayard, 1986.

The *Harkis*

Faivre, Maurice, *Les Combattants musulmans de la guerre d'Algérie*, Paris: L'Harmattan, 1995.

Hamoumou, Mohand, *Ets ils sont devenus harkis*, Paris: Fayard, 1993.

Jordi, Jean-Jacques and Mohand Hamoumou, *Les Harkis, une mémoire enfouie*, Paris: Autrement, 1999.

Roux, Michel, *Les harkis, les oubliés de l'histoire*, Paris: La Découverte, 1991.

The Arab world

Dib, Faith El, *Abdel Nasser et la révolution algérienne*, Paris: L'Harmattan, 1985.

Graniage, Jean, *Histoire Contemporaine du Maghreb*, Paris: Fayard, 1994.

Horani, Albert, *A History of the Arab Peoples*, London: Faber and Faber, 1991.

Rogan, Eugene, *The Arabs*, London: Allen Lane, 2009.

Cold war

Connelly, Matthew, *A Diplomatic Revolution: Algeria's fight for independence and the origins of the cold war era*, Oxford: Oxford University Press, 2002.

Wall, Irwin, *France, the United States, and the Algerian War*, Berkeley: University of California Press, 2001.

French Empire

Ageron, Charles-Robert, *La Décolonisation française*, Paris: A. Colin, 1991.

Aldrich, Robert, *Greater France: A history of French overseas expansion*, Basingstoke: Macmillan, 1996.

Betts, Raymond, *France and Decolonization 1900–1960*, London: Macmillan, 1991.

Chafer, Tony, *The End of Empire in French West Africa*, Oxford: Berg, 2002.

Conklin, Alice, Sarah Fishman, and Robert Zaretsky, *France and Its Empire since 1870*, New York: Oxford University Press, 2010.

Cooper, Frederick, *Decolonization and African Society: The labour question in French and British Africa*, Cambridge: Cambridge University Press, 1996.

Cooper, Nicola, *France in Indochina*, Oxford: Berg, 2001.

Dalloz, Jacques, *La Guerre d'Indochine*, Paris: Seuil, 1987.

Evans, Martin (ed.), *Empire and Culture: The French experience, 1830–1940*, Basingstoke: Palgrave, 2004.

Pervillé, Guy, *De l'empire français à la décolonisation*, Paris: Hachette, 1995.

Shipway, Martin, *The Road to War: France and Vietnam, 1944–1947*, Oxford: Berghahn, 1996.

Thomas, Martin, *The French Empire Between the Wars: Imperialism, politics and society*, Manchester: Manchester University Press, 2005.

Decolonization

Burbank, Jane and Frederick Cooper, *Empires in World History*, Princeton: Princeton University Press, 2010.

Cooper, Frederick, *Decolonization and African Society: The labour question in French and British Africa*, Cambridge: Cambridge University Press, 1996.

—— *Africa since 1940*, Cambridge: Cambridge University Press, 2002.

Shipway, Martin, *Decolonization and Its Impact: A Comparative Approach to the End of Colonial Empire*, London: Blackwell, 2008.

Thomas, Martin, Bob Moore, and L. J. Butler, *The Crisis of Empire: Decolonization and Europe's imperial states*, London: Hodder Arnold, 2008.

Israel

Kykle, Keith, *Suez*, London: Weidenfeld and Nicolson Ltd, 1991.

Shlaim, Avi, *The Iron Wall: Israel and the Arab world*, London: Allen Lane, 2000.

The legacy of the conflict

Eldridge, Claire, 'Memories of the Algerian War of Independence', University of St Andrews: PhD, 2009.

Evans, Martin and John Phillips, *Algeria: Anger of the dispossessed*, London: Yale University Press, 2007.

Hadad, Samy, *Algérie: Autopsie d'une crise*, Paris: L'Harmattan, 1998.

Hadjadj, Djillali, *Corruption et démocratie en Algérie*, Paris: Éditions La Dispute, 1998.

Hidouci, Ghazi, *Algérie: la libération inachevée*, Paris: La Découverte, 1995.

Labat, Séverine, *Les Islamistes algériens: entre les urnes et le maquis*, Paris: Seuil, 1995.

Manceron, Gilles and Hassan Remaoun, *D'une rive à l'autre: la guerre d'Algérie de la mémoire à l'histoire*, Paris: Syros, 1993.

Redjala, Ramdane, *L'Opposition en Algérie depuis 1962*, Paris: L'Harmattan, 1988.

Reporters sans Frontières, *Le Drame algérien*, Paris: La Découverte, 1996.

Roberts, Hugh, *The Battlefield Algeria, 1988–2002*, London: Verso, 2003.

Rouadjia, Ahmed, *Les Frères et la mosquée*, Paris: Éditions Karthala, 1989.

Shepherd, Todd, *The Invention of Decolonization: The Algerian War and the remaking of France*, Ithaca: Cornell University Press, 2006.

Stora, Benjamin, *La Gangrène et l'oubli: la mémoire de la guerre d'Algérie*, Paris: La Découverte, 1991.

—— *Ils venaient d'Algérie: l'immigration algérienne en France, 1912–1992*, Paris: Fayard, 1992.

—— *L'Algérie en 1995: la guerre, l'histoire, la politique*, Paris: Éditions Michalon, 1995.

Willis, Michael, *The Islamist Challenge in Algeria*, London: Ithaca, 1996.

FILMS

La Bataille d'Alger (Gillo Pontecorvo, 1966).
La Guerre sans nom (Bertrand Tavernier, 1992).
Hors-la-loi (Rachid Bouchareb, 2010).

WEBSITES

<http://www.algeria-watch.org>: A very well-informed independent Algerian website that monitors human rights issues in the country.

<http://www.charles-de-gaulle.org/page/l'homme.php>: Site for the Charles de Gaulle Foundation which contains key documents as well as documentary footage.

<http://www.el-mouradia.dz>: President Bouteflika's official website with speeches, key historical documents, and the Algerian constitution.

<http://ens-web3.ens-lsh.fr/colloques/france-algerie/>: Superb website exploring the best contemporary research on all aspects of Franco-Algerian history, based upon a conference organized by the École Normale Supérieure at Lyon in June 2006.

<http://www.ldh-toulon.net>: Website of the Ligue des Droits de l'Homme in Toulon which contains numerous articles examining the ongoing debates about the Algerian War.

<http://www.port.ac.uk/special/france1815to2003/>: This website contains the following interviews with key historians:

Algerian Nationalism and the Popular Front, Margaret Majumdar
Decolonization and the Fourth Republic, Tony Chafer
Fourth Republic Politics, Richard Vinen
French Indochina, Nikki Cooper
La Guerre d'Algérie et le Nationalisme Algérien, Gilbert Meynier
Gaullism and the Algerian War, Stephen Tyre
Decolonization, the French Empire and Sites of Memory, Robert Aldrich

Index